MW01280034

The Eisenach Epistle Selections V2: The First Sunday In Advent To Trinity Sunday

Richard Charles Henry Lenski

In the interest of creating a more extensive selection of rare historical book reprints, we have chosen to reproduce this title even though it may possibly have occasional imperfections such as missing and blurred pages, missing text, poor pictures, markings, dark backgrounds and other reproduction issues beyond our control. Because this work is culturally important, we have made it available as a part of our commitment to protecting, preserving and promoting the world's literature. Thank you for your understanding.

THE EISENACH
EPISTLE SELECTIONS

Made Ready for Pulpit Work

BY

R. C. H. LENSKI

·VOLUME II

The First Sunday After Trinity to Thanksgiving
or Harvest Home

1914
LUTHERAN BOOK CONCERN
Columbus, Ohio

THE TRINITY CYCLE.

THE TRINITY CYCLE.

The First Sunday after Trinity to the Twenty-Seventh Sunday after Trinity.

Like a great cathedral the long series of after-Trinity texts rises up before us, its spires climbing heavenward in the closing texts which deal with the consummation of the Christian life. We need not repeat at length what we have already indicated in the introductions to the previous cycles, that these epistle texts are based on the gospel texts as their foundation. The fundamental idea expressed by the latter texts is modified after the manner of the epistolary writings of the apostles in general, the whole series thus bearing a distinctive character of its own. The great theme of the Trinity series in the gospel selections is "the Kingdom of Heaven," or "the things pertaining to this Kingdom." We noted, in our description of this theme (see *The Eisenach Gospel Selections,* II, 5, *etc.*), that the gospel texts which unfold it combine the objective and the subjective elements and constantly show our personal connection with the Kingdom and the things pertaining to it. This is true also of the Trinity epistles, only these in many cases bring out more fully the subjective element, as is natural in selections taken from epistolary writings. The great theme for the entire Trinity cycle therefore is: **the Life in the Kingdom of God,** or, formulating it more simply still: **the Christian Life.** There are six texts which treat of the beginnings of this life; there are eight which show its unfolding in the individual; nine more, tracing its unfolding in the people of God; and finally four which describe its consummation. At the head of all these texts stands the one for the Trinity Festival, which, as in the gospels, closes the festival half of the year and at the same

time opens up the non-festival half, for it sets forth in a
grand summary all the blessings of the Christian life, connecting them all with their fountain, the Trinune God, "who
hath blessed us with all spiritual blessings in heavenly
places in Christ," Eph. 1, 3.

The first subcycle presents *the beginnings of the Christian life.* The six texts of this subcycle fall into two sections of three each. We have first of all a comprehensive
description of the first church in Jerusalem, the mother of
all subsequent Christendom. Here, after Christ's work
was finished and the Holy Spirit sent, the actual beginning
of the Christian life and church was made. We behold
the church as a union of believers, all resting on the Word.
This is essential for all time, and to this very day all who
come to faith and Christian life are introduced to this
same blessed union and rest upon the same Word. — The
second text goes a step forward and shows us *what constitutes membership in the Christian church,* namely the
possession of Christ's righteousness by faith. This grand
text takes in at the same time the story of how faith is
wrought, how it expresses itself in confession, and how
it saves by securing the forgiveness of sins. — The third
text centers our attention entirely upon Christ himself by
illustrating to us in the first apostolic miracle *the power
of Jesus' name.* Peter's sermon on the miracle is the chief
part of the text, and this is all aimed at producing by
Christ's saving power repentance and faith in the hearts
of his hearers.

In the first three texts the general foundation is laid:
the church — the Word — Jesus; in the next three the
attitude of men towards these three is set forth. So the
fourth text describes vividly the attitude of *opposition*:
the Jewish leaders spurn Jesus, the Gospel addressed to
them, and the church with which they are brought into
contact. It is the attitude of thousands still. — In the fifth
text we have an exhibition of *indecision.* The hour of
grace was at hand, but Gamaliel wanted to wait for further
developments. This too prevents in many the beginnings

of faith and the Christian life. — Now, closing the first subcycle, follows the beautiful text of Philip and the eunuch, a fine illustration of unhesitating, normal *acceptance* of Christ.

The second subcycle takes up the line of thought where the first closes: the eunuch, an individual, has become a Christian; how now must his life unfold? Eight texts trace out *the unfolding of the individual Christian life.* — The first of these texts is comprehensive, it names many things, yet it gathers them all into one special point, one eminently fitted to stand at the head of all Christian life: *godliness.* Every believer must direct his life toward God; that must be first, and that is always fundamental. — Paired with this first text is the second, the key to which is *service* to our fellow men. The two incidents narrated in this text bring out finely this idea of service, which may be individualized according to the features furnished by the text itself, and amplified by means of application in a more general way. This text shows in a marked way how necessary it is to study the correlation of the texts in the entire series; without such study, we fear, this text would puzzle the preacher greatly, and he could hardly hope to do justice to both of its sections. — The third text in this subcycle deals with the Christian's *testimony.* Paul on Mars Hill illustrates how all of us ought to be "ready always to give answer to every man that asketh us a reason concerning the hope that is in us." — In tracing the development of the Christian life we certainly dare not forget *faithfulness.* In this fourth text Paul enjoins it upon Timothy and points to his own past as an example of this cardinal Christian requirement. — Equally important is *certainty,* and this text is one of the very finest and strongest in all Scripture on this particular and essential subject. — This is followed by a beautiful missionary text: Paul sees the man from Macedonia and hears his call to come over and help those who need him so sorely in that land. Every Christian must have *the missionary spirit;* it is essential to the Christian life. In many cases it will be possible to connect this text with the regular mission festival of the congregation. The author has found it very profitable to preach a sermon on this subject a couple of weeks before the festival itself was held. This should be done in any case, and if it can be arranged in the regular order of texts as here presented, so much the better. — A most necessary subject is the one presented by the next text: the Christians' *priestly calling.* In fact, this is one of the very finest texts for this purpose in all Scripture, and it is so rich that no interruption ought to deprive the congregation of hearing a sermon on it. — The second subcycle ends with a text on *gratitude* or thankfulness. Paul looks back over the course of his life, and as he does so, there is no thought of complaint because of hardships and trials, no regret at having lost any worldly advantage, there is only the one deep feeling of gratitude that God in his grace has accepted him and made him what he is. This is how every Christian must feel as he looks back, now, and at last when life draws to its close. —

In the third subcycle, beginning with the Fifteenth Sunday after Trinity, the vision is wider. Here the Christian life is shown in its fuller setting: each of us belongs to the church of God, we are, all together, the people of God. Accordingly our texts trace out for us the *unfolding of the Christian life amid the people of God.* — The first text takes up the subject of *our earthly calling.* God's people are bound for heaven, but while they remain here on earth they must live orderly, earn their daily bread, and follow in this respect the fine example of St. Paul. The subject of church discipline may be incidentally introduced in connection with this text, since Paul would have us withdraw from those who walk disorderly, but the trend of the text is evidently the one indicated. — The second text deals with the other side of the Christian life, with *our exalted heavenly blessings* as a people of God. With our feet we stand on earth indeed, but with our hearts we are in heaven. Note especially that the text speaks of us as a people, the present Christian counterpart of the O. T. people of God, and our blessings belong to us as one great body. Moreover, these are the highest blessings which any people on earth can ever hope to possess. — The third text sets before us as God's people our heavenly goal, the Canaan of eternal rest. But this *our Sabbath rest* is to be attained by persevering faith. The first three texts of this subcycle thus belong together and constitute a little cycle by themselves: Christians follow their earthly calling in quiet good order — enjoy and rejoice in their heavenly blessings — and with earnest faith press forward to their Sabbath rest above.

In the following texts God's people are considered as belonging to Christian congregations. A number of very important and practical lines of thought are thus introduced, furnishing the very best kind of sermon material. The Eighteenth Sunday after Trinity urges: *that the members of a congregation must show their faith by works of love, mercy, and charity toward their fellow members.* Both doctrinally and practically this Christian requirement ought to be urged most earnestly upon our people. — The next text is in the same line: *the members of a congregation must assist each other in bodily and in spiritual trouble.* Here is a fine opportunity to expose the folly of faith-cure, Christian Science, and other errors of this class, and at the same time to describe just how Christian people ought to act when sickness comes to a home, or when one of their number goes astray. — A step further places us among *the strong and the weak members in a Christian congregation,* showing what our conduct must be when this difference, always present to some degree, comes into play. Here too the sermon ought to follow very practical lines. — The next text deals with the household: *parents and children, masters and servants in the Christian congregation.* This too opens up a subject that furnishes the finest opportunity for instruction and admonition in practical lines. Here is the place to touch the labor question, socialism *etc.* — In the following text a number of duties are combined, showing in a general way some of the more important things that must be taken care of among Christian people. We may combine the different thoughts by saying that *the members in a Christian congregation must continue in love, purity, and faithful adherence to the teaching of the apostles.* — The last text of this subcycle will be found especially interesting and fruitful when its subject is noted: *the pastor and his chief duty in the Christian congregation.* Here one pastor writes to another, showing how he must conduct himself in his holy office. The text would do for a pastoral sermon, but it is well for all our congregations to hear an occasional sermon along these lines. The subject of Christian liberty in regard to food and drink may also be handled at this place, but should certainly not crowd out the real subject of the text.

The last subcycle very appropriately deals with *the consummation of the Christian life.* There are four fine texts. Since the church year seldom contains twenty-seven Sundays after Trinity, the preacher should carefully go over the entire series of texts and drop here and there such texts as he may prefer to pass over, reducing the number to as many as the year furnishes after-Trinity Sundays. This is far better than to cut short the final subcycle, or perhaps to omit it altogether. — The subjects of these last texts are all quite evident. The first text is an exhortation to *blamelessness.* It has considerable detail, all of which is rich in sermon thoughts. The entire text refers to the end of the world, and bids us arrange our lives, so that we may meet our Lord with joy when now he comes to judgment. — This is followed by a text on *perseverance,* urging all who are liable to grow discouraged to keep on and not cast their confidence away. It is cowardly to shrink back, it is glorious to hold out to the end. — Surely, no preacher will want to skip the third text in this subcycle, the one on *final faithfulness.* The entire letter to the angel of the church in Smyrna is used, but its crowning point will always be taken to be the call: "Be thou faithful unto death!" — The close of the entire church year has a grand text on *the saints in heaven,* one that can be made very comforting and admonitory for our people. In Germany this text is used for the so-called *Totenfest,* the last Sunday of the church year being used for a sermon on the sainted dead. In the American Lutheran churches this festival has secured no hold, but the text offered here is fine for a general closing text, apart from its special use in Germany.

THE FIRST SUNDAY AFTER TRINITY.

Acts 4, 32-35.

The general trend of the first subcycle of the Trinity texts is indicated by this first text which presents to us, not the faith or godly life of some one Christian in the early days, but the first congregation, or rather the entire early *church* as such in its first development under the leadership of the entire body of the apostles in Jerusalem. Luke has two summary descriptions of the early church: the first follows the great events of Pentecost when three thousand souls were brought to faith and Christian baptism, Acts 2, 41-47; the second somewhat later when the number had grown to five thousand men alone, exclusive of women and children. It is this second description which constitutes our text. — In his first outline Luke mentions a number of important features in regard to the young spiritual life of the first church; in the second he restricts himself to two essential marks of the life of the church, essential to the church of all time: the unity of faith based on the apostolic testimony, or the Word, and the outgrowth of that faith, Christian love and its first fervent manifestation. The general theme of our text is, therefore, *the church as a union of believers;* or, if we prefer, *the church as it rests on the Word.* That Word unites all who accept it, in saving faith and in Christian love as the necessary outgrowth of that faith. A glance is sufficient to show that here we have the basis of all that follows in the long line of coming texts. Whatever is said concerning any part of our spiritual life, activity, condition, and hope, rests on the foundation here indicated. — In the text itself Luke has woven the Word and faith and love so closely together that we can draw no line of division between them. All that we can do is to combine the first two verses, since they state these essential features of the church; and likewise, the next two verses which describe the individual manner in which the faith and love of the first church manifested itself.

The church as it grew in faith and love from the Word.

The Pentecost miracle resulted in the conversion of 3,000 souls; the miraculous healing of the begging cripple in the temple and the preaching connected with it resulted in a further great increase (verse 4). Luke narrates in detail what happened to Peter and John, and how they finally returned to their companions, and with them prayed that God might uphold the church against its foes. Here Luke pauses to give us a glimpse of the inner life of the church, at the same time preparing to narrate further events. **And the multitude of them that believed were of one heart and soul: and not one** *of them* **said that aught of the things which he possessed was his own; but they had all things common. And with great power gave the apostles their witness of the resurrection of the Lord Jesus: and great grace was upon them all.**

Looked at outwardly the church at Jerusalem consisted of a **multitude,** a large number of people, naturally of the most varied kind, old and young, rich and poor, of various occupations, gifts, temperaments, inclinations, *etc.* The thing that made them one body was faith, they were the multitude **of them that believed,** and the aorist participle signifies that they had come to faith. All are meant, the apostles and all who had joined them in be· lieving. Faith is the distinctive mark of the church in its entire membership; the communion of saints always consisted of believers who embrace the saving merits of Christ. Outward adherence does not constitute true membership; it may lead to that, but in itself it does not constitute real membership. This is a ·spiritual thing, not a matter of outward association or organization. Faith, of

course, produces many visible results, for they who believe show it in a variety of ways; and these manifestations are all valuable, but valuable only as evidences and
fruit of the inner thing, the precious saving faith itself.
— The entire multitude of believers **were of one heart
and soul.** The two are mentioned to make the statement
very strong. The heart in biblical language is the organ
of thought, emotion, and will; it is the seat of the soul,
and thus the center of the personality. Oneness in heart
and soul is the most perfect inner agreement and union.
Besser writes: "They all wanted one thing: to be saved
eternally; they all thought one thing: only to be faithful to the Lord Jesus; they all experienced one thing: the
comfort of the Holy Spirit." They were bound firmly
together as if one heart beat in the breast of all, and one
soul animated all. There were no divisions, factions, con-
tentions, serious differences in regard to the saving truth
they all embraced. Moreover, there was kind and affectionate fellowship between them, with a complete absence
of quarreling, strife, and the like. In this regard the first
church stands as a model for all time. While, sad to say,
in subsequent times this complete and lovely oneness was
lost as far as the church generally is concerned, in many
individual localities and congregations it has been attained
again and again, namely a true, hearty oneness in the acceptance and confession of the truth and in the fellowship
and affection of love. — Luke records a remarkable evidence of this oneness in Jerusalem: **and not one said that
aught of the things which he possessed was his own; but
they had all things common.** Usually there is one who
thinks and acts contrary to the rest, and in a larger body
there are several, sometimes quite a minority; the remarkable thing in the first church was the absence of even one who
stood in opposition. What an admonition to the contrary
people in our congregations to-day! Moreover, in this case
earthly possessions were concerned, and we know how men
naturally cling to their personal property and incline to use
it solely or chiefly for their own distinctive personal in-

terests. While some are moved by generous, beneficent, or philanthropic feelings, still the children of this world, and great numbers of Christians, even in following such impulses, manifest a certain selfishness which shows that their motives are not at all born of Christian love. Christianity is not opposed to the possession of personal property; nowhere does Christ require that personal ownership be abolished. What it does require is that we look upon all our possessions and talents as the gift of God entrusted to us for the joint good of ourselves and others, to be administered as under the eye of our Lord. — Here in Jerusalem the members of the church had **all things in common.** This was entirely voluntary, without any legal or other requirement, a free and lovely expression of the spirit of kindness and fellowship animating the hearts of all. It did not involve the transfer of all property and possession to a common treasury, and was thus far from the communism introduced by certain communities of later times. The Christians at Jerusalem had all things in common in that every individual of means allowed others, as they had need, to share the benefit of his possessions. Every needy member could count fully upon the help of every well-provided member. A special way in which the greater wealth of some was made to avail for others is described in verses 34-35. What is mentioned to begin with is the general readiness and desire to impart any needed help and kindly assistance to others, because every person felt that what he owned was entrusted to him for the benefit of all. It is an unworthy supposition to think that this generosity was due to the insecurity of the property of believers in Jerusalem because of the hostility of the Jewish authorities, or to the mistaken expectation of Christ's coming to judgment in the immediate future. Nowhere does Luke hint at such doubtful motives. — When faith and love are mentioned it is well to indicate their source, the divine Word. **The apostles** were the preachers of the first church, and they **gave their witness** in preaching and teaching; ἀπεδίδουν, the imperfect from διδόω, they continued doing this, day by day, and the compound verb implies that this was what was due on their part. Christ had commissioned and empowered them to testify. — The subject of their testimony was **the resurrection of the Lord Jesus** (*Christ,* added in margin), the crowning work of God in accomplishing our redemption. The resurrection of Christ was the natural key-note of apostolic preaching, because it was proof positive of the divinity and Messiahship of Christ; it attested the full efficacy of his life, sufferings, and death in removing the barrier that shut us out from God, satisfying every claim of his holiness and righteousness; it showed, moreover, that the glorified Savior lived as the Head of the church to keep and bless it to all eternity. With the preaching of the risen Savior the apostles won one glorious victory after another. And to this day it is Sunday, the day of Christ's resurrection, which assembles the great host of his followers for their regular worship in honor of his name. — **And great grace was upon them all.** The context here is such that we are not warranted in making this statement parallel with the one in Acts 2, 47, where the grace and favor of men is said to have rested on the Christians of Jerusalem. Luke adds no such modifier here, but allows us to conclude that this was the grace and favor connected with the preaching of the resurrection of Christ, *i. e.* divine grace and the blessing that attested it, basing also on this grace, as an evident fruit of it, the Christian love he now describes more fully.

The special manner in which the love of the church manifested itself.

Luke writes very briefly in Acts 2, 44-45: "and had all things common; and they sold their possessions and goods, and parted them unto all, according as any man had need." Here now the matter is more fully explained: **For neither was there among them any that lacked: for as many as were possessors of lands or houses sold them, and brought the prices of the things that were sold, and laid them at the apostles' feet: and**

distribution was made unto each, according as any one had need.

This manifestation of love was an evidence of divine grace. Great as the host of believers had become, there was not among them **any that lacked,** *i. e.* the necessaries of life. Every one was provided for, either by what he himself owned and earned, or by what was distributed to him from the funds of the church. Besser writes: "The lame beggar who had been healed (Acts 3, 6-8) needed no longer to beg." In all subsequent ages this example of the first church has been considered the pattern to follow. Arrangements were made in the local congregations to take care of the poor and needy; these have been more or less elaborate and efficient, but hardly ever entirely absent. In cases of emergency special provision was made, and the spirit of brotherly love and helpfulness manifesting itself on such occasions has been notable indeed. Besides these local arrangements the work of Christian charity has been organized on a grander scale. Many congregations have coöperated, raising large sums for special purposes, building eleemosynary institutions of various kinds, providing them with steady support, educating and sending out special helpers to minister to the special needs of the poor and afflicted. In these later times the work of Inner Missions has received the special attention of the church. As long as the grace of God rules the church and fills it with living faith, so long this work of love upon any that lack will continue. — Luke tells us how the funds were provided in the first church: **as many as were possessors of lands or houses sold them, and brought the prices of the things that were sold.** The wealthier members made large, voluntary contributions. Note the imperfect tenses ἔφερον *etc.*, and the present participle πωλοῦντες, which describes what was done in succession, from time to time. It is not said that each individual gave all his possessions to the church, or that each person sold all his lands and houses and brought the proceeds. Barnabas had a field and sold it, bringing the

2

entire price of it; but what else he owned and retained for himself we do not know. In the case of Ananias and Sapphira we are told that they might have retained their property entirely, or, after selling it, might have kept any part of the price for themselves. We find too that some retained their houses (Acts 12, 12; 21, 16; compare also Jam. 1, 9 and 27; 2, 1; 3, 14). The offerings that were made were entirely voluntary; they were true gifts of Christian charity. Luther says, the apostles and disciples did not demand the strange possessions of Pilate and Herod, in order to make an equal division of goods to all. — The money that was intended as an offering was brought and laid **at the apostles' feet.** This was in the assemblies of the believers; the apostles, being the teachers, are represented as sitting before their hearers. — From these funds **distribution was made unto each, according as any one had need.** This was done by the apostles themselves until afterwards special deacons were appointed (Acts 6, 1 *etc.*). The needy ones were especially widows, as we see from the latter passage, and only those who had need received any of this charity money. The ἄν with the indicative εἶχεν denotes repetition in the subordinate clause; the classical language would employ the optative. Blass, 2nd ed., 63, 7. As often as a needy case was reported, relief was applied; the money was always ready.

HOMILETICAL HINTS.

The work of the Pentecostal Spirit in the life of the church is so varied and extensive that we must devote many a Sunday and sermon to its detailed consideration. This is our task in the after-Trinity season. We begin with a view of the church itself, when the apostles were its leaders and the Spirit of God was strong in every heart.

Would that it might never be said of us, as Jesus himself said of the church at Ephesus after its first lovely development: "Nevertheless I have somewhat against thee, because thou hast left thy first love." Rev. 2, 4.

When the apostles gave their witness of the resurrection of the Lord Jesus so effectively at Jerusalem, then the prayer of the church was fulfilled: "Grant unto thy servants to speak thy word with all boldness, while thou stretchest forth thy hand to heal." Acts 4, 29-30.

Wherever such preaching was borne of faith, there, as in the days of the first beginnings of the church, it has wrought faith. Wherever it has placed in the center of its proclamation the testimony concerning the resurrection of the crucified Lord and his glorification by the Father after the pangs of the cross, it has not been uttered in vain, it has demonstrated that, though uttered by sinful lips, heavenly powers were active in and through it, human hearts were consecrated as altars of God by it, sacred fires were kindled in them, and the barren wilderness of death was turned into fields of verdant life. The preaching of the apostles finally ceased, but the apostolic power of preaching has continued wherever its message remained intact. Give us preachers who speak because they believe, who do not tamper with the Word, but seek to impart it, whose desire is not to alter it, but to convey the power of it, and we will have to-day, as in days of old, multitudes of believers confessing the Lord and serving him in love. Rump.

Faith comes by preaching, the Word will not return void, it enters men's hearts, it prepares for the Lord a people ready for his service. A thousand dew-drops glisten on the grass in the early morning radiance, and in everyone of them there flashes the image of the sun; so thousands of Christian hearts reflect the image of the Lord who gave himself for their salvation. — All doubt of the blessed resurrection of Christ is gone, conquered by the believing testimony of that former doubter, Thomas himself. Matthes.

Call for a man's money, and you will find him not at home, or too busy to see you. You will find that about that time he is the most careful and anxious provider for his own family, in fact, you will discover him beset with all kinds of troubles and difficulties, as at no other time. Ask him for an offering, and his pleasant face will be darkened as with a shadow, and even his pride will not disdain for a little while to sit on the bench of poverty. It has been well said, conversion must be twofold, after converting a man's heart we must proceed to convert also his pocketbook.

Think a little and you will see the great difference between these first Christians and some of their spurious imitators of to-day. This modern plan to divide the good things of earth springs from the earthly desire and hunger for them, from the excessive and false value placed upon them. The heart clings to these earthly things. It demands a division of other men's goods, as robbers divide their loot. The Christians at Jerusalem were animated by the very opposite spirit. Their generous division of goods grew out of the low estimate they placed upon mere earthly things. They had found a higher treasure, a joy of possession such as the world cannot know. In the light of their spiritual and heavenly wealth they now understand what the real purpose of earthly possession is. While others shout: "What is thine, is mine!" these Christians say: "What is mine, is also thine!"

Christian love at Jerusalem achieved what the old law of Moses demanded: "There shall be no poor among you." Deut. 15, 4. At Jerusalem there was among them not any that lacked. So our abundance is to supply the wants of others, 2 Cor. 8, 14

If the heart belongs to God, all our possessions belong to him likewise. A true Christian always has money for his Lord He is God's treasurer and honors every order sent in from above.

God's Work in the First Church.

I. *The multitude of them that believed were of one heart and soul.*

II. *With great power gave the apostles witness of the resurrection of the Lord Jesus.*

III. *Neither was there any among them that lacked.*

Langsdorff.

The Church Began With a Christian Congregation, and so Continues to the End of Time.

We always find a number bound together

I. *By faith and Gospel preaching.*

II. *By love and works of charity.*

The Church Flourishing.

I. *True preaching makes faith flourish.*

II. *True faith makes love flourish.*

III. *True love makes every grace flourish.*

Behold the Communion of Saints!

I. *One in faith and doctrine.*

II. *One in love and works.*

The Treasures of the First Church.

I. *Its believers.*
II. *Its preachers.*
III. *Its lovers.*

The Bride of Christ in all her Beauty.

I. *Adorned with his Word and grace.*
II. *Crowned with faith and love.*

THE SECOND SUNDAY AFTER TRINITY.

Rom. 10, 1-15.

We have considered the church, the communion of those who believe the Gospel of Jesus Christ and manifest their faith by love. Now we are to consider what constitutes *membership in the church,* namely the possession of God's righteousness in Jesus Christ by faith. All who reject this righteousness and refuse to believe remain without. All who accept this righteousness, believe in Christ, and confess his name are members of the church, and salvation is theirs. With faith so important, it is imperative that we know how it is wrought: it is kindled by the preaching of the Gospel. — All this the apostle Paul describes to us in detail, furnishing a text exceedingly rich in Gospel truth. He shows us first of all how unbelief bars us out of the church (1-3); then, how faith brings us in (4-13); and finally, how the Gospel produces faith.

Faith — its fatal absence.

Paul is dealing with the sad story of his brethren in the flesh, once God's chosen people, but now cast out, because they would not accept his saving righteousness in Jesus Christ. He here describes their unbelief and the guilt connected with it. **Brethren, my heart's desire and my supplication to God is for them, that they may be saved. For I bear them witness that they have a zeal for God, but not according to knowledge. For being ignorant of God's righteousness, and seeking to establish their own, they did not subject themselves to the righteousness of God.**

Brethren, writes Paul to the Romans, as if he would say: "Believe me, I assure you, my feelings toward my brethren in the flesh are not resentment, ill-will, or hatred, but the very opposite !" With great sadness he records the dark facts concerning Jewish unbelief; they reject Christ and hate even his messengers, but the apostle declares (compare chapter 9, 1, *etc.*) : **my heart's desire and my supplication to God is for them, that they may be saved.** Paul's εὐδοκία, really his *good pleasure* (margin), that which would give him the greatest joy and delight, is to see the Jews saved. Nor is this an idle feeling, it goes forth in **supplication to God,** in petition and request to the God of salvation, in behalf of the Jews. Both the "good pleasure" and the "supplication" are ὑπὲρ αὐτῶν, **for them,** for their benefit or in their behalf. And this in a certain direction: εἰς σωτηρίαν, for salvation, **that they may be saved,** *i. e.* brought to faith in Christ and thus to eternal salvation. The μέν at the head of the sentence points to a δέ which should follow, but the apostle finishes his thought in a different way, still, however, bringing out the contrast. Note also the strong possessive ἐμῆς before καρδιάς, instead of a μοῦ following it: the desire of *Paul's* heart is that they be saved — but *the Jews* on their part have prevented its fulfilment. Yet that Paul still prays for them shows that they are not utterly reprobate; every converted Jew is an answer to the apostle's fervent prayer. — He explains the reason for his desire and prayer: **For I bear them witness, that they have a zeal for God, but not according to knowledge.** Paul knew his brethren in the flesh thoroughly; he had once been animated by the same spirit that he now credits them with, and later on he had himself experienced the sharp temper of that spirit. Their **zeal for God** burned in their hatred of idolatry, in their love for the temple, and especially in their scrupulous outward obedience to the law and their rabbinical traditions. Paul gives the Jews a certain degree of credit in having "a zeal for God;" they stand higher than a Pilate with his skeptic indifference: "What is truth?" or a Felix with his love of a worldly life and utter disregard of higher things. — The sad thing, however, in the case of the Jews was that theirs was a zeal **not according to knowledge.** It was strong, but entirely misdirected; it lacked the ἐπίγνωσις, true, vital knowledge and insight into divine truth. Its very strength carried them farther away from God whom it meant to serve. "This text," says the Lutheran Commentary, "is an effectual answer to the frequent statement, that it is a matter of indifference what religion one have, if he have only some form of religion, or the kindred statement that everything depends on one's sincerity." And Calvin writes: "Let us learn from this whither our good intentions carry us if we obey them." With such intentions the Jews crucified Christ, rejected his Gospel, persecuted the apostles and Christians. Misdirected zeal still leads to the most terrible results. "It is better to limp in the road, than to run eagerly outside of it." Augustine. Still, the strong zeal of many errorists is a rebuke to the coldness, indifference, and slothfulness of many who have the truth, but fail to submit wholly to its power. — Paul describes the Jewish zeal without knowledge: **For being ignorant of God's righteousness, and seeking to establish their own, they did not subject themselves to the righteousness of God.** This was their great fault, this their guilt. God had left nothing undone to place his righteousness before them, but they kept on setting up their own righteousness, "as a monument to their own glory and not God's" (Vincent), and so they knew not God's righteousness and did not submit themselves to it. The pride of their self-righteousness so blinded them (Eph. 4, 18) that they saw neither the value of God's righteousness, nor the vanity of their own. **God's righteousness** is not merely that which emanates from God (ἐκ θεοῦ, Phil. 3, 9), but that which God himself procured for us and now counts, judges, and declares to be righteousness, to meet all his demands and requirements in regard to man; "which avails before God," Luther. In the same way **their own** (righteousness) is that which the Jews themselves tried to procure and considered to be righteousness. The two kinds are finely illustrated in the

parable of the Pharisee and the Publican. God justified
the latter, the latter justified himself. He had what Paul
himself formerly gloried in: "a righteousness of mine
own, even that which is of the law," Phil. 3, 9, in reality
no righteousness at all, an *ignis fatuus;* while the publican
had the true righteousness, the actual forgiveness of his
sins, which Paul afterwards gloried in, "the righteousness which is through faith in Christ." God's righteousness is more than Christ's merits or work, objectively
wrought for us, more also than the divine acceptance of
these merits for all the world; the term signifies God's
own declaration concerning the individual sinner on the
basis of Christ's merits apprehended by faith, the *justitia
Dei imputata.* Compare the text for The Third Sunday
after Epiphany for a fuller elaboration. — For the Jews
to establish their own righteousness was to set up a righteousness by a declaration of their own based on works of
their own. This kind of righteousness is still very popular
among men; many fail to recognige its utter spuriousness.
On the other hand, for men to **subject themselves** to the
righteousness of God is to abandon all efforts at self-
justification, and to bow in the obedience of faith to what
God declares acceptable to him. Ὑποταγή *submittit se τῷ
θέλειν divino, voluntati Dei.* Bengel. To refuse such sub-
jection is not merely excusable ignorance, but the guilt of
a wicked, disobedient, and obstinate will.

Faith — its saving presence.

After stating the sad fact concerning the Jews Paul
presents at length the righteousness and salvation that
is by faith, verses 4-13. He begins with a summary
statement: **For Christ is the end of the law unto righteousness to every one that believeth.** This sums up and
settles the whole matter as between God's righteousness
and any righteousness of our own. **The end of the law**
is here not its object and aim, much less its fulfilment;
τέλος simply means "end" — the law is done with, put entirely out of force, in regard to saving righteousness. "No

man is justified by the law ($\dot{\epsilon}\nu$ $\nu\acute{o}\mu\omega$) in the sight of God,"
Gal. 3, 11. There is no way by means of law to become
righteous before God. Whatever other uses the law may
have, this is not its use. — **Christ** is the end of the law.
He was this by anticipation, when God promised his
coming, so that Abraham for instance was justified not
by works but by faith, Rom. 4, 1 *etc.;* he is this now actually since he has come and satisfied all the claims of
the law by his holy life, sufferings, and death in our stead. —
Unto righteousness to every one that believeth states
the purpose of this ending of the law by Christ. Christ's
intention was to open up a new and different way unto
righteousness, one adapted to helpless sinners who could
not possibly themselves fulfil the law. This is the way of
faith as opposed to the way of works, the way of believing
instead of doing, the way of divine giving instead of
human earning and meriting. **To every one that believeth** is universal, as in John 3, 16 and many other passages. Now the question of righteousness before God is
not one of ability, for no effort is required on our part,
only that we believe, *i. e.* let God kindle faith in our hearts.

Paul now contrasts the two ways of becoming
righteous before God: **For Moses writeth that the man
that doeth the righteousness which is of the law shall
live thereby;** compare Lev. 18, 5. The law requires a
doing, and only to him who perfectly fulfils all its requirements in thought, word, and deed, from the very
beginning to the end of life, does it hold out the reward
of life, *i. e.* eternal life with God. It need not be added
that this way of obtaining life is utterly impossible for
us who are born sinners and carry the damnable taint
of sin in us from our very first breath on. — But thanks
be to God, there is another way: **But the righteousness
which is of faith saith thus, Say not in thy heart, Who
shall ascend into heaven? (that is, to bring Christ
down:) or, Who shall descend into the abyss? (that is,
to bring Christ up from the dead.) But what saith it?
The word is nigh thee, in thy mouth, and in thy heart:**

that is, the word of faith which we preach. Paul places them over against each other: Moses, the man of the law, and the message he has to bring, and the righteousness which is of faith, the daughter of the Gospel, and the sweet message she has to bring. By **the righteousness which is of faith** the apostle means "God's righteousness," as mentioned heretofore, *i. e.* the sentence of justification which God pronounces upon faith and him who has it. The force of ἐκ πίστεως, really: *"out of* faith," must not be overlooked. In being "out of faith" this righteousness is the very opposite of that other which is out of works ("the man that doeth the righteousness which is of the law," verse 5). Paul personifies this Gospel righteousness and makes it utter its message in our ears. In doing this he utilizes words which Moses at one time employed in speaking of the law, namely Deut. 30, 11-14. It is quite evident that Paul is not quoting Moses, for he uses no formula of any kind for introducing a quotation, and he omits, alters, and adds, as suits his special purpose; he simply adapts the words of another to his own thought, just as this is done by writers generally. He is the more justified in doing this since two emphatic statements concerning the law, namely that it is "in thy heart," and that "the word is nigh thee" *(i. e.* the Israelite), are also true of the Gospel for every one who has heard it. Those expressions which are true only of the law, mentioning the doing of it, he, of course, omits. — So he makes the righteousness of faith declare to those who would despair of finding such a righteousness: **Say not in thy heart, Who shall ascend into heaven? (that is, to bring Christ down:) or, Who shall descend into the abyss? (that is, to bring Christ up from the dead.)** "To say in thy heart" is a Hebraism for "to think," and is used especially of some unworthy thought which one fears to utter aloud. Meyer makes each of the questions an expression of unbelief equivalent to a denial of the incarnation and the resurrection of Christ, but the apostle shows by his parenthetical elucidations that he conceives them, after the manner of the original in Deuter-

onomy, as expressions of an earnest desire coupled with
despair of its fulfilment. One who despairs of fulfilling
the law and thus obtaining righteousness might voice his
despair by crying: **Who shall ascend into heaven?** namely
to get righteousness there. Of course, no one can, and so
he would be left utterly hopeless and helpless. Paul uses
this question of Moses because Christ has actually come
down from heaven and brought us righteousness, which
cannot be found anywhere except in him. Whoever ignores
or sets that aside acts as if the work of Christ had never
been done and had to be done over again, in other words
as if he wanted someone **to bring Christ down** for this
purpose. — The same is true of the second question: "Who
shall go over the sea for us?" Paul alters this because he
has Christ in mind: **Who shall descend into the abyss?**
Christ actually died for our sins and arose from the dead
for our justification. Whoever ignores or sets that aside
acts as if we had **to bring up Christ from the dead** and
by our own efforts had to do Christ's work over again. The
righteousness of faith forbids us even to think of such a
thing, which would land us in utter despair, or, perhaps,
make us imagine, like the blind Jews, that after all our
efforts at fulfilling the law suffice for righteousness. —
Instead of such folly let us heed the voice of this blessed
righteousness of faith: **But what saith it?** namely in
answer to such wrong, despairing thoughts and in order to
remove them altogether. The same thing as once the law
said to Israel: **The word is nigh thee, in thy mouth, and
in thy heart.** But Paul again adds a brief explanation, for
this is not the same "word" as the "word" of the commandment mentioned by Moses, it is not a word that bids
us "do" anything to earn righteousness: **that is,** he says,
the word of faith which we preach. Instead of being left
hopeless and helpless, gazing up to the silent far-off heavens,
or trying to penetrate into the dark and voiceless shadows
of the abyss, here is our righteousness right at our side, the
blessed message of the Gospel which tells us of Christ and
his work, bids us believe, and gives us power to do so. Once

the Jews, already in childhood, learned the word of the law; thus is was put into the **mouth** of each. Its object, of course, was to enter the **heart** and control man completely. So now, Paul says of the Gospel, when it is preached it is actually put into the mouths of the hearers, they discuss it and talk of it, and into their hearts, if at all they are brought to faith. And he calls this, in distinction from the word which requires works and doing on our part: **the word of faith,** the word which requires nothing but faith and trust in its blessed offer and promise. Wherefore also it is simply preached or announced by the servants of God, for people to hear and believe.

Because if thou shalt confess with thy mouth Jesus *as* **Lord, and shalt believe in thy heart that God raised him from the dead, thou shalt be saved.** The use of the second person shows that the righteousness which is of faith is still speaking. Translators and commentators are divided in regard to the opening word ὅτι. Many, like the A. V. and the margin of the R. V. translate this ὅτι with: *that,* as if the apostle were stating the contents of what he and his fellow workers preached. And, indeed, verse 9 may be read as a brief summary of the apostolic message. But Paul has already defined the Gospel message, and that in an emphatic way in distinction from the law, as "the word of faith, which we preach." That brings out with great clearness and force the characteristic point here needed, so that no addition seems necessary. Hence Luther, Meyer, Philippi, Luthardt, and the R. V. translate ὅτι with: **because,** so that verse 9 states the reason for what verse 8 contains. This word of faith, which the apostles preach and thus put into our mouths and hearts, is all that we need, so that there is no reason for anyone to gaze with longing into heaven or into the abyss: **because** in very truth this word saves. To be sure, the law also promises that a man "shall live," but only "the man that doeth the righteousness which is of the law" (compare verse 5). The sad thing is that no man can obtain this promise, because no one can meet its condition. With the word of faith this is different;

here there is no doing at all on our part, since Christ has
already done everything for us. All that is necessary is for
us to accept him and his work, that means "confess" and
"believe"; and the result will be: "thou shalt be saved." —
Paul follows the order of the previous verse in mentioning
confession first, and believing second; in verse 10 he has the
natural order. — Confession and faith are mentioned here
side by side: **if thou shalt confess with thy mouth . . . ,
and shalt believe in thy heart,** but each involves the other,
for the proper, sincere, upright confession is always an
expression of faith, and the right kind of faith always utters
a confession.   The same is true of the objects of the two
verbs: **Jesus** *as* **Lord,** and: **that God raised him from the
dead;** each involves the other, and each is a brief summary
of the word of faith.   To confess Jesus as **Lord** is to
acknowledge him openly before men as the exalted Savior
and divine Mediator, whom we trust, worship, and obey as
such.   Bengel: *In hac appellatione est summa fidei et salutis.*
To believe **that God raised him from the dead** is to believe
and trust the crowning act of God in the work of our salvation, that act by which the efficacy and sufficiency of all
Christ's work was clearly revealed and forever sealed.   The
mention of Jesus as "Lord" harmonizes with the thought of
the first question which the apostle appropriated from
Moses; for Jesus is the Son of God who came from heaven
and became our "Lord."   The mention of the resurrection
of Christ from the dead agrees in the same way with the
second question, in the sense in which the apostle uses it;
for Christ has risen from the abyss of death and now sits
at the right hand of God forever. — If then thou shalt confess and believe: **thou shalt be saved,** delivered and rescued
from thy sins.   The law promises: "thou shalt live," a
promise utterly in vain once a man sins; it cannot say:
"thou shalt be *saved*," because the moment sin sets in and
a man needs saving help, the law can do nothing but condemn.   The blessed assurance: "thou shalt be saved," belongs only to the Gospel, and its greatest sweetness is that
it is intended for those that are lost, that need saving, namely

sinners. "To be saved" means indeed also "to live," but to live after being rescued from the death of sin.

These thoughts Paul elaborates still more fully by adding an explanation (verse 10), and by adducing Scripture proof, pointing out at the some time the universality of God's saving grace (11-13): **for with the heart man believeth unto righteousness; and with the mouth confession is made unto salvation. For the scripture saith, whosoever believeth on him shall not be put to shame. For there is no distinction between Jew and Greek: for the same** *Lord* **is Lord of all, and is rich unto all that call upon him: for, whosoever shall call upon the name of the Lord shall be saved.** — Paul now follows the natural order: faith first, confession following. The seat of faith, Calvin has well said, is not the brain, but the heart, the center of man's being. To know a thing is to exercise the sense perception and the intellect; to **believe,** in the sense of Scripture, is to exercise all the faculties of the soul. Faith is the confidence and trust of the heart that Jesus is the Savior. Such believing is **unto righteousness,** which here cannot mean merely the merits of Christ as acquired for us, or a justifying sentence pronounced on all the world, but the righteousness imputed by God in personal justification to the believer and to him alone. "Unto righteousness" = so that he who believes is now truly righteous before God and accepted as such by him. — Paul's second statement concerning confession unto salvation separates only in form what in fact always goes together. The faith that justifies always confesses, and the confession that is made **unto salvation** always has faith as its basis. A dumb faith is no faith at all; a confession without faith is a hypocritical lie. Melanchthon correctly says that Paul here requires a living and firm faith; and in the Apology to the Augsburg Confession he writes: "Paul thus says that confession saves, in order to show what sort of faith obtains eternal life; namely, that which is firm and active. That faith, however, which does not manifest itself in confession, is not firm." 158,

263. Still we must note that "righteousness" and "salvation" are distinct concepts and justify the separation Paul here makes; for we are justified the moment we believe, but we do not enter heaven and eternal blessedness until we close our earthly career in persevering faith, which includes faithful confession. The faith that justifies the sinner, if it produces no confession, is like an infertile flower, bringing no fruit, simply withering and dying; it never reaches eternal salvation, because it loses again the righteousness which alone admits to salvation. What the sinner needs is righteousness, for that alone assures him of salvation; and here he is most emphatically assured that a living, confessing faith secures this treasure.

Paul now brings Scripture proof for what he writes and notes especially that the way of faith is open to all without distinction. He quotes Is. 28, 16, which he has already used at the end of the previous chapter. In writing: πᾶς ὁ πιστεύων, **whosoever believeth,** where the Septuagint has ὁ πιστεύων, "he that believeth," he brings out the universality of the prophet's statement. For the Hebrew: "He that believeth shall not make haste," *i. e.* flee, the Septuagint has: "shall not be put to shame," apparently following the reading *yabish,* instead of *yachish;* compare Horn, *Introd.,* 7th ed., II, 304. Philippi remarks that essentially there is little difference, since he who flees is certainly put to shame. Paul also writes: **shall not be put to shame,** namely when he faces God and his judgment. Shame, confusion, fleeing from the presence of God shall indeed be the lot of all who come before God at last without the merits of Christ; but whoever brings these merits, be he the malefactor on the cross, or the greatest saint in the church, shall therein find boldness and joy in the day of judgment and unquestioned admittance into the eternal mansions. — **For there is no distinction between Jew and Greek,** as far as attaining salvation by faith is concerned. Both are in the same lost condition, both are rescued by the same means. Differences of nationality or former religious errors, in fact

all other differences do not in the least affect this vital·
point. Nor does the apostle mean that only Jews and
Greeks in general are alike in attaining salvation by faith
alone; he means Jew and Greek or Gentile as including
every individual among the two great classes of men. —
For the same *Lord* **is Lord of all;** ὁ αὐτός is the subject,
κύριος, namely Christ as the mighty and glorious Savior,
the predicate. His Lordship extends over **all,** not one
human being excepted, because he redeemed all and prepared salvation for all. — **And is rich** (being rich, πλουτῶν)
unto all that call upon him, so that no matter how great
the multitude, they cannot exhaust his saving grace and
merits; he never needs to retrench, he never reaches the
end of his resources, nor is his will to extend the blessings of his grace ever weary or unready. To call upon
him is to cry with the publican: "Be merciful to me, a
sinner." It is faith and confession in one act. The voice
may be ever so weak, his ear detects it, his heart responds.
— And there is a very direct Scripture proof for this
explanation of the apostle, namely Joel 2, 32, which, since
it is well known, he simply adds with γάρ: **for, whosoever
shall call upon the name of the Lord shall be saved.**
Here the prophet himself has πᾶς, which the apostle used
before, and also ἐπικαλεῖσθαι, which the apostle anticipated
in his explanation. Paul identifies "Jehovah" in the original with **Lord** in the sense of Christ, for the prophet's
words refer to the days of the Messiah, and Jehovah's
greatest revelation is in the second person of the Godhead
who became man and wrought our redemption. — And thus
the apostle has once more set forth in a most effective
way the saving righteousness of faith, by which alone
we are made members of the church on earth and are assured of an eternal place in the glorious church above.

Faith — its divine production.

The apostle now brings out how men are brought
to call upon Christ in true faith, namely by the preaching

3

of the Gospel through the messengers of Christ. The
Jews rejected these messengers, thus incurring the most
terrible guilt. But our text has only the first two verses
of this section, which are entirely general and apply to
all men. Since everything depends on faith, and no
righteousness and salvation is possible for us sinners
without in faith calling upon the Lord, we must know
how faith is wrought in our hearts. A chain of four
oratorical questions, ending in a striking O. T. quotation, makes this plain: **How then shall they call on
him in whom they have not believed? and how shall they
believe in him whom they have not heard? and how
shall they hear without a preacher? and how shall they
preach, except they be sent? even as it is written, How
beautiful are the feet of them that bring glad tidings of
good things!**

To call on Christ is to exercise one of the vital functions
of faith, and, evidently, no one can **call on him** who does
not believe in him. Whether we read the future indicative
πιστεύσουσιν, or the aorist subjunctive πιστεύσωσιν, and likewise in the following questions, makes no practical difference. The best authorities favor the latter, yet there is some
fluctuation even in the best texts. The former would be:
"How shall they call on him;" and the latter: "How can
they call on him." In questions of doubt and deliberation
the classics use the subjunctive, more rarely the future,
while the N. T. uses practically the subjunctive only. Blass,
64, 6, p. 210. Still Winer adheres to the future indicative
in this passage and where the third person is used, 41, 4,
p. 256. — **In whom they have not believed,** εἰς ὃν οὐκ
ἐπίστευσαν, brings out the direction of saving faith; to believe
εἰς τινα is to yield oneself in faith to someone, *fide se ad
aliquem applicare.* To call upon Christ necessitates indeed
that we turn to him completely and rely on his grace and
help. — But as faith is necessary in order to call upon
Christ, so hearing is necessary for faith. The genitive of
the person with ἀκούειν is attested by Matth. 17, 5; Mark
7, 14; Luke 2, 46; John 3, 29; 9, 31, and signifies: to hear

that person, or a word or message from him. Paul has in mind the Gospel as Christ's own word, going out from him to the hearer. Compare Winer 30, 7, p. 179. Some follow Hofmann who takes οὖ in a local sense: "*where* they have not believed;" but this does not accord with the marked personal reference in the other questions, and introduces an idea out of line with the apostle's argument. — But hearing necessitates **a preacher,** a herald who can speak in the sense of Christ's declaration: "He that heareth you heareth me; and he that rejecteth you rejecteth me; and he that rejecteth me rejecteth him that sent me," Luke 10, 16. — But this preaching necessitates a sending. Paul's argument is entirely general; he has in mind the sending of himself and his fellow apostles into all the world by an immediate commission from Christ, and then also the mediate mission of those that followed the apostles, of missionaries and pastors generally, in fact the testimony of the entire church as it rests on the general command to preach the Gospel everywhere. — Bengel calls this chain of argument a *climax retrograda. Qui vult finem, vult etiam media. Deus vult ut homines invocent ipsum salutariter; ergo vult ut credant; ergo vult ut audiant; ergo vult ut habeant praedicatores; itaque praedicatores misit.* The validity of this reasoning is beyond question: Christ has provided the necessary preachers of his saving righteousness. This the apostle expresses by a jubilant quotation from Isaiah 52, 7, using of the prophet's words what is necessary for the point in hand. The Septuagint is inexact, and Paul follows the Hebrew in this case. The prophet wrote of the messengers who came to announce the deliverance of Israel from its Babylonian bondage: **How beautiful are the feet of them that bring glad tidings of good things!** In God's great plan concerning Israel and the coming Messiah these messengers were the forerunners of the Gospel messengers, who announced a still greater deliverance, the **good things** of God's mercy and grace in Christ the Redeemer. The adjective ὡραῖος means timely, and then, referring to the time of youth and bloom, lovely, attractive, beau-

tiful. Attractive indeed to the poor captive the feet of the
runner, though treading the dust, who brings him the glad
tidings of deliverance, freedom, and all the joys that go with
these two! — Here our text stops, omitting the story of
Jewish guilt in rejecting these messengers and the "good
things" they brought. And so the preacher's aim will be to
treat positively the fine and complete answer presented by
Paul to the question, how the sinner becomes indeed a child
of God, a member of the Christian church.

HOMILETICAL HINTS.

The Jews wanted to climb up to God by their own efforts,
and pushed away his hand of grace in Christ by which he sought
to lift them up to himself. They tried to fly into heaven with
wings of their own, and spurned the ladder God set up for them
in the Savior. They intended to open heaven's portals with a key
of their own manufacture, and refused the true key which is Jesus'
blood. Therefore, the more they tried and the stronger their
efforts, the less hope there was of their success. — There are no
self-made men in the Christian religion.

Righteousness is the key to heaven, there is no doubt of that.
The perfect righteousness of the law will do the work, as Moses
truly declared. If only we could obtain this righteousness! Since
no man can — and thousands have vainly tried — our only hope
is the righteousness of the Gospel, that which God himself provided for us in Christ and offered us as a gift.

After Luther translated the Bible into German he said: "Two
weeks, sometimes three and four, I have at different times hunted
the meaning of a single Hebrew word in Job, without finding it,
and with my assistants sometimes in four days translated hardly
three lines." And you now can buy the entire Bible in your own
language for a small sum. — When the mother of Ziegenbalch, the
first misionary in Tranquebar, India, lay dying, she gathered her
children about her and said: "Dear children, I have gathered a
great treasure for you." "Where is it?" they asked. And the
answer was: "Seek it in the Bible, there you will find it, each
page I have moistened with my tears." — Behold, the Word is
nigh thee, moistened not merely with the sweat of Luther, or
with the tears of faithful believers, but with the blood of the
Savior himself. And can you let this treasure lie without the

gratitude of faithful and diligent use? Koegel. (His sermons, *Der Brief Pauli an die Roemer* are full of fine thoughts, some of which are here used.)

We count it sacrilege when the graves of our dead are robbed, but what shall we say when from our pulpits and altars men snatch the precious treasures of divine truth itself?

However stern and hard some of the sayings of Scriptures seem, no one has ever found one which says that a repentant sinner is not justified and saved.

If in the O. T. God and his Word and will were very near to Israel, much more is this true of the N. T. and its glorious Gospel wealth.

Justifying faith is the right faith. Yet we are justified, not by the fruit of our confession in word and deed, nor by the blossoms of our Christian emotions and imaginings, least of all by the foliage of our outward churchliness. All these things have their place and are necessary. But we are justified only by the root of them all, namely when with the heart and from the heart we believe. — If with the heart thou shalt believe, in spite of the Pharisees and the lying prophets within and without, thou shalt be justified.

Not with our calling on the Lord do we make him rich, but he makes us rich when he hears and answers us. So rich is he that he never complains: Are you begging so soon again? but rebukes us: Where have you been so long? So rich is he that not only with the promises of the Scriptures, but with every possible image of giving and receiving in nature he seeks to stimulate our desire to pray and receive from him. By every child that asks his parents for bread, by every lily opening its calyx to the dew of heaven, by every fledgeling opening his beak at the edge of the nest, the Lord draws us to prayer. "Open thy mouth wide, and I will fill it." Ps. 81, 10.

Faith is born with a cry on its lips. There is no continuation of faith without prayer. And faith can never reach its glorious goal unless it continue in prayer. — You complain much, you pray little, hence your lack of strength. Your enemies, within trouble you much, you are testy, you do not pray, hence your defeats. You judge others, and pray little, hence you go on arid and unblessed. The wings of prayer are eagle's wings and bear you up far above the dust and storm-clouds of time.

Our Christian profession may be a mere habit, travelling along with the Lord as long as there is no battle to fight, following the army's wake for a chance of some of the booty. These stragglers occasionally become deserters. — Where there is power, there we find results; where there is life, there we meet fruit; where there is light, we expect radiance; where there is faith, confession must follow. The mouth without the heart is hypocrisy, the heart without the mouth is deception.

The first congregation at Jerusalem forms an attractive picture. Who would not like to have been one of its members?

How are Sinners Made Members of Christ's Church?
I. *Through Christ alone.*
II. *Through the Gospel alone.*
III. *Through faith alone.*

Christ the End of the Law.
I. *A great historical fact.*
II. *A fundamental Gospel doctrine.*
III. *A blessed Christian experience.*

Langsdorff.

God's Way of Salvation for Sinners.
I. *His messengers bring us the Word.*
II. *The Word proclaims his righteousness.*
III. *His righteousness calls for faith.*
IV. *Faith utters itself in confession.*
V. *Confession leads to salvation.*

Whosoever Believeth on Him Shall not be put to Shame.
It is for this
I. *That God sends us the Gospel.*
II. *That the Gospel proclaims the riches of his grace.*
III. *That his grace kindles faith in our hearts.*

Apel.

The Word of Faith Which we Preach.
I. *A faith that relies on Christ's work.*
II. *A faith that confesses Christ's righteousness.*
III. *A faith that calls upon Christ's grace.*
IV. *A faith that insures us Christ's salvation.*

Righteousness Saves.
I. *That of the law and of works, if we could attain it.*
II. *That of the Gospel and of faith, since we can attain it.*

THE THIRD SUNDAY AFTER TRINITY.

Acts 3, 1-16.

The church — the Word — and now *the power of Jesus' name!* A great miracle in the field of physical evil at once illustrates what the saving power of Jesus is able to do, and attests the divine character and saving efficacy of the Gospel as proclaimed by the apostles through all the ages in the Holy Scriptures, and by the faithful ministry of the church. For the heart of the Gospel is Jesus' name, the Holy and Righteous One, as Peter here calls him, the Prince of life, whom God raised from the dead. — It is a mistake to spiritualize, or to allegorize this miracle in preaching on it; its own native significance, as Peter himself sets it forth to the multitude in the temple, and Luke to all the church by his faithful record in the Acts, is so great, that we should be amply satisfied with this as the burden of our sermon. The text has two parts, the miracle itself, and Peter's explanation of it.

Peter heals the lame man at the temple.

It must have been soon after the day of Pentecost that the event here described by Luke took place. **Now Peter and John were going up into the temple at the hour of prayer,** *being* **the ninth** *hour.* **And a certain man that was lame from his mother's womb was carried, whom they laid daily at the door of the temple which is called Beautiful, to ask alms of them that entered into the temple; who seeing Peter and John about to go into the temple, asked to receive an alms.** — Peter and John are mentioned together as on previous occasions; they too, in the highest sense of the word, were of one heart and mind. By nature entirely different, the one impetuous, the

39

other contemplative, they supplemented each other. Diamond polishes diamond, writes Rieger, and it may well have been that each of these two jewels enhanced the luster of the other. God has often used the friendship and association of believers for the good of the church, especially that of believers highly gifted; witness the working together of Luther and Melanchthon. — They **were going up into the temple at the hour of prayer,** as the custom of the Jews was, who had three stated periods of prayer during the day (Dan. 6, 10) : the third hour, nine o'clock in the morning in connection with the morning sacrifice (compare 2, 15) ; the sixth hour, about noon (10, 9) ; and **the ninth hour,** three o'clock in the afternoon, at the evening sacrifice (3, 1; 10, 3). The first Christians adhered to the good old custom in which they had grown up, just as we now should adhere to the good and necessary custom of two periods daily for family worship, one in the morning before the day's work begins, and one in the evening, when it ends, or before we retire. — Simultaneous with their going into the temple (notice the two imperfects) **a certain man that was lame from his mother's womb was carried** to the gate they were about to enter. He was born lame; he had never walked in the forty years of his life (4, 22). His feet and ankle-bones (verse 7) had probably never developed properly, possibly they were crooked and misshapen. His congenital lameness, especially at the age he had reached, was utterly incurable. — Friends or relatives were carrying him, **whom,** as Luke adds, **they laid daily at the door of the temple which is called Beautiful, to ask alms of them that entered into the temple.** There were to be no beggars in Israel (Deut. 15, 4), yet in the N. T. various afflicted people are mentioned who obtained their living in this way — certainly not to the credit of the Jews at this time, who had omitted the weightier matters of the law, judgment, *mercy,* and faith, Matth. 23, 23. So this poor, lame beggar had his regular station at the gate **called Beautiful,** which in all probability was the gate opposite Solomon's porch (compare verse 11), either the one leading into the court of the women (Fausset), or from this court into the upper court (Smith). Josephus (*The Wars of the Jews,* V, 5, 3) describes it as much higher than any of the other gates, the pride of the temple area, adorned with especially rich and heavy silver and gold plates. — It seems that the apostles came to the gate just after the beggar was deposited there, **who seeing Peter and John about to go into the temple, asked to receive an alms,** no doubt in the usual way in which he did his begging, holding out his hand "to receive" an expected coin or two.

Now occurs a wonderful thing. **And Peter, fastening his eyes upon him, with John, said, Look on us. And he gave heed unto them, expecting to receive something from them. But Peter said, Silver and gold have I none; but what I have, that give I thee. In the name of Jesus Christ of Nazareth, walk. And he took him by the right hand, and raised him up: and immediately his feet and his ankle-bones received strength. And leaping up, he stood, and began to walk; and he entered with them into the temple, walking, and leaping, and praising God. And all the people saw him walking and praising God: and they took knowledge of him, that it was he which sat for alms at the Beautiful Gate of the temple: and they were filled with wonder and amazement at that which had happened unto him.** — Peter is the spokesman and performs the act, and John concurs in both. Without counselling with each other they are moved by the same impulse and thought. The action of **fastening his eyes upon him** has been interpreted to mean that Peter wished to penetrate into the man's heart to discover whether he was a proper recipient for the blessing about to be bestowed upon him. This, however, puts too much into the apostle's action. Luke in no way indicates anything especial in this beggar; Peter and John saw only a poor, pitiable cripple before them. There is no hint of any advance "faith" on his part; he does only what any beggar would do when his expectation is aroused. It is best to suppose that on approaching the beggar and hearing his plea for alms the Lord put into their hearts the thought of healing him according to the promise given them. This inward motion from above made them look intently at the beggar, and made them ask him to look on them, and thus to heed closely what was now about to be done. Here is a case where faith follows the miracle instead of preceding it. — So the beggar **gave heed unto them,** ἐπεῖχεν (*scil.* τὸν νοῦν) αὐτοῖς; but the request of the apostles led his thoughts no higher than the expectation **to receive something from them,** very likely something above the small gifts that usually fell into his palm. The thought that he was about to be delivered from his affliction certainly did not enter his mind. — **But Peter said,** contrary to the man's expectation: **Silver and gold have I none.** If he thought to get a coin or two of silver, or possibly even of gold, he was mistaken. The apostles were not in a position to give him any notable gift in money. Of John at least it is generally supposed that he had moderate means, so that he could give Mary, the mother of Jesus, a home (John 19, 27), but more than that we can hardly say. — There is no time, however, for the beggar to feel disappointed, for Peter at once adds: **but what I have, that I give thee.** He had it from the Lord, miraculous healing as a seal of the Gospel message, and healing for this particular person according to the intimation of the Lord. — So without further preliminaries he says to the expectant beggar: **In the name of Jesus Christ of Nazareth, walk.** It came like a glorious flash from heaven upon the lifelong cripple! It asked no preparation, employed no other means, hinged on no conditions, proceeded through no stages of development. The priceless blessing fell directly from heaven into his lap. **In the name** states the source and fountain; the "in" links together the infinite and blessed power of Jesus and the helpless infirmity of this begging cripple. Peter utters that name himself: **Jesus,** the Savior, **Christ,** the Messiah or Anoninted of God, **of Nazareth,** the place where he dwelt so long and which the Jews generally mentioned in speaking of

him. The beggar had heard that name, no doubt, but now
all that lies in it is opened for him. — Peter waits for no
response from the beggar either in word or action:
And he took him by the right hand, and raised him up.
Perhaps the hand was still extended for the gift, it now
obtains one greater than the man had dreamed. As in the
case of one sound in his limbs, the assistance of another is
enough to bring him from his sitting posture, and he is
actually **raised up** and stands unassisted, as never before in
his life, strong and erect. — Luke adds the explanation:
**and immediately his feet and his ankle-bones received
strength.** The moment Peter uttered the Savior's name
and grasped him by the hand, the power of Jesus made the
feet and ankles of the cripple stiff, firm, and strong
(ἐστερεώθησαν, from στερεός, rigid, hard, *etc.*), so as to serve
their natural purpose. — **And leaping up, he stood, and
began to walk,** his limbs not only sound and whole in
every way, but he at once able to use them to the fullest extent. This increases the miracle. Feeling the new and
wonderful strength in his limbs he **leaped,** sprang and
jumped up before the apostles and any others near the gate,
including very likely the friends who had brought him
thither; then he **stood,** while they made ready to go on
through the gate; and as they passed in he **walked** by
their side: **and he entered with them into the temple,
walking, and leaping, and praising God.** His joy was
so great, that every little while it broke forth and made him
disport his limbs in leaping, and his heart overflowed with
gratitude so that his lips broke out in words of praise to
God. What a glorious hour of prayer that must have been
for this beggar suddenly made so rich through Jesus' name!
But what a reminder for us who have enjoyed these riches
all our lives long, so often without even thinking of what
was ours. He used his limbs for going into the temple,
and it were well if we would use ours more for the same
purpose, and always for walking in the paths of righteousness and true obedience to God. — **And all the people
saw him walking and praising God,** for he attracted gen-

eral attention in this public place: **and they took knowledge of him, that it was he which sat for alms at the Beautiful Gate,** they came to know it beyond a doubt, they were perfectly sure of his identity. The effect was that **they were filled with wonder and amazement at that which had happened unto him.** They recognized the miracle that had been wrought upon the man, and it filled them with the greatest astonishment.

Peter explains the miracle.

The evening sacrifice was ended, and the people streamed back again through the court of the women to pass on out. Peter and John and the healed man were in this multitude. **And as he held Peter and John, all the people ran together unto them in the porch that is called Solomon's, greatly wondering.** Solomon's porch, or *portico* (margin) lay opposite the Beautiful Gate and the court of the women and ran along the entire east side of the temple area. Compare the remarks in *The Eisenach Gospel Selections,* II, 348. Passing out from the inner courts it was most natural that the multitude should collect in this roomy place. Their astonishment was still at its highest pitch, they were ἔκθαμβοι, quite amazed or astounded. So they surrounded the healed beggar, who clung or **held** to Peter and John (this the only proper meaning of κρατεῖν here). Attention was thus drawn in the directest way to the apostles, and Peter was compelled to explain that the credit for this miracle did not belong to him or John personally. This is why Luke writes: **And when Peter saw it, he answered unto the people.** The question that blazed in their minds was, how this beggar was healed. — Peter's answer is quite direct: **Ye men of Israel, why marvel ye at this man? or why fasten ye your eyes on us, as though by our own power or godliness we had made him to walk? The God of Abraham, and of Isaac, and of Jacob, the God of our fathers, hath glorified his Servant Jesus; whom ye delivered up, and denied before the face of Pilate, when** he had determined to release him. But ye denied the Holy and Righteous One, and asked for a murderer to be granted unto you, and killed the Prince of Life; whom God raised up from the dead; whereof we are witnesses. And by faith in his name hath his name made this man strong, whom ye behold and know: yea, the faith which is through him hath given him this perfect soundness in the presence of you all. — The answer in itself is brief: Not we have done this wonderful thing, but Jesus, the Messiah. But while the question seemed at first to be concerning the beggar, Peter turns it entirely into a personal matter regarding his hearers. The Messiah, who wrought this miracle and thus stands glorified before them, is Jesus whom they rejected in the most shameful way, but whom God raised up and attested as the true Savior. And this personal bearing of the miracle still holds good for all who hear the story of it. The question is still: Do we acknowledge and accept this Savior in true faith, or do we repeat the fatal mistake of the Jews who delivered him up and crucified him? — The address: **Ye men of Israel,** is more than an empty honorary appellation, it is intended, as Stellhorn correctly states, to render them conscious of their position and consequent duty. They are to view this miracle as true Israelites should. — Therefore the correcting questions: **why marvel ye at this man? or why fasten ye your eyes on us, as though by our own power or godliness we had made him to walk?** Some read ἐπὶ τούτῳ as a neuter: *at this thing* (margin), but in substance there is no difference. True Israelites should not marvel merely at the man or his miraculous healing, they should consider something else. Nor should they look upon Peter and John as though in them the *causa effectiva* or *meritoria* of the miracle could be found, for they possessed no magic or divine **power,** nor was their **godliness** so great that it could claim miraculous intervention on the part of God as a reward. The genitive τοῦ περιπατεῖν αὐτόν combines the idea of result and of purpose: as though we brought this about and intended it (Winer, 44, 4, p. 292). — The one to consider in this matter, Peter tells the astonished assembly, is their own God, and he uses the old covenant name of God, so precious to the Jews on account of that covenant, and so significant as regards the new covenant: **The God of Abraham, and of Isaac, and of Jacob.** He adds: **the God of our fathers,** thus connecting himself and John with his auditors, as men who together adhere to the faith of the "fathers." — By this great miracle God **hath glorified his Servant Jesus,** τὸν παῖδα αὐτοῦ, for which the margin has: *Child,* but Peter uses the word here as it is used in verse 26, and in 4, 27 and 30, namely in the specific sense of Isaiah's *Ebed Yaveh,* Is. 40-66. For "Son of God" the N. T. always has υἱὸς θεοῦ; the specific meaning of παῖς is apparent when we note that no apostle is ever called παῖς, but δοῦλος, "servant" in the ordinary sense of the term. Christ became the **Servant** of God when in lowly and humble form he carried out the Father's saving will regarding fallen man; and this "Servant" God glorified by the resurrection from the dead and the exaltation at the right hand of power. — Now comes the personal turn of Peter's words, sudden and startling, direct and crushing: on the one side, God, and what he did, namely glorify Christ; on the other, what the Jews did — the very opposite! — disown and disgrace Christ: **whom ye delivered up, and denied before the face of Pilate, when he had determined to release him.** Note the emphasis in ὑμεῖς μέν, as if to be contrasted with ὁ θεὸς δέ, instead of which verse 15 has: "whom God raised from the dead." The Jews **delivered up** Jesus to Pilate, when they brought him to the governor with the demand to have him crucified, and they **denied** him **before the face of Pilate,** boldly, shamelessly to his very face, when they passionately declared that he was not their King, John 19, 14-15; Luke 23, 2, and insisted on his being crucified. And all this, when Pilate **had determined to release him.** The ἐκείνου (purposely used instead of αὐτοῦ) contrasts even Pilate with the Jews. God glorified Christ, Pilate at least wanted to let him go, but the Jews absolutely rejected him and wanted him killed. The Jews were shamed even by the heathen Pilate. Besser. — Now follows another and different contrast, suggested by the word "deny;" Peter shows them whom they chose and denied instead: **But ye** (unlike even Pilate) **denied the Holy and Righteous One, and asked for a murderer to be granted unto you, and killed the Prince of life.** This brings out fully the enormity of the Jewish rejection of Christ. The great Servant of Jehovah whom they denied was the **Holy and Righteous One,** sinless and consecrated to God, without fault or flaw in heart or conduct, all this also in regard to his great mediatorial work. And him, whom God had promised them so long and finally sent to them, they **denied,** a repetition of the word which shows that this was the central act of all this wicked rejection of Christ. The Holy and Righteous Servant of God was not good enough for them, they **asked for a murderer to be granted unto them** (Luke 23, 19) instead, and got what they wanted. The unreason, the utter baseness, the actual blasphemy of their act is thus brought out glaringly. The words of Peter are like sledge-hammer blows, each one delivered with crushing effect. In every term which the apostle uses there lies an unanswerable overwhelming argumnt. True Israelites ought to accord with the God of Israel, ought to delight in his holy and righteous Servant, ought to glory and rejoice in the Prince of life, ought to judge better than a heathen governor, ought to abominate a foul murderer. But they had done the exact opposite of all this, and now stand without answer and excuse when it is all brought home to them. No wonder Peter's words were effective; compare 4, 4. Here let us learn one of the secrets of effective preaching! Over against "the Holy and Righteous One" is placed ἄνδρα φονέα, "a man who is a murderer," the two nouns hightening the effect of the statement. — And the climax is: **ye killed the Prince of life,** the ἀρχηγός, the author, originator, the cause of life (compare Heb. 12, 2 in the text for Palm Sunday, also Cremer's explanation of the word), here placed in contrast to φονεύς, a destroyer of life. Christ is the fountain of true life for us because he delivered us from

sin and death and bestows true life upon us who had lost it.
He himself is "life" (John 14, 6), and whoever has life has
drawn it from him. This "Prince of life" the Jews **killed,**
nailing him to the shameful cross. Here is a new contrast.
The statement is of great value dogmatically in regard to the
person of Christ, since it shows that all human attributes
and their works are ascribed to the person of Christ,
whether this person is designated by a human or a divine
name. There is thus in Christ both a communication of natures and of attributes. Luther brings out the practical
value of this for our faith: "If it were not said, 'God has
died for us,' but only a man, we are lost. But if the death
of God, and that God died, lie in the scale of the balance, he
sinks down, and we rise up as a light, empty scale. But he
also can indeed rise again or spring from the scale; yet he
could not have descended into the scale unless he had first
become a man like us, so that it could be said: 'God died,'
'God's passion,' 'God's blood,' 'God's death.' For in his
nature God cannot die; but now God and man are united in
one person, so that the expression 'God's death' is correct,
when the man dies who is one thing or one person with
God." *Formula of Concord,* 632, 44. And this is not
merely a *praedicatio verbalis,* as Zwingli and others declare,
the Confession is careful to add. — Over against what the
Jews did stands the great, significant act of God, which
Peter states in a brief relative clause: **whom God raised
from the dead** — on which Meyer remarks: "Simply
grand!" Thus at one stroke all the wicked efforts of the
Jews against Christ were nullified, all their acts contradicted
and condemned, and God's great Servant approved of God
in all his work and sacrifice, and crowned with infinite
glory. The key to Peter's whole address, as well as to all
his preaching and teaching, is thus the resurrection of Christ
from the dead. — **Whereof we are witnesses,** Peter adds,
men who can testify from personal knowledge and firsthand
evidence that this thing is so. The genitive οὖ is best read
as a neuter: "of which thing," not as a masculine: *of whom*
(Christ), margin. To testify of Christ's resurrection, to

proclaim the risen, living, glorified Savior, is the chief duty of the apostles. Peter is thus at this very moment executing his holy office. And the great miracle just performed upon the poor beggar is a tangible, forceful evidence for all his auditors, that the apostolic testimony is true.

Now follows Peter's explanation of how the miracle was wrought: **And by faith in his name hath his name made this man strong, whom ye behold and know: yea, the faith which is through him hath given him this perfect soundness in the presence of you all.** — The first emphasis is on the "name" of Christ, the second on "faith," both words being repeated on this account. Christ's **name** is not a mere sound uttered by human lips, but the blessed word which designates to us the person whom Peter has just described. In his name Jesus himself stands before us, revealed to our hearts as the Savior he really is. Therefore, to know his name is to know him; to believe in his name is to believe in him. This is how **his name made this man strong;** Jesus himself healed the beggar, his name is the *efficient* cause, and Peter places it last in the sentence to make the repetition of it the more emphatic. — The correlative of the "name" is **faith,** for the name is intended for faith and is embraced and held fast by us in faith. And so faith is the *instrumental* cause of the miracle. The beggar was healed τῇ πίστι, **by faith,** namely the faith of the apostles, who came to him with Jesus' name. The best reading has the simple dative, and no preposition with it. In saying this Peter turns to the beggar: **whom ye behold and know** — you see him healed, and you know that it is he. And the apostle emphasizes it: **yea, the faith which is through him** hath done this, the faith which Christ himself wrought in us by all that he revealed of himself. It was no self-made faith, no confidence springing only from their own ideas, and thus gravely mistaken and disappointing. The faith Christ had wrought in the apostle's hearts he fully justified, for he used it as the instrument to give the begger **this perfect soundness in the presence of you all.**

4

By ὁλοκληρία is meant soundness in all parts, completeness. Besser thinks that this second reference to faith applies to the beggar; but his healing is nowhere conditioned on his own faith, though, no doubt, when he found himself miraculously healed, he believed. It was the faith of the apostle's that brought him the blessed name and all the healing and saving efficacy that lies in that name. So faith still goes through the world proclaiming the name of the Prince of life to all who need his help; and wherever the blessed Gospel message sounds forth there, beyond a doubt, Christ himself and all his power and grace are present. He demonstrated it here in the temple in a visible way by a physical miracle upon a helpless beggar; but his greatest desire is to demonstrate it in an invisible way upon our immortal souls.

HOMILETICAL HINTS.

In our day many say, perhaps not in so many words, but often very plainly by their deeds: Faith and love have I not, and what I have, namely silver and gold, that I give thee not!

Thomas Aquinas, the famous scholastic theologian of the Middle Ages, once saw a high dignitary of the church wash his bejeweled hands in a golden basin. Jokingly the wealthy prelate remarked: "Now, my dear sir, the church can no longer say: Silver and gold have I none." "Yes." said Thomas, "and for this very reason it cannot say: In the name of Jesus Christ arise and walk."

A healthy man is not necessarily a better man than others. — Of what use is health and soundness of limb, if we do not use both in God's service, and thank him? — How sad when even on his death-bed a man clings to his poor earthly life and begs to have it lengthened at least by minutes and seconds, which can only prolong his suffering, whereas, if he would, he might have the Prince of life at his side, and be led by him as in a sweet and gentle dream through the portals of the shadow into eternal life and light. — We do not need health in order to become truly happy people, and certainly not in order to become righteous and good in God's sight. Paul was a sufferer all his life. Yet who would say that he was not truly happy and godly at the same time?

The bodily blessing which the beggar received is secondary to the spiritual blessing which in and through the name of Jesus was held out to him and all the people in the Temple that day. That name healed the beggar so miraculously to show all the world that it is able with divine grace and help to free our souls from all that causes so much misery and distress in the world.

People are astonished to see crippled limbs made sturdy and sound at a word; they should observe with holy astonishment, fear, joy, and gratitude that souls bound in sin are made free, sound, and whole at a word likewise, even the same word: Jesus Christ of Nazareth.

The world has but poor comfort and help for the sick and suffering, the unfortunate and wretched. To a certain extent it has learned to relieve their suffering and poverty outwardly, but this is all. The church reaches out its ministering hands in the name of Jesus; it brings bodily help and relief, and this sweetened with heavenly words of comfort and healing. Even where it cannot cure crippled limbs it fills the soul with heavenly gladness and peace. And thus it meets our greatest needs and bestows eternal blessings.

Not suffering and poverty, but sin and unbelief is the worst thing in the world. To be a beggar is pitiful but to reject the Prince of life is a thousand times more pitiful. To find silver and gold may be good fortune, but to embrace the name of Jesus in true faith is eternal wealth.

The Blessed Power of Jesus' Name.

I. *Illustrated* in the healing of the lame man at the Beautiful Gate, by a physical demonstration of that power.

II. *Exercised* whenever and wherever the Gospel is preached, by spiritual results.

The First Apostolic Miracle an Example of the Blessed Work of the Church.

It shows us

I. *The field of its operation.*

II. *The power at its command.*

III. *The results it attains.*

Apostolic Care of the Poor and Sick.

I. *Money is little.*

II. *Help is more.*

III. *Christ is everything.*

Stoecker.

True Christians are the Happiest People.

I. *They may always pray.*
II. *They can always give.*
III. *They must always praise.*

Anacker.

The Prince of Life Glorified Among Men.

I. *By his resurrection from the dead.*
II. *By the miracle at the Beautiful Gate.*
III. *By the Gospel preaching of Peter.*
IV. *By the faith of all believers.*

"All Hail the Power of Jesus' Name!"

I. *Think who he is!* (God's Servant; the Holy and Righteous One; the Prince of Life.)
II. *Remember what he does.*

THE FOURTH SUNDAY AFTER TRINITY.

Acts 4, 1-12.

The church, the Gospel, the name of Jesus and faith in his name, all meet *opposition*. We have an example of it in this significant text. The tragic thing about it is that this opposition spurns the only source of salvation in all the world and thus dooms itself to eternal destruction. The text continues the story of the miracle at the Beautiful Gate, describing first the apostles' arrest by the Jewish officers, and secondly their defense before the Jewish high court.

The arrest.

And as they spake unto the people, the priests and the captain of the temple and the Sadducees came upon them, being sore troubled because they taught the people, and proclaimed in Jesus the resurrection from the dead. And they laid hands on them, and put them in ward unto the morrow: for it was now eventide. But many of them that heard the word believed; and the number of the men came to be about five thousand. Peter and John were still busy speaking to the people, when "there stood by them" (ἐπέστησαν αὐτοῖς), all unexpectedly, the officials who had come to arrest them, together with the men who were causing their arrest. Luke names them in order: **the priests,** namely those of them who were taking their turn in attending to the ministrations at the sanctuary; **the captain of the temple,** the officer commanding the Levitical temple guard, whose duty it was to keep good order (compare Josephus, *Wars of the Jews*, 6, 5, 3); **and the Sadducees,** such of them as happened to be at hand when Peter addressed the people. The Sadducees are present at this arrest because they are instigating it. This

53

Jewish sect rejected the mass of oral tradition taught by
the popular schools, claimed that this life was the whole
of existence, that there are neither angels nor spirits, and
that there is no resurrection of the dead; while small in
number, the Sadducees wielded a tremendous influence,
since they commanded wealth and social position, and
counted among them the family and connection of the high
priest and a number of other priests. They were the aristo-
crats and freethinkers among the Jews. Josephus writes:
"The doctrine of the Sadducees is this, that souls die with
the bodies; nor do they regard the observation of any thing
besides what the law enjoins them; for they think it an
instance of virtue to dispute with those teachers of philosophy whom they frequent; but this doctrine is received but
by a few, yet by those still of the greatest dignity." *Antiquities,* 18, 1, 4. — Luke explains their presence here:
**being sore troubled because they taught the people, and
proclaimed in Jesus the resurrection from the dead.** The
thing that "grieved" (A. V.) them was that Peter and John
should teach at all, and then that of all things they
should teach the resurrection of Jesus. Thus they
understood Peter's words well when he explained the
healing of the lame man at the Beautiful Gate as the
glorious work of Jesus — Jesus, who must then be risen
from the dead and glorified in heaven. It seems that
the Sadducees had stirred up the temple authorities about
the matter and are present to see what is about to be done. —
**And they laid hands on them, and put them in ward unto
the morrow: for it was now eventide.** Whether any
formal grounds were stated for this action is not indicated;
suffice it to say, the Sadducaic hatred of the doctrine of the
resurrection was so great that it meant to stop this preaching at all hazard. Night trials were forbidden to the Jewish
courts, — though in contradiction to their own law they
tried Jesus at night — and so, pending trial, the apostles
were put in ward, *i. e.* kept safe by being put in prison.
All this was done, apparently, without any disturbance;
no one interfered. — **But,** while the apostles were silenced

for the moment, and locked in prison cells, the Gospel message they had uttered went on freely doing its work, **many of them that heard the word believed:** "so belief cometh of hearing, and hearing by the word of Christ," Rom. 10, 17. **And the number of the men,** not counting all the "souls," as in Acts 2, 41, **came to be about five thousand.** Besser interprets: "Five thousand men together with their families were now added to the congregation at Jerusalem." Thus the promise Christ had given to Peter and John when he bade them launch out into the deep and let down their nets, was wonderfully fulfilled. Here the fishers of men had taken another draught for the glory of their Master, Luke 5, 9. Nor was it strange that so few believed when Christ preached, and so many when the apostles preached. He had done the sowing, they were reaping what he had sowed; and not till his work was done and crowned with glory could the fruit fully appear.

The defense.

So Peter and John had their first taste of persecution, as the Lord had told them in advance. They bore it with the utmost courage and confidence. **And it came to pass on the morrow, that their rulers and elders and scribes were gathered together in Jerusalem; and Annas the high priest** *was there,* **and Caiaphas, and John, and Alexander, and as many as were of the kindred of the high priest. And when they had set them in the midst, they inquired, By what power, or in what name, have ye done this?**

A plenary meeting of the Jewish High Court or Sanhedrin was called for the next day. This body consisted of seventy-one priests, scribes, and elders of the people, and under the Romans was presided over by the high priest. The possessive αὐτῶν, **their** rulers, *etc.,* refers to the Jews. The **rulers** here are the priests who belonged to the Council, including the high priest himself; among them, very likely, were the heads of the twenty-four courses, into which the entire body of priests was divided. **Annas** and **Caiaphas** are especially mentioned, the former no longer high priest, the latter now holding that office, and both known to us from the gospels. Annas is still named first, because he was very influential, Caiaphas is his son-in-law. **John** and **Alexander** also belong to the high-priestly class, although we know nothing further about them. There were also others **of the kindred of the high priest,** all of them Sadducees, and therefore opposed to the chief doctrine of apostolic preaching. The **elders** were the heads of large family connections and figured as direct representatives of the people; the **scribes** were the recognized interpreters of the law, the *sopherim*. **In Jerusalem** suggests that some were summoned to the city from their country places near by, where they spent part of the summer season. Thus a great and important audience was gathered together for the apostles. Bengel writes: "One almost feels as if the Passion History is to be re-enacted. These unhappy men are still illumined by the patient sun of the Lord's blessing, who is not willing that they should die in their sins. Once more the aged Annas is to hear the voice of the Prophet, who suffered a blow upon the cheek in his presence, and once more Caiaphas, the high priest of the year of all grace, is to hear Jesus, whom he condemned as a blasphemer, confessed as Christ the Lord." — Peter and John are brought before this august tribunal. What memories, what surmises must have arisen in their hearts! They are placed **in the midst,** in the center of the semicircle of elevated seats upon which the judges sat. Then, very likely through the same Caiaphas who once had questioned Jesus, they are confronted with the question: **By what power, or in what name, have ye done this?** No crime is charged against them, they are not confronted with a row of witnesses; they are asked to make a statement for themselves. **Ye,** *ὑμεῖς*, is the last word in the question; it bears an emphasis of scorn. So also the wonderful miracle wrought by the disciples, which put the multitude in utter astonishment, is here referred to by a simple *τοῦτο*, **this,** or "this thing." They would not designate or describe it in any proper way, for that would have meant an acknowledgment of its greatness or goodness. Verse 14 informs us that the beggar stood beside his benefactors at this hearing, no doubt having been confined together with them during the night. It is important to note that the reality of the miracle wrought upon him is in no way questioned. As in the case of Christ's miracles the evidence was too overwhelming for any attempt in this direction, a glaring contrast to the modern heretical imitators of the apostles, whose wonderful cures do not bear close inspection. The Jewish exorcists also claimed to do wonderful things, using the formulas of their day, the names of the patriarchs or of Solomon, which were considered proper and orthodox. The question to the apostles implies that they had used a different power and name, one that laid them open to a serious charge. What name that was, and what power it stood for the Council knew well enough; so their question to the apostles bids them condemn themselves in the eyes of their judges. Jesus of Nazareth to them is a blasphemer for having called himself the Son of God; their contention had been that he had not come in the name of God. The Sadducees among these judges could, of course, not urge that he had been in league with Beelzebub, for they denied the existence of angels and spirits; yet Josephus informs us that they were base enough, when it served their purpose, to "addict themselves to the notions of the Pharisees, because the multitude would not otherwise hear them." *Antiquities,* 18, 1, 4. **By what power, or in what name** demands to know the kind of power or name, taking it for granted in their judgment that both are wicked.

Then Peter, filled with the Holy Ghost, said unto them, ye rulers of the people, and elders, if we this day are examined concerning a good deed done to an impotent man, by what means this man is made whole; be it known unto you all, and to all the people of Israel, that in the name of Jesus Christ of Nazareth, whom ye crucified, whom God raised from the dead, *even* in him

doth this man stand here before you whole. He is the stone which was set at nought of you the builders, which was made the head of the corner. And in none other is there salvation: for neither is there any other name under heaven, that is given among men, wherein we must be saved. ˌ

In this first hour of trial the Savior's promise was fulfilled for his apostles; they needed not to be anxious how or what to reply to their judges, it was given them by the Holy Spirit what they should speak, Matth. 10, 19. Peters defense is fine in every way: it exposes the full weakness of the implied charge of the Sanhedrin, it confesses the name of Christ in a deliberate, confident way, it fearlessly exposes the wickedness and guilt of these judges, and it triumphantly proclaims salvation in his name, and in his alone. The High Council might scornfully address Peter and John as ὑμεῖς, they found them anything but men to despise. — Peter addresses his judges in an altogether respectful manner: **Ye rulers of the people, and elders,** using a briefer formula which names only two classes instead of three (Luke 23, 13; *etc.*); although "elders," like "rulers," may signify the entire Council (Luke 22, 66). — In the conditional form with which the reply begins: **if we this day are examined, etc.,** there lies a fine intimation that there is no just ground for such an examination. The emphatic ἡμεῖς answers in a dignified way to the ὑμεῖς in the question. — In a telling way the apostle at once states squarely and fully what his judge had veiled by the indefinite τοῦτο: **a good deed done to an impotent man,** and the statement of it in these words must have been greatly re-enforced by the presence of the man at their side, although the apostle uses the indefinite "a man" and does not point to him directly, allowing his auditors to look at him for themselves. **A good deed** needs no criminal inquiry like the one here instituted. — But if nevertheless such an inquiry be made, **by what means** (hardly: *in whom,* masculine — margin) **this man is made whole,** *saved* (margin), or "rescued" (σέσωσται, perfect tense), from his sad condition, the apostle rejoices to make full and complete answer. He does it with great emphasis: **be it known unto you all, and to all the people of Israel, that in the name of Jesus Christ of Nazareth . . . doth this man stand here before you whole.** Joyfully, triumphantly even, he names the name they themselves have demanded. He courts the fullest publicity in the matter, for there is absolutely nothing to hide, and all Israel may profit by the knowledge. — But as in his sermon to the multitude in Solomon's porch, Peter makes a pointed personal reference to his judges, striking for its fearless courage: **whom ye crucified, whom God raised from the dead, *even* in him doth this man stand here before you whole.** They who presume to charge the apostles with a godless deed themselves stand charged with such a deed, and one of the most terrible import. The ὑμεῖς of scorn, addressed by Caiaphas to the apostles, returns from Peter's lips upon him and his fellow judges; and this ὑμεῖς confronts them with ὁ θεός, the true God himself. They **crucified** the Messiah, inflicted the most awful death of shame upon him; and God? — God **raised him from the dead,** undid their work, glorified him with the highest possible honor, pronounced an ineffaceable sentence of condemnation upon their terrible deed. What an accusation upon these accusers! fortified by the divine evidence of God's own judgment of their deed in the beggar made whole by the risen and glorified Christ. One might think that Caiaphas and his companions would have interrupted Peter with words of blazing wrath and indignation; but the truth makes cowards of the men who cannot face its light. They let Peter speak on. — He does it by describing their deed in David's prophetic language: **He is the stone which was set at nought by you the builders, which was made the head of the corner** (Ps. 118, 22). They were indeed "the builders," called to the work of building up Israel spiritually; but the very "stone" which they needed most for their building, they "set at nought," mocked as amounting to nothing, and cast aside. Thus they demonstrated that

they were unfit to build God's temple. God himself interfered and made Christ **the head of the corner,** controlling
all the lines of the building and governing every other stone.
Compare Eph. 2, 20 in the text for Pentecost. So in the
light of God's deed and of his prophetic Word these judges
of the Lord's apostles stand convicted; nor is there any
defense they are able to offer. Besser says that Peter
loved this passage concerning the corner-stone especially
(1 Pet. 2, 4, *etc.*) and might have said: This is my passage;
for his own name Peter constantly reminded him of this
Stone. Christ himself had made use of David's prophecy,
Matth. 21, 43-44. — The apostle's aim was not by any
means merely to defend himself, and if possible to regain
his liberty. What defense he makes is all in the interest
of the Gospel of Christ, that the saving power of Jesus'
name may be made known. Whether his judges acquit or
condemn him, he testifies to them, as he would to men
everywhere, that Jesus is the Messiah glorified of God. In
charging the Jewish authorities with the murder of Christ,
with contradiction and opposition to God, he aims to call
them to repentance and thus to save also their souls. So
he adds the precious Gospel word, which has sounded with
its sweet refrain through all the ages of Christendom:
**And in none other is there salvation: for neither is there
any other name under heaven, that is given among men,
wherein we must be saved.** When the Jews asked Peter
for the name be employed, they could not have asked him
a question he delighted to answer more. The one deed
done in the temple in this name was only a sample of what
lies in this name for us all. And that is **salvation,** deliverance, rescue, in the full Messianic and spiritual sense of
the word. And this complete salvation which we all need
is not in any **other,** ἄλλος; for there is not a second one
of this *same* kind. Nor is there a name of a *different* kind,
ἕτερον, which could offer us salvation. There is absolutely
only this one, **under heaven,** as far as its canopy stretches,
among men, as far as their nations and tribes extend.
That is given . . .   wherein we must be saved points

to the divine agency in the work of salvation. The name that saves us must be "given" us from God in heaven; only so could the saving name ever come to man. And this work of being saved is God's command and imperative purpose: **wherein we must be saved.** God is insistent about it; he makes it our chief duty in giving us this name. Not, however, that now we save ourselves by means of this name, but that we **be saved,** σωθῆναι, let him save us, and not wickedly and wilfully hinder his blessed work. No wonder the Smalcald Articles put forward Acts 4, 12 and declare: "Of this article nothing can be yielded or surrendered, even though heaven and earth and all things should sink to ruin."; "Upon this article all things depend, which, against the pope, the devil, and the whole world, we teach and practice. Therefore, we must be sure concerning this doctrine, and not doubt; for otherwise all is lost, and the pope and devil and all things against us gain the victory and suit." 300, 5. The last word is ἡμᾶς, **we** must be saved — a word that reaches out to the whole Jewish Council and embraces them in saving love together with the believing apostles. Alas, they thrust it from them and judged themselves unworthy of eternal life, Acts 13, 46.

HOMILETICAL HINTS.

A sure sign of the enmity of the world is when the enemies of Jesus are our enemies. It was by no means accidental that the same High Council of the Jews which had condemned Jesus, now had before them the apostles of Jesus.

The Word of the Gospel is intended to produce faith, but when it fails to do that, it is bound to produce opposition. Let no man be surprised at this second result; for, if it should fail to appear, we would have reason to fear that our preaching is not up to the standard required by the Master.

To be sure, all these men who here appear as the enemies of Jesus are dead, and the Jewish sect of the Sadducees is no more; but their kind has not died out. We need only ask, what displeased them so about the disciples. These Sadducees claimed to be very much enlightened and were proud also of their tolerance. Many of them followed the principle: live and let live. To be sure, why not let every man proceed in religious things after his own fashion? Even for the greatest possible enjoyment of life they allowed many things to pass unchallenged, but one thing offended them, if any one spoke of the resurrection from the dead and of eternity. If Jesus was risen, then his enemies were lost, then their unblief was their guilt, his cross their judgment. When the disciples preached Christ risen, these Sadducees felt in their consciences the accusation of him whom they had crucified, who thus again insisted that they choose: either to repent and believe in him, or to smother the voice of conscience in their enmity against him. And wherever the Gospel meets the Sadducaic kind, it always stirs up enmity. Paul complains to the Philippians of the enemies of the cross of Christ, whose God is their belly, who are earthly minded. This is the kind that shows its enmity in slighting and mocking remarks, dragging into the mire what Christians deem holy. It is the kind that is so cheap to-day. But if Jesus' enemies are our enemies, this is a testimonial of honor for us and ought to fill us with new joy in confessing his name. The less men want Christ alive, the more lively our testimony of him should be. Riemer.

If Peter had said: "In the name of Jehovah, the God of Israel, we have done this thing," he would have spoken truthfully and correctly, but in his apostolic office he was bound to reply, what now we sing with joy: "Ask you: Who is he? Christ Jesus: here see Great Sabaoth's Lord! There is no other God: His is the field forever." Luther.

Either we give up all hope of rescue and admit that sin and death belong to our nature and our lot as human beings, or we accept the name which is offered us as the only fountain of deliverance and help. — Wherever a crushed life began to blossom again, a torn conscience was made whole and clean, a sinful child of man made a happy child of God, there against all doubt and enmity of men the confession rang out: Jesus is the victor; glory to his name!

Do not think that when men fail, God's plans cannot be carried into effect. The Jews may crucify Christ, but God makes him Lord of all by raising him from the dead. If we fail to recognize our opportunities, so much the worse for us; if we embrace them the glory of the work to which God calls us shall also be our glory.

God is the right Builder, and when the men he had called to the work rejected the one stone essential to the temple of God, he himself placed it in position, not merely as part of the wall, but as the head of the corner, governing the entire building.

The name is the person, but the person fully revealed, so that we may know him and believe in him.

Our Joy in the Midst of Opposition.

I. *It centers in Jesus' name.*
II. *It glories in Jesus' blessings.*
III. *It is secure in Jesus' protection.*

There is None Other Name Under Heaven Given Among Men Whereby we Must be Saved.

I. *See then what it means to reject this name.*
II. *See also what it means to accept this name.*

Our Defense of Jesus' Name.

I. *The opponents.*
II. *The defenders.*
III. *The clash.*
IV. *The victory.*

Christ's Confessors Before the World's High Council.

I. *As accused.*
II. *As accusers.*
III. *As witnesses.*
IV. *As judges.*   F. V.

Why Does Jesus' Name Meet so Much Opposition?

I. *It challenges the sinner.*
II. *It strikes the conscience.*
III. *It draws to repentance.*
IV. *It lifts up to God.*

The Only Name.

It is the heart
I. *Of all true preaching.*
II. *Of all true faith.*
III. *Of all true confession.*
IV. *Of all true rescue work.*

THE FIFTH SUNDAY AFTER TRINITY.

Acts 5, 34-42.

Gamaliel was the teacher of St. Paul (Acts 22, 3), and probably was identical with the grandson of Hillel, the son of Simeon. The Jews regarded him as one of the seven greatest teachers of the law. Later Christian tradition makes him already at this time a secret adherent of Christ, like Nicodemus, afterwards, together with the latter and his son, baptized by Peter and John; but this is mere tradition. Some have attributed his counsel on the occasion mentioned in this text to the basest of motives, but evidently without warrant. He was wise enough, and upright enough, to counsel moderation to his colleagues when they were about to give way to their passion of hate against the apostles for continuing the preaching of Christ and his resurrection, and for charging the Sanhedrin itself with opposing God in slaying Jesus. There is a certain fear of God in his advice. But the fatal defect in it is that it temporizes. Gamaliel thus stands for *indecision*, a thing as bad in its way, when the hour of grace is at hand, as open and violent opposition. Gamaliel still has many followers, men honorable enough in many ways, and yet, in the face of the full light of the Gospel, waiting, hesitating, unable and unwilling to throw themselves on the side of right, truth, salvation, God, and always with an eye to their earthly interests.

Gamaliel counsels indecision.

At their first trial before the Council Peter and John had refused to cease preaching Christ, and afterwards they made this refusal good. The activity of the apostles reached farther and farther. They wrought many signs

64

and wonders, verse 12; they met in Solomon's porch as when the beggar was healed; they won "multitudes" of new believers, "both men and women;" and they attracted the people from the cities around Jerusalem. In a word the Christian propaganda was assuming alarming proportions in the eyes of the ruling Sadducees, and they finally proceeded to interfere. This time they arrested all the apostles, verse 18, and when they brought them to trial, they met Peter's unanswerable defense: "We must obey God rather than men," verse 29, and the same telling call to repentance. Cut to the heart and ready to slay the apostles, Gamaliel steps into the breach. **But there stood up one in the council, a Pharisee, named Gamaliel, a doctor of the law, had in honor of all the people, and commanded to put the men forth a little while.** Gamaliel was a **Pharisee,** of the Jewish party who paid scrupulous regard to tradition and to the observance of all external forms and ceremonies, and in doing this separated themselves from the other Jews. The term itself means "separated." The Pharisees were esteemed by the people generally for their strict observance of the many regulations with which they hedged in the law iself; but they were proud and haughty self-righteous formalists, violently opposed to the doctrine of grace and liberty as set forth by the Gospel. In many respects the Pharisees opposed the Sadducees, but both alike refused to follow Christ. Gamaliel was an honored **doctor,** or authorized teacher of the Jewish religion and law, and his fame had spread throughout the land. His position and fame lent weight to his words, even with the Sadducees in the Sanhedrin. It was no unusual thing that he demanded when he asked that the accused men be **put forth a little while,** compare 4, 15. What he had to say was intended for the private ear of his colleagues.

And he said unto them: Ye men of Israel, take heed to yourselves as touching these men, what ye are about to do. The Jews loved to be called Israelites, a name that

5

recalled the best things in the life and character of their forefather Jacob. **As touching these men** is best construed as in the R. V. Gamaliel urges his colleagues to avoid hasty action and to safeguard themselves in what they are about to do. No doubt, some thought of the effect their action might have on the populace, since "the people magnified them," *i. e.* the apostles and believers generally, verse 13, but Gamaliel had a different self-interest in mind. The trouble was, that he did not view this interest squarely and draw the full conclusions from it in regard his own conduct and that of his associates. — He elucidates what he has in mind by two pertinent examples. **For before these days rose up Theudas, giving himself out to be somebody; to whom a number of men, about four hundred, joined themselves: who was slain; and all, as many as obeyed him, were dispersed and came to nought.** Josephus mentions a Theudas, a false prophet who "persuaded a great part of the people" and came to a miserable end, in his *Antiquities,* 20, 5, 1; but this was about ten years after the time of our text, and therefore cannot be the man here referred to. To conclude that the Acts are historically unreliable, is altogether unwarranted, the more since Gamaliel mentions the actual number of the followers of Theudas, only "four hundred," and therefore not "a great part of the people," as in the account of Josephus. This writer either has no record of Gamaliel's story, or he brings it in Book 17, 10, 5, where he tells of the deeds of the ambitious Judas, who aspired to the royal dignity, which agrees with Gamaliel's statement: **giving himself out to be somebody.** Herod caught him and disposed of him and his followers. The names Theudas, Thadeus, and Judas differ but little. There are still other conjectures, which we pass by here. — Gamaliel brings forward a second and similar case: **After this man rose up Judas of Galilee in the days of the enrolment, and drew away** *some of the* **people after him: he also perished; and all, as many as obeyed him, were scattered abroad.** Josephus gives us an account

of this Judas, born at Gamala in Gaulonities, east of the
Sea of Galilee, but called a Galilean because he lived in
Galilee and there caused his agitation against paying taxes
to the Romans, when Quirinus took the second census or
"enrolment" about A. D. 6. *Antiquities,* 18, 1, 1 and 6;
20, 5, 2; *Wars,* 2, 8, 1. Gamaliel reports that this agitator
perished, and his followers were scattered, although the
agitation which he caused revived later on and caused further trouble. — Gamaliel has been doing some thinking,
and the question he raised with himself was whether this
movement marked by the name of Jesus was merely human like the two he instances, or whether after all the
hand of God was in it as the apostles so confidently and
emphatically claimed. He is inclined to take the former
view, but is evidently not ready to give the final answer.
What it was that raised a doubt in his mind and caused him
to hesitate, as he does, we are unable to say; it may have
been the signs and wonders wrought by the apostles and following what Jesus had done himself, or the rapid spread of
the Christian movement at Jerusalem, or something that secretly touched his personal life. At least he shrinks from
taking the most violent measures against the apostles. His
indecision makes him cautious, and in an effective manner he urges the same caution upon his colleagues.
**And now I say unto you, Refrain from these men, and
let them alone: for if this counsel or this work be of
men, it will be overthrown: but if it is of God, ye will
not be able to overthrow them; lest haply ye be found
even to be fighting against God.** It is immaterial whether
we read τὰ νῦν or simply νῦν. **If this counsel . . be of
men,** ἐάν with the subjunctive, looks to the future for the
final decision; **but if it is of God,** εἰ with the present indicative, presumes this possibility now. Meyer thinks this
indicates that Gamaliel was inclined to hold the latter view,
but the form of the conditional sentences gives no hint in
this regard. Winer 41, 2. The concluding clause: **lest
haply,** μή ποτε, requires that we supply before it in thought:
προσέχετε ἑαυτοῖς or an equivalent: be careful. The καί

seems elliptical: not only against men, but **even** against
God himself. Gamaliel fears that he might fight *against*
God, and so he counsels to do nothing. This is the mark
of indecision; for the true alternative is to fight *for* God.
Little is gained if we avoid a sin of commission by falling
into a sin of omission. If it is wicked to fight against God,
it is dastardly not to fight for God. Gamaliel is waiting for
further evidence that the Christian movement is "of God."
Abraham told the rich man in hell that his five brothers
had sufficient in Moses and the prophets; Gamaliel and the
Jews had not only Moses and the prophets, but also Christ
and the apostles. "An evil and adulterous generation seek-
eth after a sign; and there shall no sign be given to it but
the sign of Jonah the prophet." Matth. 12, 39 *etc.* The
most convincing evidence does not convince this kind, even
when the fear of the truth strikes home in their hearts.
They still demand other evidence, and such as really is not
fully convincing at all. If a man had risen from the dead
and warned the rich man's five brothers, they would not
have regarded it; if the work of the apostles had wrought
still greater wonders at Jerusalem, many would still have
rejected it. True faith is satisfied with God's evidence, the
faith that is built on something else, for instance on the
show of outward success, is not true. Gamaliel's counsel
sounds wise from the standpoint of the world; in reality
its wisdom is folly. The thing that struck this Rabbi's
heart regarding the work of the apostles should have made
him ask squarely then and there: Is this counsel or this
work of God or of men? and accept unhesitatingly the
glorious evidence of Christ's words and works, especially
also of his resurrection, no matter what the consequences
might be in hatred and opposition of the Sanhedrin. His
indecision in the face of the greatest divine evidence proved
his undoing, wise and learned though he was reputed to be.
The trouble with this Pharisee no doubt was that his sins
did not harass his conscience; the veil of pharisaic self-
righteousness blinded him to the truth of the Gospel.
Peter's call to repentance did not stir his heart. He who

comes with a distressed conscience to Christ will soon see and know that Christ and his work is "of God;" all others, even if they outwardly join the church, for this or that extraneous reason, are after all no true members of it. God's providence used Gamaliel's counsel to give the young congregation at Jerusalem further respite from persecution.

The work of the apostles goes on.

What a contrast between Gamaliel's indecision and the joyful, fearless action of the apostles! — **And to him they agreed: and when they had called the apostles unto them, they beat them and charged them not to speak in the name of Jesus, and let them go.** Meyer remarks on this agreement with Gamaliel: "only *in tantum.*" They refrain from taking extreme measures. Even the unscrupulous Caiaphas, who had managed the killing of Jesus, was silent on this occasion. Nobody arose to confute Gamaliel by stating that the Sanhedrin had really decided in regard to "this counsel or this work" when it condemned Jesus as a blasphemer and had him crucified. But the apostles are not simply dismissed, they are punished for having disobeyed the Sanhedrin's orders not to preach in Jesus' name, by being beaten. Brought in before their judges, they are stripped to the waist and tied in a bent position to a pillar, whereupon an executioner applies a three-thonged whip across the back, striking thirteen times, making thirty-nine stripes (one less than the law allowed, Deut. 35, 3, compare 2 Cor. 11, 24). This penalty was used for many misdeeds, and was considered very shameful, Acts 16, 37. Christ had warned his followers: "They will scourge you in their synagogues," Matth. 10, 17; compare Acts 22, 19. — In addition the apostles receive authoritative orders **not to speak in the name of Jesus,** to cease all utterance resting on that name. And so the authorities release them, or **let them go.** For the moment the danger was passed, the future was in the Lord's hands. — **They therefore departed from the presence of the council, rejoicing that they were counted worthy to suffer dis-**

honor for the Name. And every day, in the temple and at home, they ceased not to teach and to preach Jesus *as* **the Christ.** Gamaliel also departed, but not rejoicing. If this work was "of God," would not forbidding it and scourging its agents be "fighting against God"? But there was no doubt in the hearts of the apostles. All twelve of them rejoiced **that they were counted worthy to suffer dishonor** (note the oxymoron, the bringing together of contradictory terms) **for the Name,** that supreme name Christ Jesus which filled their hearts and constantly came from their lips. Here was begun what Paul writes of, 1 Cor. 4, 9: "I think God hath set forth us the apostles last of all, as men doomed to death: for we are made a spectacle unto the world, and to angels, and to men." The marks on the apostles' backs were badges of honor. In the great and blessed fight *for* God, they had not been undecided and inactive like Gamaliel, but had done their part valiantly, and like true soldiers of the cross bore honorable wounds to attest their noble loyalty. — Never for a moment do they permit human authority, even though it be that of the highest tribunal of their nation, to interfere with that of their divine Lord and Master who bade them preach the Gospel. This false and hostile authority only stimulates them to be more active than ever. They **teach and preach,** informing their pupils and all who inquire or argue, and proclaiming the good news in public to every gathering; and this **every day** as the one great business of their lives, both **in the temple,** *i. e.* in the courts where people met daily in considerable numbers, **and at home,** in their own dwelling-places and in the houses of believers generally. They were altogether devoid of fear; thy scorned to work secretly. Nor did they complain of the injustice they had suffered at the hand of their enemies, or boast of their own courage and fortitude, or trouble to defend their own personal honor against the shame inflicted upon them; if they thought of themselves at all, they sought only to be found faithful of the Lord in working for his honor alone. The consequences they left entirely to the Lord and never tried to avoid any further persecution by meeting their enemies half-way. A finer example of joyous and confident decision for the Lord and of courageous and loyal adherence to his Word we cannot find. May it stiffen our loyalty and stimulate our energy in the Master's cause.

HOMILETICAL HINTS.

"These times call for decision,
Though foes 'gainst us inveigh;
For open, bold confession,
Whate'er the world may say:
In spite of all the glitter
Of gilded heathendom,
To praise, defend, and cherish
Christ's Gospel till he come."

"O Come, Eternal Spirit," verse 4.

The great question is still: Is this counsel or this work of God, or is it of men? Let us give credit to Gamaliel for stating the question correctly; we cannot accept his shrewd worldly answer.

The religions of Buddha and Mohammed have had great success, but does this prove their divine origin? — Who can take the time necessary to mark the issue of a movement, when life is such a short span? If a cause is divine God cannot leave us in the dark, to perish waiting for certainty; he gives us the clear and necessary evidence at once. — In questions pertaining to the soul and its eternal welfare, who can afford to stand cooly by while the decision is being made? — Gamaliel's principle: first see, then believe, reverses the principle of the Gospel: "Blessed are they that have not seen, and yet have believed," John 20, 29. — Christian faith is not wrought by watching the outward success of the Gospel; that kind of faith is mere human assent and vanishes in the day of persecution. Christian faith is wrought by watching the grace of Jesus Christ delivering poor sinners from death and damnation.

Indifference, cautious compromise, shrewd calculation, going half-way, taking the middle path between that which is of God, and that which is of men, may look like great wisdom, in reality it is the hight of·folly. He that is not with me is against me, applies in this case. You can avoid fighting against God, only by fighting for him. You can escape unbelief, only by believing. You can refrain from serving the devil's cause, only by serving God's cause. — Gamaliel's counsel is a pillow for religious ease, a cloak of selfishness and self-love.

It is easy to march out against Midian with the 32,000, but quite a different thing to be one of the 300 who with "the sword of the Lord and Gideon" attack the enemy. Who would not play safe, await the issue and then join the ranks? But to offer the confidence of faith and without seeing believe — ah, who is ready for that?

The old gospel lesson shows us Peter: "Master, *at thy word* I will let down the net." Luke 5, 5. Gamaliel would stand by first, and see how Peter fared, then too he would let down the net — but it would be too late for the catch.

What did the apostles do when they suffered such unjust and shameful treatment at the hands of the High Council? Did they call a great mass-meeting that very night of all the people and protest in the name of liberty, justice, and human rights against the treatment they had received, draw up a ringing appeal to Pontius Pilate for protection against any further violence of this kind and have it signed by thousands, and, to top it off, organize a society for the purpose of exposing to public criticism and scorn injustice and wrong such as had been inflicted upon them? Hardly: the walls of Zion are not built by these modern methods of worldly procedure. The apostles joyfully preached the Gospel. That was their best answer to the stripes they had suffered. — You cannot kill the truth by forbidding it and nailing it down in a coffin. — It is better to come away from the High Council with a bloody back and a sound conscience, than to leave it as an honored member with a conscience haunted by a secret fear. — Next to open enmity the worst thing the Gospel meets in its course is calculating indecision.

The greatest question of the age:

Is the Gospel of God, or is it of Men?

There are three answers:

I. *Unbelief.*
II. *Indecision.*
III. *Faith.*

Christ once said: "Come and see." John 1, 39; compare 46.

Gamaliel's Counsel: "Wait and See."

I. *It seems safe, and yet is dangerous — look at his fellow counsellors.*

II. *It seems godly, and yet is ungodly — look at the Lord and his blessed cause.*
III. *It seems sound, and yet it is folly — look at the disciples.*

Adapted from Matthes.

Choose Between Gamaliel and the Apostles, between

I. *Doubt and faith.*
II. *Calculation and joy.*
III. *Indecision and certainty.*
IV. *Hesitation and zeal.*

Gamaliel's Sad Mistake.

I. *He fails to see his hour of grace.*
II. *He is undecided where the evidence is complete.*
III. *He waits until it is too late.*

The Gospel Call for Decision.

I. *God's revelation is complete.*
II. *The lines among men are drawn.*
III. *Your time of grace is short.*

Gamaliel's Wise Folly.

I. *He fears to fight against God, but*
II. *He fails to fight for God.*

THE SIXTH SUNDAY AFTER TRINITY.

Acts 8, 26-38.

In the narrative of the eunuch's conversion we have a fine example of the *acceptance* of Jesus' saving name. This rounds out the first after-Trinity subcycle, the last three texts forming a trio by themselves: opposition — indecision — acceptance; all clustering about the name Jesus. Philip "preached unto him Jesus;" and the eunuch confessed: "I believe that Jesus Christ is the Son of God." — The church at Jerusalem had grown larger and larger through the preaching of Jesus' name by the apostles. Soon the work of caring for the needy became so extensive that the office of ·the deaconate was established and seven men were solemnly set apart for this special duty, among them the Philip of our text. Then the storm of persecution, held back so long, broke forth in a bloody manner; one of the seven deacons, Stephen, became the first Christian martyr. A great persecution arose against the entire church of Jerusalem, and the Christians, excepting the apostles themselves, were scattered abroad throughout Judea and Samaria. This, instead of hindering the Gospel, carried it into every town and village. Philip thus labored in Samaria, and afterwards in the old cities of what was formerly Philistia, finally he dwelt in Cæsarea; here Paul and his companions visited him, Acts 21, 8. It seems that Philip was in the city of Samaria, where he had met with great success, when he was called away to bring into the kingdom the soul of this unnamed eunuch, Acts 8, 5. **But an angel of the Lord spake unto Philip, saying, Arise, and go toward the south unto the way that goeth down from Jerusalem unto Gaza: the same is desert. And he arose and went.** It is certainly noteworthy that

74

the Lord employed the service of angels in bringing into his kingdom the first Gentiles, here the Ethiopian eunuch, and in chapter 10 Cornelius. the centurion of the Italian cohort. There are no details of the appearance of the angel to Philip. The command for Philip to **arise** does not imply that he lay asleep, it simply means that he is to make ready for his journey, compare 5, 17. God uses his angels as ministering spirits, sending them forth to do service for the sake of them that shall inherit salvation, Heb. 1, 14. In this case the heavenly agencies are revealed to us, causing what, no doubt, to the eunuch appeared as a chance meeting on the lonely road to Gaza; so God guides all his work and brings the Gospel and his Gospel messengers at the proper time to the souls of men. — **Gaza,** its name signifying "the strong one," was the southernmost and most important of the five cities of old Philistia, lying upon the shores of the Mediterranean Sea. Of the roads that lead down from Jerusalem to Gaza Philip is to take the one that is **desert,** ἔρημος, leading through an uninhabited country and therefore lonely and less frequented than the other roads. This directs Philip sufficiently, but at the same time it casts a light upon the eunuch, who chose this way in order to be undisturbed in his study of the book he had purchased at the holy city. Philip, as an obedient servant of the Lord at once proceeds on his way, certain that the Lord was directing him. Would it not have been easier for the Lord to have sent the angel directly to the eunuch and permit Philip to remain in his successful work in Samaria? The Lord has bestowed the office of the ministry upon men, not upon angels, and we will find in every case that the Lord makes use of the men he has called and honors their office and work accordingly. So Philip goes forth on his long journey afoot. The time and effort spent is not too great to save an immortal soul.

And behold, a man of Ethiopia, a eunuch of great authority under Candace, queen of the Ethiopians, who was over all her treasure, who had come to Jerusalem for to worship; and he was returning and sitting in his

chariot, and was reading the prophet Isaiah. Here is a
fine description of the man Philip is sent to meet. The
exclamation **behold** conveys a good deal, when we place
ourselves in the position of Philip: he sees before him a
Gentile, a black man! None such had been received
hitherto into the church, and we know what a change of
ideas the reception of Gentiles required on the part even of
the apostles. Without warning this grave subject is now
brought before Philip. He needed not to hesitate: the
Lord himself had sent him to this man. The supposition
that this eunuch was really a Jew who had risen 'to an
important position in Ethiopia is without foundation, ἀνὴρ
Αἰθίοψ (from αἴθω, "to burn," and ὤψ, "a countenance")
pointing not to residence merely, but to nationality.
Ethiopia lies south of Egypt and, in the wider sense, embraces a large territory, including Nubia, Abyssinia, *etc.*,
but here most likely, in a narrower sense, the kingdom of
Meroe at the junction of the Blue and White Nile. This
Ethiopian was **a eunuch,** which must be taken in the literal
sense, since δυνάστης, "courtier," or "high officer," follows,
preventing us from taking εὐνοῦχος in that sense. Eunuchs
were used not only to have supervision of harems, but also
to fill other important positions at oriental courts. So this
man was **of great authority under Candace, queen of the
Ethiopians,** the office he held being that of chief treasurer. **Candace,** like "Pharaoh," "Sultan," and "Czar" is
not a personal name, but a title; Ethiopia was ruled in these
ancient times by a line of queens. The name has become
famous in the history of Lutheran missions. In 1853
Pastor Louis Harms of Hermannsburg in Hanover, Germany, a small inland town, had a vessel built with funds
which he collected, in order to send the first missionaries
he had prepared to their destination in Africa; that vessel
he named after the Ethiopian queen, "Candace," and it
served its purpose well. This undertaking, successfully
carried into effect, stands forth as one of the great monuments of faith in the history of modern missions. — The
eunuch, whose traditional name is Indich, or Judich, **had**

come to Jerusalem for to worship, so that he must have
been a proselyte, though not a "proselyte of righteousness,"
a convert in the fullest sense of the word, because of his
mutilation; but one of that numerous class of Gentiles
called "proselytes of the gate," a stranger within the Jewish
gates, observing only the so-called Noachian commandments (Gen. 9, 4-6) against idolatry, blasphemy, disobedience to magistrates, murder, fornication or incest, robbery
or theft, and eating blood. These proselytes were nearly
always open to the Gospel. In far off Ethiopia he evidently
had come in contact with the Jews and had accepted the
essentials of their faith; the hardships and dangers of a
journey of two hundred miles had not deterred him from
carrying out his desire to see the great temple at Jerusalem,
and though because of his mutilation unable to enter the
inner courts (Deut. 23, 1), he had rejoiced in such approach
as was possible for him, and in the special promise of the
Lord: "For thus saith the Lord unto the eunuchs that keep
my sabbaths, and choose the things that please me, and take
hold of my covenant; even unto them will I give in mine
house and within my walls a place and a name better than
of sons and of daughters: I will give them an everlasting
name, that shall not be cut off." Is. 56, 4-5. — We are
unable to say what he had found in the temple, and whether
the empty formalism of the worship there satisfied his soul.
One thing, however, he had found: **he was returning
and sitting in his chariot, and was reading the prophet
Isaiah.** Had he purchased the precious scroll in the holy
city? It seems quite likely, since he is so intent on his treasure, as one who has just come into its possession and cares
for nothing else. He might have chosen a more interesting
road homeward, it seems as if he purposely chose this to
be undisturbed in his reading of the prophet. It was God's
guidance that had placed Isaiah, the evangelist of the O. T.,
in his hands and that made him turn to the very choicest
part of the entire book of this prophet. Slowly the chariot
moved on, while Philip waited to be overtaken by it. The
eunuch was reading aloud, perhaps with some difficulty, for

the writing of those ancient manuscripts was not so simple, and the tongue was not his native Ethiopian, but the Septuagint, the Greek translation widely used in those days. **And the Spirit said unto Philip, Go near, and join thyself to this chariot. And Philip ran to him, and heard him reading Isaiah the prophet, and said, Understandest thou what thou readest? And he said, How can I, except some one shall guide me? And he besought Philip to come up and sit with him.** Philip's conduct is inspired by the Holy Spirit himself, overcoming at once, by a positive inward injunction, any misgivings or hesitancy that might have arisen in his heart. To Philip, the evangelist, the Spirit speaks, but not so to the eunuch, when the way of salvation was to be expounded to him. "God does not wish to deal with us otherwise than through the spoken Word and the sacraments, and that whatever without the Word and sacraments is extolled as spirit is the devil himself." *Smalcald Articles,* 333, 10. In the preaching of the Gospel God adheres to the means and the office he himself has given us; dreams, visions, voices, and the like he may use for certain purposes, but not for this one. — As Philip hastened to the chariot he heard the reading of the familiar words, and knew that the way was open for him. His question: **Understandest thou what thou readest?** leads at once to the heart of the matter. If he read with understanding he was a Christian; if not, Christ was at his door and knocking. The interrogative ἄρα, here strengthened with γε, rather looks for a negative answer. And the eunuch's reply shows that the surmise of Philip is correct: **How can I, except some one shall guide me?** or, more closely: "For how should I (ἂν δυναίμην), except some one shall guide me (ἐάν here with the future indicative ὁδηγήσει)?" On the γάρ in the question see Winer 53, 8, under b, p. 396; Blass, p. 274, simply says it is used where we employ "then." — The eunuch's answer is coupled with the request for Philip **to come up and sit with him,** for the eunuch at once perceived from Philip's question that he must be able to give him light. This prompt invitation to

a stranger on a lonely road also indicates the great longing
for light and information in the eunuch's heart. He was
different from the haughty Jews, who declared in their
blindness: "We see," John 9, 41, and therefore could not
be enlightened.

**Now the place of the scripture which he was reading
was this,**

He was led as a sheep to the slaughter;
And as a lamb before his shearer is dumb
So he openeth not his mouth:
In his humiliation his judgment was taken away:
His generation who shall declare?
For his life is taken from the earth.

**And the eunuch answered Philip, and said, I pray thee,
of whom speaketh the prophet this? of himself, or of
some other? And Philip opened his mouth, and beginning from this scripture, preached unto him Jesus.** —
"The place," ἡ περιοχή, or rather "the contents," of "the
scripture" or writing, here the book of Isaiah (53, 7-8), is
quoted quite closely from the Septuagint, which however
differs considerably from the Hebrew original. The chief
difference is in the fourth and last lines which read respect-
ively: "He was taken from prison and from judgment;
. . . for he was cut off out of the land of the living." Here,
of course, in a historical narrative this difference need not
be noted exegetically, the questions at issue turning on the
general import of the prophet's words, not on the specific
meaning of any single word or phrase. The eunuch had
before him the best translation of his time, and Luke simply
reproduces the text of that translation, which, by the way,
agrees exactly with the Alexandrine codex of the Septuagint
(Horn, *Introduction*, II, 298). — The prophet is writing of
the *Ebed Yaveh*, the promised Messiah, see Acts 3, 13 in
the text for the Third Sunday after Trinity. He is describing his humiliation and passion, together with the
exaltation following and the glorious fruit. Patiently,
silently, without resistance the great Servant of Jehovah
is led to his death, **as a sheep to the slaughter;** his silent

patience and submission is emphasized by the added comparison of **a lamb** opening not its mouth under the hand of his shearer. But **in his humiliation,** when he had humbled himself to the death of the cross, ἡ κρίσις, **his judgment was taken away,** the judgment of God executed upon him as our substitute; having rendered full satisfaction or atonement, that judgment ἥρθη (from αἴρω), was lifted and taken from him. God's claims were satisfied, Christ's humiliation was ended and turned to exaltation. — **His generation** are those that belong to him as their spiritual head and ancestor (Stellhorn), all true believers; γενεά is not *Lebenslaenge* (Luther and others), and cannot be here the Jewish "race," which in its representatives rejected Christ. **Who shall declare** it? means: Who shall state its number? it will exceed computation. **For his life shall be taken from the earth,** shall enter upon a heavenly mode of existence and in its activity be freed from the limitations of a life on earth. So he will multiply the number of his believers with the heavenly efficacy of his grace. — The eunuch **answered** Philip by replying to the latter's question regarding the difficulty he experienced in trying to understand the prophet's meaning. And he has struck the heart of the matter, the one point on which everything turns: **I pray thee, of whom speaketh the prophet this? of himself, or of some other?** Who is this suffering Servant of Jehovah, who shall rise to heavenly glory and reap such wonderful fruit of his labors? Could it be the great prophet himself? Even the eunuch felt that there were difficulties in this supposition, too great to admit this as the solution. But who else could it be? We are unable to say how much the eunuch had heard concerning Jesus; yet his prompt acceptance of Philip's interpretation would indicate that he had learned the story of Jesus while in Jerusalem, and needed only to have the prophecies of the O. T. connected properly with what he had heard, in order to bring him to the Christian faith. This too may explain to us the readiness with which Philip proceeds to baptize him. — Everything is ready for the evangelist, who **opened**

his mouth, with due solemnity, **and beginning from this scripture** as a fine and fitting starting-point, yet bringing in what other prophetic passages he needed, much as Jesus himself once did (Luke 24, 27, and 45), he **preached unto him Jesus,** the whole blessed Gospel of salvation in Jesus' name. "What all flowed from the teacher's lips concerning the Word of life, how he preached of the Crucified One in words ever more fiery and enthusiastic, and what all transpired in the soul of the hearer, how his heart burned within him, how the scales fell from his eyes, how light upon light illumined him, how perhaps tear upon tear rolled down his cheek, all this the record does not describe, words cannot properly reproduce it. Enough, there must have been another upon the chariot, the Holy Spirit, who opened the mouth of Philip and the heart of the treasurer; and the result was that this apt pupil of the Gospel could exclaim:

'Now I have found the firm foundation,
Where evermore my anchor grounds!'

O that this might be the result of all our preaching and hearing, Bible reading and explanation, meditation and praying, the knowledge and ever firmer conviction: Jesus is the Messiah, as the prophet promised, as this sinful world needs him!" Gerok.

And as they went on the way, they came unto a certain water; and the eunuch saith, Behold, *here is* **water; what doth hinder me to be baptized?** *And Philip said, If thou believest with all thy heart, thou mayest. And he answered and said, I believe that Jesus Christ is the Son of God.* **And he commanded the chariot to stand still: and they both went down into the water, both Philip and the eunuch; and he baptized him.** — It has been impossible to determine beyond question what **water** this could have been alongside the desert road to Gaza. There is no stream or lake in this locality. Seiss, *The Baptist System Examined,* 215, states that Eusebius, Jerome, Reland, and the Baptist Mr. Samson, think that this "water"

6

was "a fountain boiling up at the foot of a hill and absorbed again by the soil from which it springs." Robinson suggests as a very probable place for this baptism the water in the *Wady el-Hasy,* between Eleutheropolis and Gaza, not far from the old sites of Lachish and Eglon. The legendary scene is between Jerusalem and Hebron, but cannot be the actual scene at all. See Smith's *Dictionary of the Bible* on Gaza. — The eunuch's question implies that he was fully instructed in regard to baptism; Philip must have included what was necessary in his preaching of Jesus. **What doth hinder me to be baptized?** implies that the eunuch knew of no hindrance, but he leaves it to the fuller knowledge of his teacher whether his own supposition is correct. — Verse 37 is omitted in the best manuscripts, and those that have this addition present considerable variation. It was probably an exegetical complement written at first in the margin to round out the story, and then inserted in the text itself by uncritical copyists. The addition is entirely in harmony with the inspired narrative itself; in fact, some direct and solemn confession of Christ, ·like the one here described, may well have been made in connection with the eunuch's baptism. There is no need of referring to the matter in the pulpit, unless quite exceptional circumstances should warrant it. — Philip, of course, consents to administer the sacrament to the eunuch, who at once **commanded the chariot to stand still,** indicating that a servant acted as the driver. **And they both went down into the water** in order to be in a position to perform the sacred act. **Both Philip and the eunuch** did this, just as both, after the baptism had been administered, **came up out of the water,** verse 39. The going *into* the water (εἰς τὸ ὕδωρ), and the coming up *out* of it (ἐκ τοῦ ὕδατος) is therefore not the baptismal act itself or any part of it. That act is described by the words: καὶ ἐβάπτισεν αὐτόν, **and he baptized him.** How? in what manner? Luke does not say. Stellhorn concludes: "A baptism by immersion," *Lutheran Commentary,* Acts; but this is only an assumption which disregards several important considerations. The reference to Acts 2, 40, which Stellhorn adds, as determining the general custom in the first church, does not speak for immersion, but positively against it, since the three thousand baptized on the day of Pentecost, in whatever way they were baptized, certainly were not immersed. See *Eisenach Gospel Selections,* I, 655-6. Cremer defines βαπτίζω as "a washing for the removal of sin," *waschen behufs Entsündigung.* This washing in some form or other the eunuch here received. The water into which Philip and his pupil went, if a pool formed by a spring, as Eusebius reports, or a small temporary stream in the wady, as Robinson suggests, afforded too little depth for immersion. There is no hint that the eunuch laid aside any of his garments; we are left to suppose that both, as they sat in the chariot, arose together and stepped into the shallow water, the baptism following by sprinkling, or pouring, or some other way. All that was necessary was "water" in the case, not a certain large amount of it or of a certain depth. Examination of the pertinent passages will show that the Holy Spirit nowhere describes the mode of baptism or indicates some special mode in a positive way. In some instances immersion was possible, but whether it was actually employed even in these is not certain or even highly probable; in more instances immersion is altogether out of the question. The practice on Pentecost and in the days following, when thousands were baptized, the number going to five thousand men alone at a very early date, and "multitudes both of men and women" (Acts 5, 14) following these, all receiving the sacrament where immersion was not feasible, established a custom which certainly governed the practice for some time to come. See the *Eisenach Gospel Selections,* I, 57; 204; 655; and Krauth, *Conservative Reformation,* 518 *etc.* for an elaborate and thorough treatment of the subject. Stellhorn voices the teaching of our entire church and many others when he declares : "that the *mode* of applying the water in baptism, and the *quantity* used, is immaterial." It is the sacrament itself that is of greatest importance, since this is a means of grace, divinely insti tuted as such. By his baptism the eunuch was made a partaker of the forgiveness of sin and of life and salvation. His baptism sealed his faith by making every baptismal promise of Christ actually his own. Tradition reports some interesting things concerning the activity of the eunuch in his own country, such as that he became an evangelist to his countrymen and that he baptized the queen herself. There is no question, he must have helped to spread the Gospel wherever he went.

HOMILETICAL HINTS.

It is the Lord's business to send angels, but not ours to demand angels.

The treasurer of the Ethiopian queen held the key to all her treasure-vaults, but he lacked the key of life, the key to the Scriptures, the key to heaven. By the aid of Philip he found the master-key to all three — the Savior Jesus Christ.

The grace of God sometimes meets us on the way to the temple, sometimes in the temple, but sometimes also when we are far away, alone with our thoughts, perhaps least expecting it.

How much delight we take in the Word of God is shown, perhaps, by the dust that accumulates on our Bibles. — All the glitter of the gold that passed through this man's hands, all the power of influence, for which many envied him, all the honor connected with his high station at court, could not fill the void in his heart, that sought for something richer than gold, mightier than power, more glorious than honor among men. — His dark skin marked him as a son of Ham on whom the curse of Noah lay, his physical mutilation debarred him from full membership with God's O. T. people, but allowed no pride or resentment on his part to shut him out from such part of Israel's blessings as he could obtain. The very richness and fulness of the spiritual privileges which we enjoy make us exacting and fastidious, so that we will not take our blessings unless they are offered us in the dainty way and with the personal considerations we think our just due.

Travel is often a weariness of the flesh; this eunuch made it a refreshing of the spirit. — A Bible in every hotel-room is the fine watchword of the Gideonites, a society of commercial travellers; may it carry Christ into many a heart. Think of the chaff that is sold on many a train! Take a better companion with you when you must journey from one place to another.

When Philip met the eunuch: There was no long preface; no stopping only in the outer court; no formal or physical conditions; no ceremonial regulations — but, what we enjoy to-day, direct entrance into the sanctuary, the soul and center of all Scripture at the first step: And in Jesus Christ, his own Son, our Lord; led like a sheep to the slaughter, suffered under Pontius Pilate; dumb as a lamb before his shearer, crucified, dead, and buried; in his humiliation his judgment taken away; the third day he rose again from the dead; he ascended into heaven; and sitteth at the right hand of God the Father Almighty; his generation who shall declare? from thence he shall come to judge the quick and the dead.

If the queen of Sheba shall rise up against this generation which hears more than the wisdom of Solomon, shall the Ethiopian eunuch be silent against those who have more than one companion for one brief day of travel, who year after year have all God's prophets, evangelists, and apostles, to help guide their spiritual course, but fail to heed their blessed instruction?

Let us get out of the cold, dreary hole of our narrow personal interest, and aid others like Philip did.

When the first star shines at evening time, it is not long till a countless host glitters in the dark sky. Who will count the Gentile hosts that followed the Ethiopian eunuch in faith to Christ? We all were blessed in the work that Philip did on that lone road from Jerusalem to Gaza.

Isaiah in the wagon, the baptismal water upon his head, the Savior in his heart, no wonder that the eunuch went on his way rejoicing.

How the Ethiopian Was Saved.

I. *When he heard of God, he went to his temple.*
II. *When he found the Scriptures, he studied them.*
III. *When he discovered Christ he believed in him.*

Who Made Candace's Treasurer so Rich?

I. *Isaiah.*
II. *Philip.*
III. *Christ.*

The First African Made a Christian.

I. *He follows God's leadings.*
II. *He uses God's Scriptures.*
III. *He inquires of God's servant.*
IV. *He believes in God's Savior.*
V. *He rejoices in God's Sacrament.*   Schultze.

The Triumph of God's Grace in the Conversion of the First African.

I. *Of God's providential grace.*
a) The temple.
b) The Scriptures.
c) The evangelist.
II. *Of God's saving grace.*
a) The Lamb led to the slaughter.
b) The way of salvation in Christ.
c) Faith and Baptism.

What Might Have Kept the Ethiopian Eunuch from Christ?

I. *His position as treasurer.*
II. *The distance to Jerusalem.*
III. *The difficulties of the Scriptures.*
IV. *The humbleness of God's messenger.*

In the Ethiopian's Conversion We See That Mission Work Is God's Work.

I. *He prepares the soil.*
II. *He points the way.*
III. *He provides the means.*
IV. *He apportions the success.*

THE SEVENTH SUNDAY AFTER TRINITY.

1 Tim. 6, 6-12.

The very first words of our text mark plainly the turn in the thought as now we are ushered into a new subcycle: "But godliness with contentment is great gain." We are now to consider the things that pertain to the Christian faith and life: "Follow after righteousness, godliness, faith, love, patience, meekness." The first text, we see at a glance, is comprehensive; "godliness" is a wide term, but the apostle puts a number of other comprehensive virtues beside it, and certainly leaves nothing untouched when he adds: "Fight the good fight of faith!" The term *godliness* dominates the text; our subject naturally will be *the Christian's godly life*.

Godliness with contentment.

The false teachers against whom Timothy had to contend "supposed that godliness is a way of gain." They used their profession and practice of religion for mercenary ends. Probably they took good pay for the false wisdom they taught; they were "greedy of filthy lucre," 1 Tim. 3, 8, against which Paul had especially warned the "deacons," compare Tit. 1, 7; Mark 12, 40. The tendency to prostitute the profession of religion, and also the office of teaching it, to commercial ends has not died out. The apostle's warnings, therefore, still apply. But he does more than warn, he sets forth the true blessings and riches of godliness. **But godliness with contentment is great gain: for we brought nothing into the world, for neither can we carry anything out; but having food and covering we shall be therewith content.** — Paul is emphatic in placing over against the base notion of godliness and its false use the true conception:

87

ἔστιν δέ. Those false teachers "supposed something (verse 5), the apostle states the fact as it is (ἔστιν δέ). Godliness is not only gain, but **great gain,** but in a different way entirely from what these self-seeking men supposed. By πορισμός is meant a means or source of gain; godliness is truly a paying business. But the apostle cuts off the false notion which so many connect with "godliness," by coupling **godliness with contentment.** He means the true reverence and fear of God, animating all our thoughts and actions, not merely an outward profession of religion or Christianity. The root of this godliness is faith in Christ; its motive power is the desire to be and do what shall please God; the thing it shrinks from is, in any way to offend him. — Part of this godliness is, of course, **contentment,** the disposition to be satisfied with what God gives us, as Paul expresses it Phil. 4, 11: "I have learned, in whatsoever state I am, therein to be content," where he uses the adjective from which we have the noun. It is evident, godliness coupled with contentment, as all true godliness must be, cannot be self-seeking and mercenary in its purposes and dealings. For godliness, therefore, to lack contentment is to show that it is inwardly false; it may secure a certain kind of gain, the true riches it cannot attain. This true riches consists in the godliness and contentment itself. To have that is to be lifted above all the vexations, temptations, dangers and disappointments of mercenary men; to rest serene and safe in God's care who ever provides what we need and what is good for us; to have that happiness and inward joy which the world in its chase after earthly treasures cannot know. — This the apostle elucidates first by pointing to our real condition in this life, and secondly by describing the loss of those who are bent on securing earthly riches. **For we brought nothing into the world** — a statement no one will care to contradict. Naked we came, and naked we shall go. The reason is: **for neither can we carry anything out.** The best reading omits δῆλον: *it is certain* (A. V.), "it is plain." The apostle is not stating merely a second undisputed fact, but is using this as a proof for the first fact which he states. We bring nothing into the world, *because* we take nothing out when we leave. "If anything earthly were of real value or use for us men, we would take it with us and enjoy it after death; for the children of God lose nothing that is essential and necessary to them when they pass over into the future world. And since nothing is essentially and necessarily connected with our future and real life, we bring nothing of this kind with us when we come into the world: we merely find it here and we leave it here, as destined only for use in this preparatory and preliminary life; therefore also we are to be content when we have what is necessary, and therefore a godly man is thus content." Stellhorn. — This the apostle adds in a direct statement, indicating the true gain of Christian godliness: **but having food and covering we shall be therewith content.** The apostle has in mind those who desire to be rich, hence this "but." "Food and covering" sums up briefly the necessaries of this life, all that the body really requires. The underlying thought is that we Christians do have this; God provides for us, why should we be "anxious," Matth. 6, 33. The passive of ἀρκέω means to be satisfied or content, and the future states this as a fact: **we shall be content** — our godliness, being of the right kind, positively has this result. This rendering is better than to give the future tense an imperative meaning: *let us be content,* Luther and A. V. To know these things and to act on them in godliness and contentment is certainly great gain.

But look at the other side, it corroborates what has just been said: **But they that desire to be rich fall into a temptation and a snare and many foolish and hurtful lusts, such as drown men in destruction and perdition. For the love of money is a root of all kinds of evil: which some reaching after have been led astray from the faith, and have pierced themselves through with many sorrows.** Paul is not speaking of those that *are* rich, but of those **that desire to be rich,** no matter how much or how little they actually possess. The American Committee translates

βουλόμενοι with "are minded," because the "desire" is really
a strong wish and a determination on their part. Their
motto is: "Seek ye the kingdom of God and his righteousness so that all these things — money and possessions —
shall be added unto you," perverting the Lord's word,
Matth. 6, 33. Their intention and striving is **to be rich,**
which means that they are determined to stay rich if they
already have riches, and to obtain riches and keep them
if they are still poor. — These people **fall into a temptation and a snare;** their desire puts them into a situation
where their evil lusts will be stirred up and control their
actions, and the figurative term **snare** indicates that they
will be caught like prey and bound fast by the sin they
commit. Paul does not say what form the temptation will
take, and we ought not to restrict the "snare" to the one
sin of securing or retaining wealth by unjust means. Once
let a man find the glittering bait of riches attractive, and
the devil will know how and where to lay his snare. Think
of Judas, and of Ananias and Sapphira in the early church.
Note the paronomasia between πορισμός and πειρασμός, also
the other alliteration. — But the one fall results in constantly falling, or in a fallen condition: **and in many
foolish and hurtful lusts,** all sorts of sinful desires which
now rule the heart and life. They have all entered in
by one gate, and now cannot be driven out. By a kind
of metonymy Paul attributes the folly of those who have
the lusts, to the lusts themselves. In their evil desires they
may think themselves shrewd, may boast of their business
judgment and ability, many glory in their success, but
the lusts they have thus allowed free play are **foolish**
nevertheless; they promise a satisfaction they never give,
they make a man pay a big price for what afterwards he
would pay even more to be rid of. So these lusts are
ἀνόηται ἐπιθυμίαι, devoid of sound reason and judgment,
especially of the moral kind. **And hurtful,** βλαβεραί, nor
is their hurtfulness a slight thing, they are **such as drown
men in destruction and perdition;** complete and total
destruction is meant by this duplication of synonymous

terms. They plunge or sink into the terrible gulf of destruction, like the rich fool the night his soul was demanded of him, like Dives when he had his last sumptuous feast, like Judas when too late he perceived his folly and went and hanged himself, like Ananias and his wife when God's judgment came upon them. This drowning is not merely moral turpitude; for this precedes it. It is the opposite of salvation and eternal blessedness. — Paul explains these results still further: **For the love of money is a root of all kinds of evil.** Evil of all kinds may grow out of various roots; one of them, and a frequent one, is "the love of money," ἡ φιλαργυρία, greed, avarice, the desire to get and hold fast money or wealth for its own sake, or for sinful gratification. Augustine: *Avarus in corde hydrops est; plus bibendo plus sitit.* The margin points to the Greek as reading: *a root of all evils,* ῥίζα πάντων τῶν κακῶν. A visit to some of our prisons will show us how many men have tasted of the bitter fruits of this one root of evil. The fair apples they reached out to pluck turned out to be apples of Sodom when they put them to their lips. Human passions in countless forms blaze around the desire and love of money. It is the inner motive of civic, political, legal, commercial, sexual and other corruption. — How this deadly root operates the apostle pictures in a sentence: **which some reaching after have been led astray from the faith, and have pierced themselves through with many sorrows.** The relative ἧς refers to "the love of money;" it is hardly proper to say that the apostle here construes carelessly, wanting to say that some reach after money, and sáying instead that they reach after "the love of money." Wohlenberg is right when he takes the word as it stands; when people want to become rich this love of money seems attractive to them, they actually reach out and get more and more of it; they go where this love rules and return with more of it in their own hearts; they even boast of it as something creditable to themselves. — But in doing so they **have been led astray from the faith,** or rather, since the passive aorist has the intransitive meaning: "they wandered away." The apostle has in mind men who at first had true faith in their hearts (note the article), but more and more they turned from it when the idolatry of money-love took possession of them. "True faith cannot be without true love, and the love of money is the very opposite of the love of God and our neighbor: the lover of money makes money and property his god, puts it in place of God, loves it like him and instead of him, and closes his heart against the need of his fellow men, which in love he ought to alleviate. Accordingly, no man who lets the love of money rule his heart can live in true faith; and this love rules a man as soon and in so far as it prevents him from doing what his love to God and his neighbor demands of him." Stellhorn. Compare Eph. 5, 5; Col. 3, 5-6. "No man can serve two masters . . . Ye cannot serve God and mammon," Matth. 6, 24. — The loss of faith is the most terrible of all, but in addition: **they have pierced themselves through with many sorrows,** not only pangs of conscience, but all the thorns and arrows that wound those who depend on earthly things: care, worry, anxiety, disappointment, and the like. The chase after money leads to anything but happiness, even when men call it fairly "successful." When the love-light goes out and the metallic glitter of gold takes its place, all the joys of love flit away, and the demons of evil passions assemble, soon to pounce upon their helpless victims. Bengel, however, adds: *Horum dolorum remedium fides.*

Godliness with her sister virtues.

Emphatically and squarely Paul turns his faithful Timothy against all these evil results and the ungodly sources whence they spring: **But thou, O man of God, flee these things; and follow after righteousness, godliness, faith, love, patience, meekness. Fight the good fight of the faith, lay hold on the life eternal, whereunto thou wast called, and didst confess the good confession in the sight of many witnesses.** — There is a strong argu-

ment in the appellation **man of God,** which refers not to
Timothy's office as a pastor and teacher, but to his faith
as a true Christian. Godliness and all godly virtues are
the proper adornments of a "man of God." To be sure,
every pastor has a double obligation to show himself a
man of God. The more worldly-minded preachers seek
their own earthly advantage, the more must true Christian
pastors let the light of their faith shine in godly bearing
and conduct. — Timothy is to **flee these things,** like
poisonous serpents, like a dreadful pestilence, like the
snares of the devil. It is hardly safe to conclude from this
admonition that Timothy was inclined to the love of money,
as Wohlenberg intimates; the very passage he quotes,
Phil. 2, 19-23, points in a different direction. But "let
him that thinketh he standeth take heed lest he fall," 1 Cor.
10, 12. Above all let us who are pastors and teachers of
others never presume that we have no need of the warnings we sound in the ears of others. Let us ever be rich
in God, and grow in this wealth, then, whether we have
much or little of earthly wealth, we will be safe. — There
is a contrast between "flee" and **follow after,** or pursue;
yet both are two sides of the same act: in fleeing we are
to follow after. The virtues which the man of God must
pursue and secure for himself in ever greater measure are
named in three pairs: **righteousness, godliness — faith,
love — patience, meekness;** yet they form one chain, and
ever the second is dependent on the first. **Righteousness,**
as the opposite of what Timothy is to flee, is his entire
Christian relation and conduct toward God and men, Rom.
6, 13; 16; 18. The righteousness of the Christian life is
meant, which consists in the right disposition and conduct.
Its companion is **godliness,** the fear and love and trust
that ever looks to God, obeying his Word and will, pleasing him in every possible way, and fearing to offend him
in any degree. The heart of true righteousness is godliness.
— Both rest on **faith,** which draws all its comfort from God
in Christ, and is active in **love** toward God and man. Love
will appear as **patience,** steadfastness, perseverance, and

quiet endurance when affliction and persecution make their
appearance. And **meekness** will be added, a gentle temper,
to shut out any bitterness or resentment when men in
some way wound our feelings. These are the chief characteristics of the "man of God," and the more he attains
of these virtues the greater is his abiding wealth. We,
indeed, bring nothing of it into the world, but if we pursue
it aright we shall surely take it with us when we leave the
world. And while we have it we shall always find it a
blessing, a protection besides, a root of all that is good,
sweet, noble, heavenly, never disappointing, never wound-
ing us. — But we cannot pursue these virtues unhindered
and unmolested; we will meet both foes and obstacles —
hence: **Fight the good fight of the faith** (compare 2 Tim.
4, 7 in the text for the Third Sunday in Advent; 1 Cor. 9,
24, *etc.*). It is the fight which true faith cannot avoid
(note the article), the fight which always goes together
with faith. He who believes and becomes a man of God
steps into the arena, and the contest is on. But his weapons
are so keen, his strength from the Lord so ample, that
the victory is assured for him. He who himself had
fought the good fight here encourages his younger companion in arms to do the same. It is indeed a **good**
(καλός) fight, beautiful in the eyes of God and his angels
and saints, fought in a good cause, in a clean manner, for
a precious crown. — To the latter Paul refers when he
adds: **lay hold on the life eternal,** as the contestant in
the arena grasps the prize of victory and holds it as his
own. No man can earn for himself eternal life, even in
the slightest measure; it is wholly and in every part a
gift of God. But the great Giver of it bestows it only
upon those who believe and maintain their faith by his
grace to the end. When we reach the hour of death nothing but the hand of faith will be able to grasp eternal
life. — To make this fight and to gain this prize, Timothy,
as Paul reminds him **was called** when the efficacious
power of the Gospel touched his heart and kindled the
first spark of faith in it. That the call was effective in

his heart he evinced by his confession: **and didst confess
the good confession in the sight of many witnesses.**
The article: τὴν καλὴν ὁμολογίαν, makes it certain that the
apostle has in mind the confession Timothy made at his
baptism. There is no reason to suppose that this was
a very special confession or statement on the part of Timothy; it was the confession of faith in Christ which was
regularly made at that time by those who received baptism,
just as we now require the same thing. Its ancient form
we cannot state, but its contents is beyond question. Paul
calls it a **good** confession, beautiful before God and men.
How base would be a denial following it! A later suggestion is that this was Timothy's ordination confession,
but there is no direct reference to his office here, so that
the old view is in every way preferable. Our confession
is the answer to God's calling; as the call stands firm on
his side, together with the prize of life to which he calls,
so let our confession never waver, but grow stronger and
stronger by the working of his grace in our hearts and
lives. — Timothy made his confession **in the sight of
many witnesses,** before the assembled congregation, as is
the precious privilege and solemn duty of every adult
convert to this day. Paul wants him to keep that in mind,
and Bengel finely states the reason: *Coram multis testibus,
qui contra te, si deficeres, testuari forent.*

HOMILETICAL HINTS.

Contentment always has enough. — Down along the shores of
the Mediterranean where the sunny coasts of France and Italy invite
and attract the traveller every spring, there stands a little lonesome
house bearing an inscription of only two words, which translated
read: "Enough for those appointed to die!"

"To whom does your house belong?" You reply: "Why, to
whom but to myself?" "Well, since when?" "Since I inherited it
from my parents." "Why did they will it to you?" "Because they
could not take it along." "Who is going to have it later on?"
"Why," you reply, "I hope my children." "Why are you going to

leave it to them?" "Because I cannot take it along!" Matthes. —
An old spoon shown in the Kolberg Dome bears the inscription:
"Too few build where they expect to dwell."

The cradle: "We brought nothing into this world;" the coffin:
"Neither can we carry anything out." — A fool who drinks salt-
water to slake his thirst. You cannot quench the love of money
by feeding it gold.

Rump gives a scathing description of bankers, trustees, speculators, and others who sear their consciences, harden their hearts,
kill their moral sense of right and wrong, all for the sake of money.
What do they care for the pleadings of the inexperienced widow,
the timid inquiry of frightened orphans. They take the last savings
from the quivering hand of old age, the few dollars that form the
stay of the sick and helpless. They hoodwink the law and know
how to avoid its terrors; *etc.* — There is no commandment of God
which the desire to be rich has not transgressed a thousand times.
— Money is power, but often it is the powerful snare which holds
the bird it has caught, so that it cannot escape.

How are we to distinguish, since worldly men also use godliness
for gain. There is a sure way to distinguish. Paint a fire as
naturally as you possibly can, or get a great artist to do it; have it
so that looking at it you cannot distinguish the flames from those
of real fire. Then take the picture into a dark room and let the
flames light up the room. True fire spreads light and heat.

Wealth is no sin, poverty no virtue. Both may be either — it
depends on the heart. — If poverty were godliness, monks and nuns
would certainly be saints.

Paste diamonds deceive many, but so do stones of the purest
water. You can wear them only between the cradle and the grave.
Secure the diamonds that you can wear to all eternity: righteousness and godliness. — Be satisfied with what you have, not with
what you are.

Here are two rich men: A laborer with his wife at his side,
his little flock about the table, a frugal meal before them. They
fold their hands and bow their heads as grace is said and Jesus
invited to their board. They are happy and content, care knocks in
vain at their door, their treasure-chest lies upon the tidy shelf
against the wall — a well-worn Bible. — An old man with feeble
steps enters his cosy little room in the Home which his church
has provided for such as he. There lies his Bible and hymnal, there
are his few belongings; thankfully he looks at the sunset in the
west and thinks of pleasant by-gone days, thankfully he praises God
who has fulfilled his promise: At eventide it shall be light. From
his little hoard of savings he finds it possible to give a silver coin
each week to the Lord's mission work — far more than the wealthy

farmer across the way. — These two have learned the great secret of true riches: godliness with contentment is great gain.

Paul pictures true happiness and blessing as altogether independent of money. But many Christians refuse to believe him. They worship God, but somewhere they have hidden away a little idol, to whom they offer daily sacrifice. — The fight for existence is the only one some people know; its principle is: Money is thy fortune! The fight of faith is the true issue, and its principle is: God is thy fortune! — Righteousness is better than riches; godliness more precious than gold; faith nets more than finance; and love never needs to worry about lack.

"Fight the Good Fight of Faith!"

I. *According to your calling* (Baptism).
II. *With your God-given power* (faith and godliness).
III. *Against your deadliest foes* (lusts).
IV. *For the heavenly prize* (eternal life).

Heffter.

The Surest Way to the Greatest Wealth.

I. *Righteousness and godliness.*
II. *Faith and love.*
III. *Patience and meekness.*

Would You Like to Be Rich?

I. *Only temporarily?*
    a) Then put your foot into the snare.
    b) Then fill your heart with lusts.
    c) Then thrust your head into sorrows.
    d) Then drown in destruction and perdition.
II. *Or eternally?*
    a) Then heed the Word.
    b) Then fight the good fight of faith.
    c) Then practice godliness.
    d) Then continue in the good confession.
    e) Then lay hold on eternal life.

Paul's Call to the Man of God.

I. *Flee!*
II. *Fight!*
III. *Follow!*
IV. *Lay hold!*

7

"Godliness With Contentment is Great Gain."

It secures for us:

  I. *A good conscience.*
  II. *A happy heart.*
 III. *A worthy life.*
 IV. *A blessed death.*

An Outline of the Godly Life.

  I. *Faith.*
  II. *Communion with God.*
 III. *Christian virtues.*
 IV. *War against temptation and lusts.*
  V. *A blessed end.*

THE EIGHTH SUNDAY AFTER·TRINITY.

Acts 16, 16-32.

The point at which this text stops helps to indicate what this text intends. The entire story of the jailor's conversion is not told, two verses are omitted. The stop is made with the final statement of service rendered to this unhappy man; and that is the key to the text as fitted into this second after-Trinity subcycle. After "godliness" as the first grand and comprehensive result of faith in our hearts and lives, we may well consider that part of it which is embraced in the term "love," namely *service to our fellow men*. Two instances of such service are here presented, an unfortunate maid is freed from the spirit that abused her, and an unfortunate man on the brink of despair and suicide is led to Christ. The unity in this double narrative is service, namely the highest and best service, rendered in the name of Jesus, prompted by the love of Jesus, and leading the unfortunate to the mercy of Jesus. The excellence of the text when considered from this point of view will be appreciated by the preacher. The most natural thing will be to divide the text according to the persons to whom the service is rendered, but the source of the service, the love of Christ in Paul's heart, must dominate both parts.

Paul's service to the maid with a spirit of divination.

The apostle is on his second great missionary journey, in the first European city at which he makes a stop for work. He has had his first success, Lydia, a Jewish seller of purple was brought to faith in Christ. Paul continues his labors and follows up this first success. **And it came to pass, as we were going to the place of prayer, that a certain maid having a spirit of**

divination met us, which brought her masters much gain by soothsaying. The same following after Paul and us cried out, saying, These men are servants of the Most High God, which proclaim unto you the way of salvation. And this she did for many days. — Such was the poor girl upon whom presently the apostle bestowed the great benefaction of deliverance. **The place of prayer,** to which Paul and his companions **were going,** and made it a practice to go, is the same as in verse 13, either a building or an open place where the Jews assembled for prayer in cities or towns where there was or could not be a synagogue. The locations near rivers were preferred on account of the lustrations connected with the Jewish prayers. Josephus, *Antiquities,* 14, 10, 23. While going out to the place of prayer, **a certain maid having a spirit of divination met us.** This was a case of demoniacal possession, such as are recounted in the Gospels. Meyer would reduce it to an instance of mental derangement giving certain faculties a peculiar sensitiveness or keenness, but this agrees neither with what Luke says here or in verse 18. The spirit dominating this girl is designated by the apposition: "A Python" (margin). Python, in Greek mythology, was the name of the Pythian serpent or dragon that dwelt in the region of Pytho at the foot of Parnassus in Phocis, and was said to have guarded the oracle of Delphi and been slain by Apollo. Grimm-Thayer. Then the word became a common appellation for those who professed to reveal future events, like the Delphic oracle, especially those who delivered their oracular utterances by ventriloquism. To this class, it seems, this girl belonged. The demon controlling her made her utter remarkable statements concerning secret and future things. This terrible affliction was turned into gain by **her masters,** apparently two or more, who probably owned her as a slave, and may have bought her as such in order to use her for **soothsaying;** they charged a price for any one who wished to get an answer from her, and secured **much gain** by this ungodly procedure. But the world has not changed in this respect. It is ready to use every sin and vice, and to pander to every delusion and lust, simply to get "much gain." As far as the unfortunate instruments of its trade are concerned, it cares absolutely nothing for them, except to coin money out of them. We meet the same spirit in the industrial world, where thousands of masters care not a whit for the real welfare of their workers, as long as they can richly profit by their labor. — The maid followed after Paul and his companions and continued to **cry out** (ἔκραζεν, imperfect): **These men are servants of the Most High God, which proclaim unto you the way of salvation.** The remarkable thing is the truth and correctness of this utterance. Even if we accept the supposition that this maid was a Jewess, we must admit that of herself she could not have had the full clear knowledge she here expresses. As in the Gospels, when the demons declared Jesus to be the Son of God, so here the demon possessing the maid is the real speaker. And these demons know both who Christ is and who the servants (*bondservants,* margin) of Christ are, and what their mission is. But why do they proclaim aloud this knowledge of theirs? Either from abject or servile fear, that with fawning and flatteries would fain avert from itself the doom which the presence of Christ or his servants announces to them (Grotius); like the fugitive slave, dreaming of nothing but stripes and torments when he encounters his well-known lord, and then seeks by any means to deprecate his anger (Jerome); or, better still, the explanation Trench himself gives after quoting the others: in order to injure the cause of Christ, by bringing upon it the discredit and suspicion which must ever be attached to any demoniac utterance. This last is undoubtedly best: when the devil tells the truth, he cannot have a good motive or a good purpose. So also Christ silenced the testimony of the demons, Mark 1, 23-27; Luke 4, 35; Mark 3, 12; and Paul here does the same. — But not at once, he let her go on **many days.** Why? The matter of working miracles, from all that we can gather in the

Scriptures, was not left entirely to the will and judgment of the apostles; they followed the direction of the Spirit also in this regard. So Paul suffered the annoyance for a good while, then finally interfered.

But Paul, being sore troubled, turned and said to the spirit, I charge thee in the name of Jesus Christ to come out of her. And it came out that very hour. — This describes the benefaction bestowed upon the pitiable maid. The apostle was **sore troubled** not through personal vexation at her annoying cries, but because of her sad condition — the helpless victim of a wicked spirit. He had waited till he was entirely sure as to what the Master wished him to do in the case. With this settled he **turned,** not to the maid, but **to the spirit** with the command: **I charge thee in the name of Jesus Christ to come out of her.** Whenever we can act in Christ's name and by his authority, it is as if Christ himself acted; but whenever we lack his authority, then we may shout his name till we are hoarse, and nothing will come of it, except his displeasure with us. The spirit **came out that very hour,** the spirit, and not the *fixe Idee,* as Meyer thinks. The result itself was instantaneous, but Luke writes "hour," because after that she never spoke by divination again, and the change in her was dated from that hour. One would suppose that all men would acclaim this deed of the apostle, see in it the hand of "the Most High God" and a sample of the "salvation" his messengers bring; but worldly eyes always take a different view.

But when her masters saw that the hope of their gain was gone, they laid hold on Paul and Silas, and dragged them into the marketplace before the rulers, and when they had brought them unto the magistrates, they said, These men, being Jews, do exceedingly trouble our city, and set forth customs which it is not lawful for us to receive, or to observe, being Romans. And the multitude rose up together against them: and the magistrates rent their garments off them, and commanded to beat them with rods. — This was Paul's reward for the priceless service he had rendered the poor victim of the devil. That the maid was owned by at least two and possibly more **masters** is shown by the plural here, when they proceed in unison. **The hope of their gain,** the great sums they still hoped to get, **was gone.** Luke very finely uses the same word and form: ἐξῆλθεν, for the coming out of the spirit from the maid, and for the disappearance of the hope of gain with that spirit. The greedy eyes of the world always look for gain; knowing not the true gain (recall the previous text). Touch the unconverted money-bag, and you will see the full activity of its wicked possessor. A fine example is Demetrius at Ephesus. — How soon these men perceived their great "loss" we are unable to say, it must have been quite soon. Perhaps Paul and his friends were coming back from the place of prayer, when these men pounced upon these two: **Paul and Silas,** and using violence **dragged them into the marketplace before the rulers.** Luke and Timothy for some reason were not molested. The marketplace was the public place, the square, or forum, where the public generally gathered, not only for business, but also for other purposes. The magisterial offices, the courts, were usually located at or near the marketplace. The ἄρχοντες are **the rulers** of the city, the police-court, we might say. Luke reports nothing of what transpired before these judges. It is hardly to be supposed that they saw nothing in the case and therefore turned it away; nor is there any hint that the accusers changed their charge against Paul and Silas in order to get a better hearing before the higher judges. The rulers, however, seem to have themselves referred the case to the higher judges, namely to **the magistrates** or *prætores, the duumviri,* as Cicero calls them, who held the highest authority in the colonial cities and handled infractions of the Roman law. The term στρατηγοί, "commanders," was preferred by them as indicative of greater honor, and as the true equivalent of "prætors." For full details see Conybeare & Howson, *Life and Epistles of the Apostle Paul,* chapter IX. — And now we hear the accusation, which says nothing of the maid that was freed, but a good deal about something else: **These men, being Jews, do exceedingly trouble our city, and set forth customs which it is not lawful for us to receive, or to observe, being Romans.** The inflammatory character of the statement that Paul and Silas were **Jews** will be noted when we recall that the Jews were recently expelled from Rome (Acts 18, 2), and that it was the pride of every colonial city to copy the doings of the capital. "Being Jews" made those two stand in the worst possible light. The fact that there were no Jewish men, or hardly any, at this time in Philippi, made the presence and activity of these two "Jews" the more noticeable, and now that full attention was drawn to them, dangerous. The statement that these men **do exceedingly trouble our city** is a violent exaggeration; the only advertisement they had received to make their presence generally known was not by what they had done, but by the maid's daily shouting after them. As to the **customs,** which Paul and Silas preached, being **not lawful** for Romans (note the proud contrast to the preceding "Jews"), it was a fact that the letter of the Roman law was opposed to any religious innovation or the introduction of a new religion. There were exceptions, as in the case of the Jews themselves, but a strict application of the Roman legal principles would have held Paul and Silas liable. In the bloody persecutions which followed later the Christian religion was condemned as a *religio illicita.* — But whether the charge was in any measure true or not, these "magistrates" are not left to decide, for **the multitude rose up** in a tumult against Paul and Silas, as if to give the magistrates an ocular demonstration of how the city was exceedingly stirred up. The magistrates were thus carried away into hasty action against the accused, **rent their garments off them, and commanded to beat them with rods.** Both acts were orders to the lictors, the upper part of the body of the victim being bared for the scourging. The imperfect ἐκέλευον describes the event as happening before the narrator's eyes (Winer 40, 3); and the present infinitive ῥαβδίζειν denotes continued action. So

the apostles received **many stripes,** no one keeping record
or limiting the number.   .

Paul's service to the jailor.

In the very midst of his shameful reward for one
kind deed, Paul performs another. As regards the maid
that was released from the evil spirit, nothing more is
said; it is possible that she too found complete release
from all the devil's power, spiritual as well as physical.
Not so much she and her possible fate, but the service
rendered her and so shamefully requited, is to occupy
us here. So also in the case of the jailor. **And when
they had laid many stripes upon them, they cast them
into prison, charging the jailor to keep them safely:
who, having received such a charge, cast them into the
inner prison, and made their feet fast in the stocks.** —
The severe measures already taken are followed by others.
The magistrates intend to look into this case more fully
later on, so they remand the apostles to **prison.** The Roman prison usually had three distinct parts, the *commu-
niora*, where the prisoners had light and air; the *interiora*,
shut off by strong iron gates with bars and locks; and the
tullianum or dungeon, for executions and prisoners condemned to die. The jailor receives the special charge **to
keep them safely,** which of course made him especially
responsible and liable. So he not only **cast them into
the inner prison,** behind bars and doors where the worst
criminals were kept, but also **made their feet fast in the
stocks,** at once a fetter and an instrument of torture, for
the feet were spread wide apart and locked fast in this position. The middle voice ἠσφαλίσατο implies that the jailor
made them safe and fast on his own account. No negligence should be charged to him. Paul himself well remembered the cruel treatment he received on this occasion,
for he refers to it 1 Thess. 2, 2: "having suffered before,
and been shamefully entreated, as ye know, at Philippi."
His condition must have been distressful in the extreme:
bleeding, bruised, and sore, without anything to assuage his

wounds, and now the miserable prison-cell, with its harsh floor and its painful stocks! It would seem, if any one needed help and service, it would be Paul and Silas. But instead they render service — and the very greatest possible — to their own tormentor.

But about midnight Paul and Silas were praying and singing hymns unto God, and the prisoners were listening to them; and suddenly there was a great earthquake, so that the foundations of the prison-house were shaken: and immediately all the doors were opened; and every one's bands were loosed. And the jailor being roused out of sleep, and seeing the prison doors open, drew his sword, and was about to kill himself, supposing that the prisoners had escaped. — *Nihil crus sentit in nervo, quum animus in coelo est.* Tertullian. What else could they have done in pain and wretchedness of body but pray to God? writes one commentator. And their prayer was not a weary wail, a dismal complaint. It was, no doubt, a petition for deliverance according to the good and wise counsel of God, but especially a petition for fortitude and strength to bear their cross, for the furtherance of God's work in the midst of his enemies and for the conversion of many. And soon their praying turned to singing. What **hymns** they used we are unable to say, but the Psalms of David have ever been dear to those who suffer, especially also to those who suffer wrong. Besser thinks Ps. 18 strikes the right note. Such actions a Roman prison had never seen, but, of course, it had never held such Christians before. The imperfect tense ὕμνουν shows that the singing accompanied by prayer continued some time. — No wonder that **the prisoners were listening to them.** The jailor had forgotten to fetter their lips, their hearts he could not have reached at all. "And if among those captives there was a malefactor like the one at the right side of Christ's cross, Paul and Silas sang him into Paradise." Besser. Stoecker in his city mission work in Berlin employed bands of singing boys each band under a good leader, and sang the precious Gospel into many a cold and

arid heart; and this work of the *Kurrendensaenger* continues still. But for himself Paul was learning here what
afterwards he put into such comforting language in his
eighth chapter of Romans. In the heat of affliction, like
gold, faith is refined. — The **great earthquake,** while a
natural phenomenon and due to natural causes in the usual
order, was nevertheless a direct providential intervention
in the course of events in Philippi, in favor of his apostles
and their work. Those two in prison had not prayed for
an earthquake, probably that would have beeen the last
thing they would have thought of as helpful to them. But
God always knows best what means to employ, at what
time, and in what manner. The earthquake was severe
enough to shake the **foundations of the prison-house,**
and thus to rend and leave open **all the doors,** and to loose
every one's bands or fetters. The stocks were burst apart,
chains shaken out of their wall-fastenings, other δεσμά likewise. The fetters mentioned in the context and the entire
description shows that Luke means by the **bands** that were
loosed such as held the prisoners fast in the prison, not such
as they might have carried with them. Winds, waters,
earthquakes, as well as other disturbances of nature, often
perform the strangest feats, but all under God's directing
providence. It was not otherwise here, only here we see
more of the inner purposes and aims of God than we can
under ordinary circumstances. — The jailor was fast aleep
when these events so important for him occurred. They
were to help usher in his own release from a prison-cell and
bonds worse than those he had laid upon the apostles. His
first thought is of his duty, his responsibility. Himself, no
doubt, frightened and unnerved by the earthquake, he now
sees **the prison doors open,** and jumps to the conclusion,
entirely natural under the circumstances, that **the prisoners
had escaped.** That meant his utter undoing, for the Roman law dealt severely with jailors who permitted their
prisoners to escape, and he had been especially charged
with the keeping of two. At once the pagan thought of
suicide leaps into his brain: he **drew his sword,** the short

Roman μάχαιρα he always wore at his side, **and was about to kill himself.** What a difference between the singing, happy apostles, in the midst of suffering, shame, and danger of the greatest kind, and this great Roman coward, who flies to suicide before he really knows whether misfortune has befallen him or not! But this was true Roman teaching, for had not Cassius when defeated covered his face and ordered his freedman to kill him in his tent here at Philippi? Had not Titinius, his messenger, done the same thing, as properly "a Roman's part?" Brutus likewise, and many others. This is the wisdom of the world, this is its comfort when its little earthly castle of fortune is wrecked. It is the devil's own inspiration; a Judas dies by his own hand!

Now comes the story of Paul's great benefaction to this poor fool. **But Paul cried with a loud voice, saying, Do thyself no harm: for we are all here. And he called for lights, and sprang in, and, trembling for fear, fell down before Paul and Silas, and brought them out, and said, Sirs, what must I do to be saved? And they said, Believe on the Lord Jesus, and thou shalt be saved, thou and thy house.** — Paul saves his life, and what is infinitely more, his immortal soul. We need not wonder that none of the prisoners had fled. The effect of the praying and singing of Paul and Silas was still in their hearts, and combined with that the tremendous effect of the earthquake itself, which to them all could not but appear as a direct intervention of the God to whom these two had prayed. So they all stood together, and Paul's shout stopped the desperate deed of the jailor. — No wonder that he was **trembling for fear,** his heart torn with conflicting emotions in that terrible midnight hour. **He called for lights,** to assure himself of the truth of Paul's words, and when he **sprang in,** discovering that it was even as Paul had said, he was completely overcome. **He fell down before Paul and Silas,** the jailor before his prisoners, the man who had made them suffer extra tortures before those who had saved him from eternal torment. What a scene for those other prisoners! What thoughts must have mingled in their hearts? Besser exclaims at sight of this jailor prostrate before Paul and Silas in dumb gratitude: "Behold, the man from Macedonia! And if he had been the only one in all Macedonia, to be brought to salvation, Paul and Silas would gladly have suffered the scourging and the pain of the stocks for this one." — Lifted up with gentle yet firm words the jailor **brought them out;** whither he brought them is not said, nor whether the other prisoners accompanied them. Luke is not concerned about all the details. And now an unexpected question falls from the man's lips: Κύριοι, τί με δεῖ ποιεῖν ἵνα σωθῶ; Beneath the man's rough exterior there beat a poor, wretched human heart. For all his rough and often cruel job he had higher aspirations. And now, all suddenly, his whole inner nature had been shaken up; he had been tossed between life and death. God had reached into his life, this God of Paul and Silas who was greater than any Jupiter or god of Olympus. We may be sure that the jailor knew the entire story of these two prisoners whom he was to guard so especially. He may not have heard any of their singing and praying during the night, wooing sleep instead, but he had heard of that maid and her constant shouts about a ὁδὸν σωτηρίας. So the greatest and most blessed question any human being can ask came to this man's lips: **Sirs, what must I do to be saved?** The title κύριοι shows the humility of the speaker and the reverence he has for those addressed. The ποιεῖν implies that he is ready to do the severest penance, to bring the most painful sacrifice, to undertake the most arduous labor, in order to obtain salvation. As imperfectly as he knew the way to be saved, so imperfectly he very likely also knew what this salvation meant. Yet he had a glimpse of it in Paul and Silas, undisturbed by fear, undismayed by their punishment, courageous, and helpful even to him. He knew at least this, that he needed salvation, and that salvation was a most precious thing. — The answer he gets has gone on ever since it was spoken, and later recorded, on its mission of light and deliverance: **Believe on the Lord**

Jesus, not on us as κυρίους but on him as κύριον. The very first word: πίστευσον corrects the wrong idea that may lie in ποιεῖν. The aorist imperative is used, instead of the present, because the moment a man believes, that moment salvation is his; then too the aorist is stronger than the present would be. To **believe** is to put all our hope and confidence **on** (ἐπί) **Jesus,** on him and his merits, as satisfying God, making us acceptable to him, and giving us eternal life. The way of faith seems much easier than the way of works; it is, and it is not. The way of faith lets God do everything for us, the way of works tries to do everything, or nearly everything, itself. That is harder, much harder; in fact an impossible task and effort. They who try works make the thing easy, they simply tie a few apples on the Christmas tree; but they who try faith find that an entirely new tree must be grown if there is to be fruit. That is harder, and yet easier, because God's grace grows the tree. — The result is always certain: **thou shalt be saved, thou and thy house;** σὺ καὶ ὁ οἶκός σου puts both side by side for special emphasis. This reference to the **house** of the jailor includes his wife, children, servants, and any relatives who may have made their home with him. Paul is preaching family religion. And the entire family, it seems, is his audience: **they spake the word of the Lord unto him, with all that were in his house.** What a midnight service! With wounds untended, with limbs still aching from the stocks, with bodies wearied and crying for rest, these two unwearied hearts proclaim all the main points of the Gospel to their willing hearers. The love of true preachers, and of true Christians in general, forgets self in extending the highest benefactions to others. They find their work its own sweetest reward. — Here the text ends: the last glimpse we catch of the group in the jailor's house shows us the love that delights to serve, and a service the highest and holiest of all, rendered in the purest and most unselfish love.

HOMILETICAL HINTS.

Unbelief loves to go hand in hand with superstition. Faith is the enemy and death of both. — The devil possessed the poor maid at Philippi and made her utter strange things by a sort of ventriloquism. The devil controlled her masters just as much, making them use the basest means to secure money. The one was a divining devil, the other was the devil of unscrupulous greed. Both devils are still at work, often in the same person, who by the lying arts of mind-reading, fortune-telling, clairvoyance, spiritualism, and other deceptions, prey upon the gullibility and superstition of thousands and for their own gain draw money from their deluded victims. Alas, that there are so-called Christians who also help to enrich these deceivers, and buy for themselves falsehood, delusions, sins, an evil conscience, the displeasure and wrath of God!

God is very particular as to the means by which he builds his kingdom. He has provided the means himself, his Word and sacrament, messengers whom he himself calls, hearts filled with love and devotion, deeds prompted by true obedience, noble generosity, pure unselfishness. He wants no testimony of devils, no service or gifts from worldly men whose hearts care nothing for Christ. And yet how often Christian people forget this divine rule! If the devil condescends to do "good," they offer him a place. If the church can profit by worldly men, methods, practices, they are willing to make room for them. Many an unblessed dollar has been thankfully received and receipted by those who should have spurned it and cast it out.

Let us answer the question honestly. What would pain us more, to lose the Gospel, or to lose our income? The actual test, if God should make it, would search us far more closely than the effort to give an honest answer at the moment, for we always rate the power of resistance our will is able to offer as far greater than it really is.

What reward do you expect for the service you render? Acknowledgment, praise of men, honor, appreciation, money, position? And when what you think the due measure of such reward is withheld from you, what complaint do you think yourself entitled to? One look at Paul and Silas should teach us how to bear the greatest ingratitude with a joyful heart and the one desire, not to reap any reward for ourselves, but to extend to those that abuse us some new service, even greater than the one already rendered.

One is with us when we serve him faithfully. The night is not too dark, the prison not too strong, the shame we suffer not too great, our pain and bodily misery not too violent, our condition not too hopeless. As he is the one help of those in the power of the devil, sin, and death, so he is the one stay of all his followers in affliction.

The jailor was himself held in terrible bonds, and the devil, this jailor's jailor, thought to bring him to execution by his own hand. Then Jesus opened his prison bars and gave him the true freedom he had never had.

The world believes in social service, but in no more. Nor does it care much for social service connected with spiritual service. The chief aim of the church is spiritual service. All other service it makes subservient to this.

One believes, all are saved. How is this possible? One light in the house, and all walk in the radiance thereof. One child of peace, and all are touched and drawn to the fountain of peace. One son of God in a home, and all see and learn the blessedness of sonship.

Many a providence of God is meant to rouse up the sleeping conscience. Alas, when men allow it to fall asleep again!

Blessed Are They That Serve in Jesus' Name!

I. *Because of their Lord.*
II. *Because of their service.*
III. *Because of those whom they serve.*
IV. *Because of their reward.*

The Power Which Real Disciples of Christ Possess.

I. *Against the powers of darkness.*
II. *Against the threatenings of danger.*
III. *Against the terrors of conscience.*

Rump.

God's Servants are Called for God's Service.

I. *God has put the right motive for such service into their hearts.*
II. *God has equipped them with the right power for such service.*
III. *God opens the door for such service on every side.*
IV. *God strengthens them in every trial they meet in such service.*

The Work Christ Has Set His Disciples to Do.

I. *To drive the devil and his works out.*
II. *To bring Christ and his gifts in.*

What Have God's Servants a Right to Expect?

I. *Success.*
II. *Ingratitude.*
III. *Divine Comfort and Help.*
IV. *Reward.*

Sorrows and Joys in Serving the Lord.

I. *There are great sorrows.*
II. *But they lead to greater joys.*

Deichert.

THE NINTH SUNDAY AFTER TRINITY.

Acts 17, 16-34.

Ready always to give answer to every man that asketh you a reason concerning the hope that is in you," 1 Pet. 3. 15. This word fits the action of Paul at Athens exactly. When the Epicurean and Stoic philosophers began to inquire and led Paul unto the Areopagus, he willingly went and cheerfully gave them answer, with the result that some believed. The occasions when answer is demanded of us concerning our faith and the hope we base on it are not usually as grand as was the one here at Athens, but they are just as real and important, both for us and for those who require the answer; we must be equipped to give answer, to render it promptly, cheerfully, and skilfully, like the apostle. It is frequently the wisdom of this world, in some form or other, which either with a show of scorn, or with good-natured tolerance, calls us to an account. The Gospel is the highest wisdom of all, and we must be fortified with its superiority and free from any fear in the presence of opponents. Human reason is still blind in religious things; philosophy, especially also the common cheap philosophy of to-day, has no satisfactory answer to the highest questions of the soul; the Gospel alone has the true light and is able to satisfy the soul. All this, and more in the same direction is shown us by Paul's answer to the Athenian inquiries.

Paul called upon to make answer.

Silas and Timothy remained at Berœa, while Paul at the instance of the brethren left the city and proceeded to Athens, where he ordered his companions to meet him as soon as possible. **Now while Paul waited for them at Athens, his spirit was provoked within him, as**

he beheld the city full of idols. So he reasoned in the
synagogue with the Jews and the devout persons, and
in the marketplace every day with them that met with
him. And certain also of the Epicurean and Stoic
philosophers encountered him. And some said, What
would this babbler say? other some, He seemeth to be
a setter forth of strange gods: because he preached
Jesus and the resurrection. And they took hold of him,
and brought him unto the Areopagus, saying, May we
know what this new teaching is, which is spoken by
thee? For thou bringest certain strange things to our
ears; we would know therefore what these things mean.
(Now all the Athenians and the strangers sojourning
there spent their time in nothing else, but either to tell
or to hear some new thing.) And Paul stood in the
midst of the Areopagus, and said.

Paul was alone in **Athens.** He spent his time looking about this famous city, "the eye of Greece, the mother
of arts and eloquence." "The once famous center of Greek
thought and culture, long the dominant power among the
varied states of which ancient Greece was made up, whose
name and influence at one time was all-powerful in so many
rich and flourishing cities round the Mediterranean Coast,
in Asia as well as in Europe, had become after many vicissi-
tudes a simple provincial city of the province of Achaia in
the empire. Rome, in memory of its past splendid history,
had accorded it the privilege of a 'free city,' *urbs libera."
Popular Commentary.* But much of its ancient glory still
lingered in the famous city when Paul paid it this memorable
visit. But it did not attract him or fill him with pleasure:
**his spirit was provoked within him, as he beheld the city
full of idols.** The pagan Lucian might indeed exclaim:
"When I first came to Athens I was astonished and delighted
to see all the glory of the city;" Paul looked at Athens
with Christian eyes. And these saw it κατείδωλος, **full of
idols,** a word found only here, but formed after the analogy
of others in frequent use. Even pagan writers have drawn
especial attention to the overabundance of temples and

statues in the Athens of these days. Petronius satirically remarks that in Athens it is easier to find a god than a man. Pausanias in his fine description states that Athens had more images than all Greece put together. Xenophon calls Athens "one great altar, one great offering to the gods." And Livy writes: "In Athens are to be seen images of gods and men of all descriptions and made of all material." In the Agora, or market-place, every god in the Olympus found a place; every public place and building was at the same time a sanctuary, dedicated to one or more gods; and besides the ordinary gods there were deifications of Fame, Modesty, Energy, Persuasion, *etc.* — Paul no doubt appreciated the wonderful beauty and art that gave
· these temples, sanctuaries, public buildings, and statuary the wonderful distinction they possessed, but, if anything, this lavishing of beauty and skill upon objects of idolatrous worship, made him the more indignant. But **his spirit was provoked within him,** not at the people as such, but at the delusion of the devil that held them, at the blindness, ignorance, folly, and wickedness in which they lay, proud of their shame, boasting of their depravity. — It seems that Paul had intended to wait quietly for the arrival of his companions in Athens, but when he saw this display of idolatry he could not remain quiet; **he reasoned,** in conversation or discussion, first **in the synagogue with the Jews and the devout persons,** *i. e.* the proselytes of the gate, who assembled there; but he did not stop with this, he began the same kind of discussion and argument **in the market-place every day with them that met with him,** *i. e.* with any that happened to be present with him. This *Agora* (market) was by no means like the market-sections of to-day, devoted only to the selling and buying of all sorts of provisions, and frequented by a bustling, busy crowd occupied with nothing else. The Athenian *Agora* was the meeting-place of philosophy and idleness, of conversation and business. Under the plane trees were the statues of some of the most famous men of the city, such as Solon, Conon, Demosthenes; the *Agora* was full of the memories

of history. All around the buildings were decorated with sculpture and impressive figures; some of the more prominent were graced with porticos and cloisters, beautified with paintings and statuary. Here there was the finest kind of opportunity for conversation and discussion, and Paul made full use of it.

Besides others **certain also of the Epicurean and Stoic philosophers encountered him,** συνέβαλλον, imperfect, on various occasion; they got together with him in discussion, not necessarily in a hostile manner. **The Epicureans** were quite atheistic in their philosophical speculation; they thought the world was formed by an accidental concourse of atoms, not created, not even formed by divine power. While they permitted a certain belief in the gods, they treated them as phantoms, without influence upon the world and life; they mocked at the popular mythology, but presented nothing better. Their view of the soul was materialistic, at death it was dissolved and dissipated in the elements, ending forever the existence of man. Life therefore was not regulated by any higher moral or spiritual considerations; its highest aim was gratification: gross and sordid, even vicious and criminal, if one was inclined that way; or refined and esthetic, if one had tastes and aspirations in this direction. *Pleasure,* not duty, was the substance of this philosophy. Its founder, Epicurus, was born in Samos 342 B. C.; his idea of the supreme good was the ἡδονή, pleasure, and the means to attain it, virtue, a doctrine which could not possibly produce anything but selfishness and sensuality as men tried to put it into practice. Note how little advance certain schools of to-day have made as compared with the old Athenians. — **The Stoics** were pantheists; they condemned the worship of images and the use of temples, considering them only as ornaments of art. God to them was merely the Spirit of Reason of the universe; matter was inseparable from this deity, and he was conceived as impressing order and law upon it, since he regulated it as an inner principle. The Stoics considered the soul to be corporeal, at death it would

be burnt or absorbed into God.   Their moral code was
higher than that of the Epicureans, their ideal being an
austere apathy or unconcern, holding itself superior to passion as well as circumstance; pleasure was no good, pain no
evil; reason was their guide and decided what was good or
what was evil.   He who followed reason was perfect and
sufficient in himself.   When reason saw no more in life, it
dictated suicide, as the most reasonable thing.   Its first two
leaders died by their own hand, and the Romans who felt
attracted especially by this sterner philosophy often followed their example.   Stoicism was the philosophy of
human *pride*.   Zeno, a Cyprian by birth, taught in Athens
about 300 B. C.   Both of these philosophies were naturally
diametrically opposed to Christianity with its doctrine of
God, the soul, sin, redemption, salvation in Christ, the resurrection of the body, and eternal life.   Reason is still the
god of many to-day. — Luke does not say what line the
discussions in the *Agora* followed.   He reports only the outcome.   **Some said, What would this babbler say?**   They
were of the supercilious or scoffing kind: calling Paul a
σπερμολόγος, a bird that picks up seeds, one who gathers up
scraps of knowledge (σπέρματα λέγειν) ; a chatterer, like a
crow or daw. — **Other some** were inclined to be more
serious : **He seemeth to be a setter forth of strange gods,**
δαιμόνια *demons* (margin) in the sense of divinities : **because
he preached Jesus and the resurrection;** not that they
considered the resurrection a divinity, but naturally spoke
of "gods" whenever a new divinity was mentioned.   This
had been quite dangerous in the days of Socrates, but now
the Greeks were more tolerant, and ready to accord the
divinities of other nations a certain place. — The outcome
of these preliminary skirmishes in the *Agora* was that **they
took hold of him and brought him unto the Areopagus,**
in order to hear his doctrine in full.   No violence is implied ;
there is no hint of a trial.   Paul is formally invited to lay
the Gospel before the most influential and important per-
sonages of the city.   The Ἄρειον Πάγον is the hill of Mars,
an elevation to which rock-hewn steps led up from the

Agora; this was the seat of the highest tribunal bearing the same name "Areopagus," the judges sitting in seats hewn out of the rock. A temple of Mars stood on this elevation, and below the judges' seats in a broken cleft there was a sanctuary of the Furies. The associations of the place were all of a solemn nature; the moment for Paul must have been a serious one. — His audience is grave and deliberate; the apostle rises to the occasion. **May we know what this new teaching is, which is spoken by thee?** Its newness especially attracts these Athenians. **For thou bringest strange things to our ears,** and their strangeness surprises them. **We would know therefore what these things mean,** literally: "what these things want to be," what they are intended to mean. — But lest we expect too much of these inquiring Athenians and the importance they give to this hearing of the apostle, Luke adds that it was a characteristic of the Athenians in general, and even of the strangers sojourning in Athens for a time and catching their spirit, to spend their time ($εὐκαιρεῖν$ = to have time or leisure) **for nothing else, but either to tell or to hear some new thing.** For other things they were too busy, but never for this — like the American Athenians who spend hours reading "the news," wading through huge "dailies," but are too busy for a few moments daily of prayer and Bible reading in family worship. The comparative $καινότερον$ is like the common $νεώτερον$ in the question regarding the news, asking in reality for what is "newer" than they had heard so far, *i. e.* for the latest news. Winer, 35, 4. Thucydides and Demosthenes both rebuke the old Athenians for this greed for news; it tended to make them exceedingly superficial and to treat the greatest news in the world, the Gospel itself, as something to be quickly crowded out by some newer sensation. — So the great moment came upon which Luke concentrates our attention: **Paul stood in the midst of Areopagus, and said.** What a pulpit he had found! Above him, on the Acropolis, with its shrines and works of art, there towered the great statue of Minerva, rising above all as the tutelary divinity of Athens and

Attica; around him, the solemn expanse of the Areopagus, likewise marked for paganism, and now filled with the disciples of the "Painted Porch" (in the *Agora* itself, where Zeno had taught), and of the "Garden" (the school of Epicurus not far from the market), with such others as had been attracted to listen likewise; below him the idolatrous city itself, shorn of much of its former grandeur, but still bearing the glitter of its singular fame, its famous "market" lying at his very feet. Here Paul gave answer to those who asked a reason concerning the hope that was in him.

Paul's answer.

In every way it is a masterpiece, in its introduction, in its line of argument, in its fitness for his audience, in its climax. It is bold, but it does not unnecessarily offend; it refutes, but it does this so as to win; it states the truth squarely and fully, and this so as to lift it far above the follies of error; it is reasonable, but it aims at the heart; it seeks to win men, but above all it glorifies God and the Savior Jesus Christ. It remained unfinished, but it did not fail of divinely given fruit. **Ye men of Athens, in all things I perceive that ye are somewhat superstitious** (*very religious*). **For as I passed along and observed the objects of your worship, I found also an altar with this inscription, TO AN UNKNOWN GOD. What therefore ye worship in ignorance, this set I forth unto you.** — Note the directness of this introduction; his hearers want to know what he sets forth, and he makes that his theme: the true God, whom they do not know. He proceeds in an interesting way, bound to hold the attention and to stir his hearers' thought. He addresses them as Athenians, a title they were proud of and one in accord with the fact. The one thing that Paul singles out as attracting his attention is **that ye are somewhat superstitious** ὡς δεισιδαιμονεστέρους ὑμᾶς, which is rendered far better by the American translators: **very religious.** The word may be taken in a good as well as in an evil sense, the comparative here pointing to the former. Athens had the fame

of being more religious than any other Grecian city, a fact
of which even these philosophers, though they made so little
of the old gods, were no doubt proud. Blass is undecided
whether the comparative here has the classical sense: "un-
usually (too) god-fearing," or simply "very god-fearing;"
the latter is preferable. See also Winer, 35, 4. — But the
apostle at once adds the unexpected thing he has in mind. He
has inspected their σεβάσματα, **objects of worship,** temples,
altars, idol-statues, and has found **an altar,** whether in
some temple or not is not said, **with this inscription:**
ΑΓΝΩΣΤΩ ΘΕΩ. Zoeckler reports something similar in a
Vedic hymn ("the nameless god"); in old Egyptian docu-
ments ("Great god, whose name is unknown;" "God, whose
name is hidden;" *etc.*); among the Aztecs (a nine-story
teocolli, or mound, dedicated to the "unknown god, the
cause of all causes." In regard to Athens, Philostratus, A.
D. 244, testifies that there were altars to unknown gods; and
Diogenes Laertius, A. D. 275, relates "how, when once the
Athenians were afflicted with a pestilence, Epimenides stayed
the plague by sending white and black sheep from the Areopagus, and then sacrificing them on the various spots in the
city where they lay down, to the unknown god who sent the
pestilence. Therefore, this writer adds, there are nameless
altars at Athens." *Popular Com.* The margin, like the A. V.,
reads the inscription definitely, although the article is missing, as may be done, because one special deity is doubtless
meant. It was immaterial for the apostle's purpose just
what thought the Athenians connected with the strange altar
he had found; in turning from all their known gods to one
unknown, even if they meant this one in the usual polytheistic sense, they set aside these known gods as useless. But
this indirect conclusion the apostle drives home to his hearers by unfolding to them who this unknown God, the one
whom indeed they do not know, really is. — **What therefore ye worship** (εὐσεβεῖτε, in the good sense of the word)
in ignorance this set I forth unto you. Paul uses the
neuter, ὅ . . . τοῦτο, because he intends to reveal not
only the name of this God, but whatever else is necessary

for a true knowledge of him. Alas, that God should be unknown, in his truth and saving grace, to many even in Christian lands. They worship at the altars of the world and the
flesh, satisfied with the profession of "God" as made by
some secret order, but the true God they do not know, except that conscience, when aroused, smites them perhaps
with a secret fear of his holy and righteous judgments.
I declare unto you, says the apostle with clean-cut emphasis. He uses no "if" or "and," no false humility about
"trying to declare;" he knows the truth, and he rejoices to
declare it.

Forthwith he plunges into his theme: **The God that
made the world and all things therein, he, being Lord
of heaven and earth, dwelleth not in temples made with
hands; neither is he served by men's hands, as though
he needed any thing, seeing he himself giveth to all life,
and breath, and all things; and he made of one every
nation of men for to dwell on all the face of the earth,
having determined** *their* **appointed seasons, and the
bounds of their habitation; that they should seek God,
if haply they might feel after him, and find him, though
he is not far from each one of us: for in him we live,
and move, and have our being; as certain even of your
own poets have said, For we are his offspring. Being
then the offspring of God, we ought not to think that
the Godhead is like unto gold, or silver, or stone, graven
by art and device of man.**

Paul proclaims to these Athenians the true God, ὁ θεός,
as the omnipotent Creator, Ruler, and Benefactor, absolute,
and sufficient in himself. He lays special emphasis on
man's relation to God, as his creature, altogether dependent
on him and his gifts, and intended to worship God, whose offspring he is. All this he does in a simple, direct, and mighty
way, depending on the great power of these truths concerning God to enlighten and convince his hearers' hearts. —
Over against the vain gropings of heathen philosophers Paul
sets the first chapter of the Bible: **The God that made
the world and all things therein.** "The world" is the or-

dered universe; not only that, but "all things in it," great
and small, visible and invisible, God made. Nothing came
of itself, nothing was before God, nothing has its origin outside of him. The philosophy of science still needs this
Pauline statement to brush away its ignorant speculations.
— As the great Creator he is **the Lord of heaven and
earth,** their master and ruler, greater than both. This
overthrows the entire foundation of idolatry, which drags
God down from this supreme eminence. Paul states this
finely, by using a concrete form of expression, at once understood by his hearers: This God **dwelleth not in
temples** (or: *sanctuaries*) **made with hands.** How could
the Maker of all be confined in one of the little spots he himself has made? 1 Kgs. 8, 27. How could he who made all be
confined in a dwelling we, his own creatures, have made? —
Parallel with this is the heathen idea of worship: **neither
is he served by men's hands, as though he needed any
thing;** this is evident the moment we have the right conception of God, **seeing he himself giveth to all life,** our
very existence and greatest treasure, **and breath,** the
continuance of life, **and all things,** every other possession
that goes with our being and earthly existence. Since we
must take everything as a gift (διδούς) from him, how can
he really need anything that we have? This shatters the
whole conception of heathen offerings and sacrifices, which
always is that the gods need these things, and are therefore
so insistent on their being supplied with them. — Paul's argument is especially fine as applying to the philosophers who
had learned to scorn the gods of Greece. They were shown
the true reason for scorning them, not a veiled atheism, nor
a supercilious skepticism, which left the great question of
the cosmos, of man, of the course of men and nations *etc.*
unanswered in helpless ignorance, but a full, clear, efficient
grasp of the truth: the one true and only God; before him
all idolatrous debasements of God had to vanish. — In a
similar way, allowing the power of the great truth itself to
win its way against the perversions of error, the apostle puts
forth his thoughts concerning anthropology, especially con-

cerning the intentions of God regarding man. God is not
unconcerned about him, has not left him to his own devices:
**he made of one every nation of men to dwell on all the
face of the earth.** The best texts omit the word "blood,"
but ἐξ ἑνός strongly, if very tersely, declares the unity of the
human race; a fact often disputed even in these later days,
but also by the old heathen mythologies and philosophers. We
must read ἐποίησεν κατοικεῖν as belonging close together. Paul
has spoken of the creation above, here he deals with God's
providence. How God proceeded is shown by the added
participial clause, in which the aorist ὁρίσας indicates the
same time as the main verb ἐποίησεν: **having determined
appointed seasons, and the bounds of their habitation;**
allotting to every nation its period of time and its geograph-
ical location, according to the wisdom and beneficence of
his providence. But the chief stress is on the infinitive
ζητεῖν, which expresses the divine purpose in all this dealing of God with men: **that they should seek God.** There
is most certainly the implication here that man had lost
God, a thought implied already in the previous reference to
idol worship, in fact already in the theme of the entire
address: The unknown God. It is not God's will to remain unknown, he wants men to seek and find him and
enter into communion with him. All God's dealings with
men show that this is his great purpose; God's creation of
man and his providence place this beyond doubt. Atheism
and skepticism militate against the proper conception of God
as well as of man and of the purpose God has set for man. —
When the apostle speaks of our seeking God in our fallen
condition he has in mind the natural revelation of God and
the divine purpose connected with that. Man is not a
brute that this revelation should be entirely useless and pur-
poseless for him. So he adds: **if haply they might feel
after him and find him, though he is not far from each
one of us.** Blind though man is in his natural state, yet the
nearness of God to him is such that man, groping and
reaching out his hands, may know of his presence and thus
find him. On the optatives, εἰ ἄρα γε ψηλαφήσειαν αὐτὸν καὶ

εὕροιεν, which are used after a secondary tense to indicate a subjective possibility, compare Winer 41, 4. On the subject itself compare Romans 1, 18 *etc.* No man can be saved by his natural powers; but God wants all men to use what he has given them, the revelation of nature, including what pertains to his own constitution, his reason, moral nature, and conscience, if he have no more, and then, of course, the revelation of grace, if that be vouchsafed to him. When man refuses to do this, he incurs a special guilt before God, a guilt in which the apostle's hearers lay. — The fact of the true God's nearness to man, even in his natural state of sin and blindness, the apostle proves by a concrete fact; he does not appeal to the abstract omnipresence of God, but as on other occasions when speaking to Gentiles, to his universal benefactions: **for in him we live, and move, and have our being.** Chrysostom uses the comparison: he surrounds us on every side like the atmosphere. To **live** is more than to **move,** which even inanimate creatures may do; to move is more than merely **to have our being,** that is merely to exist. So here we have a fine anticlimax. Man certainly should be cognizant of God, for without him he could not live for a moment, could not move a hand or foot, could not in any way even exist. This is a cardinal passage on the divine providence of God, including the *præservatio* as well as the *concursus.* **In him** is more than "through him;" it expresses a wonderful immanence, yet, as the clear enunciation of creation and providence and the absolute self-sufficiency of God shows, without a trace of pantheism. — Mindful of his audience, learned in Greek literature, the apostle brings in a quotation from their poetical writers, a comprehensive word which covers the entire subject of man's relation to God: **For we are also his offspring.** Aratus, a countryman of Paul himself, has exactly these words as the first part of a hexameter: "Ever and in all ways we all enjoy Jupiter, for we are also his offspring." But the Athenian Stoic Cleanthus (like Aratus 270 B. C.), and also Pindar (about 500 B. C.), say the same thing. Paul leaves the line unchanged with its γὰρ καί.

The article τοῦ in epic poetry has its original meaning, namely that of a demonstrative pronoun. Winer 17, 1. The quotation is used by the apostle like an *argumentum ad hominem.* Zeus is not the true God, but the head of the mythological gods; but if the Greek poets declared man to be "his offspring," that was a faint glimmer of the real truth, that the true God called us into being, preserves, and keeps us, so that we indeed are his offspring and are treated as such by him. Paul here shows that he has some knowledge of Greek literature, and that he knows how to put it to good use. The reference to several poets (τινές) as making the declaration referred to, instead of indicating that Paul had no special knowledge of their writings and quoted only from general hearsay, shows exactly the opposite; he must have known these different poets. That one of them was an Athenian his hearers must have remarked with especial pleasure.

Drawing the great conclusion he had in mind in his elaborations, the apostle now comes to the revelation which God made in Christ; so he weaves together, first theology and anthropology, then these two and Christology or soteriology. **Being then the offspring of God, we ought not to think that the Godhead is like unto gold, or silver, or stone, graven by art or device of man.** — Here Paul explodes the entire folly of images. If we are the offspring of God, God must be infinitely greater than we are, hence he cannot be like what is far beneath us, metal and stone, even though formed by man's art and thought. Paul grants the "art" and also the ideas or thought (ἐνθύμησις) connected with the statues of the heathen divinities, but he makes plain in an unanswerable way that this entire effort does so little justice to God, that it does not even do nearly justice to man. The idea of the apostle is not like that of Isaiah 44, 9 *etc.,* that the image made by man is itself considered to be a god by its maker, but that it really represents and pictures the god. This is the proof which the Athenians needed, and it had its force even for the atheistic and skeptic philosophers present, as it showed them the true reason for rejecting the old pagan gods, namely the reality and infinite greatness of the one true God, revealed for one thing in the greatness of man as his offspring. — With these fundamental truths settled the apostle takes up the revelation God has made in Christ. He passes over the revelation of the Old Covenant, showing his hearers at once what God offers them now. **The times of ignorance therefore God overlooked; but now he commandeth men that they should all everywhere repent: inasmuch as he hath appointed a day, in the which he will judge the world in righteousness by the man whom he hath ordained; whereof he hath given assurance unto all men, in that he hath raised him from the dead.** — One God, one human race, one way of salvation, one judgment, these are the lines of the apostle's address. There was no need for Paul to say that the purpose of God, that men should seek God, was not fulfilled on the part of the Athenians; their polytheistic sanctuaries and statues were evidence enough. What did God do? Besser replies: "Had he looked at the Athenians with the fire-flames of his holy eyes, there would have been no Athens this many a day." But God **overlooked the times of ignorance** by looking at Christ and the plan of salvation for the coming ages. He bore the idolatry of the Gentiles, he ceased not to reveal himself to them in nature and providence, he even made them feel his wrath for plunging into special wickedness and depravity. At last the great day for which God had prepared and waited in patience and love so long arrived: redemption was complete, the Gospel could go forth to all the world. — That day had arrived for Athens: **but now he commandeth men that they should all everywhere repent,** ἀπαγγέλλει, "he gives the word," not to a few but to "men" generally, as the God of all, that they should **all everywhere repent.** At this moment God was giving the word to this effect to the Athenians. It has sounded since wherever God's messengers went. The verb μετανοιεῖν signifies a change of heart; in what respect, Paul's previous words make plain. They are to realize their sin and past neglect of God's revelation of himself in true sorrow of heart and turn to him for forgiveness. — This they are to do **inasmuch as,** in accordance with the fact that, **he hath appointed a day in the which he will judge the world in righteousness.** As he appointed certain times and locations to every nation, so he has appointed a day of judgment for all the world of men. He is a righteous God and his judgment will be **in righteousness,** in harmony with this principle of his being. It will be a judgment which all men will acknowledge as right; for it will condemn all those who persist in turning away from God, and clear all those who allow themselves to be brought to God by his revelation and grace. By this reference to God's just judgment the apostle aims directly at the consciences and hearts of his hearers. All his reasoning pressed in this direction, and now it is driven home deep and true. "Think of the souls of such hearers of the apostle's address as was that of Dionysius: were they not bound to succumb beneath the weight of their long ignorance and to ask with a terrified conscience, how they might succeed in turning from their false gods to the living God, and so find God as to be able to stand in the revealed day of his righteousness?" Besser. — The judgment will include τὴν οἰκουμένην, *the inhabited earth* (margin), every dweller on it. — But the great thing concerning this judgment is that it will take place ἐν ἀνδρὶ ᾧ ὥρισεν, **by the man whom he hath ordained,** really: "in the man," in his person. The case of the relative is assimilated to that of its antecedent. Paul here emphasizes the human nature of Christ after the manner of John 5. 27; he who died for us on the cross and rose again for our justification shall be our judge at the last day, according to the eternal decree of God. — **Whereof he hath given assurance unto all men, in that he hath raised him from the dead;** πίστιν here is not saving faith in general, but the faith or assurance that this "man" will be our judge; and this faith God has offered to all by raising him from the dead. What a remarkable man — who can this be? is the natural question which the apostle's words provoke. It was the question Paul wanted in his hearers' minds, in order to tell them the better of Jesus who is appointed our Judge because he is our Savior. But, instead of asking this question, the old spirit of scoffing and skepticism asserted itself again. They interrupted the apostle and dismissed him.

Paul's answer not in vain.

At first it seemed so. **Now when they heard of the resurrection of the dead, some mocked; but others said, We will hear thee concerning this yet again. Thus Paul went out from among them.** It is impossible to say whether these were Epicureans or Stoics; the idea of any one rising from the dead seemed ridiculous to them all. "If the judge before whom you cite us is one risen from the dead, we little fear him!" Besser. The others dismissed him politely; whether they were impressed to any degree we cannot tell. **Thus** Paul left — apparently with nothing to encourage him. — But even in this city of idols and philosophers the Gospel proved its efficiency, for Luke reports: **But certain men clave unto him, and believed: among whom also was Dionysius the Areopagite, and a woman named Damaris, and others with them.** It seems that these men were among the auditors on Mars' hill, and among them was one notable person, one of the Athenian judges of the high court; whether he was a philosopher we do not know. Tradition has made much of him, as that he was the first bishop of Athens and received the martyr's crown. Real facts we have none to report. Beside him a woman is named, not as Chrysostom states the wife of Dionysius. Some think that she is named because she was an ordinary unlearned person, but if anything the opposite is true. Both were important persons. And **others with them** seems to imply that the other discussions of Paul also bore fruit. There was a circle of believers in Athens, although we hear nothing further concerning them.

9

HOMILETICAL HINTS.

Culture without God, and art without God, and science without God never lead to salvation, but when they have reached their highest development only reveal the great need of salvation. — It is the devil's irony that man should waste so much of his finest skill and highest genius in the service of idolatry and delusion. This is what stirred the heart of Paul and inspired him to set before the blind Athenians the glory and blessedness of the Gospel truth.

The most profound philosopher needs the simple elements of the Gospel; they answer more questions than all his reasoning and speculation, and they satisfy the soul.

The mark of our time is still to seek diversion, change, new sights and sensations. In fact, this is the mark of the world generally, a constant fluctuation, alteration, passing on from the old to the new, and from the new as having grown old quickly to something newer. For the world passeth away and the lust thereof, and this now already is its passing. We Christians have something that remains unchanged, old and yet ever new, that shall comfort and bless us forever, for it shall never pass away.

As a child at once indicates its parents, even when these are not present at the moment, so every human being is a living, eloquent testimony of God and his dealings with us. Can we think of a child without a father and a mother? So man is unthinkable without God. For our being, our development and growth, our very existence goes back to God. Rump.

The unity of the human race, so often denied and derided, has finally been established even by the science of man. Biology teaches it, also the science of language, in fact, all comparative study of man. — But so much of this study still labors with degrading conclusions, because it has not grasped the glory of him who called us into being, and the grandness of his creative act.

The act that makes us forget God or turn away from his truth and guidance is accursed. — When God inwardly draws nigh to us, or when we are inwardly drawn near unto him, a judgment passes through the soul. This we are always inclined to evade, and yet everything depends on our humble submission. God's inward judgment would bow our hearts in repentance and so free us from our sins.

What did the great apostle Paul tell his learned hearers on Mars' hill? Why, the simple elements of the Gospel, such as even a child among us knows. When we are asked to testify of our faith, we need not stammer and excuse ourselves; the things that God wants us to say, and that men need to hear, are the simple rock-bottom facts of the Gospel. These we believe, these let us state without hesitation and fear.

Was the Gospel ever preached wholly in vain?

Why Should We Cheerfully Face the World With Our Testimony?

I. *It is a woefully ignorant world.*
II. *It is a sadly deluded world.*
III. *It is a miserably helpless world.*
IV. *It is a world which our testimony alone can save.*

Paul's Visit to Athens.

I. *What he found there.*
II. *What he took there.*
III. *What he left there.*

What Was Wrong at Athens?

I. *Many gods — but no God.*
II. *Much learning — but no truth.*
III. *Great art — but no peace.*
IV. *Vast pride — but no faith.*

The Wisdom of God Makes Answer to the Wisdom of the Word.

On the highest questions:

I. *Concerning God.*
II. *Concerning man.*
III. *Concerning salvation.*

If We Are God's Offspring:

I. *We must know God.*
II. *We must be like God.*
III. *We must be one with God.*

The Story of the Altar to the Unknown God.

I. *A chapter on blind groping.*
II. *A chapter on dire need.*
III. *A chapter on imperative duty.*

THE TENTH SUNDAY AFTER TRINITY.

Acts 20, 17-38.

This is as fine a text on *faithfulness* as the Scriptures contain. Here we have both the duty enjoined upon us and a living example of faithfulness set beside the duty to stimulate and encourage us. The whole text receives a special solemnity from the fact that Paul was taking what he thought was his final leave of the Ephesians and so looked back upon his labors there as closed for good and all. Paul, indeed, is an apostle, and his faithfulness exhibits what is the duty and ought to be the constant effort and finally the joy and satisfaction of every pastor; but as Paul admonished the Philippians: "Brethren, be ye imitators together of me, and mark them which walk even as ye have us for an ensample," Phil. 3, 17, so in its wider range Paul's faithfulness as exhibited at Ephesus and set forth in his farewell address to the Ephesian elders applies to us all. Blau in Reylaender's work on these texts hits the right mark when he makes his first theme on this text: *Paulus ein rechtes Musterbild christlicher Treue bis an den Tod.* The body of Paul's address may be conveniently divided into four sections: Paul's labor and devotion in the past, verses 18-21; his expected trials in the future, 22-27; his admonition to feed and protect the flock, 28-31; his pleading for unselfish devotion, 32-35. The introductory and the closing verses round out the whole.

Paul faithful in past labors.

Conybeare and Howson describe in detail the journey of the apostle which took him to Miletus, the sea-port entrance to Ephesus. He landed there in the early morning. **And from Miletus he sent to Ephesus, and**

132

called to him the elders (*presbyters*) **of the church.** "The excitement and joy must have been great among the Christians of Ephesus when they heard that their honored friend and teacher, to whom they had listened so often in the school of Tyrannus, was in the harbor of Miletus within the distance of a few miles. The presbyters must have gathered together in all haste to obey the summons, and gone with eager steps out of the southern gate, which leads to Miletus. By those who travel on such an errand a journey of twenty or thirty miles is not regarded long and tedious, nor is much regard paid to the difference between day and night. The presbyters of Ephesus might easily reach Miletus on the day after that on which the summons was received. And though they might be weary when they arrived, their fatigue would soon be forgotten at sight of their friend and instructor; and God also 'who comforts them that are cast down' (2 Cor. 7, 6), comforted him by the sight of his disciples. They were gathered together — probably in some solitary spot upon the shore — to listen to his address. This little company formed a singular contrast with the crowds which used to assemble at the times of the public amusement in the theater of Miletus. But that vast theater is now a silent ruin, while the words spoken by a careworn traveler to a few despised strangers are still living as they were that day, to teach lessons for all time and to make known eternal truths to all who will hear them, while they reveal to us, as though they were merely human words, all the tenderness and the affection of Paul, the individual speaker."
— And when they were come to him, he said unto them,

Ye yourselves know, from the first day that I set foot in Asia, after what manner I was with you all the time, serving the Lord with all lowliness of mind, and with tears, and with trials which befell me by the plots of the Jews: how that I shrank not from declaring unto you anything that was profitable, and teaching you publicly, and from house to house, testifying both to Jews and to Greeks repentance toward God, and faith toward our Lord Jesus Christ. — The **ye** is emphatic; others

might not know, these elders did. **Asia** is here the west
of Asia Minor with Ephesus as its capital, including
Mysia, Lydia, Caria; here were the seven churches addressed in the Revelation. All the conduct of the apostle
during his labors in this territory was thoroughly well
known to the believers at Ephesus, especially the elders.
— Paul singles out several important features: **serving
the Lord with all lowliness of mind;** as a true δοῦλος, or
bondservant of the Lord, not as a master, apostle though
he was; and thus, mindful of his position and work: "with
all lowliness of mind," humbleness in all things, a soil
that steadily produces the flowers of patience, gentleness,
friendliness, and the like. The root of this humbleness is
the true knowledge of sin, repentance, and gratitude for
divine forgiveness. That makes us lowly slaves of Christ,
faithful in humility. — **And with tears,** wrung from his
eyes not by the hostile treatment of his enemies, for in the
Philippian prison we hear him singing, but by his tender
solicitude for the church and the welfare of its members.
These were tears of love and deep concern, not of personal
pain. Paul put all his heart into his work, he knew nothing
of cold professionalism. — But, of course, there was also
an abundance of suffering from persecution: **and with
trials which befell me by the plots of the Jews,** who hated
and opposed him with murderous intention. Paul was a
proper theologian according to the rule of *oratio, meditatio,*
and *tentatio;* he knew the theology of which Luther says
that it cannot be learned so quickly, but one must constantly
campaign and war against the devil, and so attain it. Such
trials, not only for those who teach, but also for those
taught, are blasts of wind, not to blow out, but to fan the
flame into a bright blaze. — From his own person Paul
now turns to those whom his service concerned: **how that I
shrank not from declaring unto you anything that was
profitable, and teaching you publicly, and from house to
house,** literally: "how I concealed, or kept back, nothing of
what is profitable in order not to declare it to you and to
teach you, *etc.*" In τοῦ μὴ ἀναγγεῖλαι we have what would

have been the apostle's intention, if he had wanted to withhold any thing. One consideration alone prompted Paul's action, the desire to give his hearers what really profited them; he was not shielding his own skin, or seeking the approval and rewards he might secure, he was seeking the benefit of the people. They who really knew his work, knew that. And he labored diligently in this: teaching **publicly,** in public places and assemblies, and privately, **from house to house,** wherever a door opened itself to him. Paul believed in visiting, but in visiting for the purpose of teaching something spiritually profitable. I do not think he made any fashionable pastoral calls. — Note the climax: **declaring,** which is a simple announcement; **teaching,** which is a connected elucidation and explanation; and now **testifying,** which is a declaration of personal experience easily connected with both the other activities. This testimony Paul offered **both to Jews and Greeks,** making no difference between them, for all alike needed whereof he testified, namely **repentance toward God, and faith toward our Lord Jesus Christ,** *i. e.* the repentance by which a man turns to God in order to get rid of his sins; and the faith, by which a man turns to Christ in order to obtain salvation. In both *εἰς* indicates the direction, and with πίστις it is used as one of the regular constructions. Faith to be true and saving must be directed to Jesus Christ, to the divine Redeemer and his saving grace and work. To preach repentance and faith is the one great business of every pastor, of every church, of every Christian. If we are not called to do this work publicly, we all have God's call to do it privately in whatever circle God has put us, and we should do it by putting our heart into it in personal testimony. These are the things that profit, and Bengel is right: "These are to be taught, the rest are to be cut off, or cut short."

Paul faithful in expected trials.

From the past which the apostle has thus summarized, he turns to the prospects of the future: **And**

now, behold, I go bound in the spirit unto Jerusalem, not knowing the things that shall befall me there: save that the Holy Ghost testifieth unto me in every city, saying that bonds and afflictions abide me. But I hold **not my life of any account, as dear unto myself, so that I may accomplish my course, and the ministry which I received from the Lord Jesus, to testify the gospel of the grace of God.** And now, behold, **I know that ye all, among whom I went about preaching the kingdom, shall see my face no more. Wherefore I testify unto you this day, that I am pure from the blood of all men. For I shrank not from declaring unto you the whole counsel of God.** — The two exclamations **behold** mark the special thoughts which Paul here makes known to the elders, the second (verse 25) even more serious than the first. When he says that he goes to Jerusalem **bound in the spirit** (not "Spirit" as in the next verse), he means that an inner constraint binds him; he is not going merely of his own accord, so that he might change his plans and go elsewhere instead. He felt that he ought to go. And this weighed the heavier because of what certainly awaited him there. — The details he did not know, **save that the Holy Ghost testifieth unto me in every city, saying that bonds and afflictions abide me.** This was through prophetic utterances, as we see from Acts 21, 4 and 11; compare also 11, 28; 13, 2. Imprisonment was directly foretold, the rest was veiled in the term "afflictions," or "oppressions," in their very indefiniteness allowing room for the gravest fears. — What has Paul to say to this dark prospect: **But I hold not my life of any account, as dear unto myself;** οὐδενὸς λόγου, "not of one word," in the sense that he would not speak a single word to save his life (ψυχή), yet with the limitation "as dear to myself." Others are on their own account frantic when danger threatens their lives, Paul, as far as his own love of life is concerned is ready to die; whatever value his life has is in connection with the service of the Lord. — This is brought out by the addition: **so that I may accomplish my course, and the ministry which**

I received from the Lord Jesus. Meyer is ready to retain ὡς with the infinitive τελειῶσαι as the only case of a purpose clause of this peculiar form in the N. T. Compare Blass, 223, who conjectures ὥστε instead of ὡς; the R. V. reads ὡς τελειώσω, a regular purpose clause, but offers in the margin a solution of the reading with the infinitive: *in comparison of accomplishing my course.* The idea expressed by the apostle is that his chief concern is not the prolongation of his earthly life, but the proper completion of his course as a minister of the Gospel. That might require that he should die at Jerusalem; if so, well and good. But whatever it required, the apostle was ready and willing for that. "To finish the course" is a favorite figure with Paul; compare especially 2 Tim. 4, 7. **The ministry** is the office or work of the apostleship to which Paul was especially called, 9, 15; Gal. 1, 1; hence the statement that he received **it from the Lord Jesus.** We see how highly Paul valued his office and his work, it was dearer to him than his life. What a rebuke to all time-servers in the ministry who are "faithful" for the dollars there are in it, and have no conception of the true glory of their calling and of the real inwardness of ministerial faithfulness. — As in verse 21, so here again the apostle summarizes what his office really included: **to testify the gospel of the grace of God,** to assure men of that in the most earnest and effective way. "The gospel of the grace of God" is the good news that God forgives our sins for Christ's sake; all other gospel is false, however much it may attract some preachers who substitute it for Paul's Gospel of grace. The inner motive of the apostle's faithfulness, besides his own faith in Christ and love to him, is the appreciation he had of the origin, nature, requirements, and blessings of his office. It was far greater than Paul, great though he was; and far greater than any who hold this office to-day. Let it ever lift them far above unworthy thoughts and reasonings, to the full light of true faithfulness. — How dark the future really seemed to the apostle he now indicates by emphatically stating to the elders: **I know that ye all, among whom I went about preaching the kingdom, shall see my face no more.** This does not say nor mean that Paul expected to die in Jerusalem. We must also observe that he does not refer what he says to a direct revelation of the Holy Spirit. A good many ancient and modern exegetes conclude that Paul was freed from his first captivity and visited again the scenes of his labors in Asia. Stellhorn writes, *Die Pastoralbriefe Pauli*, I, 7: "This we see clearly and distinctly in several passages of his letters written during his first captivity, in which he utters the confident conviction that he would be freed again from his captivity and see once more the Corinthians in Asia Minor and Europe, namely Phil. 1, 23, *etc.*; 2, 24; Philem. 22. That Paul also could err in such things, and was not constantly inspired in them, is really self-evident, and is made evident by Acts 27, 10 compared with verse 24. The ending of the Acts, 28, 30, *etc.*, also rather favors the assumption that Paul was freed from his first Roman capitivity. For if this had not been the case, why should Luke not have added the brief remark to his Acts that Paul finally praised the Lord by a martyr's death? But if he again attained his liberty and thus could undertake a fourth missionary journey, and then suffered death in Rome, it is easy to understand why the Acts close as they do. It would also be somewhat unexpected, if, after all the Roman officials who examined Paul's case (Acts 23, 29; 24, 26, *etc.*; 25, 18 and 25; 26, 30, *etc.*) declared positively that he was innocent and not to be punished according to the imperial law, the emperor himself should have condemned him to the very severest penalty. Stellhorn adds the further historical evidence for this view. Paul must then be taken as expressing his personal conviction to the Ephesian elders, when he said that he knew they all among whom he had labored here would not see his face again. Nor is it necessary to reason with Besser and some others, that Paul indeed was to die, but that the prayers of the churches intervened and thus secured for him a prolongation of life. With ὑμεῖς πάντες the apostle includes all his disciples in Asia; to conclude that a few others, outside of the elders themselves, were present at this farewell, is not necessary as far as these words are concerned; a few strongly attached friends of Paul may have accompanied the elders, as Irenæus asserts. — **I went about preaching the kingdom,** Christ's kingdom of grace, is another fine definition of Paul's apostolic work, applicable especially to the work of missionaries to-day. — **Wherefore,** διότι, is used indirectly here. "for which reason," since Paul thought this his final farewell. **I testify unto you this day,** one that the elders would surely never forget, **that I am pure from the blood of all men** (compare 18, 6), according to the word of Ezekiel 3, 18-21, which see. While καθαρός usually has the simple genitive, it also may have ἀπό, which is no Hebraism. **The blood of all** is a pregnant, metonymical expression for the guilt involved in bringing about a death, and here the death of eternal destruction. On the great judgment day none of the lost in all that territory shall be able to point to Paul and say that his is the guilt. Whoever else may be guilty, Paul is pure from this terrible stain. — Nor is this a recent thought of Paul, a late effort to safeguard himself; it animated him in all his ministry, it was one of the great motives of his unfailing faithfulness: **For I shrank not from declaring unto you the whole counsel of God.** In the word "shrank" there lies a hint that if Paul had considered men only, or selfish personal advantages, he might indeed have kept back this or that part of his teaching, for it often ran counter to Jewish bigotry and heathen prejudice, and it often offended Christian ignorance and narrowness. But Paul ever bore in mind the accounting he would have to render at the last day to his Lord. So he preached **the whole counsel of God,** the entire will of God, every doctrine and truth he had received from God, each part in its proper place, with its proper emphasis. He had no pet doctrine, no peculiar personal views, no dislike or disinclination toward any doctrine. He did not omit what was difficult and hard to set forth, unpalatable and obnoxious to human reason, out of harmony with the spirit of the

times. He put justification by faith into the center because
God put it there, but he treated numberless minor questions
in the light of divine truth as well. Now he looks at his
work as completed here and therefore closes it with this
solemn testimony which meant so much for him. Yet it
must have had its effect also on the men who were to continue his work after him and in his place. Count yourself among them, brother, and read Heb. 13, 17, especially
the clause: "as they that shall give account." Christian
faithfulness in general will make us live so close to "the
whole counsel of God" that no one shall be able to point
to any deviation in word or in conduct on our part as the
cause for his erring from the faith and losing his soul.

Paul faithful in admonishing others to faithfulness.

He turns now to the elders themselves, to leave them
a precious legacy. **Take heed unto yourselves, and to
all the flock, in the which the Holy Ghost hath made you
bishops, to feed the church of God, which he purchased
with his own blood.** — While the addition of "therefore"
makes a fine connection with the preceding, the best reading omits it. He who is set to take heed to others must
first take heed to himself. "Be yourself a sheep of the
Good Shepherd, and you will not be a false shepherd; let
repentance and faith be your own daily practice, and you
will truly testify of both; give heed to reading (1 Tim. 4,
13) and searching in the Scriptures and discover for yourself that by every word that proceedeth out of the mouth of
the Lord doth man live (Deut. 8, 3), and you will be able
and joyful to declare the whole counsel of God." Besser.
Be clean yourself, before you cleanse others; be taught
yourself, before you teach others; be light yourself, before
you lighten others; be near to God yourself, before you
attempt to bring others near. — **And to all the flock** follows the beautiful figure which Jesus himself used, John
10, 11 *etc.;* Luke 12, 32. The addition of **all** is important.
Pastors must not devote themselves only to a part of the
flock, their friends, the faction that sides with them, and

neglect those whom for some reason or other, they personally may not like. The true shepherd's heart knows no such dividing lines, is superior to all factional spirit, loves every sheep, especially those that need help and attention. If your heart is not big enough to embrace "all the flock," you are not big enough to be the shepherd of any of the flock. — Paul brings out the sacred obligation and trust connected with the ministry by adding: **in the which the Holy Ghost hath made you bishops,** ἐπισκόπους, for which the margin has the translation of the A. V.: overseers. "In which" implies that they themselves are members of the flock, a special work being assigned to them. And this is to be **bishops,** to have oversight, charge, and direction of the flock, to care for it and provide for all its spiritual needs. The word was afterwards used as a title and was distinguished from the term "elder" or presbyter (verse 7), as denoting those who had oversight over a number of congregations including their elders. But here "bishops" and "elders" refer to the same persons, the pastors at Ephesus. **The Holy Ghost** made, ἔθετο, set them as such in the flock. He is mentioned (compare 13, 4) because the entire church is under his guidance, John 14, 16; 16, 12 *etc.* In every right call, ordination, and installation we must see the work of the Holy Spirit himself — a great comfort and support to every true pastor. — But Paul is careful to mention just what these overseers are to heed well: **to feed the church of God,** ποιμαίνειν, to tend, cherish, mind the flock, which is here defined as the **church,** or assembly of believers. This work includes feeding in the narrower sense, instruction by teaching and preaching, but it includes besides the work of guiding, guarding, controlling, *etc.* As shepherds they are "to shepherd" the flock. The two oldest manuscripts read **God,** also some other authorities, the rest read instead "Lord," which perhaps was put for "God" because of the addition: **which he purchased with his own blood;** yet others think the orginal was "Lord," and was changed to "God" because Paul almost invariably writes "church of God" (1 Cor. 15, 9; Gal.

1, 13; 1 Tim. 3, 15), and not "of Christ," or "of the Lord"
(only Rom. 16, 16, and here in the plural). But this second
observation has little weight. It is a wonderful statement
that "God" purchased, or acquired for himself as his
property (περιεποιήσατο), the church "with his own blood;"
it designates Christ according to his divine nature, and
predicates of him something human, "blood," also an act involving blood. Thus is shown the mysterious communication of natures in Christ and of their attributes. Practically
this is of the most vital importance, for no mere human
blood could have purchased the church; it had to be a blood
of divine efficacy and power, "God's own blood." When
"bishops" keep in mind the price paid for the souls entrusted to them, they will be mightily moved to faithfulness; when believers consider the price of their own souls
they will likewise walk in faithfulness.

The first admonition is to faithfulness in general;
it is followed by a particular reference to coming
danger. Paul expected a severe trial for himself; he
expects something similar for his fellow laborers: **I
know that after my departing grievous wolves shall
enter in among you, not sparing the flock; and from
among your own selves shall men arise, speaking perverse things, to draw away the disciples after them.
Wherefore watch ye, remembering that by the space
of three years I ceased not to admonish every one night
and day with tears.** — This knowledge, unlike that concerning his never seeing again the Ephesians, is based on
the Spirit's revelation: "The Spirit saith expressly, that in
later times some shall fall away from the faith, giving heed
to seducing spirits and doctrines of devils, *etc.*" 1 Tim. 4.
1 *etc.* The danger shall be double, wolves from without,
perverse speakers from within. Paul keeps well to the
words of Christ when he continues the figure of the flock
by describing its enemies from without as **grievous
wolves . . . not sparing the flock,** (Matth. 7, 15:
"ravening wolves;" Luke 10, 3; John 10, 12). False
teachers are meant, some of whom were already baying

about the church; they would grow much bolder after Paul was gone and they had to deal with lesser men. Paul calls them βαρεῖs, heavy, in the sense of a burden hard to bear, hence **grievous; not sparing** — destroying, rending the flock. This is exactly what false teachers invading the church from without are, though they come in sheep's clothing. But the saddest thing is that from among the members of the church themselves, and from the bishops themselves there should arise enemies of the flock. Paul scorns to call them "teachers," he says they are men talking twisted, distorted, perverted stuff, διεστραμμένα (διαστρέφω), **perverse things,** no doubt here Gnostic speculations, that extravagant mixture of Christian ideas and pagan imaginings, which later had its stronghold in Ephesus and Asia Minor generally. — **To draw away the disciples after them** means to divide the church to cause schisms and sects. What a long procession of these two classes of foes the church has had to suffer during these past ages and especially also in the present age! They have torn and rent her holy body again and again, fattening like wolves on her flesh, and using the deluded disciples for their own selfish purposes. — **Wherefore watch ye,** says the apostle, like true shepherds who never grow careless or indifferent. 1 Cor. 16, 13; Col. 4, 2; 1 Thess. 5, 6: "Let us not sleep, as do the rest." It may be arduous, but faithfulness requires it. — Paul's example is to stimulate them: **remembering that by the space of three years I ceased not to admonish every one night and day with tears.** What he had done they could and should do. The "three years" are approximate. **Night** is mentioned first, for wolves prowl at night, and watching must be done especially at night; **day** is added, because this shepherd-care never relaxes. **To admonish,** νουθετέω, means to put in mind, and thus to warn. **With tears,** as in verse 19, with such solicitude and affectionate care that his whole heart was in this work. And this Paul did with **every one,** watching over each individual soul and keeping it from going astray.

Paul faithful in admonishing others to unselfish service.

Such service always marks true faithfulness. It rejoices in its heavenly reward, and never trades that for earthly silver and gold. **And now I commend you to God and to the word of his grace, which is able to build** *you* **up, and to give** *you* **the inheritance among all them that are sanctified.** This is the final **now;** Paul has done what he could, his comfort is God and the power of his gracious Word. He commits (παρατίθεμαι) the elders to **God,** and in the church God keeps, guards, strengthens, and blesses with **the word of his grace** (compare verse 24), that Word which contains and dispenses his grace and all its gifts as a true means of grace. As long as a pastor lives in communion with God through this Word, he will be a faithful shepherd; as long as any Christian does the same, he will be a faithful member of the flock. — The participial clause belongs to the word "God": **which** (who) **is able to build you up** as a spiritual temple, Eph. 2, 22, keeping you in the church and ever true to it. And this to the end that ye may attain the eternal **inheritance,** the final state of blessedness and glory awaiting all true believers. This inheritance is of course a gift, due entirely to grace; but it is bestowed only upon children, who are the true heirs, and these Paul describes as those **that are sanctified.** As the land of Canaan was apportioned by lot to the children of Israel, each getting the gift of his inheritance, so all God's saints shall receive their portion in heaven (κληρονομία from κλῆρος, lot). Only they who are and remain **among all that are sanctified** by the imputed holiness of Christ in justification, which brings forth a holy life through the activity of the Spirit and the word of truth (John 17, 17), shall at last receive the heavenly inheritance.

All those who keep in true sanctification and rejoice in the promised inheritance will be preserved from one of the worst hindrances to faithfulness, namely covetousness or selfishness. **I coveted no man's silver, or gold, or apparel. Ye yourselves know that these hands min-**

istered unto my necessities, and to them that were with
me. In all things I gave you an example, how that so
laboring ye ought to help the weak, and to remember
the words of the Lord Jesus, how he himself said, It is
more blessed to give than to receive. — This is Paul's
own exposition, on the basis of his own practice, of the text
I Tim. 3, 4: "no lover of money;" and Tit. 1, 7: "not
greedy of filthy lucre." Even to **covet** earthly wealth is
secret unfaithfulness to the holy office. Let us ponder well
the example of Paul that we may be kept from this foe of
faithfulness in all our ministry. Clerical speculators are an
abomination unto the Lord; self-seekers in the ministry
disgrace the holy office; to scheme for "fat" calls, to use
our position of trust for mercenary ends, to commercialize
our holy labor — all these things and others like them call
forth God's displeasure, damage the church, and injure the
soul. — Paul supported himself while preaching and
teaching. When he said **these hands** he probably extended them in an appropriate gesture; they showed
the marks of his trade as a tent-maker. **My necessities,**
not luxury, is significant; but also: **to them that were
with me,** showing how Paul applied his surplus. —
Why he accepted no pay from the people he served
he tells us, here holding it up as an **example** for unselfish service: **that so laboring ye ought to help the
weak.** The spiritually weak would have stumbled if
Paul had made use of the Gospel rule in his apostolic
missionary labors that they who preach the Gospel ought to
live of the Gospel, I Cor. 9, 14. It is the same to-day in
foreign mission fields, where mercenary motives are quickly
attributed to missionaries who require remuneration for
their labors. Paul's wisdom is unquestioned in this respect,
and his faithfulness shines the brighter for this attribute of
unselfish devotion. But while the same spirit must animate
all preachers of the Gospel, the apostle himself has indicated
in his writings what the practice should be in normal situa-
tions in established and fully regulated congregations. —

10

The apostle fortifies his injunction by adding that thus he
has shown these elders how **to remember the words of the
Lord Jesus** in this regard, **how** (ὅτι) **he himself said,** to
sum up all his sayings in this line in one especially pithy and
telling sentence: **It is more blessed to give than to receive.**
It is blessed also to let others give while we receive in the
right spirit and manner. Paul shows us this in Phil. 4, 10-17
in his own receiving. But there is a greater blessedness,
of which he has tasted abundantly in his life and labors, and
that is to give to others, especially the highest and greatest
gifts which the Lord has first given to us. It is this giving
that makes the ministry blessed above other callings. May
we all taste of this blessedness in the fullest measure! And
so Paul closes his address, sealing it with a word of Jesus
himself, which though nowhere recorded in the gospels must
actually have been uttered by the Lord, and is also used by
some of the old fathers. The special use which the apostle
here makes of it is only an illustration of its application to
all Christians generally who desire to be found faithful in
the Master's service.

**And when he had thus spoken, he kneeled down and
prayed with them all. And they all wept sore, and fell
on Paul's neck, and kissed him, sorrowing most of all
for the word which he had spoken, that they should behold his face no more. And they brought him on his
way unto the ship.** — After speaking to the elders of the
Lord, he now speaks to the Lord of the elders. In this
prayer he commended them and all the church unto God.
Christians do well to part with a prayer upon the lips. Paul
left the elders a fine last impression in that final kneeling
posture. Luke writes literally: "But considerable weeping
there was of all." These tears and kisses of strong, earnest
men are a fine testimonial for the apostle and his work.
There is a time to give room to the feelings, as here, and a
time to hold them in check. The imperfect κατεφίλουν denotes repeated tender kissing; and θεωρεῖν, **behold,** is from
the standpoint of the elders, here implying a beholding with
affection and delight, not simply "see," as Paul humbly puts

it in verse 25. In the imperfect tense of προέπεμπον, "were bringing," there is a lingering reluctance. So faithful Paul was parted from his faithful elders, but God and his grace was parted from neither.

HOMILETICAL HINTS.

As is your living, so shall be your leaving. — The past is not gone, it returns again, as the seed sown into the ground returns in the harvest. Only the seed of faithfulness returns blessedness. — Paul was not only a preacher, he was a sermon, and this text gives us the quintessence of it. — If Paul had taken much silver and gold and apparel with him as the net gain of his missionary and pastoral work, what a poor cargo it would have been; but he took what no gold or silver could buy, and what was fairer and finer than the richest raiment, the love and gratitude, the blessings and prayers of hearts which he had brought to Christ.

Behold, the apostle who had received the world as his field of labor and who cared for all the churches (2 Cor. 11, 28) did not think it beneath him to train catechism-scholars in Ephesus, and to follow up the old and the young here and there in the houses to give each what he required.

"Paul calls his entire doctrine the Gospel, but he embraces the sum of his doctrine under two heads: 'Repentance toward God, and faith toward our Lord Jesus Christ.' And in this sense the general definition, *i. e.*, the description of the word 'Gospel,' when employed in a wide sense, and without the peculiar distinction between the Law and the Gospel, is correct, when it is said that the Gospel is a preaching of repentance and remission of sins." *Formula of Concord*, 590, 4-5.

A great many work hard in the church, and yet with all their exertion fall short of faithfulness, for they are not faithful to the whole counsel of God. — Others are altogether orthodox and the form of their teaching is outwardly correct and complete; but they fail to put their very hearts into their words and work, they are strangers to tears, they have never take the full measure of the word "testify."

Wilberforce, to whom countless slaves owe their liberty, said that a useless Christian is an actual. monstrosity. — Think of the martyrs of all ages whose delight was the office of the ministry, and who counted not their own lives dear, beginning with Stephen, continuing with Peter and Paul, on down to our days, when the

Chinese Fan Szu, gaining consciousness again after severe tortures, said to his tormentors, who threatened to cast him into the fire if he did not recant: "You need not trouble yourselves, I can go into the fire myself." And calmly he entered the flames and his death.

All faithful hearts rely on a faithful God. When parents must part from their children, missionaries from their young converts, great leaders from those whom they have led, what is their comfort and stay at thought of coming dangers and trials? God and the word of his grace.

Many a preacher casts the blame on his people when his ministry lacks the proper success. Let him look at his hands in the light of the Word; he will find some spots of blood. — Acts 20, 26 makes a good farewell text — if the right ministry is about to be closed. — Paul is a fine example for preachers, but he intended his faithful work as an example for the entire flock.

The world is quite sure that it is better to receive than to give, but the world always' was a fool. — The secret of the blessedness of giving shines clearest in the infinite blessedness of the Giver of all good and perfect gifts. All the blessedness of giving includes that of receiving and goes beyond it, for we must have received, and received aright, to be able to give.

Paul, a Model of Christian Faithfulness Unto Death.

   I. *His faithfulness in work.*
  II. *His faithfulness in suffering.*
 III. *His faithfulness in love.*

                                         Blau.

The Faithfulness Required of a Pastor and his People.

They must both be faithful

    I. *To God.*
   II. *To his Word.*
 III. *To his church.*
 IV. *To each other.*
   V. *To themselves.*

Is Their Blood on Your Hands?

   I. *What doctrine have you stood for?*
  II. *What example have you given?*

The Church of God Purchased With His own Blood.

I. *Its value.*
II. *Its care.*

Paul's Legacy of Faithfulness.

I. *The example he left.*
II. *The admonition he added.*

The tenth Sunday after Trinity is marked by Christ's weeping over Jerusalem, Luke 19, 41-48, the regular gospel lesson.   Hence Blau takes as a theme:

O Church of God, Remember the Things That Belong to thy Peace!

I. *Think of the grace thou hast received.*
II. *Think of the dangers that lie in wait.*
III. *Think of the duty thou canst not escape.*

THE ELEVENTH SUNDAY AFTER TRINITY.

Rom. 8, 33-39.

Quid usquam Cicero dixit grandiloquentius? asked
Erasmus. He might well ask, Cicero never had such a
theme and therefore never could reach such heights of
eloquence. The eighth chapter of Romans is the great chapter of comfort, and the highest, strongest, deepest comfort
of all Paul unfolds in the last section of this chapter, verses
31-39, where he presents the Christian's *certainty of salvation*. Our text restricts itself to the special elaboration in
which the apostle unfolds this certainty. There are three
thoughts: we need fear no accusers, no persecutors, no
powers of any kind.

We need fear no accusation.

The opening question in verse 31: "If God be for us,
who is against us?" governs all that follows, the apostle
merely specifying in detail who and what might attempt
to be against us. So also the answer in verse 32 covers
all that follows in giving us the strongest possible certainty and assurance of God's love, *i. e.* of forgiveness,
life, and salvation. See the last section of the text for
New Year's Day. The first specific question then is this:
**Who shall lay any thing to the charge of God's elect?
It is God that justifieth; who is he that shall condemn?
It is Christ Jesus that died, yea rather, that was raised
from the dead, who is at the right hand of God, who also
maketh intercession for us.** — When Paul thinks of anyone or anything being "against us," his first inquiry is
always in regard to the court-room of God. Woe to us
if anything can be successfully brought against us there.
So here he inquires, but with a blessed certainty in his

heart: **Who shall lay anything to the charge of God's elect?** The verb ἐγκαλεῖν, really: "to call in," has a forensic use: "to lay to one's charge," "to accuse," "to prosecute." **God's elect** are those whom God chose out of the world, John 15, 19; 17, 6; those "whom he foreknew and fore-ordained to be conformed to the image of his Son," verse 29. There is no article with ἐκλεκτῶν, because their quality as such is to be marked. They are **God's** elect because he chose them and they now belong to him as such. The question is very wide, including any and every accusation that might be made by hostile powers, of which Philippi mentions Satan, the law, conscience, the world, *etc.* The fact is that these enemies think they can accuse us, for we are by no means sinless. Satan is the great accuser who likes to bring every fault against us before the tribunal of God; our fellow men have much to charge against us; our own conscience condemns us; and the law, which searches out our most secret faults, has one fearful charge after another against us. Godet asks concerning the apostle himself: "Did Paul himself, when writing these words, not think of the cries of pain uttered by the Christians whom he had cast into prison and scourged, and especially of the blood of Stephen?" Still the triumphant question implies positively; No one can lay anything to their charge. — The reason is already indicated in the word "God's elect," but the apostle states the answer in so many words: **It is God that justifieth.** The possibility of reading this as the margin does: *Shall God that justifieth?* is based only on a supposed logical connection of the different sentences; and the logic in this case is not very lucid. No accusation can hold against God's elect, because **God** himself (note that θεός follows hard on θεοῦ) **justifieth** them, *i. e.* pronounces them free from guilt and declares them just for the sake of his Son's merits. It is not that God ignores our sins, or refuses to entertain proper charges against us. There is no unjust partiality on his part, no trace of favoritism. The sins are there and their full gravity in the sight of God, but there are also the atoning merits of Christ em-

braced by the faith of the elect; and on the basis of these
God justifies. The apostle, in writing as he does, may have
thought of Is. 50, 8-9, applying what is there said in regard
to the Messiah, to the elect. — Paul repeats the question in
an intensified form, and brings in a fuller answer: **who is
he that shall condemn?** The R. V. appends this question
to the previous answer as part of it and explaining it, but
the A. V. has the preferable arrangement of a parallel question to the one already stated. Some read the present participle κατακρίνων, "condemneth;" our version has the future
καταρινῶν, harmonizing with the tense in the first question.
The sense then is not: God justifies; who then shall condemn? adding the reference to Christ as the reason why
such condemnation would be impossible; but, independently:
"Who is he that shall condemn?" with its independent
answer, both question and answer parallel to the preceding.
Many may accuse, only one can **condemn,** declare the accused guilty and pronounce judgment. — The apostle does
not say it, but he seems to imply that he is thinking of the
one real Judge, Christ, in asking this question. The answer
then is the more effective: This very Christ, our Judge,
is our great Advocate, shielding us against condemnation. **It
is Christ Jesus that died** to atone for all our sin and guilt.
We again decline to turn this declarative statement into a
question, as is done in the margin. — But Paul in a manner
corrects himself: **yea rather, that was raised from the
dead, etc.** He finds he can say more than that Christ died
for us. Not that his dying is not enough; quite the contrary. But his resurrection, session at God's right hand,
and intercession show forth the full power and fruit of his
atoning death in shielding us from condemnation. For in
that he was raised from the dead we see that he was indeed
the Son of God, "and the blood of Jesus his Son cleanseth
us from all sin," 1 John 1, 7. Moreover, his resurrection
attested that his sacrifice on the cross was indeed sufficient
to atone for all sin, to conquer death and hell. So Paul adds
the resurrection in an emphatic way. — But there is more
to say in this line: **who is at the right hand of God,** ex-

alted as to his human nature to the fullest participation in the divine majesty and power. On the right hand of God see the text for Ascension; compare Philippi on Rom. 8, 34. This glorious position of the crucified and risen Christ is not intended to convey the idea that he can and will by his power shield the elect in judgment against a possible condemnation, as some seem to think. The question of condemning and acquitting is not one of power and might, but of right and wrong. So Christ's being exalted at God's right hand refers to his relation to God: he is of equal glory and majesty with the Father, near to him, mighty with him, and in all that he does for us infinitely superior to any who could possibly oppose us. — This indicates that the session at God's right hand is connected with the intercession: **who also maketh intercession for us.** This is the *intercessio specialis,* for believers, John 17, 17 and 11 (as distinguished from the *intercessio generalis,* for all the living), in which Christ prays for the believers that they may be preserved and grow in faith and holiness. In Paul's argument the intercession is viewed as in 1 John 2, 1: "If any man sin, we have an advocate with the Father, Jesus Christ the righteous: and he is the propitiation for our sins: and not for ours only, but also for the sins of the whole world." No condemnation can possibly touch us as long as this great Advocate makes his merits count in our favor. His intercession cannot fail of success, since he has propitiated God by an all-sufficient obedience. — So we are safe against any and every juridic attack.

We need fear no persecution.

There is another set of dangers, assailing us directly with violence, not indirectly with accusations. Our salvation is safe also against these. **Who shall separate us from the love of Christ? shall tribulation, or anguish, or persecution, or famine, or nakedness, or peril, or sword? Even as it is written,**

For thy sake we are killed all the day long;
We are accounted as sheep for the slaughter.

Nay, in all these things we are more than conquerors through him that loved us. — As long as we are united with Christ (and God), so long no accusation or condemnation can rob us of salvation; but may not somebody break this connection between us and Christ? Paul emphatically and triumphantly denies it. **Who shall separate us from the love of Christ?** The answer is: No one can! The interrogative τίς leads to expect that persons will be mentioned as trying this, instead Paul mentions impersonal forces. He either personifies them, or he writes pregnantly, thinking of the foes that bring such inflictions upon us. **The love of Christ** (or as some have it: *of God,* margin) is his love to us, not ours to him; compare verse 39. We can be separated only from that with which we are connected; from something that exists outside of us and does not depend upon us. **To separate us** from the love of Christ is to turn that love from us and make us stand forsaken and alone. The question really is: Can anything make Christ cease loving us and showing his love to us? Paul raises this question not theoretically, but as a matter of experience. He is thinking not of a question to be argued in the schools, but of a question pressed out of the hearts of those who are tasting the bitterness of the evils he here mentions. The world especially likes to point to such afflictions as evidence that Christ has ceased to love us; just as under the cross the Jews mocked Christ: "He trusted in God, let him deliver him now, if he will have him; for he said, I am the Son of God." So they say to us, and the tribulation in which we are plunged, the anguish, persecution, *etc.* seem to rise up like mighty waves overwhelming our little bark, like the boat of the disciples on the Sea of Galilee, while Christ seems to be asleep and unconcerned, or far away and forgetful of our dire need. Do these things, can they really separate us from the love of Christ? Is his arm ever too short; does his heart ever grow cold? Stoeckhardt misses the point entirely by bringing in the question of faith: Can anything sunder the tie of faith that connects us with the love of Christ? He answers this by saying that the elect

cannot lose their faith. But Christ loves even those who
lose their faith and his love reaches out to them to save
them. Besides there are many other things that try to extinguish our faith besides the tribulations mentioned by
Paul. — The apostle mentions in detail: **tribulation,** θλίψις
from θλίβειν, to press or straiten; **or anguish,** the feeling
caused by being completely hemmed in. These two often go
together, Rom. 2, 9; 2 Cor. 6, 4; compare Trench, *Synonyms*,
II, 20 *etc.* **Or persecution,** διωγμός from διώκειν, to chase,
hunt, pursue; **or famine, or nakedness, or peril,** danger
of any kind, **or sword,** which points to death, and to
which Bengel adds, that Paul here names the method of
his own death. When these things come upon us, they
hardly look like the caresses of love, they look like the
blows of wrath; but none of them, nor all of them together,
separate us from the love of Christ. That love shines in all
its power and comfort behind them, yea, in and through
them. — In putting together this catalog of afflictions the
apostle was not drawing upon his imagination; we know
what he had experienced himself, but instead of referring to
anything in his own life he quotes Ps. 44, 22: **Even as it is
written,**

For thy sake we are killed all the day long;
We are accounted as sheep for the slaughter.

Paul uses the Septuagint, which agrees closely with the
original. The fate of God's children is the same in all ages;
in what happened to those of the old Covenant we have a
prophecy concerning those of the new. God's enemies did
not care at what time of the day they slew the people of
God. "Persecution, like death, has all seasons for its own."
The wicked, when their passion against God's people breaks
loose, count them no better than sheep to be slaughtered. —
One thing, however, remains for God's children: the love of
Christ. However dark their experiences, that sun shines
undimmed. So Paul testifies, and we hear the note of
triumph in his words: **Nay, in all these things we are
more than conquerors through him that loved us.**
Amplius quam victores sumus, quoniam in cruce etiam

gloriamur. Beza. Paul himself wrote, Rom. 5, 3: "Let us
also rejoice in our tribulations." The cross is the Christian's badge of distinction and honor. The apostles "rejoiced that they were counted worthy to suffer dishonor for
the Name," Acts 5, 41. Christians of the right kind do not
only suffer persecution, but suffer it with a spirit that
makes them more than conquerors. But all this **through
him that loved us,** διά with the genitive, which is better attested than the accusative: "on account of him that loved
us." The aorist participle ἀγαπήσας is used because Paul is
thinking of Christ's death in which he showed most completely his love for us. "A Christian is thus a king, *i. e.* lord
over all, and to him all creatures must be obedient, but
spiritually. Externally, life and its possessions may be taken
from him, but he labors for and does what is commanded
him. And even though everything were taken from him,
yet he is always benefited thereby, and his faith is ever
growing and ruling in his heart; so that neither riches nor
poverty trouble him, or make him sadder or more joyful
(Phil. 4, 12). Whether he be maligned or praised, it is all
the same. This is accomplished by the mind which he has,
i. e. the joyful, firm faith whereby he cleaves to God. Such
a lord is a Christian heart, which no one can change or
trouble; it always retains its self-possession. Such lords
faith makes of us. But where are such Christians? St. Paul
was one of them." Luther.

We need fear no foe of any kind.

All that Paul has said concerning persecution and its
accompanying terrors rests on a broader basis still: no
created thing of any kind is able to separate us from the
love of God and thus deprive us of salvation. But it must
be noted in this entire song of triumph, that the apostle
says nothing about us ourselves, our own wicked will, and
what this might do. Besser rightly observes: "From the
love of Christ, which is one with the love of God, only unbelief can separate us." And Philippi's observation must
always be heeded. "When Paul says in verses 35-39 that

nothing is able to separate us from the love of God, this establishes no inamissibility of grace and, farther up, absolute predestination, just as little as does John 10, 28-29. For although it is true that no one and nothing can tear us out of the hand of God and Christ, because their omnipotence and grace is stronger than all earthly powers, this by no means excludes our being able wilfully and voluntarily to tear ourselves out of their hand. Though tribulation may not separate us from God, still sin may." This too is why the elect are constantly admonished and warned to fight against sin and to prove faithful by using the grace bestowed upon them. In other words, our certainty of salvation is not absolute, but conditionate; and the conditionate factor is not God or his grace, or any power or foe outside of us, but our own heart; as the *Formula of Concord* states it, 653, 21: "That the good work which he has begun in them he would strengthen, increase, and support to the end, *if* they observe God's Word, pray diligently, abide in God's goodness, and faithfully use the gifts received." To say that this certainty is no certainty, because it includes the condition indicated, and to demand a certainty without such a condition, is to side with Calvinism in this important question. — Paul now reaches his climax: **For I am persuaded that neither death, nor life, nor angels, nor principalities, nor things present, nor things to come, nor powers, nor hight, nor depth, nor any other creature, shall be able to separate us from the love of God which is in Christ Jesus our Lord.** — The general includes the specific; because no creature of any kind can separate us from God's love, therefore tribulation *etc.* cannot do it. This is the force of **for.** But now the apostle is not satisfied merely to state the great fact itself, that no creature whatever can separate us from the love of God, he puts in the personal note: **I am persuaded.** Instead of stating the objective fact as such, he states what its effect is on himself: it completely persuades and convinces him, it fills his heart with the most blessed certainty. And such must be the case with us. Truth is good in itself, but it is not made fruitful until it persuades us. When Paul writes: "I am persuaded," he does not merely declare or teach, he goes beyond both and testifies; he lets his heart speak. — The question in the apostle's mind is still the same as in verse 35, because there is and can be nothing worse for us than **to separate us from the love of God.** Only here the possibility itself is denied: **shall be able to separate us;** and the love **of God** is put in place of "the love of Christ," though there is no special difference. That this is God's love to us is plainly shown by the addition: **which is in Christ Jesus our Lord,** *i. e.* manifested to us in him and ever flowing out to us in him. And this love is itself mighty and efficacious to hold us and keep us in its blessed embrace, mightier than all the forces which the apostle names. — The effort to arrange the apostle's catalog of forces which might separate us from God's love in pairs, each with contrasting members, meets with insuperable difficulty and must be given up. Meyer thinks there are two pairs, and then two others to each of which a general third member is added. Zahn prefers to read "height" and "depth" as specifications of "powers." All the best manuscripts place "powers" where the R. V. has it, not where the A. V. has it. Paul is persuaded that **neither death, nor life** shall be able to separate him from the love of God. Death comes first to his mind, because in verse 36 he ended with "sword." Neither the power of death which so many dread, though it appear with fire or sword, lion's teeth or executioner's rope, nor life which so many prize, though it invite with a thousand attractions, shall rob us of God's love. Christ has destroyed the power of death, broken its sting, removed its errors; Christ has given us a new life, higher than any the world knows, and has shown us the vanity and emptiness of the life whose treasures are merely of earth. — **Nor angels, nor principalities** in the invisible world. Whenever evil angels are meant the N. T. indicates the fact; so "angels" here can hardly mean demons. Nor are we justified in interpreting: good angels and bad angels, for nothing indicates that "principalities" are so restricted. On angel ranks, which also are not indicated here, see Eph. 1, 21 in the text for Exaudi.

Both terms here are to be taken in the widest sense, as the entire context shows, and the best distinction seems to be that suggested by Zahn: "angels" = spirits who serve; "principalities" = spirits who rule. But both in the good sense. If the question be asked, how good spirits, whether serving or ruling, could possibly separate us from God, the only answer is that Paul is speaking hypothetically as in Gal. 1, 8. He is making a list of all the mighty forces outside of us and declaring that none of them, whether in heaven, earth, or hell, is able to sunder us from God. — **Nor things present, nor things to come,** Vulgate: *instantia,* in the act of happening, no matter whether terrible or delightful; or still hidden in the bosom of the future and pictured by the imagination in fearful or in attractive colors. We may often be disturbed by them, but God's love is mightier than all of them and lifts us up where we can confidently face no matter what comes now or in remoter times. — **Nor powers** stands alone and cannot mean a class of angels as when it is ranged alongside of "angels" and "principalities." Zahn suggest: the powers of nature which often show themselves in terrible calamities; but while these are included, "powers" is even more general. Possibly on this account the apostle added no companion term, his effort not being fine literary form and balance. — **Nor height, nor depth,** in the sense of anything that can come upon us from above or from beneath. Since "powers" might do this, Zahn connects these three; only "powers" may be viewed also as coming upon us in "things present" and in "things to come." It is best, therefore, not to try to find such special connections. — **Nor any other creature,** or *creation* (margin) is summary and general: anything of any kind outside of God. So mighty is God's love, so firmly attached to us, so constant in all its operation, so triumphant in all its purposes! What a comfort for every Christian, what a rebuke to our littleness of faith!

HOMILETICAL HINTS.

Here comes the army of our past sins, marshalled by three mighty generals, the devil himself, the world, and our own accusing conscience. Must we not flee in consternation as utterly unable to face their dreadful onslaught? Not for one moment. The blood of Jesus Christ, his Son, cleanseth us from all sin. Our general is Christ and leads the glorious army of his merits in the defense of all his believers. The issue is never in doubt for a moment. — In the hour of doubt it is of no avail to tell my heart that in spite of all my sins I still love God, still mean to do the good and to hate the evil, *etc.* My terrified conscience asserts the contrary and has an advocate from the bottomless pit. I am lost unless I learn to believe that God loves me, has loved me from eternity, has chosen me in Christ my Redeemer. And this not through an angel, not even through Gabriel, who greeted Mary and announced to her the birth of the Savior. No other ladder into heaven, or down from heaven, does Paul show us than Jesus Christ in the Gospel. "It is God that justifieth; who is he that shall condemn? It is Christ Jesus that died, yea rather, that was raised from the dead, who is at the right hand of God, who also maketh intercession for us." Besser.

Some have invented the idea of an "unconscious Christianity," a cloak for worldly ignorance and indifference in the highest matters of the soul. By it they would save for Christianity the names of famous men, and others less noted, who scorned to bear the cross of Christ. Little baptized children have an unconscious Christianity, and some poor Christian in the dark hour of suffering when the mind is clouded. But it is the business of all true faith to know, to be conscious, to be mightily certain of the love of God in Christ Jesus. And lest this ever slip from our hearts, when doubts, afflictions or hostile powers surround us, the apostle has furnished us the mighty support of this eighth chapter of Romans, with its conquering, triumphant conclusion.

We may stumble and fall into sin, but Christ's intercession never stumbles or falls. — The scars may remain, the wounds are healed.

Here comes the army of afflictions to lay siege to our hearts. It hems us in with anguish, it shoots its darts of persecution, it makes us suffer with famine and nakedness, it threatens us with the sword of death. But we are safe under the banner of Christ's love, which leads us through much affliction into the kingdom of God.

He who is one with God is frightened by no creature. When a board creaks, when a mouse runs, when it thunders, conscience quakes: Oh, oh, the beam creaks and knows my sins, all creatures are against me! But Christ orders it preached to all creatures that he gives the conscience rest, so that they must leave it in peace. . . . So the Gospel tells all creatures: Let the man alone and do not frighten him in the least. I am his friend, harass him no more! Then follows peace, joy, rest. Luther.

Our certainty is not an idea that we have, perhaps altogether unfounded, a deduction, perhaps, like so many of science resting on insufficient evidence, a philosophy, drawn from the speculations of thinkers who are subject to error as we are. Our certainty is God's own Word and promise, planted into our hearts by the Holy Spirit himself. Like a mighty anchor it holds the vessel in the severest storm. Heaven and earth may pass away, but this Word, and he who makes it our own, cannot pass away.

A Christian must know that he has Christ; next, what he has in Christ; then his certainty of salvation is fully established.

The Certainty of Salvation in Christ Makes us Christians.

For

I. *We must know that we are Christians.*

II. *We must know what we have as Christians.*

Riemer.

The Believer's Song of Triumph.

I. *A gloria* (33-34).

II. *A hosanna* (35-37).

III. *A halleluiah* (38-39).

According to Eberle and Bunke.

Faith's Triumphant Song.

I. *Many are against us.*

II. *God is for us.*

III. *Christ is over us.*   Heise.

Nothing Shall Separate us From the Love of God.

I. *Not the consciousness of guilt — God's love pardons.*

II. *Not the pressure of affliction — God's love strengthens.*

III. *Not the power of death — God's love gives us eternal life.*

From Florey.

11

The Christian's Joyful Certainty of Eternal Salvation.

I. *It rests on the love of God and the merits of Christ.*
II. *It is established in the heart by the Word through faith.*
III. *It fills us with comfort and joy in the face of every ill.*

The Mighty Arm of God's Love in Christ Jesus.

I. *Whom does it embrace?*
II. *How does it hold fast?*
III. *Against what does it shield?*

THE TWELFTH SUNDAY AFTER TRINITY.

Acts 16, 9-15.

Certain of his own salvation, the Christian hears the cry of the man from Macedonia: "Come over and help us!" So this text, breathing *the spirit of missions*, was allotted this very proper place. We hear the call that reached Paul; we see how he answered it; and we hear the story of his first promising success.

The call from Macedonia.

Paul is on his second great missionary journey; he has finished his visit to the congregations established by his first efforts, and by the repeated guiding of the Holy Spirit he has finally reached Troas (Alexandria Troas), the sea-port of Mysia, through which the trade with Macedonia went. The name reminds us of ancient Troy, which lay a little to the north; no doubt Paul also knew the tale of the conflict waged there by the heroes whom Homer has immortalized. But his heart was taken up with a far more important question: Where did the Holy Spirit want him to continue his labors? Here is the answer: **And a vision appeared to Paul in the night. There was a man of Macedonia standing, beseeching him, and saying, Come over into Macedonia and help us. And when he had seen the vision, straightway we sought to go forth into Macedonia, concluding that God had called us for to preach the gospel unto them.** Here then is Paul's call and direction, and he shows that he understands it. — **A vision,** ὅραμα, is something that is seen, a spectacle. Paul had a number of them. Acts 18, 9; 23, 11; 27, 23; 2 Cor. 12, 1, *etc.* This one appeared **in the night,** whether in a dream or not is

163

not said, the circumstances are rather against such a supposition. — **There was a man of Macedonia,** or more exactly: "a Macedonian man," **standing** before the apostle (ἐστώς, second perfect participle), **beseeching him,** possibly with appropriate gestures, **and saying, Come over into Macedonia and help us.** The petition itself, if nothing more, as for instance his manner of dress, his accent, or the special information of the Spirit, indicated the man's home. He asked for help from the apostle of Christ, which could mean only one kind of help, namely the spiritual help and deliverance offered by the Gospel. And this the apostle is asked to bring in person, he is to cross over into that province of Europe and preach there. The man asks not for himself alone, but for all his people: **help us.** It is certainly not necessary to suppose with Brenz and some other old commentators that this "man from Macedonia" was one of the good angels in the form of a man, fighting in Macedonia against the spirits of Satan, and calling Paul to his aid. The vision needs no other explanation than that God placed this figure before the apostle's eyes and made his ears hear the appeal. As such it is a divinely given type of the entire heathen world, the tremendous spiritual need of which ever cries in our ears. Alas, that so many eyes, even in the shadows of night, cannot see, or see too faintly, the shining figure with outstretched hands; and so many ears, open to all sorts of other invitations, cannot hear, or hear only too faintly, this pleading invitation to come with the Gospel. Let us note especially the petition to "come over." "How shall they preach, except they be sent?" Rom. 10, 15. Someone must "go," Matth. 28, 19; nothing less will suffice. — Paul does not hesitate or wait for a second invitation; **straightway** he is ready. The word: **we sought to go forth** shows that the apostle's companions were of the same mind, and the first person plural, appearing here for the first time in the Acts, shows that besides the two companions who had accompanied Paul to Troas, Silas and Timothy, Luke, the writer of the Acts, had also arrived there. In this unobtrusive way he indicates his presence. — So Paul's aim was Macedonia, **concluding that God had called us for to preach the Gospel unto them.** This is the conclusion which Paul draws (συνβιβάζειν, to bring together), and that rightly. God's call was everything to him, as it must be to every minister of the Gospel and every missionary. When he makes his will known, as now he does by providential indications added to the voice of the church, "straightway" we must follow. And there is only one thing to help the heathen world, not culture, education, our own customs and advanced ways, whatever value these may have, but the preaching of the Gospel. This and this alone saves souls, builds God's kingdom, meets his good and gracious will.

The response from Troas.

This is immediate. **Setting sail therefore from Troas, we made a straight course to Samothrace, and the day following to Neapolis; and from thence to Philippi, which is a city of Macedonia, the first of the district, a** *Roman* **colony: and we were in this city tarrying certain days.** — The middle and passive of ἀνάγω means to put to sea, to set sail; hence ἀναχθέντες: **setting sail.** Paul and his companions found a vessel for the journey across to Europe and were off immediately. They **made a straight course** (εὐθυδρομέω from εὐθύς, straight, and δρόμος, course) on the first day to the island of **Samothrace,** and on the next (τῇ ἐπιούσῃ, used with and also without ἡμέρᾳ) to the seaport on the mainland, **Neapolis,** from which a well-paved road led across the intervening ridge to the apostle's first destination, **Philippi** in Macedonia, a distance of about 10 miles. This city was founded by Philip of Macedon, the father of Alexander the Great, in a place called from its marvelous streams "The Place of Fountains." It became famous as the place where the last battle was lost by the republicans of Rome, under Brutus and Cassius, both sacrificing their lives. Augustus gave it the privileges of a *colonia,* making it a border garrison of Macedonia and a perpetual memorial of the victory over Brutus. When Luke adds that Philippi is **a city of Macedonia,** he indicates why Paul did not stop on the island, or in the seaport Neapolis; the latter still belonged to Thrace, not being joined to Macedonia until the time of Vespasian; and the apostle's call was Macedonia. The addition: **the first of the district** cannot mean that Philippi was "the chief city of that part of Macedonia," A. V. Thessalonica was chief city of the province, and Amphipolis of the **district,** Macedonia Prima, called thus as lying farthest to the east. Luke simply means that Paul began his work in the **first** city in Macedonia which he could reach; he took the first one in "the district" or "the section," *i. e.* the eastern quarter of Macedonia. Luke accurately adds that Philippi was a Roman **colony,** which means a city with the special privileges of the citizens of Rome itself; its inhabitants possessed the rights of Roman citizenship, of voting in the Roman tribes, of having their own senate and magistrates, of being under Roman law (the *jus Italicum*), and having the Roman language. The colonies tried to reproduce Rome in miniature and succeeded admirably, especially also in the less admirable features. — So Paul reached his first Macedonian field of labor; he had come quickly and directly, with no delay of any kind. To make a straight course in a sailing vessel means to have the most favorable wind; it seemed as if God himself speeded the journey. — Yet after Paul and Silas, themselves Roman citizens (Acts 16, 37), together with their companions Timothy and Luke, had entered this town of their fellow citizens, Luke records: **we were in this city tarrying certain day,** διατρίβοντες, spending a number of days without at once preaching the Gospel. Paul is not over-hasty; he carefully looks over the field before he begins his operations. Though several days were used up, they were thus well spent.

And on the sabbath day we went forth without the gate by a river side, where we supposed there was a place of prayer; and we sat down, and spake unto the

women which were come together. This was in all
probability the first Sabbath since the apostle's arrival.
Following his usual custom he begins his work by hunting
up the Jews. But here in Philippi their number was evidently small. There was no synagogue in the town, and
the remark that Paul "went forth without the gate, where
we supposed there was a place of prayer," indicates that
even here there was no building, but only an open place
where the little band of Jews was accustomed to assemble.
Paul had probably failed to find out exactly from those he
asked, where this place was. He knew it would be by a
river side, since the Jews always sought such places on account of their ceremonial washings. The river in this case
was most likely the little Gangas or Gangites, certainly not
the Strymon or Nestos, both of which are too far away.
Following the indefinite information he had secured Paul
and his companions succeeded in finding the προσευχή, but
only a few **women** were present. Why no men has been
variously answered; it seems that there were very few Jews
in the city, and though some decline to admit it, it may be
that the decree expelling the Jews from Rome (Acts 18, 2)
had been copied by the colony cities. Perhaps Paul asked
himself when he saw these few women, proselytes some of
them like Lydia, or Jewish women married to Gentiles like
Timothy's mother (verse 1), whether thus the vision of
the "Macedonian *man*" was to be fulfilled. But there is
no hesitation; before this simple little audience in this in-
significant place the four Gospel messengers **sat down,**
as was the custom of teachers, **and spake the word.** And
here was fulfilled the Savior's promise, that where two or
three are gathered together in his name he will be in their
midst.

The success at Philippi.

**And a certain woman named Lydia, a seller of
purple, of the city of Thyatira, one that worshipped God,
heard us: whose heart the Lord opened, to give heed
unto the things which were spoken by Paul.** — Paul's

first convert in all Europe is a woman; no wonder her name is cherished by her sisters in the faith and all believers generally. **Lydia** was her personal name, as Luke indicates by saying she was so **named.** Ptolemy indeed calls Thyatria, her home city, a Lydian town, but if this were correct, it would certainly make it superfluous to state that she herself was a Lydian. But Thyatira lay on the confines of Mysia and Ionia, and it exists even to-day with 17,000 inhabitants. The place was noted for its trade in **purple,** and Lydia herself, having come from there, was **a seller of purple.** This dye was obtained by the Tyrians from the shellfish *Murex purpura,* and conchylium, and the waters at Thyatira were considered as especially suitable for producing the brightest and most permanent hues. Scarlet fezzes made there are still thought to be superior. In three inscriptions dating back to the time between Vespasian and Caracalla a corporate guild of dyers is mentioned as being established in this city. Lydia sold the goods shipped from her home city in Philippi, and her having a "household" and a place large enough to furnish lodging for four male guests indicates that she must have been quite prosperous. She was a successful business woman, which meant much more in those olden days, when the liberties of women were still greatly restricted, than it would mean now. — But Luke adds: **one that worshipped God,** which describes her as a proselyte of the gate; see Acts 8, 27, Sixth Sunday after Trinity. We would like to know her whole story in detail, but we have only these salient facts. The worship of the sun god Tyrimnas, to which her native city was given, had lost its hold upon her, for she knew now the great Creator himself of the sun, moon, earth, and all things. Her business, resting as it seems entirely on herself, does not keep her away from the little place of prayer with its few women visitors. Her husband is nowhere referred to, and all conjectures are that she was a widow, conducting the business her husband had established and conducting it well. The lessons that lie here for the preacher are obvious; let him use them well. Compare the author's *Biblische Frauen-*

bilder, p. 349, for some of them. — Luke writes of this woman: she **heard us.** Little did she dream that Saturday morning what treasure she would find in that quiet retreat by the river side: but she heard the great apostle of the Gentiles himself set forth the blessed Gospel of Jesus Christ with all fervor and conviction, and she heard this corroborated by his three able followers. She had come upon the pearl of great price, and its glory captivated her heart. — **Whose heart the Lord opened, to give heed unto the things which were spoken by Paul.** The Lord opens the heart so that a person believes; but the hand with which he presses the latch and draws the door is the Word which we hear. No man can open the door of his heart himself, nor can he help the Lord open it, by himself pressing the latch or himself pushing at the door. The one thing he can do is to push the hand of the Lord away, *i. e.* to refuse to hear, to refuse to heed; and thus he can hold the door shut and bar it even more effectually than it was at first. This is wilful resistance and prevents conversion. All the women at the river side heard Paul speak, but all did not heed like Lydia. The grace of hearing, however, none of them thrust away, and they may have come to faith later. The heeding may have followed, when afterwards they called the apostle's words to memory, discussed them perhaps with Lydia, or when they heard the same things preached once more. "The grace of hearing," Besser writes, "no man is able to ward off." But we must let God work the heeding through the hearing, then will his blessed purpose be accomplished. In heeding, in holding her mind attentive to Paul's words when the divine truth was exerting its power upon her, Lydia came to believe. This is a fine example of the operation of God's Word and grace in bringing about adult conversion. There is no emotionalism, no ranting and beating upon the hearer by the preacher, no shouting and agitation by the hearer: only the silent touch of the Spirit as the ear conveys the blessed truth to the heart, the true inward consent, the blessed confidence and trust, which presently manifests itself in an honest confession.

Luke is reticent, he goes into no detailed description: **And when she was baptized, and her household, she besought us, saying, If ye have judged me to be faithful to the Lord, come into my house, and abide there. And she constrained us.** In due order Lydia's baptism followed, but just when, and where, and how Luke does not say. The addition καὶ ὁ οἶκος αὐτῆς even leaves us in doubt whether she and all her household were baptized together, or whether she was at once baptized, and her household shortly after. The former seems more probable, because a definite point of time is indicated, the time when she insisted on the apostles' lodging at her house. It is probable that at the solemn service in her house, when she and her household were baptized, that then and there she insisted on these her teachers making their headquarters with her. The fact that **her household** was baptized with her is used as an argument for the baptism of children, especially since there is repeated mention of such baptism of entire families. The argument is good in a general way, as it presents to us the idea of family religion in the apostolic church. All the members of the household, with no exception stated or implied anywhere, were thus received into the church of the Redeemer. If a special class, as for instance children, were excluded, we certainly have the right to expect that the holy writers should have indicated as much; they indicate, if anything, the contrary. We have no means of discovering whether Lydia had any little children either of her own or of some servant among the members of her household. Besser, assuming that she had, asks: "What would she have said, if the preachers of the Gospel had refused the water of Baptism to the little ones in her house? She would have had to grow doubtful of her own faith, the gracious gift of God. But she learned Jesus Christ aright from Paul, the Savior of all sinners, of the old as well as the young, and since she herself became as a child in receiving the grace of life, she is certain too that the heart of the smallest child is just as accessible to the Lord, or even more so, than her own." — Lydia at once attests the sincerity of her faith. She asks her teachers to lodge at her house; perhaps they at first declined, but **she constrained** them in Christian love, by the following argument and appeal: **If ye have judged me to be faithful,** and this they had and could not deny, in admitting her to baptism, **come into my house, and abide.** This was not merely woman's logic, it was the true logic of Christian love, gratitude, and generosity. That made it so convincing for Paul. In this Lydia, from the very beginning, set a mark for the church at Philippi. This was the one congregation which remembered the needs of the apostle in future days and sent him kindly personal gifts, especially when in captivity in Rome. How Paul appreciated such remembrance he himself records Phil. 4, 15 *etc.* This is an example which is worthy of emulation by all who share the faith of Lydia and the Philippians whom Paul won for the Gospel.

HOMILETICAL HINTS.

Behind that man from Macedonia what an army! From the marble halls of Athens and the judgment seats of Rome, from the sunburned fields of Spain and the verdant pastures of the British Isles, from the Alpine cliffs of Switzerland and the great oak forests of the German lands, even to the distant steppes of the giant Russian empire, the snow and ice-fields of Norway, and the green meadows of Ireland, there sounds the echo of the cry at Troas: "Come over and help us!" Behind the one man there stands an entire continent. And behind the one generation there stands another, and another — all doomed to the same blindness, superstition, depravity, wretchedness, and death, if this cry is not answered and the divine help sent. And — listen! To-day we still hear the same echo, coming across the land and the sea, to us who like Paul have the help and know the power of that help — and yet often hesitate in sending it. — This cry of the man from Macedonia is not a mere man's appeal for human pity and assistance; it rang in Paul's ears and heart as the voice of God. It was only a different form of the Master's own command: Go, preach the Gospel!

If in that hour, writes Matthes, someone in the philosophic schools at Athens had proclaimed it as the latest piece of wisdom that out before the gates of Philippi a travelling Jewish tent-maker was weaving the shroud for the corpse of their defunct world-wisdom; and if in the imperial palace at Rome someone had told the story that a woman purple-seller from Asia Minor was buying a mantle of scarlet before which all the imperial pomp and lordly power of Rome in the hight of its glory would have to fade — what a roar of mocking laughter he would have had for answer! Yet the things that are weak and despised in the world God has chosen to confound the things that seem great. 1 Cor. 1, 28.

Do you know that name: Thyatira? John tells us what the Lord bade him write to the angel of the church at Thyatira, Rev. 2, 18, *etc.* Some think that Lydia was instrumental in planting the Gospel in this her old home town.

Paul never arrogated to himself the power to open human hearts; yet, though he could not open them, the Gospel which he preached, being the power of God unto salvation, could do this wonderful and blessed thing.

Faith cometh by hearing. But to hear only half will not do; nor to prick up the ears in idle curiosity. The ear is the avenue to the heart; and right hearing permits the Gospel to reach its real inward destination. — God sends the apostle to proclaim help and salvation, and he guides Lydia to the place where the proclamation is made. To bring together the help and the helpless is ever his delight.

Were there no children in so many houses? And the Jews, accustomed to circumcise their sons on the eighth day, and even the Gentiles, to dedicate them unto the gods, could they have forgotten their children when Baptism was to be administered to the household? Caspari.

Rump compares Lydia to the chalice of the lily turning to the sun for light. So must the soul be attracted by the heavenly rays of the Word.

All believers are not grateful, but they all should be. The rose without its delightful odor would lose much of its beauty. When Lydia had received so much her heart was bent on making some fitting return.

The Christian is Bound to Hear the Missionary Call.

   I. *For it is God's own voice;*
  II. *And we have open ears and a responsive heart.*

Why do we Still do Mission Work?

   I. *We still hear the call.*
  II. *We still have the Word with which to answer the call.*
 III. *We still see the fruit which the Word brings forth.*

"Come over and Help us!"

I. *The world's need.*
II. *God's will.*
III. *Our own desire.*

You hear much said about the missionary spirit among Christians, especially that so many lack it.

The Secret of the Missionary Spirit in a Christian's Heart.

There is always

I. *An eye open to the world's need.*
II. *An ear open to the Lord's call.*
III. *A heart open to the world's salvation.*

Lydia: An Answer to the Question: Does Mission Work Pay?

I. *A soul saved.*
II. *A household made Christ's.*
III. *A congregation started.*
IV. *An entire continent opened up for the Gospel.*

Lydia, a Model for our Women.

I. *She receives the Word of God.*
II. *She serves the kingdom of God.*

Koegel.

THE THIRTEENTH SUNDAY AFTER TRINITY

1 Pet. 2, 1-10.

Langsdorff takes this as a text on spiritual growth, following the lead of the commentators who usually take the first three verses together under the caption: "that ye may grow thereby;" and the next seven as summarized in the statement: "Ye also, as living stones, are built up a spiritual house." It would accord with the general trend of the previous texts to introduce at this point the subject of spiritual growth or edification in a more or less general way. But Conrad's observation is worthy of attention, when he points out that here we have the chief passage in the N. T. on the spiritual priesthood of believers, that precious doctrine brought forth in its fulness of truth by Luther, and yet so often misunderstood and so little applied by many who bear his name. Already in verse 5, in connection with our edification as "a spiritual house," we are told "to be a holy priesthood, to offer up spiritual sacrifices, acceptable to God through Jesus Christ." And then comes the ninth verse with the positive declaration: "Ye are an elect race, a royal priesthood . . . that ye may show forth the excellencies of him who called you out of darkness into his marvelous light." It is self-evident that priests, and especially priests with such glorious functions to perform, must attain the proper spiritual growth and development according with their high and holy calling. A richer sermon will result if these thoughts are kept in mind and our subject be made: *the Christian's priestly calling.* The first three verses state the general requirement for this calling; the next five, its connection with Christ and his holy temple; and the last two its exalted character and its sacred functions.

174

The general requirements of our priestly calling.

These are both negative and positive. **Putting away therefore all wickedness, and all guile, and hypocrisies, and envies, and all evil speakings, as newborn babes, long for the spiritual milk which is without guile, that ye may grow thereby unto salvation; if ye have tasted that the Lord is gracious.** This is a general admonition, pertaining to all Christians alike. We all have the same holy calling, and therefore, once we are Christians, we must put away all evil things, and must grow spiritually unto salvation. This general character of the admonition in no way conflicts with the special characterization of our calling · in what follows; while it would fit other characterizations just as well, it certainly also fits this. The οὖν, **therefore,** connects this admonition with what Peter has just said concerning our "having been begotten again, not of corruptible seed, but of incorruptible, through the word of God, which liveth and abideth," verse 23 preceding. Having been reborn, our desire should be to grow and develop. This will require that we **put away** what now no longer is a proper part of ourselves, however closely it belonged to our nature heretofore. In fact, the things which the apostle mentions are all so hostile and antagonistic to our new nature, that they and it cannot exist peacefully side by side; one or the other must go. Having just spoken of brotherly love in the preceding 22nd verse, the apostle mentions such sins as would conflict especially with this love, but we must remember that this love to others is the outgrowth and the evidence of the right love to God. So we are to put away **all wickedness,** every form of the inclination or desire to do evil; **and all guile,** wile, craft, or cunning, intended to deceive and mislead others to their hurt. δόλος properly meaning a bait for fish; **and hypocrisies,** every form of falseness in our conduct; **and envies,,** all the ill-will that crops out at sight of the good fortune of others; **and all evil speakings,** every utterance prompted by evil thoughts or motions, slanders, derogatory statements, backbiting. Wickedness, says Augustine, delights in harming others, envy is pained at their good fortune;

guile fills the heart with duplicity, hypocrisy the tongue; and evil speaking destroys the good name of others. If we are reborn, what have we to do with these vices? Our hearts must be completely controlled by love. — Having stated the negative requirement in a participial clause, Peter now brings out the positive in the main sentence: **as newborn babes, long for the spiritual milk which is without guile.** The readers of Peter were by no means all beginners in the Christian life, a goodly number of them having followed Christ some ten or fifteen years when this letter was addressed to them; so we must not introduce the idea that the **babes** here meant now require **milk,** the elementary instruction of Christians, and afterwards may also receive "strong meat," the more difficult teachings of the Word. All Christians, whether old or young, beginners or veterans in the faith, will always be **as newborn babes;** and so Peter admonishes them all to continue thus, and therefore to "long for the spiritual milk," which the Lord offers them. The comparison "as newborn babes" is to keep before us the new state into which the grace of God has brought us by regeneration; it is a state which always requires **spiritual milk** as nourishment. The adjective λογικόν shows that γάλα is figurative, a milk, as Luther says, "which the soul takes, which the heart seeks." While it is true that the apostle means the Word by this "milk," yet λογικόν does not express this, as Bengel has it: *lac verbale,* or Weiss: "derived from the Word;" see Meyer. The Word of God is both the seed of regeneration and the food of the regenerate; the mother who brings forth the child, and the mother who nourishes the child at her breast. This Word can so nourish and strengthen because it is **spiritual,** enters the mind and heart with divine power and grace, and because it is **without guile,** altogether pure and unadulterated, with nothing foreign admixed. From the precious Gospel of Christ we draw nothing but the pure milk of God's saving truth, "unmixed with the plaster of Paris of heresy," as Irenæus adds. Peter bids us **long for** this milk, as babes cry until they are satisfied. The 119th Psalm is a fine example of this longing, for instance verse 20: "My soul breaketh for the longing that it hath unto thy judgments at all times;" verses 28; 40; *etc.* To cease hungering for the Word is a sign of spiritual decline, which, if continued, must end in death. A strong and robust appetite for the Word is an indication of spiritual health. — **That ye may grow thereby unto salvation** shows what must prompt the longing of our hearts for the milk of the Word. While the new life is complete in itself at regeneration, being life, it always seeks growth and development. Like the branch on the vine its nature is to put forth leaves, tendrils, and fruit, increasing in size and strength constantly. To cease growth is to decline; to rest is to rust. There is no neutral state. One of the worst spiritual diseases is consumption, to draw awhile from the milk we have formerly taken, but finally to take no more, and thus to decline steadily, though perhaps unconsciously, until the spark of inner life is extinct. **Unto salvation** means the glorious salvation to come; for this we were reborn, and for this we are fed and nourished. Our whole spiritual being tends toward that last and final communion with God. — But Peter adds: **if ye have tasted that the Lord is gracious,** making what, of course, is a fact conditional in form, in order to have each one of his readers raise the question in regard to himself and thus to realize that he has actually tasted the Lord's graciousness. The verb keeps to the figure of the milk; it points to the actual experience of faith in dealing with the Word. To find the Savior there and peace for the soul and a thousand gifts of grace is indeed to taste something sweet; and really to taste that once will make us desire to taste it again and again, for nothing can so satisfy the soul. Yet instead of saying anything about the "milk," or its equivalent the Word, the apostle mentions **the Lord,** Christ, the substance of the Word, and concerning Christ, that he is **gracious,** kind and benignant. The attribute χρηστός fits both the person here spoken of and the figure employed in speaking of him. The apostle utilizes Ps. 34, 9: "O taste and see

12

that the Lord is good," not quoting the words as such, but merely appropriating from them what here fits his thought. There is no need to restrict the apostle's meaning to either or both of the Sacraments, as if he referred especially to them as evidences of the Lord's goodness; Peter speaks in a general way, embracing any and every. experience of Christians by which they taste the Lord's graciousness in feeding upon his Word.

The connection of our priestly calling with Christ.

All Christians are born again, desire the milk of the Word, taste the graciousness of Christ.   Peter now changes his imagery, but he keeps the thought of life, "living stones," and he emphasizes more fully our connection with Christ; at the same time he advances from the idea of "babes" who merely receive the Lord's care, to that of priests who render him acceptable sacrifices. **Unto whom coming, a living stone, rejected indeed of men, but with God elect, precious, ye also as living stones, are built up a spiritual house, to be a holy priesthood, to offer up spiritual sacrifices, acceptable to God through Jesus Christ.** — Peter is describing the high, blessed, glorious position and office of his readers.   This explains his change of figures: we are a temple, a wonderful spiritual temple; but even more: as the priesthood is more than a temple, so we are even the spiritual priesthood itself. — **Unto whom coming** expresses the constant activity of faith, from its first inception on.   When Christ invites us to come unto him, John 3, 20-21; 5, 40; 6, 3; Matth. 11, 28, he offers us the power to do so in the very invitation itself.   Usually προσέρχομαι is construed with the dative; here we have πρὸς ὅν, a stronger form, for we are not merely to come to him and stand in his presence, but to be joined unto him.   Christ is described as **a living stone,** according to the figure of a spiritual temple which Peter has in mind, utilizing again O. T. imagery as found in Ps. 118, 22; Is. 28, 16.   The article is omitted, not in order to render the term indefinite, since the added attribute makes it definite enough, but in order to emphasize the quality indicated by the designation. Christ is the great corner-stone of God's temple, and as this is a living structure, so this chief stone is a "living" stone, having life in himself and acting as a fountain of the true spiritual life ($\zeta\omega\eta$) for us. — In further description Peter adds: **rejected indeed of men, but with God elect, precious,** or, as the margin has it: *honorable.* Christ was rejected by the builders themselves, as Peter says Acts 4, 11 in his address to the Jewish High Council; here, however, men generally are said to have rejected him, because blind human wisdom always does the same thing. "Men" thus stand in contrast to "God;" the idea that believers accept Christ is conceived as due to God, since they of themselves did not accept him. The rejection was prophesied Ps. 118, 22; God's election Is. 28, 16. In God's sight, **with God,** whose great plan was carried out in spite of the blind hostility of men, this wonderful stone was **elect,** and counted as **precious** in being thus chosen to be the head of the corner, *honorable* in God's eyes. The same thought is often concretely expressed by pointing to the crucifixion of Christ by the hands of men and to his resurrection through the power and glory of God. — Peter now turns to his readers: **ye also, as living stones, are built up a spiritual house.** We are **living stones** in a secondary sense, since we derive our life from Christ through faith; yet we have thus true life, and are like Christ, the original "living stone." It is best to read οἰκοδομεῖσθε as the indicative, not the imperative (Luther, the margin of the A. V., and some others, who would conform it to verse 2), and as a true passive: **ye are built up.** This denotes a continuous activity in regard to those who by God's grace are now living stones; not the addition of new stones, but the spiritual work of God continuing on in the old ones. The spiritual growth and development of believers is meant, edification in the highest sense of the word, an ever fuller, deeper, and more intense connection of believers with Christ. The means for this, since an activity of God is meant (note the passive) is his Spirit, Word and Sacrament; its result is

stronger, fuller faith, a life more and more sanctified, a
spiritual enrichment every way. The whole work is mediated through Christ: "unto whom coming." — Without describing it particularly the apostle's thought is that all true
believers are joined together thus in one, they are built up
a spiritual house, "the church of the living God," 1 Tim.
3, 15. Peter writes οἶκος, not ναός, on account of the preceding verb, although the idea of a temple is suggested
beyond question by the reference to the priesthood. This
"house" is **spiritual** because the entire structure is the opposite of material, a joining together of our spirits with Christ,
the glorified Redeemer, through the Spirit of God. — But
Peter goes a step higher. No activity can be ascribed to a
"house," even to a "temple," but our spiritual communion
and union with Christ brings forth a very important activity
on our part, one intended of God and in which he delights,
a glorious and exalted privilege for all believers. To this
the apostle rises by changing his figure and adding in the
form of an apposition: **a holy priesthood, to offer up
spiritual sacrifices, acceptable to God through Jesus
Christ.** The margin reads: *for a holy priesthood,* but the
εἰς has nothing especial to recommend it. By ἱεράτευμα we
must not understand the office only, but a body of priests.
All believers, by virtue of the work of Christ, have the high
and blessed prerogative of priests, direct access to God, as the
priests of old went in and out of the temple of God, where
God dwelt in the Holy of Holies, and the right and duty to
offer sacrifices to God, as was the special office of the O. T.
priesthood. What was reserved in a special way to a particular class in the old covenant, has now become the high
privilege of all believers. And all the outward regulations
of the priestly service have been changed into spiritual functions. Even the Jewish priests were held back by these outward ceremonial forms, for Christ had not yet removed the
veil that hung between them and God. But now, through
his blood, the way is open, and we are all "a holy priesthood" with all that that implies. — There is an emphasis on
holy, for such only as are sanctified and cleansed can ap-

proach a holy God and render him acceptable service and
sacrifice. Our holiness is in the removal of our sin by justification, and this always has as its fruit a life of holiness.
— The main work of the O. T. priesthood was the offering
of sacrifices, material, animal sacrifices. These pointed to
Christ's great sacrifice to come. As such they have come
to an end and need no repetition in any form, since Christ
has made his all-sufficient sacrifice once for all. But there
remain, and are called for more imperatively than ever, the
sacrifices of praise and thanksgiving, seeing that all the
treasures of God's grace are now poured out upon us. So
Peter writes: **to offer up spiritual sacrifices,** ἀνενέγκαι from
ἀναφέρειν, to carry or bring up, namely upon the altar. What
is meant by these sacrifices we read Rom. 12, 1: "to present
your bodies a living, sacrifice, acceptable to God," *i. e.* to
give our bodies with all their members and powers into
God's service; Heb. 13, 15: "a sacrifice of praise to God
continually, that is, the fruit of lips which make confession
to his name;" to which the next verse adds "to do good and
to communicate," "for with such sacrifices God is well
pleased;" Phil. 4, 18; and Rev. 8, 3: "the prayers of all the
saints upon the golden altar which was before the throne."
The public preaching is not included among these sacrifices
of the universal priesthood of believers, because this work,
while also to be rendered as a sacrifice to God, requires a
specific call and is allotted only to those so called. — These
sacrifices, like the "spiritual house" in which they are rendered, are to be **spiritual,** produced in us by the Spirit of
God and bearing the quality and marks of his work. They
are **acceptable to God through Jesus Christ,** because rendered in his name and for his honor, as evidences of the
life he has wrought in us, and freed from all the faults and
shortcomings of the flesh which still clings to us, by his
perfect merits. Our entire priesthood rests on Christ, and
only through him may we draw near and offer anything to
God. — In Peter's words there lies an implied contrast with
the O. T. people of God: they had a house of God, but we
are to be this house ourselves; their temple was of dead

stones, we are living stones; they approached God through a priesthood, we are to be the priesthood ourselves; they offered material sacrifices, ours are to be spiritual.   Rome insists that we approach God still through a specific human priesthood, the papal hierarchy; others have similar ideas concerning the office of the ministry as an intermediary between the believers and God.   Against these errors compare the Confessions 349, 65 and 69; 263, 25 *etc.*

Peter establishes and explains what he has written by referring to the O. T. Scriptures: **Because it is contained in scripture,**

Behold, I lay in Zion a chief corner stone, elect, precious:

And he that believeth on him shall not be put to shame.

For you therefore which believe is the preciousness: but for such as disbelieve,

The stone which the builders rejected,

The same was made the head of the corner;
and,

A stone of stumbling, and a rock of offense;
for they stumble at the word, being disobedient: whereunto also they were appointed.

The freedom of these quotations is to be explained by the apostle's purpose, which is twofold: proof, but at the same time explanation, and this extending to the proof-passages themselves. **Because** shows that what the apostle has written is founded on Scripture; περιέχει, impersonal: **it is contained.** — The first quotation is from Is. 28, 16, to which reference was already made. Peter is concerned especially about what is here said by the prophet concerning **a chief corner stone,** namely the promised Messiah. Delitzsch interprets the prophecy: "This stone is the true seed of David who appeared in Jesus." On the thought of what "the chief corner stone" signifies see Eph. 2, 20-22 in the text for Pentecost, and Acts 4, 11, the Fourth Sunday after Trinity. Only the two attributes which he used above does the apostle now touch upon in

the quotation: **elect, precious.** — As important in regard
to believers he adds the line: **And he that believeth**
(adding: **on him,** for which the margin has: *it,* the stone)
shall not be put to shame. The original has: "shall not
make haste," which is explained in Rom. 10, 11, the Second
Sunday after Trinity. The believer is he who comes to
the living stone, verse 4; built on this stone as the rock of
salvation he shall not be put to shame, he shall be safe and
secure "unto salvation," verse 2. — Peter drives this home
to his readers: **For you therefore which believe is the
preciousness;** note the emphasis on ὑμῖν, and the emphatic
position of τοῖς πιστεύουσιν at the end, immediately next to
the opposite ἀπιστοῦσιν. In ἡ τιμή Peter takes up the attribute of the stone ἔντιμον, at the same time expressing positively what lies in καταισχυνθῆναι: the value, the honor which
the chief corner-stone has in God's eyes is ours also as believers, since faith joins us to this stone; so nothing can make
us ashamed. No outward prerogative, such as the Jews
boasted, is of avail; their own Scriptures ascribe the honor
that avails before God only to faith. — And this is clinched
by further quotations dealing with those who do not believe: **but for such as disbelieve,** — Ps. 118, 22 speaks
of them — what is this precious stone to them? For them
too, only in a different, hostile sense this stone **was made
the head of the corner.** It was done of God in spite of
them, and in fact in order to confound them. Peter uses
Is. 8, 14 to show it, simply attaching it to the previous
quotation by **and: A stone of stumbling, and a rock of
offense,** compare Rom. 9, 33; also Luke 20, 17-18, where
the Lord explains Ps. 118 by adding: "Every one that
falleth on that stone shall be broken to pieces; but on
whomsoever it shall fall, it will scatter him as dust." The
verb προσκόπτειν means to stumble, also used metaphorically
of moral stumbling, and πρόσκομμα is the hindrance against
which one stumbles. So Christ, placed by God as the head
of the corner, is in the way of those who do not believe.
They cannot avoid him, and refusing to be built upon him,
they strike against him. Since he disagrees with all their

wickedness they even rage against him, to their own destruction. — The same thought lies in **a rock of offense;** σκάνδαλον, the crooked stick in a trap to which the bait is fixed and which causes the weight to fall upon the victim, is also used metaphorically for "offense." Commentators debate whether Christ is such a stone of stumbling and rock of offense objectively or only subjectively, in God's intention, or only because of man's folly. The best answer is that the two belong together; for God intended Christ for the salvation of all, not for their destruction. The latter is God's will not _antecedens,_ but only _consequens,_ when he takes man's perversity into account. — Peter brings this out by the explanation: **for they stumble at the word, being disobedient: whereunto also they were appointed.** It is 'through "the word," the Gospel, that these opponents come in contact with Christ; to this they refuse to yield in the obedience of faith. The margin connects as follows: _being disobedient to the word._ The position of the words makes the other connection preferable, although he who "stumbles at the word" because of disobedience, is evidently disobedient to that very Word. Not unto such disobedience, but because of it the children of disobedience were appointed to stumble. This is the judgment upon them, fixed already in advance. God cannot and will not change his great plan of salvation, least of all will he take away his Son our Savior to please wicked men; that would be to abandon all his believers to destruction. So they who will not be obedient in faith when all the grace of God is brought to them, are to stumble, they are to fall. Christ is thus indeed "set for the fall of many," Luke 2, 34; "he that believeth not shall be damned," Mark 16, 16.

The exalted character of our priestly calling and its functions.

After the digression regarding those who disbelieve Peter turns again to the main theme, the exalted position of true believers: **But ye are an elect race, a royal priesthood, a holy nation, a people for** _God's_ **own posses-**

sion, that ye may show forth the excellencies of him who
called you out of darkness into his marvelous light:
which in time past were no people, but now are the
people of God: which had not obtained mercy, but now
have obtained mercy. — Here all the secret glory of
God's true children stands revealed; but it requires the eye
of faith to see it. In the world unbelievers often act as
great lords, the power, authority, and honor that impresses
the world being in their possession, but in. reality they are
already disgraced, defeated, outcast, and condemned in the
sight of God, and soon enough their shame shall appear.
Instead of following out either the old figure of a building,
or introducing a new one, the apostle shows the exalted.
position of believers by applying to them the inportant
designations for the true people of God in the O. T. These
are not quotations in the regular sense of the term, but
appropriations, setting forth at the same time the highest
reality contained in those ancient statements. — The first
honor title: **an elect race**,, briefly summarizes what was
said of the true Israel of old in passages like Deut. 7, 6-7;
Is. 43, 10 and 20; 44, 1-2. As God chose Abraham for his
own, and the Abrahamitic nation, so he has chosen us. But
Israel was chosen with the condition, that they should be
God's own if they continued in his law and statutes. When
they turned from these, God also cast them off. But in us
the condition of God's choice is fulfilled through the operation of his grace: as believers we are "a chosen generation"
(A. V.). That this choice or election was made in all
eternity, God foreknowing his own, Peter does not say;
it is the present blessed state that he lays stress on throughout. The terms **race, nation, people** show that Peter views
the believers all as one body; it is the *una sancta ecclesia*
which he is here describing. Whatever differences there
may be among the individuals are here lost sight of; the one
thing that we are, and that we ought to be proud and happy
to be, is here emphasized. — **A royal priesthood** recalls
Ex. 19, 5-6, from which Peter also draws the next designation. The Hebrew reads: "a kingdom of priests." Ours

is "a priesthood," a union of such as are called and empowered to draw nigh unto God and to render him acceptable sacrifices, as shown in verse 5; and this a "royal," kingly priesthood, because it belongs to the King of kings himself and its duties are to honor and magnify him. The idea expressed by Peter is not that we Christians are a kingdom composed altogether of priests, for the fundamental idea is that we are a "priesthood," and this is described by the adjective "royal." So also the first meaning cannot be that we are priests with a royal mind, or with royal honor, *etc.;* the idea of royalty must be referred first of all to our connection with the King: we are kingly only because of this King. Then, of course, it may be added, that being his and serving him in his kingdom, we have no business to be beggarly in our mind and bearing, and that he himself treats us royally. But all these and similar thoughts are in the line of deductions and applications, and therefore require as a basis the first meaning we have indicated. — **A holy nation** means a nation separated unto God and dedicated wholly to him. As a holy God we his people must be holy, else we could not belong to him. Christians must once for all give up the desire to be like "other people," for the moment this desire is carried into effect they lose their distinct and exalted character. Our holiness is by imputation, and resting on that by gradual acquisition. — The final designation: **a people for** *God's* **own possession** is drawn from Is. 43, 21; compare Deut. 7, 6; Ex. 19, 5; Mal. 3, 17. Stoeckhardt who uses every opportunity to bring in his idea of a sure and certain election "unto faith," takes this designation in the sense that God will always retain us as his property. The true sense is not such a deduction, but the one Besser already indicates, and so finely sets forth in Tit. 2, 14: "Our great God and Savior Jesus Christ, who gave himself for us, that he might redeem us from all iniquity, and purify unto himself *a people for his own possession,* zealous of good works." The word: for his "own possession" points to redemption and the resultant ownership. Our value in God's eyes is the price he paid for us;

our glory is that we are now truly God's own. As between the terms γένος, ἔθνος, and λαός there is no specific
difference here; all of them, as also ἱεράτευμα, express a
communion and fellowship embracing all the individuals
alike who are here had in mind. — It would be a decided
mistake to suppose that we can be all that Peter says here
of us, and at the same time sit down quietly and contem-
plate our honor and excellence. These are by no means
static terms, but dynamic ones, they all include what Peter
puts into a purpose clause, which however contains an
undertone of admonition: **that ye may show forth the
excellencies of him who called you out of darkness into
his marvelous light;** compare above: "To offer up spiritual
sacrifices." Peter again uses Is. 43, 21; compare Is. 42,
12. The ἀρεταί of God are those attributes and qualities of
his which make him excellent and thus praiseworthy; here
his love, mercy, grace, and goodness are especially meant,
all those attributes which manifested themselves in his act
of "calling us out of darkness into his marvelous light."
The effective and successful call is meant, for we are now
in the light. The **darkness** is not merely our former state,
but, parallel with "his light," the terrible state of the world
under the prince of darkness, a state of blindness, lifeless-
ness, death which still exists in the world about us. God's
call, operating through the Gospel, brought us out of that
and into **his marvelous light,** *i. e.* the light of truth, life,
blessedness found in the kingdom of grace. The more we
see what all this "light" of God contains, the greater must
be our wonder and marveling. The excellencies of God
with which we ourselves have thus come into closest personal contact, it is God's purpose that we proclaim, announce out to the world, to **show forth.** All that we are
demands it; for this especially we are priests of God. By
word and deed, by our profession and conduct, at all times
and under all circumstances, we are to perform this highest
and most blessed work on earth. God's excellencies are to
shine out from us into men's hearts, that they too may be
won and become people of God. Alas, how often we fall

short in our holy office; we show forth too often and too much the flesh, the world that is still in us, the imperfections and sins that still cling to us. — The closing words of our text, an adaptation of Hosea 2, 23, are used like the previous O. T. references: **which in time past were no people, but now are the people of God: which had not obtained mercy, but now have obtained mercy.** Peter here sums up all that he has said in verse 9, and even farther back, verse 4 *etc.* To be **no people** is to be like sheep without a shepherd, a prey to every foe; to be **the people of God** is to be under him as King, Protector, Provider, and Benefactor. This is our blessed state now. And the heart of it all is that then we **had not obtained mercy,** had not become partakers as yet of the pity of God by which he tries to remove our wretchedness; but we **now have obtained mercy,** our wretchedness has been removed by this mercy and we are thus in the state Peter has so eloquently described. Paul uses this passage to show what God did for the Gentiles, Rom. 9, 25; Peter brings out that God has done this for all Christians alike.

HOMILETICAL HINTS.

Many read a great deal; but instead of the pure milk of the Gospel, which produces growth, they swallow all sorts of fancy mixtures, which destroy the digestive organs. Besser. — The sign of regeneration is not merely firmness; firmness might be a hardening, a petrifaction. The sign of regeneration is hunger for the milk of the Word, desire to grow and gain strength, ability to fight and overcome the old sins and faults.

"That is to taste, when I believe with the heart that Christ has given himself to me, and that he has become my own, and that my sin and misfortune are his, and that his life is mine. When this enters my heart, thus I taste it. For how could I fail to have joy and delight in it? Do I not grow exceedingly glad if a friend of mine presents a hundred gulden to me? But he who does not receive it into his heart cannot rejoice in it. And they taste it best of all who lie in the agonies of death, or are oppressed by an evil conscience; there, as we say, hunger is the best cook, making all food taste good. The heart and conscience, when it feels its misery, cannot hear anything more lovely; that makes it eager, and it smells the roast from afar, and cannot eat enough of it." Luther.

What stones! They have not only been dressed by having piece after piece chipped away, and every corner and edge beveled and made true; the great Master-builder has penetrated them through and through and filled them inwardly with life, so that they are not only outwardly joined and connected with the chief corner stone, but grow together with it in the most intimate inward union. Matthes.

Many think they are edified when some pious thought or emotion is stirred within them. But here we are shown that edification consists in being built upon Christ; hence the more I rest upon Christ through his Word and Sacrament, the more I am edified. At the same time we are shown that edification includes our connection with others. Every sermon that I hear, every hymn that I sing, every instruction that I receive, every confession in which I join, every example of holy living and dying that I witness, every fraternal aid that I receive: all this brings out to me that I am one of many living stones who are all being built up into a spiritual house. So true edification can be had only in communion with others. A hundred or a thousand scattered stones are no building. — We do not edify ourselves; we are edified.

Our proper burnt offering is now repentance and faith, by which we die daily together with our sin-offering Christ, and live again to have our entire lives cleansed and purified by the fire of the Holy Spirit and taken possession of by God to be consumed by him. Kliefoth.

How fine to see the father of a family exercise his priestly office in the midst of the priestly members of his family, with the fire of devotion, like the morning and the evening sacrifice, burning daily upon the family altar. — Where the burnt offering of complete devotion to God is brought, there the thank-offering of praise and adoration will also be added.

"Here you see," writes Luther, "that St. Peter clearly says there is only one light, and concludes, all our reason, however intelligent it may be, is nothing but darkness. For though reason is able to count: one, two, three, and to see what is black or white, large or small, and to judge outward things, it cannot see what faith is. Here it is stone-blind. Therefore Peter speaks of a different light, one altogether marvelous, and tells us all straight out, that we are all in darkness and blindness unless God calls us to his true light."

The doctrine of the universal priesthood of believers is the scriptural corollary of the doctrine of justification by faith. When Christ died for our sins, the chief function of the priestly office was fulfilled once for all, Heb. 7, 26-27; 10, 14. Full and free access to the throne of grace was opened for all. From that moment on there has been but "one Mediator between God and men, the man Christ Jesus," 1 Tim. 2, 5. All believers are now essentially equal in their enjoyment of the privilege of approach to God: "a royal priesthood, a holy nation." This abolishes every special priesthood forever. To think of still making sacrifice for sin is to spurn the sacrifice of Christ; to thrust in priestly mediation between God and man is to count the mediation of Christ as insufficient. There remains for us now the sacrifice of service and praise. Consecrated by the water of Baptism and by the unction of the Holy Spirit, we may thus daily minister before the Lord. We are to comfort the brethren, to distribute to the necessity of the saints, to proclaim the Gospel to the world in word and deed. The Christian ministry rests on the universal priesthood of believers; it establishes no special order or rank, but allots the administration of certain public functions, according to Christ's own will and direction, to certain persons by means of a special call.

"Ye are a Royal Priesthood."

I. *Yours is the priestly dignity.*
II. *Yours is the priestly calling.*

Conrad.

The New Israel in its Festive Beauty.

I. *A chosen race — crowns on their brows.*
II. *A royal priesthood — light and truth in their hearts.*
III. *A holy nation — prayers on their lips and offerings in their hands.*
IV. *A people for God's own possession — Canaan before their eyes.*

Jeremias.

Our Priestly Prerogatives.

I. *On what do they rest?*
II. *In what do they consist?*
III. *And what do they require?*

The Wonders of God's Spiritual Temple on Earth.

I. *Its living walls.*
II. *Its royal priests.*
III. *Its acceptable sacrifices.*

What has the New Birth Made of us?

I. *Living stones, to be built on Christ.*
II. *Babes, to be fed with spiritual milk.*
III. *Royal priest, to offer spiritual sacrifices.*

True Edification.

You must be built

I. *On Christ.*
II. *By means of the Word.*
III. *In fellowship with others.*
IV. *To the praise of God's grace.*

THE
FOURTEENTH SUNDAY AFTER TRINITY.

1 Tim. 1, 12-17.

The second subcycle of the after-Trinity texts closes
with a fervent text on *gratitude,* and the cause of this gratitude is the deepest of all, the grace of God that pardons
the sinner and takes him into his service. The heart of the
text is verse 15, with its classical announcement of the
doctrine of grace, the experience of which so deeply moved
the heart of Paul in thankfulness. The apostle is occupied,
first, with the grace which he has experienced in his own
person, and then with the intentions of this grace in regard
to others.

Paul grateful on his own account.

In fortifying Timothy against certain false teachers,
whose doctrine was agnostic speculation and whose
practice legalism, but who could not tell how a poor
sinner obtains pardon and peace for his conscience, Paul
refers to his own blessed experience of grace, thus putting the truth in glaring contrast to falsehood. **I thank
him that enabled me,** *even* **Christ Jesus our Lord, for
that he counted me faithful, appointing me to** *his* **service;
though I was before a blasphemer, and a persecutor, and
injurious: howbeit I obtained mercy, because I did it
ignorantly in unbelief; and the grace of our Lord
abounded exceedingly with faith and love which is in
Christ Jesus.** — Paul begins with a strong personal note;
these false doctrines are not only intellectual errors in his
estimation, they strike at his own heart and life, and in
warding them off his own heart speaks out, thanking God
for what has become inexpressibly dear to him. Χάριν ἔχω
is not altogether the same as εὐχαριστῶ or χάρις τῷ θεῷ other-

wise used by Paul; it expresses his continued thankfulness
in the sense: "I feel grateful." His gratitude goes out to
him that enabled me, that is gave him strength, in the
widest sense of the term, for his entire career as a Christian
and in particular as an apostle. All his spiritual strength
and ability Paul refers to its true source, even **Christ Jesus
our Lord,** Jesus of Nazareth who is the Messiah of God and
by virtue of his saving work and exaltation our blessed Lord
and Master. Bengel refers this strengthening to Paul's
conversio et vocatio, Chrysostom to his suffering, others to
his miraculous deeds; but restrictions are out of place: all
Paul's spiritual strength, and the very life with which it
was connected he has, holds, and uses in gratitude to the
divine Giver and his grace. "I can do all things in him
that strengtheneth me," ἐν τῷ ἐνδυναμοῦντί με, Phil. 4, 13;
compare 2 Tim. 4, 17, where the same verb occurs. Some
read the present participle: *that enableth me* (margin),
which would refer to a constant and continuous strengthening, while the aorist points to one special divine act. What
act, as to outward circumstances, the apostle does not say,
and it is in vain to speculate. — Paul mentions especially
as a reason for his feeling grateful: **that he counted me
faithful, appointing me to** *his* **service.** This is not an explanation of the strengthening, for it is something in Christ
himself. The Lord did not doubt him, treat him with
suspicion, as well he might have done, considering his record
before his conversion; the Lord **counted,** or considered, him
faithful, worthy of trust, and showed this by the signal
honor he conferred upon him, **appointing me to service,**
which may mean the actual installation into service, or the
preliminary designation of Paul for future service, according to what force we give εἰς. Paul does not say that he
showed himself worthy of such trust on the Lord's part;
he refers the matter entirely to him, as Peter did when the
Lord asked him: "Lovest thou me?" John 21, 15-17. The
aorist participle θέμενος expresses time simultaneous with
the aorist main verb ἡγήσατο: in so appointing him the Lord

13

showed his confidence in Paul. There is no article with διακονίαν; Paul means service in general, of which Augustine finely says: *Servitium Domini summa libertas.* All service demands faithfulness, and for the Lord to use Paul at all for service showed his gracious confidence in him. — And in Paul's case this is especially noteworthy: **though I was before a blasphemer, and a persecutor, and injurious.** Here Paul openly confesses and acknowledges his sins, nor does he soften his words. He blasphemed Christ, by using wicked and hateful language against him, trying even to force others to do the same, Acts 26, 11; he pursued (διώκτης, only here in the N. T., from διώκειν) the followers of Christ, as one chases wild animals, Acts 22, 4 and 7; he wantonly, insolently hurt those who fell into his hands (ὑβρίστης, from ὑβρίζειν, to outrage, insult, maltreat, *etc.*). This memory of his past sins served to humble Paul all his life long, to magnify God's grace in his own case, and thus to keep ever flowing his stream of gratitude. In this Paul differed from those great sinners who after their conversion love to recount, and even exaggerate, their past wickedness with a sort of pride, as if this were a peculiar distinction others could not boast of. — But how could Christ trust a man like this and appoint him to service? Paul tells us: **howbeit I obtained mercy.** He marks the contrast with the strong adversative ἀλλά, "but." In ἠλεήθην Paul points to the ἔλεος of Christ, his mercy which pitied his sad, sinful, lost condition, and thus saved him. Stellhorn reminds us that if Paul had been judged according to the teaching of Timothy's opponents in Ephesus, he would have been absolutely condemned under their legalism. In the law there was no hope or help for him; his one and only hope was the Gospel, the mercy of the Lord. And this he obtained. On the way to Damascus Christ's mercy found him and in the preaching and teaching of Ananias in Damascus its saving power took hold of him completely. Paul repented and believed; he was converted. It was thus that he received mercy. And now we see how Christ could trust this former blasphemer

and persecutor and appoint him to service; Christ's mercy
had changed the man and made him a fit instrument for
the Lord's work. — When the apostle adds: **because I did
it ignorantly in unbelief,** he is not endeavoring to excuse
his guilt, or to explain it away, as though when a thing is
done in ignorant unbelief, perhaps with the intention to
do God service (John 16, 2), it cannot be wrong, or at
least not very wrong. Both Paul's ignorance and his unbelief were full of guilt in God's eyes. It is not the lessening
or removal of his terrible guilt that Paul has in mind,
but an explanation of how the mercy of God overcame his
wickedness. Paul did not sin against better knowledge:
he raged against Christ and the church **in unbelief,** ἐν ἀπιστίᾳ,
rejecting Jesus and his teaching, and all the claims of the
church. But in this he acted, not against better knowledge,
which would have brought him perilously near the sin
against the Holy Ghost, or plunged him into it, like some
of the Pharisees, Matth. 12, 31-32, but in his unbelief he
acted (ἐποίησα, without an object) **ignorantly,** in sheer
blindness. The implication is that unbelief may act in different ways, but in Paul's case the terrible outbreaks he
was guilty of were due to ignorance. And thus the mercy
of God was able to reach Paul's heart and overcome it.
It could do this without using violence or operating with
irresistible power, a thing which it never does. However
black Paul's guilt was, he did not go straight against better
knowledge, he did not oppose wilfully, else the Holy Ghost
could not have had his work in him (*Formula of Concord,*
526, 12; 568, 83). When the hour had come God sent the
light of truth to dispel Paul's ignorance, and he himself
tells us, Acts 26, 19, that he "was not disobedient unto the
heavenly vision" which made the divinity and glory of
Jesus plain to him once for all. — But in recalling how the
Lord dispelled his ignorance the apostle acknowledges
and praises the riches of the grace vouchsafed unto him:
**and the grace of our Lord abounded exceedingly with
faith and love which is in Christ Jesus.** This sentence
still depends on ὅτι, **because.** When Paul speaks of sin,

Rom. 5, 20, he says that it "abounded," ἐπλεόνασε, but of grace, it "did abound more exceedingly," ὑπερεπερίσσευσεν; but now he expresses the same thought by ὑπέρ added to πλεονάζειν : ὑπερεπλεόνασεν. He ascribes his conversion entirely to **the grace of our Lord,** his love to those who have in no way deserved it, and what this love does in reaching out to rescue such unworthy persons. And in his case, Paul says, it required the largest measure of this grace. Instead of intimating in any way that he had made it easy for the Lord's grace to convert him, he intimates the opposite. Some sinners yield 'to the slightest touch of divine grace. Paul in his ignorant unbelief required that this grace should abound, overflow in its richness, in order to save him. And the twofold thought, that the Lord offered him his grace, and that he offered it so abundantly, filled his whole life with the deepest feeling of gratitude. — That the grace of God was successful with Paul is brought out by the addition: **with faith and love.** The preposition μετά simply states that grace was accompanied by faith and love. It produced them in Paul's heart: where before he acted in unbelief, grace now substitutes faith; where before he hated Christ's followers, grace now works love. The two words show what a tremendous change grace succeeded in working. **Which is in Christ Jesus** belongs to both faith and love, which are here taken together: both have their foundation, their source, and the sphere of their activity "in Christ Jesus," Stellhorn. The preposition ἐν must be left in its native force. Wohlenberg's objection that faith and love would each require a different meaning of ἐν is not correct; and his idea that "love" must here mean Christ's love to Paul, instead of Paul's love to Christ, is made impossible by the juxtaposition of "faith and love" and the added prepositional phrase.

Paul grateful on account of others.

When the apostle speaks thus of himself, he does it by way of example and illustration, using the actual work of the Gospel of grace to overthrow the legalistic teach-

ings of the Ephesian errorists. ·This too causes him to
look beyond his own personal case, to put the doctrine
of grace into a general, universally applicable statement,
and even to follow up the Lord's gracious intention in
regard to others when he came with his grace to Paul.
**Faithful is the saying, and worthy of all acceptation,
that Christ Jesus came into the world to save sinners;
of whom I am chief: howbeit for this cause I obtained
mercy, that in me as chief might Jesus Christ show forth
all his longsuffering, for an ensample of them which
should hereafter believe on him unto eternal life.** — The
absence of any connecting word makes the new statement the more effective. **Faithful is the saying** expresses
the reliability and trustworthiness of the saying in so
far as it is in itself divine truth. Compare the remarks
on 2 Tim. 2, 11 for Cantate. The addition: **and worthy
of all acceptation,** *i. e.* of complete, full approbation,
emphasizes the former statement by showing how we ought
to treat such a faithful saying. It would be wrong to doubt
it in any way; whatever it may contain, perhaps at first
sounding strange to our ears, it deserves the fullest confidence on our part. This is Paul's testimony, based on his
personal experience, but it is more, God's own assurance to
us concerning his Word of grace. — The saying itself is
that Christ Jesus came into the world to save sinners.
It summarizes the Gospel of grace in as brief a fashion as
possible, and in this reminds us of John 3, 16; 1 John 4,
9-10, and a few other pithy Gospel passages. It is difficult
to say, whether Paul here actually quotes a saying current
among the Christians at that time, as not a few are inclined
to assume, or whether he here formulates this saying for
the first time as a terse expression for the true Gospel
doctrine. It is certainly possible, and even probable, that
in his oral teaching Timothy and others had heard this sentence before from Paul. Christ himself had said: "I came
out from the Father, and am come into the world," John
16, 28; and again: "The Son of man came to save that
which was lost," Matth. 18, 11; John 3, 17. "To come into

the world" is like John's expression: "he was manifested"
to take away sins, I John 3, 5. The eternal Son of God
was born of the Virgin Mary and became a man in this
earthly world **to save sinners.** This was the great purpose
of his coming, and upon this rests the emphasis. The word
ἁμαρτωλοί must be taken in its widest sense, any and all who
are **sinners,** who have missed the mark set by God's holy
law, who have thus come in conflict with his holiness and·
righteousness and are subject to· the death threatened by
the law to every transgressor, these Christ came **to save,**
to rescue from their danger, to deliver from their terrible
fate. They do not deserve it, they do not even ask for it,
it is altogether the grace, mercy, abounding love of Christ
that impels him to carry out this work of rescue. In the
one word σῶσαι is contained all that Christ has done and
still does for us sinners: his life, suffering, death, resurrection and exaltation in their mediatorial, atoning, converting
effects. — To this grand and simple Gospel statement, Paul
adds the personal confession: **of whom I am chief,** πρῶτος,
the first in the long line, the foremost, and here in the sense
of the worst. The effort to reduce this statement by
cutting it down to "one of the first," or "the first of those
saved," is blocked by the simple force of what the apostle
says. Paul humbly confesses himself the chief of sinners,
because he was formerly a blasphemer of Christ, a persecutor of the church, wantonly doing it injury; the memory
of all this makes itself felt again and again in his life, see
I Cor. 15, 9; Eph. 3, 8. But this fact, while on the one
hand it humbles Paul, on the other it makes him relish the
more the salvation which Christ brought for sinners, and
for sinners alone. If· he was the chief of sinners, heading
the procession, he would be first also in obtaining the salvation intended for sinners. Bengel notes the present tense
of εἰμί: *Sum, inquit, non fui, ipsum scriptionis momentum
includens;* but this should not be pressed, as it refers in a
general way to Paul's entire life when measured by the law.
It would contradict the specific sense of the apostle's word
for each of us now to claim to be the chief of sinners; in

fact, only one can be πρῶτος. Any application we may make in regard to ourselves must bear this in mind and must state definitely in what sense a repentant sinner can now indeed call himself "chief," namely in that he knows his own sins, and hears their accusation against him, as he cannot know and feel the sins of any other sinner. — Though Paul was such a great sinner, nevertheless, as he has already said, he "obtained mercy;" beyond question, first of all, because Christ loved also him. But there is a second reason, which Paul had in mind already when he declared himself πρῶτος of sinners: **howbeit for this cause I obtained mercy, that in me as chief** (πρώτῳ) **might Jesus Christ show forth all his longsuffering, for an ensample of them which should hereafter believe on him to eternal life.** This is the special use that Christ made of the "chief" of sinners. In saving him by his mercy his intention (ἵνα) was to exhibit **all his longsuffering,** by which, instead of striking the wicked down as he deserves, he bears his wickedness and gives him room for repentance. In μακροθυμία we must note the element of time, and Trench observes that it is used in regard to persons. In Paul's case Christ's longsuffering was finally crowned with wonderful success, when he was won by the grace that had borne with him so long. But in thus bearing with Paul Christ used him **for an ensample,** ὑποτύπωσις, a sketch or adumbration of other sinners, namely **of them which should hereafter believe on him unto eternal life.** In every one of them the same longsuffering of Christ would be apparent, but all that would thus be exhibited in them was already outlined and pictured in advance in Paul. The American translators prefer *thereafter* to **hereafter,** as expressing better the point of time in Paul's finding mercy. "In Paul, the furious foe and saved sinner, Christ once for all wanted to draw a sketch of all those who yet would and should believe on him in order to obtain eternal life." Wohlenberg. Paul thus is not only an example or an illustration, he is the supreme type of all converted sinners. As he was chief among sinners, so he became chief among pardoned

sinners. Every one of us may look upon Paul and
see in him what has been done in us also by the grace
of Christ; and there is none of us, either originally so
great a sinner, or now so rich a believer, who exceeds
the measure of Paul. In him Christ's grace showed how
deep down it can reach, and how high up it can lift. On
μέλλω with the infinitive see Blass, 204 *etc.;* it expresses
imminence and has the advantage of being able to express
what is about to happen, also in sentences referring to past
time. In πιστεύειν ἐπ' αὐτῷ faith is pictured as resting on
Christ as its foundation. **Unto eternal life** indicates the
goal.

　　Ex sensu gratiae fluit doxologia, writes Bengel. The
apostle's heart is deeply moved by the sense of his own
unworthiness and of the wondrous grace of God which
did so much for him and does so much for others likewise: **Now unto the King eternal, incorruptible, invisible,
the only God,** *be* **honor and glory for ever and ever.
Amen.** — **The King eternal,** or more closely: *the King of
the ages* (margin) describes God as the Ruler of all the
ages and what transpires in them. Weiss draws attention
to the distinction often made between this present age, in
which the conditions of salvation are arranged by our King,
and the blessed age to come, in which salvation shall be
brought to its consummation by him. **Incorruptible** describes God as superior to all corrupting powers; "who only
hath immortality," 1 Tim. 6, 16; whose life is in himself,
·and who therefore is the sole author of true life. immortality, and incorruptibility. He is **invisible,** for he is a
spirit, supreme over all, for us the object not of the senses,
but of faith. See Heb. 11, 27; Rom. 1, 20; Col. 1, 15;
1 Tim. 6, 16. **The only God** denies the existence of any
other being of the quality of θεός; to none other may we
look for divine help and salvation. If our faith fails to find
him, it will never find stable support. — And to God so
described in his supreme greatness Paul ascribes **honor,** the
esteem he deserves in his person and in all his work, **and
glory,** here the ascription of glory by men, especially all his

saints, who recognize and adore the sum of all his excellencies, namely his glory, Rev. 7, 12. And this **for ever and ever,** or, margin: *unto the ages of ages,* the genitive being added in Hebrew fashion to indicate the superlative degree of duration (Cremer), namely endless duration, eternity. This our finite minds can conceive only as an endless succession of ages, although in reality it is the negation of time itself and of all the limitations connected with it. **Amen,** "verily," seals this doxology with the stamp of truth and verity, even as Christ himself sealed many of his most important sayings.

HOMILETICAL HINTS.

People do not like to hear about sin. It is remarkable how the word is shunned especially where people shun least what it stands for. In the church its constant use has blunted its edge considerably. Outside of the church the terrible self-confidence of men hardly allows them to entertain the idea of sin. Small imperfections are admitted, things which time covers up, or which the every ready love of God is expected easily to pardon. But to speak of sin which causes a man to be damned and lost, this many consider an exaggeration of times long past. — And yet, we may add to these words of Riemer, unless we really know what sin is, we will never know what grace is, nor the true gratitude of the sinner who has tasted of the riches of grace.

Jesus makes us sinners in our own eyes, just as we are sinners in the eyes of God. That was Paul's first impression in the meeting before Damascus. It was a plunge into the abyss from the high throne of his self-glory.

I can never know any one more thoroughly than myself and my own depravity. As long as someone else seems to me to be more sinful, something of self-righteousness still covers up the bottom of my heart. Think of the possibilities of sin that slumber in your bosom; think of the conflagration that lurks in the banked fires of your passions and desires; think of the proud, desperate thoughts that would contradict God himself if your reason were left unchecked by his Word and Spirit.

Jesus — the sinner — to save: these three God has joined together, let no man sunder them. — The unique significance of Jesus is that he redeems us from the power and guilt of sin, from its curse and penalty. Paul's entire religion can be compressed into two words: Christ crucified.

If Paul, a blasphemer, persecutor, injurious could be saved, then can I. — He sits in prison, long months of captivity behind him. There were many who pitied his sad, dreary lot. But a great light shines in his heart. It has followed him everywhere, and in the darkest night of persecution it shone out with its wonderful beams: it is the light of grace, that ever brings forth the song on the apostle's lips: "But I have obtained mercy!" As he looks back over his life, its dark part when he was still a Pharisee, and its light part since he became a Christian and an apostle, that moment at Damascus when the change was wrought in his soul is ineffaceably graven upon his memory, and his heart swells with gratitude: "I thank him that enabled me!"

Heffter draws a fine parallel between the old gospel lesson for this Sunday and our epistle text: there a despised Samaritan, here a trusted Jew; there the most terrible bodily disease, leprosy, here the worst spiritual ailment, pharisaic fury; there as well as here, help and deliverance by the heavenly physician; there as well as here, the deepest and most lasting gratitude.

The Heart of True Christian Gratitude.

I. *When you understand the greatness of your sin,*
II. *The richness of Christ's pardoning grace,*
III. *The honor bestowed in his service,*
IV. *His merciful intentions in regard to others*
V. *Then you too will thank and praise God.*

How can you Know that you are Converted?

Learn of Paul

I. *To thank the Lord.*
II. *To confess the Lord.*
III. *To draw others to the Lord.*   Rump.

The Chief Chapter in Paul's Autobiography: I have Obtained Mercy.

I. *Before his conversion.*

   a) A blasphemer, *etc.*
   b) An ignorant unbeliever.

II. *In his conversion.*

   a) The chief of sinners.
   b) The chief of the saved.

III. *After his conversion.*

    a) An apostle of faith and love.

    b) A Christian filled with deepest gratitude.

Heffter

Chief of Sinners Though I be, Jesus Shed His Blood for me.

I. *Died that I might live on high;*
Lived that I might never die.

II. *As the branch is to the vine,*
I am his, and he is mine.

Looking Backward

the Christian sees with St. Paul:

I. *The mountains of grace.*

II. *The paths of service.*

III. *The signs that encourage others.*

The Most Reliable Thing in the World.

The Gospel of grace:

I. *Backed by Christ himself.*

II. *Proved by the chief of sinners.*

III. *Found worthy of acceptation by all who have believed.*

THE FIFTEENTH SUNDAY AFTER TRINITY.

2 Thess. 3, 6-13.

The Christian life as traced out by the foregoing eight texts dealt primarily with the believer as an individual. Even when the plural was used, the many were considered as units, in each of whom the different features of the Christian life were to appear in their proper development. The nine texts which now follow are governed to a marked extent by the thought that we belong together. The Christian life has important features which rest on our mutual relation to each other, on our union with each other, and these are now to be brought forward. Some of them reach to lofty heights, while others, especially those which deal with duties, are exceedingly practical in their bearing. The first of these texts has to do with *our earthly calling*, its quiet, orderly pursuit and its practical purpose. God's people are to be found doing their daily work, earning their own bread, shunning all disorderly conduct and refusing to tolerate it on the part of any one in their midst. — Paul comes to insist on these things because of the disorders which had crept into the church at Thessalonica shortly after he had gone on from there to Greece. Immediately on receiving the first report he wrote his First Epistle to the Thessalonians, and when the instruction and admonition thus given did not accomplish its purpose in all his readers, he followed it up with a Second Epistle, telling at length what developments must intervene before the Lord's return to judgment, 2 Thess. 2, and using sharper words and a more imperative tone in his admonition against all disorderly procedure.

Thessalonica, formerly Therma, and now Saloniki, has always been a famous place. Paul rightly gauged its im-

portance when he founded a church there, for he writes of
the effect 1 Thess. 1, 8: "From you hath sounded forth
the word of the Lord, not only in Macedonia and Achaia,
but in every place your faith to God-ward is gone forth."
A look at the map explains this importance. The city was
given its biblical name from the sister of Alexander the
Great. Cicero was an exile here. Anthony and Octavius
were here after the decisive battle at Philippi, granting the
city "freedom," as the coins struck at that time still attest.
Here was the virtual capital of Theodosius the Great, and
from here he sent out the decree abolishing the ancient
paganism. Thessalonica served as a bulwark against the
Goths, and then as the last stronghold against the Turks.
And it has continued as a place of great prominence in the
Levant down to the recent war in which Turkey lost most
of its European territory by the victory of the Bulgarians,
Greeks, and other allies. Just what caused the disorderly
conduct of some of the first Christians in this famous city
we are unable to say. It seems that they thoroughly misin-
terpreted the apostle's words and looked for Christ's immediate return. Some stopped their daily work altogether;
when death called away one and the other from their midst,
they feared that these would not share in the coming kingdom and glory, 1 Thess. 4, 13 *etc.;* false reports concerning
letters of Paul supporting such views were circulated, 2
Thess. 2, 2. Paul treats the whole trouble in a very efficient and masterly way. In our text he takes up the practical question of orderly conduct and quiet labor in our
Christian calling. He is confident that the Thessalonians
will do what he commands and prays that the Lord will
direct their hearts, verses 4 and 5. So we have, first of all:

The command to the congregation as a whole.

Paul takes it that the entire congregation is concerned in this matter. He therefore gives his command
to all: **Now we command you, brethren, in the name
of our Lord Jesus Christ, that ye withdraw yourselves
for every brother that walketh disorderly, and not**

after the tradition which they received of us. — In his
first letter the apostle had used the term "exhort,"
παρακαλοῦμεν, "We *exhort* you, brethren, . . . that ye
study to be quiet, and to do you your own business, and to
work with your hands," *etc.* 1 Thess. 4, 11-12. "And we
exhort you, brethren, admonish the disorderly, encourage
the fainthearted, support the weak, be longsuffering toward all." But already in the first of these exhortations
the apostle refers to his teaching when he was still with
them as a charge or command: "even as we charged you,"
παρηγγείλαμεν, 1 Thess. 4, 12. He now uses this word with
its fullest emphasis: **we command you,** παραγγέλλομεν. The
word is used of the issuing of military orders in the classics,
yet it is not as strong as κελεύειν; it may mean also to admonish, but the entire context here shows that Paul is
speaking with the tone of apostolic authority. There are
times when nothing less suffices; compare 1 Cor. 5, 4. The
address: **brethren,** however, indicates that this authority
is one of love. Paul is not arrogating to himself the lordship of an earthly ruler or master; he is a brother among
brethren, and under authority as well as they. The command then which he lays upon his brethren, and not he
alone, but his assistants with him (Silas, Timothy, Luke),
has a higher source; it comes **in the name of our Lord
Jesus Christ,** as if signed by his name, as the expression of
his will. Obedience to this command, then, is obedience to
Christ the Lord himself. It is well and good for Christian
ministers and others to appeal to the Lord's authority, and
to use his mighty name in doing so, when the doctrine and
the conduct they insist on are truly the Lord's will and
Word; but to use his name to enforce what he has not said,
what perhaps he has actually forbidden and condemned, is
to commit one of the most terrible and damaging sins. —
When the apostle commands **that ye withdraw yourselves
from every brother that walketh disorderly, etc.,** we
must not overlook what he has written previously in regard to admonishing such brethren, 1 Thess. 5, 14; nor
must we fail to note his own admonitions, 1 Thess. 4, 11

etc., our text verses 11-12, and the two letters in general. Only when such admonition proves in vain, when in spite of it a brother walks disorderly *etc.,* are we to withdraw ourselves from him. Paul chooses his words very carefully; he does not say that the Thessalonians are forthwith to expel a brother walking disorderly, he uses a negative term: στέλλεσθαι ὑμᾶς ἀπό, **withdraw yourselves from,** "stand away from." What he means he explains in verses 14-15: have no company with him, continue admonition, yet show him by standing aloof from him that the matter is so serious, that if he persists in his evil conduct, complete separation and expulsion must result. In other words, discipline is to be begun, with the motive if possible to win the brother: "to the end that he may be ashamed." This withdrawing and refusal to have company with him naturally includes that he be excluded from the Lord's table, because these Christians have the fullest, highest, and holiest company with each other and the Lord. — And this the congregation is to do in the case of **every brother that walketh disorderly,** ἀτάκτως, not in line with his brethren. The word is used of soldiers who forsake the ranks, of citizens who do not obey the civic ordinances, and then in general of men who are disorderly. In this case the order or regulation is specified: **not after the tradition which they receive of us;** the Gospel doctrine and requirements are meant which the apostle and his assistants handed down to their pupils from the Lord, both by their oral teaching while in Thessalonica, and by the instructions in Paul's two letters, compare 1 Thess. 4, 11-12. Some authorities read: *which ye received;* the preferable reading is παρελάβοσαν, a plain *constructio ad sensum,* the plural for the collective idea in "every brother, and the ending -οσαν as in the Septuagint, Papyri, and modern Greek, Robertson, 60; comp. Blass 21, 4. There is no idea here of an unwritten "tradition" after the manner of Rome; rather the fixed and established form of instruction which the apostles adhered to in all their work, and which they fully recorded in their writings. To deviate from this "tradition" was to

err from the path of truth and right, and to invite all sorts
of dangerous consequences.

The appeal to Paul's personal example.

Verba docent, exempla trahunt. Paul depended for
his temporal support on the labor of his own hands. He
thus meant to cut off any slander as if he preached the
Gospel only to enrich himself at the expense of his
followers. But here he finds his practice serviceable in
another direction: **For yourselves know how ye ought
to imitate us: for we behaved not ourselves disorderly
among you; neither did we eat bread for nought at any
man's hand, but in labor and travail, working night and
day, that we might not burden any of you: not because
we have not the right, but to make ourselves an ensample
unto you, that ye should imitate us.** — The idea in γάρ
is not to establish the "tradition" of which Paul has just
spoken, by showing that he himself observed it, but rather
to substantiate his "command" by his own example, and to
make the Thessalonians more ready to heed his words and
thus to justify the apostle's confidence in them. **Yourselves
know how ye ought to imitate us** means that Paul really
should not have to remind them. His conduct while in
their midst was still fresh in their memory, and this was
throughout a careful observance of proper Christian order, intended as an easy example for the apostle's followers. The value of example cannot be estimated too
highly. Every pastor especially has reason to ask constantly whether his conduct is such that he can ask of his
people that they "ought to imitate" him. The force of all
our preaching is lost, if by our conduct we give it the lie. —
None of those who "walked disorderly" at Thessalonica
could justify himself by pointing to Paul or his assistants:
for we behaved not ourselves disorderly among you;
ἀτακτεῖν only here in the N. T., the aorist speaks of Paul's
conduct as a definite fact in the past. — With this general
statement is paired a more particular one: **neither did we
eat bread for nought at any man's hand,** *i. e.* get our

support, our food and drink, from some one else, without earning it with our own labor. Paul and his helpers did not accept the invitation of any of their converts to lodge with them and share their table δωρεάν, "as a gift," an accusative used adverbially, "gratis." Instead of this they ate their bread **in labor and travail, working night and day, that we might not burden any of you.** The word κόπος, from κόπτω, signifies "a striking," "a beating," and is used for toil, weariness, and the like; the synonym μόχθος, from μοχθέω, to be weary and wornout with toil, signifies "hardship," "distress." The two words together give us a vivid picture of how Paul and his companions ate their bread. Their twofold task of preaching the Gospel, often amid hostile people, and suffering all kinds of persecution, and working with their hands at their ordinary trade to earn their support, left them tired and worn out. Those disorderly brethren, who stopped working and went about as busybodies, certainly had a much easier time of it. **Working night and day** likewise refers to this twofold occupation, and "night" is mentioned first because the day was counted as beginning with the setting of the sun. When others rested these men worked, either preaching and teaching, or plying the weaver's art in making tent-cloth or carpets and rugs. It goes without saying that Silas and Timothy followed Paul's example while traveling with him, and worked as he did. It makes little difference whether we take "in labor and travail" by themselves, as modifying the main verb and contrasted with the preceding "for nought," or draw the phrase to the following participle: "working in labor and travail;" the former seems more natural. — This the apostles did: **that we might not burden any of you;** their consideration was for others, not for themselves. And yet Paul does not want to be misunderstood in this proceeding on his part. No one has a right to demand that the preachers of the Gospel shall receive no support from those whom they serve. Paul therefore adds: **not because we have not**

14

the right, namely to eat bread given us by others. He treats this question at length in 1 Cor. 9, 1-18, where he explicitly says: "Nevertheless we did not use this right; but we bear all things, that we may cause no hindrance to the gospel of Christ," verse 12; and again: "so as not to use to the full my right in the gospel," verse 18. The "right" thus referred to is also plainly defined: "Even so did the Lord ordain, that they which proclaim the gospel should live by the gospel," verse 14, and the reference is to Luke 10, 7-8. Paul then wants the Thessalonians to understand clearly, that in not making use of his "right" he by no means annulled or abrogated that right, nor did he want it to be lost sight of among believers. — He continues: **but** (we did eat bread in labor and travail *etc.*) **to make ourselves an ensample unto you, that ye should imitate us,** in earning your own bread and not eating that of others. The reflexive ἑαυτούς, used regularly of the third person, is also employed for the first (as here) and the second where there is no danger of misunderstanding. Winer, 22, 5. When Paul assigns different reasons for providing his own livelihood, these all belong together, the one growing out of the other, and thus in no way contradictory. Thus his desire to burden no one hangs closely together with his determination to give no one an opportunity to say that he made merchandise of the Gospel; and in burdening no one, but rather working hard himself in order to help others, he certainly also was an **ensample** for others to imitate in their respective callings, τύπος, a form, pattern, or type, like ὑποτύπωσις in 1 Tim. 1, 16 in the previous text. **To imitate** is not necessarily to copy, but to be like in a general way. The Thessalonians were not all apostles and teachers, and yet all could and should imitate their first great teachers in diligently working at their calling and earning their own bread, instead of living disorderly and being a burden to their fellow Christians. — **For,** the apostle adds, bringing the matter to a point, **even when we were with you** (as you yourselves know, verse 7), **this we commanded you, If any will not**

work, neither let him eat. Some of the old Jewish proverbs said as much, and the principle itself goes back to Gen. 3, 19: "In the sweat of thy face shalt thou eat bread." Compare the strong condemnation of slothfulness in Prov. 6, 6 *etc.;* 21, 25; 24, 30-34; also the injunction Eph. 4, 28; and the statement on providing for one's own 1 Tim. 5, 8. The dignity of labor is higher in the Gospel than anywhere else; for not only is it God's will that we should work, but he enables us to do even the work of our earthly calling in his name, in the spirit of Christ, and for his glory. The imperative μηδὲ ἐσθιέτω is very positive and strong; he who sets himself against God's order and follows his own perverse will (οὐ θέλει): let him find no pity, let the painful consequences by their castigation teach him to change his course. Evidently Paul was opposed to the Thessalonians feeding the drones in their midst. There are many applications of this old principle in our own day. By ἐργάζεσθαι the honorable work of any Christian calling is meant; it may be very humble, but God's blessing rests upon it.

The command and exhortation to the erring.

With the heart of a true pastor Paul turns to these especially. **For we hear of some that walk among you disorderly, that work not at all, but are busybodies. Now them that are such we command and exhort in the Lord Jesus Christ, that with quietness they work, and eat their own bread. But ye, brethren, be not weary in well-doing.** — Paul had received a report of the situation in Thessalonica from the bearer of his first letter; he was not going on mere hearsay. **For** justifies what he has just said in the previous sentence: there were actually such in Thessalonica to whom his words applied. Their disorderly conduct consisted in not working at all, and, since man must have something to occupy him, in being busybodies. There is a fine paronomasia in ἐργαζομένους and περιεργαζομένους: not busy with legitimate work, but busy with other people's affairs. There was a sin of omission and one of commission, and these two frequently go together. "To be a busybody" is to be taken up with things that are none of our business, and in the case of those at Thessalonica the term means to say that they went about and agitated themselves in a fanatical and extravagant way about Christ's second coming. They were busy disturbing other men's minds and interfering with labor. — Paul directs his command in the Lord Jesus Christ to them especially; but he adds his pastoral exhortation in the same holy name. He combines firmness with gentleness, authority with love. Some pastors lack the former, some the latter; we must have both, for both are founded on our Lord, true products of his Word and manifestations of his spirit. — Paul insists **that with quietness they work, and eat their own bread;** abandoning their idle talk and running about, with a quiet mind and quiet manner they are to follow their regular avocations and earn their own livelihood. This has always been the Christian's ideal and desire; hence he prays for the government, "that we may lead a tranquil and quiet life in all godliness and gravity," 1 Tim. 2, 2; he opposes sinful disturbances of all kinds, and especially also in his own mind he cultivates the spirit of trust and obedience toward his Lord, which gives him the "quietness" that brings happiness in his "work," and the blessing of God in "bread" and prosperity. "The Lord our God hates the slothful. For no one of those who are dedicated to God ought to be idle," *Apostolic Constitutions,* 2, 63. — The final word of our text is directed to the **brethren** who have been true to Paul's teaching. The evil example of "some" is not to disturb them: **be not weary in well-doing** encourages them to go on in their quiet and orderly conduct in attending to the proper duties of their calling. The context points strongly to this specific meaning of καλοποιεῖν, which otherwise often means to do good unto others in works of charity and kindness. The verb ἐκκακεῖν means to be or become altogether bad and cowardly (κακός), hence: to grow fainthearted, to lose courage. Whatever disturbances arise round about us, whatever foolish thoughts others may follow, however hard and tiresome, lowly and humble our tasks may be, Paul bids us go on and not lose heart. The Lord's approval is ours, and that with his blessing should satisfy us completely.

HOMILETICAL HINTS.

What a mistake to forget heaven because of our earthly interests! But what a mistake likewise to think of reaching heaven without the faithfulness and obedience of our round of daily duties. — Like every Jewish scribe and rabbi Paul had learned a trade, and when he served Christ as an apostle he made the best use of his trade: not only did he earn his daily bread and have to give to the needy, he protected his work from slanderous accusations, and he gave his hearers and us all a fine example of faithfulness in our daily vocations.

Our epistle matches well with the old gospel lesson. The one bids us trust completely to our heavenly Father's care, the other bids us do our daily duty with all faithfulness. Likewise our epistle matches the old epistle, both following several similar lines. We are to restore the brother overtaken by a fault, and therefore we are to look well first to ourselves. "And let us not be weary in well-doing: for in due season we shall reap, if we faint not."

A Pharisee asks: What is forbidden; what is allowed? A Christian asks: How may I best serve my Savior, my brethren and fellow men, and myself? — If love is not false, it must cast off what is evil; and only so will it foster and encourage what is good. What a blessing are strict parents and teachers! We remember them gratefully years after they are in their graves. And those that were lax, we feel that they cared little for us, and if they did not harm us too much, we are ready to forget them.

Who can count the evils that grow out of idleness and love of a soft life? It has filled our prisons and almshouses; it has started many a young man and woman on a path of vice and wickedness; it has filled many a drunkard's grave and wrecked the prosperity and happiness of many a family; it has given us the idle rich, a menace to society and an object of envy and jealous hate to those whose work is not sweetened by the grace of God. All this idleness has done, besides filling many a weak brain with perverted religious thoughts, dangerous speculations, and detrimental dreams.

In Paradise God appointed man to dress the garden and keep it, that meant to work. Sin cursed work by adding to it bitterness and pain of a thousand kinds. Separated from God man treats work as a necessary evil, degrades it by selfish interests, perverts it by sinful aims, and in all that he does work loses the comfort and cheer of God's help and the blessing that turns work into a service of God with a heavenly reward in this life and in that to come. Besides this, sin produces those tyrants who make slaves of their fellows and in robbing them of the just reward of their labors here heap unto themselves the tortures of hell hereafter.

The Christian ideal is: "That with quietness we work, and eat our own bread." That means some honorable occupation, under God's providential care and blessing, in which we can serve him, aid our fellow men, provide for our own, help build the kingdom of God, keep bright our hope of heaven, and finally fold our hands in eternal peace and rest.

How do you do Your Daily Work?

   I. *In the name of God?*
   II. *With the help of God?*
  III. *Under the blessing of God?*
  IV. *For the glory of God?*

The Gospel Answer to the Labor Question.

   I. *Combine labor with Christian faith.*
  II. *Dignify labor with Christian obedience.*
  III. *Ennoble labor with Christian love.*
  IV. *Crown labor with Christian hope.*

Go To Work!

   I. *For God's sake.*
  II. *For others' sake.*
  III. *For your own sake.*

In the Tent-Maker's Shop.

We see
   I. *A man who eats his own bread.*
  II. *A man whose chief interest is the bread of life.*

The Christian Church the True Home of the Laboring Man.

Here he finds:
   I. *The truest help.*
  II. *The greatest uplift.*
  III. *The noblest example.*
  IV. *The best blessing in his labor.*

If any Will not Work, Neither let Him eat.

I. *Sound economics.*
II. *Sound philanthropy.*
III. *Sound religion.*

THE SIXTEENTH SUNDAY AFTER TRINITY.

Heb. 12, 18-24.

There is a mighty contrast between this and the fore-going text. Alongside of our earthly calling are now placed *our heavenly blessings.* Our feet stand on the earth, amid its labors and toils, but our heart rises to heaven and glories in heavenly riches. In this we are far advanced even above the people of God in the times of the old covenant; indeed we are on the highest plane beyond which no future earthly age can lift the church. The writer of Hebrews has a prac-tical purpose in introducing this impressive description of our heavenly blessings; he wants us to heed the more readily and willingly the admonitions he has been urging upon us, namely to bear as children the chastening of the Lord and not to fall short of the grace of God, verses 13 and 15, which, all he sums up once more at the end in verse 28: "Let us have grace whereby we may offer service well-pleasing to God with reverence and awe." But these practical consid-erations are not included in our text, which is satisfied with the one great purpose to have us realize once for all the heavenly wealth of our possessions in Christ Jesus. One thing, however, we must note well, the thought that all these blessings are for us as the people of God, as the church of Christ, as many members all bound together in one. While each individual has and enjoys these blessings in his own soul and life, yet he does so as the member of one great body, for whom as such these blessings exist. The whole text is one grand period, carefully and symmetrically built up, with first a negative and secondly a positive description.

The negative description.

This deals with the chief characteristics of the old covenant, grand and impressive indeed, but bearing

216

throughout the stamp of the law, and thus terrifying to
God's people of old. Yet the old covenant with all that
established it was a blessing to Israel, lifting that nation
far above all the surrounding Gentiles. But what then
shall we say of the new covenant and its still grander
and more impressive features, all of which shine with the
glory of God's grace and thus attract and satisfy our
souls? **For ye are not come unto** *a mount* **that might be
touched and that burned with fire, and unto blackness,
and darkness, and tempest, and the sound of a trumpet,
and the voice of words; which** *voice* **they that heard intreated that no word more should be spoken unto them:
for they could not endure that which was enjoined, If
even a beast touch the mountain, it shall be stoned; and
so fearful was the appearance,** *that* **Moses said, I exceedingly fear and quake.** — The writer of Hebrews
refers to the time when his readers became Christians, and
the perfect tense: οὐ προσεληλύθατε, implies that as they have
not come unto a mount *etc.*, they are now not there. While
the best texts omit ὄρει, commentators generally incline to
think that this is due to an early oversight in copying
(Delitzsch, Riggenbach, *etc.*), since the word is made necessary by the parallel in verse 22, and by the O. T. passage
to which reference is here had, Deut. 4, 11 *etc.* Mount
Sinai is meant, and the allusion is to Israel of old of whom
Moses wrote: "And ye came near and stood under the
mountain." If ὄρει is not restored, it is by far best to take
ψηλαφωμένῳ by itself: "something that is touched," and not
to combine it with πυρί as the margin suggests: *a palpable
and kindled fire,* since we know of no fire that can be
touched without burning. The Greek commentators and the
oldest translators into other languages all take the word by
itself. The absence of the article is important, and this for
all the nouns in this and the next verse. God's people of the
new covenant are not come to any mountain like that of
Sinai, physical, touched by men's feet or hands; the mountain we have come to is of an altogether different and higher
kind. — Instead of the translation of both English versions:

and that burned with fire, which is possible if ὄρει is part
of the text, it is far better to make this a separate member in
the sentence: "and to a fire that has been kindled." The
writer is not repeating the descriptions of the mountain in
Deut. 4, 11; 5, 23; 9, 15, but is listing those features of the
old covenant which the new has left far behind. So we are
not come to a physical, tangible mountain, nor to a fire that
something has actually kindled, like earthly fire in general.—
And unto blackness (Ex. 19, 16-18), or "a cloud-gloom,"
"a wrack of clouds;" **and darkness** (Deut. 4, 11), such
as surrounded the lower part of Sinai, while its top
burned with fire; **and tempest,** or a storm of the worst
kind, like a hurricane or whirlwind (θύελλα from θύειν, to
rush along); **and the sound of a trumpet** (Ex. 19, 16),
a reminder of the last trumpet which will call men to
final judgment according to the divine law; **and the voice
of words,** God's own voice by which he spoke to Israel
the Ten Commandments, Ex. 20, 1. To none of these
have we N. T. believers come. — As regards the voice a
relative clause is added to describe its terribleness:
which (voice) **they that heard intreated that no word
more should be spoken unto them** (Ex. 20, 19; Deut.
5, 25; 18, 16). Here παραιτέομαι is "to ward off by entreaty," and is properly followed by μή, which a few texts
omit; see Blass, 75, 4; and προστεθῆναι, passive aorist from
προστίθημι is used in the sense of "add." The Israelites
begged and implored that no word should be added unto
them (αὐτοῖς referring to ἀκούσαντες and not to ῥημάτων),
beyond the ones they had already heard. — The reason for
this earnest petition is stated: **for they could not endure
that which was enjoined, If even a beast touch the
mountain, it shall be stoned** (Ex. 19, 12-13). The verb
θιγγάνειν is here used, as often in the classics, of touching
or handling a sacred object which may be desecrated or
profaned. The great severity of all the words spoken to
them from the mount is illustrated by this one which
impressed the Israelites especially. "The ordinance that
even a beast approaching the mount was to be stoned, as

guilty of an act of sacrilege, made the whole prohibition which was principally aimed at human presumption, the more terrible, and therefore the only point mentioned here." Delitzsch. "Or thrust through with a dart" (A. V.) must be omitted as, without authority at all. — But even Moses himself, who mediated between God and the people, was overcome with terror: **and so fearful was the appearance,** namely all that has just been described as taking place on the mount, *that* **Moses said, I exceedingly fear and quake.** There is no account to this effect in the Pentateuch itself. Some have thought that the author of Hebrews drew his information from tradition, and Riggenbach states that this is quite possible. Others refer to Deut. 9, 19, where Moses says, when he saw the people sinning in worshiping the golden calf: "For I was afraid of the anger and hot displeasure, wherewith the Lord was wroth against you to destroy you." They think that the writer of Hebrews applied this statement, made by Moses when he saw the first terrible transgression of the law, to his feelings at the time when the power and majesty of God manifested itself so mightily in first giving the law. But it is best not to make ingenious combinations which leave the impression on some minds (Meyer for instance) as if the truth of the matter is that the holy writer had a lapse of memory. As regards the construction, καί must be connected with Μωνσῆς εἶπεν, the remainder forming an explanatory clause by itself: "and, so fearful was the appearance, Moses said" *etc.* Even he was a man and a sinner, and in "the appearance" which he beheld there was nothing either to fortify his heart against fear and terror, or to lessen the impact and force of it upon his heart. — Let us note before going on: Israel indeed had come to great things as compared with the Gentiles, to Israel God had revealed himself in a glorious and mighty manner. The center of that revelation was Sinai, when the covenant of the law was established. The greatness of what took place on the mount is vividly and strikingly portrayed in a few cardinal

words. And yet this was an outward revelation, marked
by natural manifestations and physical effects; it was for
the eye and the ear of those that stood by, and for their
children after them the story of these manifestations and
events. Moreover, this was ·a revelation which filled the
hearts of Israel with fear, it was the drawing nigh of
the omnipotent and holy God to a people who could not
fully approach him because of their sins. They had not
yet the full atonement and propitiation of Christ; or rather
they had it only in symbol and promise. Great, wonderful, and blessed, as this revelation certainly was, considered in its full bearing and connection, it was not and
could not be final. Still greater and far more blessed
things were to come.

The positive description.

Between the negative and the positive there is a
contrast, and yet the contrast is only one feature; the
other that must be taken together with it and as giving
it the right setting and bringing out the full significance,
is the parallel. We have both the opposite of what
Israel had and the counterpart of it, yea, the complement. And this is what makes our blessings so un-
speakably great. **But ye are come unto mount Zion, and
unto the city of the living God, the heavenly Jerusalem,
and to innumerable hosts of angels, to the general assembly and church of the firstborn who are enrolled in
heaven, and to God the Judge of all, and to the spirits
of just men made perfect, and to Jesus the mediator of
a new covenant, and to the blood of sprinkling that
speaketh better than** *that of* **Abel.** — Delitzsch adopts
Bengel's discovery that here we have seven "heavenlies"
(ἐπουράνια), to which seven "earthlies" (ἐπίγεια) on the part
of Israel at Sinai correspond, and while dropping some of
the latter's fanciful grouping he feels sure that at least the
first and the last two pairs of these sevens match each other
exactly. Riggenbach calls this fanciful, although he leaves
the fact of there being two sets of seven unaccounted for,

and himself emphasizes the parallel between the two mountains, Sinai and Zion. The verb **ye are come** is emphatically repeated. In coming to Christ we have come, and now
are, in the presence of the heavenly blessings here enumerated, enjoying their unspeakable richness. More compre-
hensively still, this is true of the entire N. T. church since
the days of its founding, to continue till the end of time,
just as the blessings of Israel continued for the entire church
of the O. T. from the establishment of the covenant at Sinai
on till its abrogation by the new covenant in Christ. — The
first of these blessings is **mount Zion;** the καί following introduces the second blessing, which it is a mistake to confuse with the first. There is a clear distinction between
mount Zion on the one hand, and "the city of the living
God," also called "the heavenly Jerusalem," on the other.
In Israel Zion was the mountain or height on which the
temple stood, the dwelling-place of God among his people;
Jerusalem was the city round about Zion. When not distinguishing between the two, Jerusalem, of course, included
the sanctuary of Zion which gave it its special sanctity, and
Zion itself could be taken in a broader sense to embrace
also the city which it sanctified. But here the writer of
Hebrews distinguishes the two and uses them as designations for still higher and holier places. We Christian believers have come to the "mount Zion" which bears the
heavenly sanctuary, where God dwells eternally in invisible
and unapproachable glory, and into which Christ, our High
Priest, entered, making complete atonement for our sins.
Heb. 9, 12 and 24. We may add too that this "mount Zion"
is the seat of Christ's eternal throne, where by his session
at God's right hand, and by his rule in infinite power and
majesty over all creatures, he fulfills the prophesied eternity
of David's throne. Is. 9, 6; Luke 1, 32. Delitzsch rightly
observes that this "mount" has no fixed sensible locality. It
is like "heaven" itself, exalted above our ordinary conceptions of space, and yet more real than any earthly place or
locality can possibly be. To this "mount Zion" we have
come, not physically, as Israel once came to Sinai and to

the sanctuary in Jerusalem, but spiritually, and thus really
and truly, by faith, and the blessing of God's presence, of
his divine grace and government in Christ Jesus are ever
ours. — **And unto the city of the living God, the heavenly
Jerusalem,** views this as situated around the heavenly
mount. As a **city** it has inhabitants, and these are mentioned presently; it is the eternal·abode and home of God's
people. The builder and owner of this wonderful city is
the living God, lifting this city infinitely above all those
founded by mortal men; it is an eternal city, where no sin,
death, or any evil ever enters to work decay or destruction.
In the earthly Jerusalem the communion of God with his
people was only imperfectly realized; in this heavenly city
all that was prefigured and begun here below shall reach
its fullest and most enduring perfection. The other name:
the heavenly Jerusalem, brings out that this is the true and
enduring City of Peace, where the Prince of Peace reigns
over his own in eternal blessedness. This "Jerusalem which
is above" is "the mother of us all," we aré her true children,
she is our real home, Gal. 4, 26. It is the home of those
that "desire a better country, that is, a heavenly;" nor is
"God ashamed of them, to be called their God: for he hath
prepared for them a city," Heb. 11, 16. Upon those that
overcome, Jesus says, that he will write "the name of the
city of my God, which is new Jerusalem, which cometh
down out of heaven from my God," Rev. 3, 12. We are
come thus by faith to this blessed city; her portals are open
to us, our place within has been prepared (John 14, 3), and
presently our feet shall stand within her gates. — Next to
the city her inhabitants are mentioned: **and to innumerable
hosts of angels, to the general assembly and church of
the firstborn who are enrolled in heaven.** It is possible
to read these words in a variety of ways according to which
of them we group together; but it is certain that καί separates the two classes mentioned, and that πανηγύρει refers
to angels and not to the firstborn whose names are recorded
in heaven. The best grouping is that offered in the margin:
and to innumerable hosts, the general assembly of angels,

and the church of the firstborn etc. That μυριάσιν may thus
stand alone is attested by numerous examples from the
Septuagint (Vincent). It is a plural form, and also in significance it forms no true counterpart to the two singulars
πανηγύρει and ἐκκλησίᾳ. A myriad is ten thousand, and
this plural stands for an uncounted host; so great
are the inhabitants of the heavenly city. First among
them are the angels: *the general assembly of the angels.*
The word stands for "a festive assembly," a general public
gathering as for the celebration of some solemnity, some
great festive occasion. Delitzsch finely remarks: "The
angelic life in the divine presence is a never-ceasing festival;
the angelic choirs are represented in Scripture as perpetually
engaged in antiphonal songs of praise, or in movements
of a sacred dance to heavenly music." "On Sinai the hosts
of angels through whose ministration the law was given,
Heb. 2, 2; Gal. 3, 19, officiated at a scene of terror. Christian believers are now introduced to a *festal* host, surrounding the exalted Son of man, who has purged away
sins, and is enthroned at God's right hand." Vincent. —
By *the church of the firstborn* we cannot understand the
church triumphant, for this is mentioned later in "the
spirits of just men made perfect," and the modifier "whose
names are enrolled in heaven" plainly points to such as
have a right to enter heaven, but have not yet actually
entered it. Still less does "church of the firstborn" mean a
distinguished class of saints, such as the patriarchs
(Bengel), contrasted with other saints born after them.
The ἐκκλησία, or assembly or body, of the firstborn are all
those who share sonship and heirship with Christ, who is
"the firstborn of all creation," "the firstborn from the
dead." The entire church on earth is meant. The firstborn in Israel were consecrated to God, Ex. 13, 2; Luke
2, 23; Israel as a people was called the Lord's "firstborn,"
Ex. 4, 22; there also seems to be an implied reference in
the term to Esau, verse 16, who sold his birthright
(πρωτοτοκία) and thus forfeited the privilege of the firstborn. The Christian church is called "the assembly of the

firstborn, because its members are truly consecrated to God by the Spirit; because not only as a nation, but also as individuals they are sons and heirs of God; and because they all keep their birthright, esteeming it their most precious possession. While not yet partakers of the festive assembly of the angels their names **are enrolled in heaven,** Luke 10, 20. The expression is very likely taken from the genealogical records kept by the Jews. To be so enrolled is to be justified by God, to be adopted as his child, to have a place in heaven assured. Compare the more elaborate explanation in the *Eisenach Gospel Selections,* I, 398-400. The angels are already in heaven, our names are there. Again by faith have we come to these blessed myriads of angels and children of God. They belong together, and faith connects us with them; now these angels as ministering spirits serve those who shall be heirs of salvation, and presently they will welcome and help receive us as we take our mansions in the skies. — **And,** we are come, **to God the Judge of all,** or, as the order of the words demands: "to a Judge the God of all." This designation may surprise us, as we are liable to think of the sternness of the Judge and the sentence he must pronounce upon the wicked. This is a thought that evidently does not agree with the line of thought here pursued. But there is no mention of the wicked here at all; the thought progresses from those who are recorded in heaven to him whose act in justifying them and pronouncing them free from guilt made it possible to enter their names on the heavenly records. This is the Judge who justifies the righteous. "We make a mistake," writes Schlatter, "when we try to highten the attractiveness and sweetness of the Gospel by hiding from our sight the judicial majesty of God. Look at it, and see how great it makes grace! The great polity in which we have citizenship, is governed throughout by righteousness." Grace is so great because it assures us of joy before the great Judge who is none less than the God of all. Already in the O. T. God is spoken of as "a judge of the widows," Ps. 68, 5, who safeguards their case against the oppressor; "the Lord executeth righteousness and judgment for all that are oppressed," Ps. 103, 6. We constantly hear those who are wronged cry to him and appeal to his judgment. Cremer shows how this is the fundamental idea in the word δίκη and its various derivatives in the Scriptures. This just Judge, who has already justified us in Christ Jesus, whom we will meet with joy on the last great judgment day, is **the God of all,** the supreme judge, above and beyond whom there is no other, and his judgment and acceptance of us in Christ Jesus therefore stands for all and can and will be changed by none. It is a mistake to make "all" here mean only the children of God (Kuebel, Vincent), or to restrict it to all who desire and accept his help (Riggenbach); it is unlimited in its sweep and shows the greatness of God and the universal final authority of his gracious judgment upon those who are in Christ Jesus. — Next are named **the spirits of just men made perfect,** whom Delitzsch calls "the chief witnesses to and partakers of the comfort derived from communion with the righteous Judge." They have received their gracious sentence in death, the prelude to that final public sentence at the end of the world, for they are **spirits,** their bodies slumber in the grave. The word **just men** is entirely general and refers to all, whether of the old or new covenant, who are just in the sight of God. They are further described as τετελειωμένοι, **made perfect,** "who have been brought to completion or perfection," namely by the grace and mercy of God. This does not refer specifically to their ethical perfection, that now they are altogether holy and above sin and temptation, but in general to their having reached the goal which is set for all of us. Their battle is fought, they are glorious victors; their course is run, the crown of righteousness is theirs. We have come unto these spirits, the noble church triumphant; faith has brought us to them, they are our brethren. We are not yet actually in their midst, but we are on the same road, they at the goal, we hastening toward it. — "As the thought of the militant and

15

suffering church on earth led to that of the Judge, the God
of all, by whom their wrongs would be one day avenged,
so that of the spirits of the just made perfect in heaven
to the thought of him to whose redeeming saving work they
owed their perfecting." Delitzsch. **And to Jesus the
mediator of a new covenant** puts the very greatest of our
N. T. blessings before us.   The writer to the Hebrews
loves the name **Jesus,** Savior, and here he views him with
all his mediatorial work complete and all the fruit of it
fully available for us.   The old Israelites only had the
promise of a Messiah; we have that Messiah himself and
his name is Jesus.   For **covenant** the margin has *testament,*
and exegetes have disputed considerably on the exact meaning of διαθήκη in the Septuagint and in the books of the
New Testament.*   The verb διατίθημι means to make a disposition or arrangement, and the noun διαθήκη is thus in
general a disposition, arrangement; just what the nature
of it is in any given case the context must show.   So here
the reference to Christ's blood immediately following suggests the explanation which precedes in chapter 9, 15 *etc.,*
where the rendering "testament" seems necessary.   And
yet the general significance of the word suffices: God
made a new disposition or arrangement, one mediated by
Christ, especially by his atoning death, whence he is called
the mediator of the new διαθήκη.   In this new disposition
there was provided the full cancellation of our sins, a free
access to God for sinners by faith in Jesus, Heb. 10, 19-20.
This is **new,** different from the old arrangement which
God had fixed for the times preceding.   Here and only
here the word νέα (*recens*), is used instead of the usual
καινή (*novus*), but the distinction can hardly be pressed,
since in later Greek, as the papyri show, the words were
used interchangeably.   We have come to this blessed Mediator; trusting in him, all the blessings he has secured by
his work are ours. — And in this the chief and essential
thing is that we have come **to the blood of sprinkling that
speaketh better than** *that of* **Abel.** Abel's blood, shed by

*See Behm: *Der Begriff* διαθήκη *in Neuen Test.*

wicked Cain in wilful murder, that is Abel through his blood, cried to God for vengeance (Gen. 4, 10) ; there is no hint anywhere in Scripture that it cried for pardon (Seeberg). Christ's blood cries for grace and pardon. But if God heard the voice of Abel's blood in his righteousness and punished Abel's murderer, he hears far more the voice of the blood of his own Son crying for pardon in behalf of all who believe. The reading κρείττονα, *better things,* A. V., is ill-supported. Whether we take κρεῖττον as an adverb or adjective makes little difference in the sense, since both the contents of the cry of Christ's blood and its effect exceeds that of Abel. He was merely a righteous man whose wrong God did not forget, while Christ as God's own Son with his divine blood entered into the holy place and obtained eternal redemption for us, Heb. 9, 12. It is the blood **of sprinkling** because, like the blood of sacrifice which accompanied the old διαθήκη, Heb. 9, 19, it is applied to all those who are to share in its blessed effects. This is done through faith, "purging our conscience from dead works to serve the living God," Heb. 9, 14; 10, 22; remitting our sins, 9, 22. The reading: "than Abel" is better than the one in the English versions: "than that of Abel," which appears to be an effort at correction. Over against the voice of the law on Sinai, verse 19, we have now the blessed voice of Christ's blood. That voice could speak only of condemnation upon sinners, but this speaks of pardon and peace. And to this we have come indeed, and come ever anew, in repentance and faith, for only by the blood of Jesus do we hope to be eternally saved.

HOMILETICAL HINTS.

Not how little the Jews had, but how much is shown in this text; and when all their special treasures, blessings, honors, and prerogatives are brought together, then our heavenly treasures are placed by their side, exceeding them all in glory, power, duration, and especially in saving effect. — The Japanese convert Kanso

Utschimura warns us likewise, not to picture paganism as altogether debased, miserable, wretched, and poor; it has many lofty things of which it is proud. But take all that it has, its very best jewels, all of them together are as nothing beside the heavenly treasures of our Christian faith. Ours is a diamond of such luster that all the bits of shining glass, which others think sparkle so grandly in the sun, are utterly lost and outdone beside it.

What a difference between Moses, the mediator of the old covenant, and Christ, that of the new! Moses himself trembled before the terrors of God's presence on Sinai, for he was only a man and a sinner; but our Mediator is the Son himself, who needs no sacrifice for himself and whose work is the highest pleasure of God. Matth. 3, 17.

Remember the joy of the Jews when they beheld their Zion and entered into the streets of the Holy City and into the courts of the temple of God. There was outward beauty and grandeur indeed, but we know it was the inward, spiritual reality that formed the real attraction for them. Our Zion is the throne of God itself; our Jerusalem heaven with its glories. Shall we not rejoice as in our devotions and worship we ever and ever again draw nigh to these?

Long ere child of man could enter the golden streets, these had their inhabitants. Long ere human hands were folded in prayer, or human heart longed for the home of the soul in light, or one born of dust was made to face the question: "Where wast thou when I laid the foundations of the earth, when the morning stars sang together, and all the sons of God shouted for joy?" these were there above, the choirs and companies of angels. Their service is sacred joy, their obedience a festal celebration. A thousand thousand serve him, and ten thousand times ten thousand stand before him. All of them ministering spirits sent forth to minister for them who shall be heirs of salvation. They belong together, these helpers above, and those who need help here below. Blessed assurance indeed that we are not alone in our severe conflict, not against flesh and blood only, but against principalities, against powers, against the spirits of evil in high places. We rejoice in the help of these blessed spirits above; and those that are with us are greater in number than those that are against us. Matthes.

Deeds are recorded, and once the record is properly entered upon the court files our possession of the property is established. So our names are written in heaven; so our property there is made surely ours. A man may own many acres and yet not actually live upon them; they are his nevertheless. So, though we have not entered upon our heavenly estates, they are ours none the less. — Compare also *Formula of Concord*, 652, 13, 25, 66, 89.

Men need mediators. But it is a sad mistake, even among evangelical Christians, to suppose that the work of mediation belongs to pastors only, whose profession is to deal with divine things, and that all others are free to devote themselves wholly to earthly business and interests. This idea of mediatorship we must oppose wherever we meet it. No, none of us is excluded here, none dare say that he cannot approach God. We may all freely go to the throne of grace and plead and intercede for each other on the strength of the one great Mediator whose blood speaketh better than that of Abel.

"Christ's blood that cries for vengeance is an altogether different and more precious blood than Abel's, which cried for vengeance only upon *one* murderer, as a type of the blood of Christ, which cries daily for the judgment of condemnation upon the devil and death because of all the blood of his saints shed from the beginning of the world, for whose sakes he gave himself and thus with his own blood and death avenges all the other blood and death upon the devil." Luther.

"Glorious Things of Thee are Spoken; Zion, City of our God."

I. *Of thy sanctuary.*
II. *Of thy inhabitants.*
III. *Of thy God.*

The Richest People on Earth.

God's people:
I. *They have always been rich.*
II. *Their riches now are infinite.*

A Look Through the Open Portals of Heaven.

I. *There is the heavenly sanctuary.*
II. *There are the homes of the blessed.*
  (Jerusalem with its mansions.)
III. *There are the books with our names.*
IV. *There are the angels, our friends.*
V. *There are the spirits of the blessed.*
VI. *There is the Judge who acquits us.*
VII. *There is the Mediator who makes us welcome.*

The body — the soul; our daily toil — our heavenly inspiration (contrasting the text for last Sunday and the present text).

Citizens of the New Jerusalem.

I. *Their home.*
II. *Their friends.*
III. *Their King.*

"I Believe in the Holy Christian Church, the Communion of Saints."

I. *My home.*
II. *My joy.*
III. *My eternal hope.*

The Two Covenants.

I. *Both great.*
II. *The latter greater.*

THE
SEVENTEENTH SUNDAY AFTER TRINITY.

Heb. 4, 9-13.

Both the old gospel lesson and the Eisenach gospel text for this Sunday deal with the Sabbath question. In a higher sense our epistle text speaks of *our Sabbath rest,* the eternal rest that remaineth for the people of God. There is but one way to enter into that rest: faith that perseveres to the end. Read the entire section from 3, 7 on and this will be found to be the underlying thought. All through the holy writer's words there rings the warning against unbelief and the hardening of the heart that rejects the Word. In our text itself the admonition to enter into that rest is coupled with the exhortation not to fall after the old example of disobedience; and the second half of the text is an impressive description of the Word which unbelief rejects and with the power of which all who harden themselves against it will have to reckon. Two things must be held fast: the one that we are now the people of God called to this rest by the Word of God as Israel was of old, and all of us as one great body, not a man falling behind, ought to press forward in faith and attain that rest. The admonition is not merely to the individual, but to us as a church, a body. The other thing is that this text supplements the preceding one which gave us a cheering view of heaven. It is well to rejoice in our great treasures, but the essential thing is to believe, and there is nothing more terrible than to have the Canaan of eternal rest and blessedness open just before us, and we through disobedience and unbelief of the Word fail to enter in.

Let us give diligence to enter into that rest.

God's people of old failed to do this; they failed to yield faith and obedience to his mighty and blessed

Word. So it was with those who had been with Moses
at Sinai and had witnessed the manifestations of God's
majesty in the giving of the law, described in the preceding text; God could not let them enter his rest, 3,
18-19. So it was with the people under Joshua after God
had brought them into the promised land; there was the
same persistent disobedience due to unbelief. God then
through David defined another day, when again the call
should go forth far and wide: "To-day if ye shall hear
his voice, harden not your hearts." This is the day of
grace in Jesus Christ, the day of the Gospel message in
Christendom. The heavenly rest invites us all now as
God's people; let none of us fail to enter. **There remaineth therefore a sabbath rest for the people of God.
For he that is entered into his rest hath himself also
rested from his works, as God did from his. Let us
therefore give diligence to enter into that rest, that
no man fall after the same example of disobedience.** —
The classics never put ἄρα first as the N. T. writers do
repeatedly. The conclusion is drawn from the previous
extensive elaboration, and it is that **a sabbath rest** remaineth for the people of God. For κατάπαυσις, "rest,"
the exceptional word σαββατισμός is used, summarizing in
the one word what is explained in verses 4-5. The rest
spoken of all along is none other than that of God himself after he had finished the work of creation. Gen. 2, 2,
a rest that means for us a complete cessation from all
labor and toil, the fullest satisfaction and joy at having
finished our day's work, a holy sabbatical enjoyment of
perfect, everlasting communion with God. This rest
remaineth, since heretofore only a few in Israel appropriated it, and so many failed to enter upon it. It is still
waiting to be occupied by **the people of God,** such as are
truly his people by enduring faith. — Verse 10 explains
what this blessed sabbath rest means: **For he that is
entered into his rest,** namely that of God, **himself also
rested from his works,** his duties, labors, sufferings, and
all the burdens connected with this our earthly existence,

as God did from his works, though these have a higher and different character, he being God. The sentence is entirely general, ὁ εἰσελθών referring to any one who has really attained the heavenly rest. The aorist in the participle and especially in the main verb κατέπαυσεν may be taken to imply that some did actually attain God's rest. There were some who believed, like Moses himself, Joshua, and David, to mention no others, although no special reference is made of such in the elaborations of the sacred writer at this place; but compare chapter 11. It is certainly badly wide of the mark to think that Christ is meant (Ebrard). As to the ἔργα in our case and in God's the point of similarity is simply this, that God set himself a task to perform in the six days of creation, and when he had finished it he rested in the contemplation of his work and its glorious perfection, and so there is a task set for us, a vocation assigned us of God, and when we complete it as God desires, we are made partakers of his rest, with all that that means of heavenly satisfaction and joy. In our case there is, of course, bound to be toil and pain, not so with God. We look back to many an error and fault in what we have done, not so God; but all our shortcomings are made good by the mercy and pardon of our Savior. God's rest is not idleness, nor shall ours be in partaking of his. It is idle to speculate farther, for who can make plain what the perfect delights of heaven shall be like? Unworthy is the thought of a *dolce far niente,* and certainly false the idea of an endless development whose final goal shall never be reached. — After thus summing up the main thoughts concerning this rest of God, that it still invites us and that it contains the highest blessedness, the admonition already begun at the head of the chapter is most earnestly renewed: **Let us therefore give diligence to enter into that rest,** σπουδάσωμεν, "let us labor," A. V., or be earnest and zealous. God's grace alone can save us and bring us to heaven, but it does this by giving us spiritual life and power, both of which it stimulates to the fullest activity in faith and devotion to God and in opposing all hostile influences. When then we grow slack, cold, indifferent, slothful in our spiritual activities, we are repelling the grace of God, losing our spiritual health, and slipping back into the death and doom of sin. So we must ever be active and full of diligence to move forward toward our goal, which is **that rest** set before us in the future. — **That no man fall after the same example of disobedience** points to the danger. It is impossible to fall in an example, so exegetes generally read the verb as expressing a complete concept by itself: "lest anyone fall," *i. e.* perish. The margin has *into* for *ἐν*, which is hardly acceptable. The idea is that he who falls would furnish the same example of disobedience as the disobedient Israelites. It is only an effort to give the *ἐν* a name that will express this Greek conception in English, when one says it is the *ἐν* of state or condition; another, of form; another, of the sphere, *etc.* By *ὑπόδειγμα* is meant a sign, or token, and thus a pattern or **example;** the Attic used only *παράδειγμα* in this sense. "The pilgrimage of the church of the N. T. out of the world, and through the world towards the final rest, corresponds antitypically to Israel's journey out of Egypt and through the wilderness to Canaan. The church is exhorted to endeavor zealously to advance on the way to this end with steady step, lest any stumble and fall." Delitzsch. The word **disobedience** stands emphatically at the end; it is the manifestation of unbelief. We must not overlook that it implies a word or command that is disobeyed, just as the unbelief underlying it implies disregard or distrust of a word or promise. Concerning this Word the writer of Hebrews has more to say, namely something that mightily reenforces his admonition.

Let us not underestimate the Word.

This is what all those do who disobey and disbelieve it, and they imagine they can do this with impunity. What a mistake! **For the word of God is living, and** active, and sharper than any two-edged sword, and piercing even to the dividing of soul and spirit, of both joints and marrow, and quick to discern the thoughts and intents of the heart. And there is no creature that is not manifest in his sight: but all things are naked and laid open before the eyes of him with whom we have to do. — In Ps. 95, which is used in this and the previous chapter with such emphasis, the admonition and appeal centers in the words: "To-day if ye will hear *his voice.*" Now what this voice speaks is **the word of God.** As regards the medium used nothing is said; with any medium it is still God's own voice. The idea that ὁ λόγος τοῦ θεοῦ here means the Son, the personal Word, is spread among the Greek and also a number of the Latin fathers. It is a fact that in verse 13 a person is meant, although he is not called the Word. Nor would it be out of harmony with the Christology of the letter to the Hebrews to have the Son called the Word. When some, like Delitzsch, point also to similar expressions on the part of Philo, this can have no weight, because the sacred writer in no way depends on this philosophizing Jew. But the fact remains that Hebrews does not use the term Logos as does John; it does not appear in passages where it would evidently be appropriate in the highest degree, if it was to be used at all; and its sudden introduction here would only confuse by taking the readers unawares. Moreover, what is said regarding this "word of God," especially the comparison to a sword, does not fit very well if a person is meant. There is no reason to limit the meaning of the term to the N. T. Word (Kuebel), or to the word of the 95th Psalm as here urged upon the readers. It is God's Word in general, especially the Word of revelation that was spoken to the fathers of old and now to us. This is not a mere sound that disappears, although when spoken by human lips its sound continues only during the speaking. The true speaker of it is God himself who must never be separated in our thoughts from his Word. This explains how the next verse comes

to speak of the person of God himself. — So the Word
of God is ever **living,** like its author, *quick,* A. V., in the
old meaning of the term.   This word heads the sentence
and in its emphatic position dominates all that is said in
further explanation.   What God speaks is an expression
of his thought and will, and therefore is altogether like
God himself.   It is an outflow of his life and therefore
instinct with life, either to kindle, similar life elsewhere
or to react against any opposition. "God does not
separate himself from his Word.   He does not disown
it, as if it were a foreign thing to him.   His it remains
also when it comes into our ear, into our heart, into our
mouth, into our book.   He knows it well as his own
Word, as the expression of his own life.   Therefore it
is never dead matter, insensible to what is done with it;
for it is a bond of union with the living God." Schlatter.
— Being living or alive, it is also **active,** ἐνεργής, later for
ἐνεργός, full of energy to carry out the will of God, either
in blessing or in cursing as the case may be.   What a mistake to disregard this living Word, to spurn the grace and
gifts which it offers, or to think we can escape its punishing
power when we do spurn it! — This is further explained:
**and sharper than any two-edged sword, and piercing
even to the dividing of soul and spirit, of both joints and
marrow, and quick to discern the thoughts and intents
of the heart.**   The Word is not only like a sword,
μάχαιρα, a short sword, a large knife, and one with two
cutting edges, δίστομος, with two στόματα or mouths wherewith to devour, but is even sharper.   The comparison is
made with something that penetrates man because the
Word thus penetrates.   The comparison is made with an
instrument that penetrates most quickly and effectually,
because the Word exceeds even this.   The sword is frequently used for this purpose of comparison and illustration in Scripture: Is. 49, 2; Eph. 6, 17; Rev. 1, 16; 2,
12; 19, 15.   Some suppose that only the destructive power
of the Word, as exercised against the disobedience, is
here meant; but while it is certainly included, the two

designations which precede, and those that follow are
indeterminate, especially also the statement: "quick to
discern the thoughts and intents of the heart." The great
truth regarding the Word here brought out is its ability
to penetrate the innermost part of man. For that the
Word was given, namely to free the soul of man from sin,
and this by exerting its power upon his innermost spirit.
Of course, if man resists wilfully and opposes that Word
in its salutary work, it will work his destruction, laying
his whole inwardness bare and thus exposing all' his
terrible guilt. — The **soul,** ψυχή. as distinguished from the
spirit or πνεῦμα is the life which the spirit gives to the
body as long as the two are connected; hence it is the seat
of the thoughts, emotions, feelings, desires, volitions and
actions pertaining to our earthly and bodily existence;
while the "spirit" is the immaterial part of our being
created and breathed into us by the breath of God, and
therefore the real seat of all his gracious operations in
regenerating and renewing us. The **dividing,** or *dividing
asunder* (A. V.) which the Word effects is therefore not,
and in no case can be, a separating of the soul from the
spirit, for these are not two entities that can be cut apart.
This applies also to the figurative terms which are added
for illustration: **of both joints and marrow,** for the
joints where the bones of the body articulate and the
marrow which is inside the bones themselves, are not
next to each other so that one could speak of cutting
them apart. To pierce to the dividing of soul and spirit
is that activity of the Word upon man by which it
separates and shows up in its true nature all that inheres
on the one hand only in his earthly life (ψυχή), and on
the other in his spiritual existence (πνεῦμα). And this it
does just as a physical sword lays bare both the joints
where the bones meet and the marrow within the very
bones themselves. Soul and spirit are not parallel with
joints and marrow, or chiastically with marrow and joints,
for these are joined by τε καί, so that the illustration of
joints and marrow belongs as well to soul on the one

hand as to spirit on the other. All the links of our soul-life, of our thoughts, emotions, *etc.*, as well as all the inner substance of them is penetrated, laid bare, exposed in its true character by the Word. It is the same with the spirit and all that God works there. And the Word is the only power that can penetrate so deeply and expose to our view the entire inwardness of our being. The practical applications are easy to make: in the light of the Word we recognize the vanity and sinfulness of many of our earthly thoughts, strivings, purposes, and achievements. The world may laud these as good and acceptable to God; the Word shows that they are anything but that. So it reveals the things of the spirit, its bondage under sin, its liberation by grace and all that belongs to our regeneration and renewal, repentance, faith, sanctification and their influence over the entire man. The Word makes us see the very joints and marrow of all these things. The notion of Delitzsch that the Word exposes the corrupting power of sin even in our body (joints and marrow taken in a physical sense, as contrasted with soul and spirit) is rightly rejected by commentators as in no way justified by the language and thought of the text itself. Some bring in here also thoughts from Philo, but these are only parts of his speculations and are not even properly illustrative. Hofmann makes the genitives "joints and marrow" depend on the preceding genitives "soul and spirit," but they evidently form a subordinate apposition. — The entire statement is rounded out by the illuminating addition that the Word is **quick to discern the thoughts and intents of the heart,** able to judge both his "reflections" as he meditates, ἐνθυμήσεις, and the "conceptions" and definite notions resulting, ἔννοιαι. **The heart,** the central organ of the personal life, is the seat of both. The difference between "thoughts" and "intents" is slight, and Riggenbach says that it can hardly be brought out. Kuebel would distinguish the two terms as the movements of the θυμός or soul, hence feelings and volitions; and the concepts of the νοῦς or mind, hence judgments and principles. All that is in our hearts the Word judges, nor is it necessary to think only of ethical feelings and judgments, since all that is in our hearts is judged as to its character by the Word. — The power of the Word is due to God himself, its author. The Word penetrates so deeply because God himself is omniscient and all-seeing. This final thought is added: **And there is no creature that is not manifest in his sight;** even beyond man, there is not a thing that God has made that is invisible or non-transparent to him. The genitive αὐτοῦ refers to τοῦ θεοῦ above, not to λόγος, for the context requires that we understand a person. **But all things are naked and laid open before the eyes of him with whom we have to do;** this is the positive side. "All things" shows how far his vision extends. To his **eyes,** that is to his infinite power of perception, all things are **naked** and without a covering that could possibly hide them, or anything concerning them, from him; and **laid open,** τετραχηλισμένα, from τραχηλίζειν, bent back like the neck of a victim in order to expose it to the knife. The verb itself means to bend the neck back, and the meaning of the participle "opened" (A. V.) or exposed is assured although there is much difference, already among the Greek expositors, as to just how this meaning is derived. — A personal turn is given this final sentence in the clause: of him **with whom we have to do;** some read: "with whom is our reckoning," *i. e.* to whom we have to give an account; and this is God. "The readers are to realize how closely what has just been said concerning God touches them. They are not to imagine that they will be able to hide from God the real and innermost reasons of their discouragement and their unbelief or the slightest stirrings of their resistance against him, and to present themselves before him as other than they are. The penetrating criticism, which the divine Word exercises upon their entire being down to the innermost parts, illustrates to them the piercing sharpness of the divine vision, and warns them not to subject themselves by indifference and disobedience to the judgment of God, whose verdict is proof against every bribe and unaffected by anything that would cloud or deceive it." Riggenbach.

HOMILETICAL HINTS.

"Man that is born of a woman is of few days, and full of trouble (*Unruhe*)," Job 14, 1.

"No rest!" the complaint of many. See the feverish restlessness in all the departments of life. What shall we call our age? The age of machinery? the age of steam? the age of electricity. In any case the age of unrest. How speeds the pulse of life! Nobody has time. — They cry: To rest is to rust! In the battle for existence there is no respite, no hesitation, no halt. To stand still is to slip back. No respite, no rest. And this is not merely the outward unrest of an activity exceeding that of the past, the utilization of every moment and every opportunity, the ceaseless pressure of work and the never satisfied lust for pleasure, the staggering of desire toward satiety and of the satieted to new desire; the children of this world are filled with unrest down to their very souls, and they pretend that this is nature, the self-evident lot of man. They hug the thought that the poor heart tossed with many a storm can have no rest or peace until it cease to beat. And then they sing in soft and sentimental tones: "There's a rest in the grave!" and think that such dreams of rest can satisfy the poor, deluded, restless soul. (Adapted from Matthes.) — The fear of death gives the lie to all such dreams of rest in the grave. No man ever attained rest or peace simply by dying. Else all Israel, all who perished in the wilderness during those forty long years of journeying, would have come to rest. Else God's own oath would be false, who swore that none of them should enter his rest. Else mere dying would be salvation, and death himself our Savior.

All sin is unrest, plunges into pain, spoils peace. A thousand experiences corroborate it. Never did sin bring rest, it never can. — The road of unbelief does not lead to rest. To be inactive in the work of the Lord, slothful and sleepy, cold and indifferent, to grow weary of suffering and affliction, of battle and warfare, this means most surely to lose God's rest. To yield to the temptation of sin, to forget the living God, is to run on the road that leads to eternal unrest.

Is that rest when conscience is silent? It might be, if there were no sleeping consciences, no erring consciences; if one could not deaden his conscience. The foolish virgins were quite easy in their minds and consciences, for they thought they were fully prepared, until there came the sudden terrible awakening — they were not ready, their rest had been folly.

Some have sought rest in monastic cells, but they took their restless hearts with them; some in far away private seclusion, but the shadow of their sins followed them; some in the silence of the tomb, but death only lied to them. Far mightier and more comprehensive is the thought of rest in the New Testament. It is not flight, but victory; not weariness, but power. For according to the promise it is the great day of God, when he himself will bring his kingdom and his rule to victory, the day of judgment for his foes, the day of grace for his friends, the day that will open, or close, the door of his glory forever.

You may wish for rest, and dream of rest, but it is all empty, because you only think away what makes your life restless. This sort of rest is little more than death. — If the Word of God would only show us the goal, it would plunge us into greater unrest than ever. But in the Word of promise there is more. I can honestly promise only what I myself have the actual means to bestow. God's Word promises rest, and at the same time it gives that rest. That does not mean that at once it proves restful to us. It must first destroy all false rest and plunge us into great unrest; for through such unrest lies the way to rest.

The Word is never without its effect. We may be indifferent and act as though it made little difference whether we heard it or not, whether we heeded it or not, always there is an effect, either one of blessing or a curse. Nothing less lies in the balance than life and death for time and for eternity. — Do you want to see the effect? Christ said to the unbelieving Jews: "Ye shall die in your sins." Behold, they died!

Behold the blessed power of the Word: it closes the dark gate of death; it opens the shining portal of life. And then it turns to us and says: "Come! here is eternal rest." Will you come? — Rest and peace and happiness can be only where God's will, his judgments, and his kingdom are victorious. So repentance and faith bring rest to the soul, Matth. 11, 29, that preliminary rest which is followed by eternal rest. — "Blessed are the dead which die in the Lord from henceforth: Yea, saith the Spirit, that they may rest from their labors; and their works do follow them." Rev. 14, 13. What great things then have they done? They stood for God and his Word here on earth. He who does that shall not fail of final rest.

There remaineth a rest for the people of God. What inexhaustible comfort for many a weary pilgrim, tired fighter, tried laborer, giving them new courage and strength.

16

Let us Give Diligence to Enter Into God's Rest!

I. *The precious truth, that there remaineth a rest for the people of God.*
II. *The sacred duties involved in this truth.*

C. C. Hein.

Rest and Unrest.

I. *The rest that works unrest.*
II. *The unrest that leads to rest.*

God's Rest Depends on God's Word.

I. *As a promise of that Word.*
II. *As a product of that Word.*

Riemer.

"There Remaineth a Rest for the People of God."

I. *A prospect of peace in death.*
II. *A call to battle in life.*

Langsdorff.

Or:
I. *Rest in the Lord.*
II. *Rest with the Lord.*

Ahlfeld.

Amid all the Unrest of Time the True Rest of Christian People.

I. *The rest of the sabbath.*
II. *The rest of God's grace.*
III. *The rest of heaven.*

Stoecker.

THE
EIGHTEENTH SUNDAY AFTER TRINITY.

James 2, 10-17.

James (Acts 12, 17; 15, 13 and 19; Gal. 2, 9; Acts 21, 18-19; Josephus, *Antiquities* 20, 91) wrote his Epistle to a circle of Jewish Christian congregations, the members of which fell sadly short in furnishing the true evidences of faith, namely the love of the brethren. These people are not only admonished to change their sinful course because sinful, but are warned at the same time that their faith, failing to produce the works of love, mercy, and charity toward the brethren, is a dead faith and useless for salvation. Our text resembles the old gospel lesson for this Sunday with its two questions: "Master, which is the great commandment in the law;" and "What think ye of Christ?" So here we have the law and the Gospel side by side: "Whosoever shall keep the whole law, and yet stumble in one point, he is become guilty of all;" and: "Faith, if it have not works, is dead in itself." The unity of the text lies in the thought that a dead faith is unable to save us from the judgment of the law, one commandment of which is sufficient to condemn the transgressor. The text is an evident warning against a dead faith. We may sum it up in a positive instead of a negative statement: *The members of a congregation must show their faith by works of love, mercy and charity toward their fellow members.* This they must do lest they fall under the merciless judgment of the law, verses 10-13; and lest their faith be found dead and unable to save, verses 14-17.

Beware, lest you fall under the merciless judgment of the law.

James has already warned his readers (1, 22): "Be ye doers of the word, and not hearers only, deluding

243

your own selves." And again, at the head of our chapter: "Do ye, in accepting persons, hold the faith of our Lord Jesus, the Lord of glory?" (compare the translation in the margin). This regard to persons, flattering the rich, disregarding and humbling the poor, James regards as a deplorable lack of true love and mercy, indicating that something is radically wrong with the faith of all those members in a congregation who go on in this sin. He shows us what the result must be, the merciless judgment and condemnation of the law. **For whosoever shall keep the whole law, and yet stumble in one** *point,* **he is become guilty of all. For he that said, Do not commit adultery, said also, Do not kill. Now if thou dost not commit adultery, but killest, thou art become a transgressor of the law. So speak ye, and so do, as men that are to be judged by a law of liberty. For judgment** *is* **without mercy to him that hath showed no mercy: mercy glorieth against judgment.** — The case of one keeping the whole law and stumbling only in one point is in the nature of it hypothetical, for no such case can actually occur. We might therefore expect ὅστις ἄν with the subjunctive, but the ἄν is absent in the best texts, Blass 65, 7; Winer explains the omission by supposing that James positively thought of such a case (p. 275), and this seems the best solution. By **the law** James means the opposite of the Gospel, the law as summed up for us in the Ten Commandments. The idea that all the requirements of the ceremonial law are also included is certainly incorrect. Reylaender's supposition to this effect is answered by the Lord's own repeated definitions of the law, notably the one he used when he dealt with the rich young ruler who imagined he had actually observed the whole law from his youth, Mark 10, 19-20. **The whole law** is the entire sum of its requirements. The verb τηρεῖν, **keep,** is really "observe," keep an eye on with the result of performing every bidding of the law; in substance it is the same as the other expressions in Scripture: πληροῦν, to fulfil; φυλάσσειν, to keep or guard; τέλειν, to bring to fulfilment; ποιεῖν, to perform. — **And yet to stumble in one** *point* supposes the lightest case possible: only in *one* point some slight transgression, and this due only to *stumbling,* to an inadvertent action, without wicked and wilful intention. It seems best to take both ἐν ἐνί and πάντων as neuters, instead of trying to supply "law" with each, which seems quite impossible, considering that "the whole law" is not a plural but a collective. — So grave a matter is it to stumble even only in one thing, that the man who does it **is become guilty of all,** γέγονεν, "he has become" and therefore now is "guilty," ἔνοχος, equal to ἐνεχόμενος, held in, bound by, no less than all. No matter what commandment is violated by the one point, this one violation involves the guilt of violating all the points of the whole law. Reylaender thinks this can only be when a man violates one commandment intentionally, but James indicates the opposite with the verb "stumble." In fact the entire context refers to such as deceive themselves (1, 22), who think they are religious (1, 26), who say they have faith (2, 14); they are people involved in a great error. The immediate connection furnishes us an illustration of what James means by sinning "in one point," namely "having respect of persons," verse 9 and the foregoing. They who gave the rich a good place in the synagogue, and told the poor to stand there, or to sit under my footstool, did not think they were doing anything wrong, least of all that they were sinning against the royal law of love, but James challenges their sin nevertheless and charges against it the guilt of breaking the entire law in all points. In the case of James' first readers the fault was even more serious, as verse 14 *etc.* shows us, for this sin against the royal law of love, as well as others of the same sort, showed that the true fruit of faith, love, was absent, hence that their faith itself was dead and a mere shadow and sham. In order to drive them to repentance James smites them with the full force of the law, for so only can their dead or dying faith be revived. They dare not go on deceiving themselves, they must realize their full danger in order to be brought to escape it. Let us note what a serious fault lack of love is, and how in any case it makes us guilty of the entire law of God. This will ever keep us in true, humble repentance, and will stir up our faith to exercise itself strenuously in all the activities of love toward our brethren. — It sounds paradoxical that a sin in one point should make one guilty of all points of the law; but James explains by illustrating: **For he that said, Do not commit adultery, said also, Do not kill. Now if thou dost not commit adultery, but killest, thou art become a transgressor of the law.** Note all through the concrete and practical way in which James argues. He uses for his illustration the first two commandments which deal with love toward our fellow man generally; and the sixth commandment is placed before the fifth as in Rom. 13, 9; Luke 18, 20; Mark 10, 19, supposedly according to an ancient Jewish tradition which had this order, followed also in the Septuagint and by Philo. The two divine prohibitions are expressed by the second person of the aorist after μή; in the condition: "if thou dost not commit adultery" οὐ denies the fact. There was hardly any danger of these Jewish converts falling into the pagan sin of adultery, as was often the case with Gentile converts who might be drawn back to the vices and shameful practices connected with their former idolatries. But it was plain that they were liable to break the fifth commandment, by hatred and malice, and evil speaking (compare 4, 1-2), all of which Christ had explained as constituting the sin of murder (Matth. 5, 21 *etc.*). Even by his new illustration James thus strikes home in the heart of his readers. The point is that whichever sin they committed they offended the one Lawgiver, whose one will expressed itself in both commandments alike. In either case they became transgressors of the law. The word παραβάτης (παράβασις) always refers to a law which is transgressed; there can be no transgression or transgressor without a definite and positive law. Trench, *Synonyms*, II, 75. To transgress the fifth commandment, James says, is to be **a transgressor of the law,** not merely of part of it, but of the law as such.

It avails nothing to be able to say: "I did not transgress the
sixth commandment;" for it is one and the same God who
gave both. You cannot divide up God or his law; they are
always one, no matter from what side the sinner may oppose them. Hunter adds that James might have brought
forward the intimate connection and inner unity of all the
commandments, also that transgressing one of them shows
a lack in us which makes obedience to the rest impossible;
but he did not do this, and if we use these thoughts — as certainly we may — they can only be additional explanations,
not the thoughts of James himself. — James now adds the
admonition: **So speak ye, and so do as men that are to
be judged by a law of liberty.** It seems hardly pertinent
to refer the speaking here meant to the fifth commandment
just mentioned, and the doing to the sixth; the admonition
is general, and the speaking and doing is that required by
all the commandments. James castigates the sins of the
tongue in a special section of his Epistle, 3, 1-12; here he
puts in an advance touch of what he has in mind. Some
refer οὕτως to what precedes: "So speak, and so do, as I
have stated," and Huther returns to this view. But James
has not laid down any rule for our conduct in verses 10-11,
he has only explained the greatness and danger of the sin
committed by so many of his readers. So we draw the
word to what follows: **So,** namely as people who are to be
judged by a law of liberty, **so speak ye, and so do.** The
consciousness of the blessed law by which we are to be
judged is to govern our every word and action. — **The law
of liberty** is called "the perfect law, the law of liberty"
in 1, 25; this is the Gospel in so far as it constitutes the
motive power and norm of the believer's life. It is a law
"of liberty," because it does not operate like the Mosaic
Law with a set of commands, but with the liberating power
of Jesus Christ, setting the heart free from the slavery of
sin and furnishing it spiritual life and strength, by which
freely, and of its own accord, in a blessed new liberty, it is
able to do the will of God. According to this law we shall
all be **judged** of Christ at the end of the world, even as he

says regarding the man that rejects him: "The word that
I spake, the same shall judge him in the last day," John 12,
48. What a mistake then to neglect and forget faith and
the love toward our brethren which must ever flow out of
it, and to try, without faith, to obey the old law of Moses,
one transgression against which must already condemn us,
and all of whose commandments together cannot put a
spark of true life and love into our hearts. — **For judgment** *is* **without mercy to him that hath shewed no
mercy.** He who has no faith, and is therefore without
mercy, kindly, helpful tenderness and pity, when he sees
those who are poor and in need, as for instance "the
fatherless and widows in their affliction," 1, 27, shall, according to Christ's own word, receive no mercy at the last
day. "Verily I say unto you, Inasmuch as ye did it not
unto one of these least, ye did it not unto me." Matth. 25,
45. — In a terse positive statement James repeats this
truth: **mercy glorieth against judgment.** "Blessed are
the merciful: for they shall obtain mercy." Matth. 5, 7.
"Verily I say unto you, Inasmuch as ye did it unto one of
these my brethren, even these least, ye did it unto me."
Matth. 25, 40. **Mercy** here is the same as in the previous
sentence, that produced by the mercy of God in the believer's heart and life. **Judgment** is the application of the law
to the sinner, especially that at the last day. Then mercy,
even as now already, **glorieth against** judgment; as an
evidence of true faith Jesus will publicly acknowledge that
mercy, and that is how it "glories against judgment."
Koegel has finely summed it up: *Jesu Barmherzigkeit
ruehmt unsere Barmherzigkeit wider das Gericht.*

Beware, lest you be found with a dead faith.

A new line of thought begins with verse 14. It is
latent already in the entire preceding part of the chapter, the thought that where true love to the brethren
and our fellow men is absent, there true faith itself must
be absent. This is now set forth directly, the works of
love being named instead of the love itself. **What doth**

it **profit, my brethren, if a man say he hath faith, but
have not works? can that faith save him?** If **a brother
or sister be naked, and in lack of daily food, and one of
you say unto them, Go in peace, be ye warmed and filled;
and yet ye give them not the things needful to the body;
what doth it profit?** Even **so faith, if it have not works,
is dead in itself.** — James asks a question that at once
goes to the heart of the matter, following it up with
equally telling explanation: **what doth it profit,** what
advantage or benefit is there? The implied answer is:
Absolutely none! The address: **my brethren,** urges the
question earnestly upon the readers, and the honorable,
fraternal title suggests to them that they certainly
should not be like the man here introduced. — **If a man
say he hath faith, but have not works?** Faith itself
cannot be seen, it makes its presence known by a proper
confession and by its proper and natural works. Now here
is a man who claims he has this true and proper **faith,** but
he admits that he has not the **works,** that belong to it. He
is like the man in 1, 26 "who thinketh himself to be religious," only this man actually says so and names the
grounds for his claim. Yet he is one who has not the
works, who for instance bridles not his tongue (1, 26),
does not keep himself unspotted from the world (1, 27),
makes no true effort to fulfil the royal law of love (2, 8),
has respect of persons (2, 9), fails to show mercy (2, 13).
— **Can that faith save him?** ἡ πίστις, *that* faith which he
says he has, but fails to prove that he has, no matter as to
what sort of faith he actually has. Beyond question
"faith" as here used by James means exactly what it does
in Paul's Epistles, when he declares that we are justified
by faith without the deeds of the law: a true and living
trust in the Savior Jesus Christ. It is not that Paul has in
mind one kind of faith when he says that faith without
works saves, while James has in mind another kind of
faith when he says that without works it does not save.
Both mean identically the same faith, and both attribute to
it, and to it as such and alone, regeneration, justification,

and salvation, only Paul emphasizes against all Pharisees that this faith saves without the works of the law, and James emphasizes that this faith does not save without the works of the Gospel, since lacking these works it would be dead. Paul nowhere contradicts James in his teaching that a dead faith is useless for salvation, and James in no way contradicts Paul in teaching that dead works are useless for salvation. Both attribute salvation to a living faith, but Paul lays stress on what must be removed before a man can attain this faith, and James lays stress on what must certainly not be absent if man is to possess and retain this faith. James quietly presupposes what Paul has uttered so fully and clearly, and Paul quietly touches upon what James brings out with all fulness and clearness. When Huther and Reylaender claim that James here speaks of a different faith from that mentioned by Paul, they are thinking of the faith this man may actually have when he admits that he has no works along with it, and that of course is only an intellectual assent. But who would be so foolish as even to claim such a faith for his own, or to think that it would save, or to say that it is without works, when it could not possibly have any real works of love? The faith the man claims to have is the true faith, the one that saves, only his claim is without foundation, for in the judgment the Lord will ask also for the works that go with such a faith — and lo, they will be absent, just as absent as the real faith itself. — The matter is finely illustrated by a case of charity that is no charity at all: **If a brother or sister,** one or the other member of the church, whom we are doubly bound to assist in their need, **be naked,** have insufficient clothing against the cold, **and in lack of daily food,** without enough nourishment for the day; **and one of you,** bringing the thing closely home to the readers, no doubt also because they were guilty of indifference to their needy brethren, **say unto them, Go in peace, be ye warmed and filled,** yea, and say it ever so tenderly and kindly, with a most holy and unctious tone, **and yet give them not the things**

needful to the body, clothing and shelter, food and drink,
the things their need cries for and true chairty would at
once think of and provide: **what doth it profit?** Why
the whole thing is a farce! To tell people to be warmed,
and not to warm them, is not only useless but heartless; to
tell a hungry brother or sister to be filled, and not to fill
them, is despicable in the bargain. See, what sort of
charity a charity without works would be? Perhaps you
have seen that kind of charity yourselves, James implies.
Well, to say the least, it is a dead, useless thing; people
can freeze to death, and starve to death, under it. — And
now the telling conclusion, so convincing that nobody can
evade it: **Even so faith, if it have not works, is dead in
itself.** Instead of keeping only to the parallel: "is of no
profit" or use, James at once inserts the reason why it is
profitless and useless: it is dead in itself. This is the real
reason why it has no works. It is like a dead tree, or
branch; how could they bear fruit? Here James says
plainly what sort of faith he really has who claims to have
true saving faith, but has not its proper works. It may be
some sort of faith: *fides generalis,* like that of people who
in a general way believe in God and in Christianity; a *fides
historica,* like that which knows a great deal about the
Gospel history; or a *fides dogmatica,* posted even on doctrine and keen perhaps to argue it, like the faith of some
scientific theologians: it is and can be nothing more than a
mere *notitio* and *assensus,* a dead thing that never even
reaches the heart; to say nothing of filling it with Christian
graces and virtues. And this deadness is emphasized:
dead in itself, καθ' ἑαυτήν, dead in and on account of its
being limited thus to itself. It is like a fire that goes out
because its flames are smothered. The idea is by no means
that works in some way help to constitute faith, that they
are a vital part of it, that being added a *fides formata* results. These Gospel works are the natural and necessary
fruits of faith; and that faith, which in itself as faith saves,
just as it has the power to save, so also it has, inhering in
it and ever active, the power to bring forth love and all the

good Gospel works of love, which wherever they appear show that faith, the real saving faith, is present indeed.

HOMILETICAL HINTS.

Paul says: Dead words bring no justification; James says: Dead faith brings no justification. — Paul says: No man is justified by the works of the law; James says: No man is justified without the works of faith. — Paul rejects the works of the law, James requires the works of faith. — Paul deals with what precedes faith and is without living connection with it; James with what follows faith and is a living product of it. — The works of the law are not only not necessary to salvation, they prevent it; the works of faith are not only desirable for salvation, they are essential to the faith that obtains it.

Even the malefactor on the cross served his fellow men with good works. He rebuked his partner in crime, he confessed Christ aloud before men; his confession has gone as a blessing down through the ages.

How we like to pick and choose among the commandments of the law! We boast of having done this and done that, while we say nothing of what we have left undone. To select your own commandments is to be your own law-giver, and to provide convenient room for sin. The chain of pearls that is torn at any point spills all the pearls. Destroy faith and love at one point, and you will look vainly for it at another.

It is amazing when we hear how mercy of the true kind will be ranked at the judgment day and then note how we all try to evade such mercy when it beckons us here. Is some brother in trouble, how glad you are to get rid of him, to pass him on with some inefficient little gift, to look for others who ought to help him. The mercy you deny others will be the mercy you will need most at that day.

The root that sends up no shoots rots in the ground. — A corpse is not a man, although at first glance it still may have that appearance and mourning friends may bid it farewell as if it were a man still. Decay is already at work upon it, soon it will be such a putrid mass that even the most affectionate will have to turn from it. That's what a dead faith looks like to God.

Our age demands a "practical Christianity." We have no use for it when it is put in place of faith; we have every use for it when it crowns faith. — To fulfil a thousand biddings of the law cannot cover up a single sin. To say Lord, Lord a thousand times is not even the beginning of faith.

None of these shall enter into the kingdom of heaven: the man who was too busy to trouble about doctrine and faith; the man who was so busy about doctrine and faith that he had no time to do mercy; the man who is so sure of his faith that he loses his works; the man who is so sure of his works, that he loses his faith; the man who is so taken up with the Gospel that he fails to submit to the law; the man who is so concerned about the law that he fails to submit to the power of the Gospel.

Beware of a Worthless Christianity!

I. *Of worthless works.*
II. *Of worthless love.*
III. *Of worthless faith.*   Matthes.

Good-for-Nothing Christianity.

I. *With its good-for-nothing obedience.*
II. *With its good-for-nothing faith.*

Faith and Works.

I. *You may be satisfied with faith without works.*
II. *The world is well satisfied with works without faith.*
III. *God alone is satisfied with faith and its works.*

"Judgment is Without Mercy on Him That Showed no Mercy."

I. *The terrible charge,* verse 16.
II. *The weak defense,* verse 14.
III. *The impending sentence,* verse 17.
IV. *The only deliverance,* verse 12.

Adapted from Segnitz.

Bury Dead Faith!

I. *It deludes its possessor.*
II. *It offends the brethren.*
III. *It is an abomination to God.*

The True Story of Practical Christianity.

I. *A sad story, when practical Christianity crowds out faith.*
II. *A glad story, when practical Christianity crowns faith.*

THE
NINETEENTH SUNDAY AFTER TRINITY.

James 5, 13-20.

The previous text insisted on a living, active faith and indicated that its activity would be in works of mercy. This text describes some of these works in detail. *The members of a congregation must assist each other in bodily and in spiritual trouble.* Three cases are set forth, and they occur in innumerable forms, so that the text has the widest application: sickness, coupled perhaps with a distressed conscience; distress of conscience in general; defection from the truth. The text is of special value in dealing with the congregational life and the way our faith must show itself in aiding the souls of the brethren. It furnishes the finest kind of an opportunity for wholesome instruction and for a number of very necessary admonitions and explanations.

Suffering and sickness.

James admonishes his readers to patience in verses 7-11. This applies both to the suffering which others bring upon us, as the prophets suffered from their own people, verse 10, and to the suffering which the Lord himself sends us, as Job suffered, verse 11. Verse 12 interrupts this train of thought, but verse 13 and the following take it up again and develop the conduct which both those immediately concerned and the other members of the congregation should manifest. **Is any among you suffering? let him pray. Is any cheerful? let him praise. Is any among you sick? let him call for the elders of the church; and let them pray over him, anointing him with oil in the name of the Lord: and the prayer of faith shall save him that is sick, and the Lord**

**shall raise him up; and if he have committed sins, it shall
be forgiven him.** — The questions here put by James
place the different conditions in which a Christian may find
himself vividly before us. They are really conditional sentences: "If one suffers, *etc.*," with the conditional form
omitted. This asyndeton, or omission of the connecting
particles, makes the expression more lively and striking.
It is best to punctuate as questions, but this is not absolutely
necessary; we may also read: "Some one suffers among
you — let him pray;" and the other statements in the
same way. — The first two suppositions are entirely general; any suffering or ill is meant, and any cheerfulness
of mind. The two thus take in our whole life, all its
shadow and all its sunshine. James would direct it all
God-ward. If any person suffers, **let him pray,** προσευχέσθω,
turn his heart in devotion and worship to God. The word
is general and does not mean specifically to ask things of
God. Compare 1 Tim. 2, 1 for Rogate. The general communion with God is meant which prayer as an act of worship affords. This already, aside from the special request
for relief, which, of course, will be one form of such
prayer, must refresh, strengthen, and help the sufferer.
— But we are not always in distress, sometimes we are of
good cheer, everything going well with us and pleasing
us. James says: Is any cheerful? **let him sing praise,**
ψαλλέτω; the verb denotes the action of touching the
strings of a harp, and then to sing to the harp, to sing
praise in general. This happy singing is to be of praise
to God, a singing of Psalms in his honor. There is
no need to insist that this means, the singer is to compose
his own songs (Reylaender); he will do what James says
when he sings some happy Psalm of David, some Christian
hymn of uninspired composition. He will distinguish
himself from the children of the world by not singing
their foolish, giddy, frivolous, fleshly songs as expressive
of his happiness. — So James would turn our whole life
upward to God, from whom all true comfort and blessings
flow. He now singles out special cases: **Is any among**

you sick, suffering from some ailment of the body?
What an army of such there are! We all belong to it at
times and can never tell how soon we will join this army
again. Huther thinks that James could not have meant
every case of sickness, but only those that involve spiritual
trouble and distress; but this is not indicated. Real sickness, of course, is meant, not slight indisposition. — When
struck down by some painful and dangerous disease, what
are we to do? **Call for the elders of the church,** summon
them to your bedside. Other helpers may and should, of
course, be also called, especially the physicians who may
be able to administer direct bodily relief and prescribe a
remedy for the ailment. James leaves this to the good
sense of his readers, his concern is the spiritual aid the
sick should have. A Christian should be entirely different
from the children of the world who think only of their
bodies when they become sick and call only the doctors
and nurses; he will make use of his Christian brethren
to comfort and refresh him in his illness, but especially
also of **the elders of the church,** the pastors of the congregation to which he belongs, called "elders" originally like the "elders" in the Jewish synagogue who
together with the "ruler" managed its affairs. Such
were appointed by the apostles in the early church
and were also called "overseers" or bishops, until later a
difference was made between them, and the names used
accordingly. See on Acts 20, 28 for Tenth Sunday after
Trinity. — The elders are **to pray over him** who is sick,
anointing him with oil in the name of the Lord. Huther
thinks this means the entire body of elders in each case
of sickness, and since there were usually several in each
congregation at this time, that invariably they would appear together at the bedside of every sick man; but this
again presses the words beyond what is necessary. The
article τοὺς πρεσβυτέρους points only in a definite way to
the persons who held this office and thus had a special duty
toward the sick. Whether one or several or all would
come to a sick person, circumstances certainly were

naturally left to decide; where the flock was large, cases of sickness numerous, and the elders very busy, the τούς as James wrote it did not forbid a distribution of the work of the elders to the best advantage. The chief thing was the prayer, as we see by the attached promise which mentions only "the prayer of faith" as that which "shall save him that is sick." The prayer was uttered **over** the sick because it especially referred to him; in many cases it was literally spoken over the prostrate form, perhaps with folded or outstretched hands extended over him. Winer, p. 363. — The aorist participle **anointing him,** ἀλείψαντες really: *having anointed him,* shows that the prayer followed the anointing. We read in Mark 6, 13 that the twelve, when out on their first mission of proclaiming the kingdom, anointed with oil many that were sick and healed them." We read nowhere that Christ commanded such anointing, much less that any promise was attached to it. James likewise attaches no promise to it, while he does to the prayer in the strongest manner. In the anointing of the sick we simply have an ancient Eastern custom which applied oil in this manner in order to refresh, strengthen, and heal the body. Its use was not confined to the hands of physicians, anyone could apply the oil. No sacramental idea of any kind was connected with it, James mentions it only as an accompaniment of the spiritual ministration of the elders. In drawing a lesson from this ancient use of oil for our hearers to-day this general medicinal effect attributed of old to oil must suffice as pointing us now to a similar use of medical means for the refreshing and relief of the body. — The Christians of the time of James used doctors and many remedies besides, which James had no especial occasion to mention here; the use of oil lies in the same plane. Later on here and there superstitious ideas connected themselves with the use of oil for the sick; not until the twelfth century was the sacrament of extreme unction established. Now the Catholic custom is to have

17

pure olive oil consecrated by the bishop, assisted by twelve
priests, on Maundy Thursday, and then distributed to the
priests of the diocese. If the quantity does not suffice
some unconsecrated oil is added; if oil is left over at the
end of the year, it is burnt on Saturday of Holy Week.
Only a consecrated priest may administer extreme unction,
to a person very sick and in danger of death; he does it
by applying it to eyes, ears, nostrils, mouth, hands, body,
and feet of the sick person, praying at each part: *Per
istam sanctam unctionem indulgeat tibi Deus quicquid
oculorum (aurium cet.) vitio deliquisti.* The sacrament
may be repeated, if the patient recovers and again becomes
seriously ill. The blessing of the sacrament, which if at
all possible is to be administered after confession and communion, is supposed to consist in the forgiveness of venial
sins, the strengthening of faith, and in bodily recovery if
conducive to the welfare of the soul. Maeusel, *Han-
dlexicon: Letzte Oelung, etc.;* Chemnitz, *Examen, XII.*
The Catholic error consists in making a sacrament of a
mere ancient custom. James speaks of sickness in general.
Catholicism refers this only to cases in which death is
imminent. James connects no spiritual results with the
anointing, Catholicism does. James makes the forgiveness
of all sins depend on repentance and faith in Christ.
Catholicism makes the forgiveness of certain sins only depend on an outward priestly performance. Just as Christians must do everything in the name of the Lord Jesus
(Col. 3, 17), and to the glory of God (1 Cor. 10, 31) they
must apply also remedies for bodily relief, here the customary use of oil, **in the name of the Lord,** in order that
he may add his blessing thereto, for unless he does so no
benefit can result. The phase "in the name of the Lord"
modifies the participle "anointing," not the main verb "let
them pray." — Some have tried to find a symbolic meaning in the application of oil to the sick as here mentioned
by James; they suppose that the oil and its application was
to symbolize the restoration prayed for. James himself
in no way indicates anything of the kind, nor do the Scrip-

tures in other places. The N. T. prescribes no symbols; it would be strange to find an exception in this place. The verb which James uses, ἀλείφω, *beschmieren, bestreichen,* in no way favors the idea that a symbol is meant; if the latter had been meant James would have used χρίω, which both the N. T. and the Septuagint employ in every case where a spiritual, religious, or symbolical application of oil is intended (compare χρίσμα and χριστός, anointed). Ἀλείφειν ἐλαίῳ = to oil with oil; it points away from any symbolical anointing of kings, priests, *etc.,* and clearly refers to the application of oil as in cases of sickness, weakness, wounds (comp. the act of the good Samaritan), *etc.,* or in cases where oil was used to refresh and stimulate the body. The idea of a symbol arose among some of the early fathers and formed the transition to the Catholic extreme unction. Just what kind of oil was to be employed James does not state, nor how and to what extent it was to be employed. The idea that the oil was considered by James as a universal remedy or an all-around medicine is unfounded; only its natural refreshing and stimulating effects as employed at that time come into consideration. The act was to be done "in the name of the Lord," since a Christian does all things in the Lord's name, and here the accompanying prayer makes it the more appropriate to mention the Lord especially. Nothing of a sacramental or symbolical nature lies in this reference to the Lord's name. — **And the prayer of faith shall save him that is sick, and the Lord shall raise him up.** This promise attaches to "the prayer of faith," and to that alone, namely to the prayer which faith utters, here the believing prayer of the elders. It goes without saying that James includes also the prayer and faith of the sick person himself. Such prayers can ask only what the Lord has promised. They will center in the petition: "Thy will be done," and cannot include unconditionally the recovery of the sick. When James writes that the prayer of faith **shall save him that is sick,** and explains that **the Lord shall raise him up** from his sick-bed, he does not mean

that this shall be done invariably, nor that it shall be done
at once and miraculously. The promise here is like that
of Jesus, John 16, 23: "If ye shall ask anything of the
Father, he shall give it you in my name;" and Matth. 21,
22: "And all things, whatsoever ye shall ask in prayer,
believing, ye shall receive." While σώσει καὶ ἐγερεῖ point to
a deliverance and a raising up which in many cases means
restoration to bodily health, they include also a deliverance
and raising up which consists in a final removal from this
vale of tears.   All those interpretations which assume
that James and the apostles and first Christians generally
were sure that Christ would return in glory during their
lifetime, and that therefore they all thought they could
live till that great day came, contradict what Paul especially
says so plainly concerning his own death, that of other
believers, and of the uncertainty of the Lord's final return.   The instructions which James here gives do not
rest on the idea that all his readers could be kept alive
until the end of the world.   He knew the promises of
Christ to prayer and the promises of Christ in regard to
his own return far better than that. — **And if he have
committed sins, it shall be forgiven him,** making him
rest easy whatever the Lord may decide as to the outcome
of the disease. Huther is mistaken when he thinks κἄν (for
καὶ ἐάν) must mean: "even if," so that the sickness would
appear as a result and penalty of sins committed by the
patient.   The context suggests nothing of the kind, and
κἄν may be either: "even if," or simply: "and if" (see
Blass), with the latter   preferable here in every way.
When sickness prostrates us, then frequently our sins
worry us.   The worst of all ailments is a disturbed and
distressed conscience.   The prayer of faith will cure that.
And here it becomes apparent that James thinks also of
faith as in the patient's heart, and of prayer as upon his
lips.   "If he have committed sins," ᾖ πεποιηκώς, refers to
special sins which trouble the heart, sinful acts of one
or the other kind which rise up in the memory and make
their accusing voice heard.   For all such distress there is

but one cure: God's pardon and forgiveness for the sake of Christ's merits. And this, together with the peace and comfort which it brings is assured to all who believe, and who cry for it to God in earnest prayer. Both in making such prayer and in keeping their faith true and strong the help of the elders will be of great benefit.

Distress of conscience in general.

Not only the sick, also those in good health may have a distressed conscience. **Confess therefore your sins one to another, and pray one for another, that ye may be healed. The supplication of a righteous man availeth much in its working.** — "Therefore" = because of the promise to faith just expressed. We are to confess our sins, because we can obtain forgiveness, because the promise is held out to our faith. The statement of James is quite general, and we must not introduce restrictions that would alter this. **Your sins,** τὰς ἁμαρτίας, include not only wrongs against our brethren, but all our sins, by which in any way we have missed the mark set by God's law. **Confess** does not mean enumerate, but it does mean that we do not lock up our sins in our hearts, but acknowledge them with expressions of their offensiveness to God and of our sorrow because of them. **One to another** by no means refers only to the persons just mentioned, a sick man and the elders, and even this with the restriction that the sick person confess to the elders. James is addressing all Christians in general. "He sets up a strange confessor," writes Luther, "his name is *Alterutrum*. The pope and the papists do not like him at all. *Alterutrum* means one to the other or among each other, and signifies us all together. That includes that the confessors are to confess to the confessants; and that they are not only priests, bishop, and pope, but every Christian would be pope, bishop, priest, and the pope would have to confess to him." The papists accordingly give up this passage as a proof-passage for their sacrament of confession. "Here the reference is not to confession that is to be made to the priests, but in general concerning the reconciliation of brethren to each other" (but even more general still, as pointed out above). "For it commands that the confession be mutual." *Apology*, 197, 12. — **And pray one for another,** just as the elders pray for the sick, here evidently for forgiveness and the peace and comfort that goes with it. Whenever a brother pours out his confession to me, I am not only to speak the word of absolution and comfort to him as his fellow Christian, but to pray for him, taking his case to the throne of grace above, lifting up his heart to the heavenly source of all forgiveness, that his assurance of forgiveness and comfort may be the greater. — **That ye may be healed** must not be misunderstood as referring to bodily healing; it is like Heb. 12, 13; 1 Pet. 2, 24, a healing of the inward spiritual hurt from sin. James is speaking to all his readers, and not only to the sick; the healing he means is such as we all need constantly. — The more to encourage such fraternal confession and prayer James positively asserts its efficacy: **The supplication of a righteous man availeth much in its working.** Here we have the word for request or entreaty in general ($\delta\acute{\epsilon}\eta\sigma\iota\varsigma$), as addressed by a petitioner to God and to men. This when brought to God by **a righteous man,** one whom God so accounts, namely a true believer declared righteous for Christ's sake, **availeth much in its working,** it will in its working, and it is indeed always full of energy and active in working, succeed in doing a great deal. The participle $\acute{\epsilon}\nu\epsilon\rho\gamma o\nu\mu\acute{\epsilon}\nu\eta$ is not the equivalent of the adjective and a mere adjective modifier of $\delta\acute{\epsilon}\eta\sigma\iota\varsigma$, as in the A. V.: "the effectual fervent prayer;" nor the equivalent of the infinitive: "availeth much to work" (Burger); nor a condition: *wenn es ernstlich ist* (Luther); but a participle retaining its native meaning attached to $\delta\acute{\epsilon}\eta\sigma\iota\varsigma$: "working," *i. e.* in its working, in its natural and proper activity. We may think the effort of prayer nets us little or no result, in reality its effort always succeeds greatly.

This James illustrates by a concrete example: **Elijah was a man of like passions with us, and he prayed fervently that it might not rain; and it rained not on the earth for three years and six months. And he prayed again; and the heaven gave rain, and the earth brought forth her fruit.** — Elijah, though a prophet, must not be thought far above us in the matter of prayer; he is of like nature, of like feelings, in like case with us; we thus belong in the same class. Yet see what his prayer did, and learn what our prayers may do! **He prayed fervently,** or *with prayer* (margin), is a better rendering than the Septuagint way of giving the Hebrew infinitive absolute: praying he prayed, meaning that he did so with the greatest earnestness, but, of course, employing only prayer. Blass 74, 4. His prayer **that it might not rain** resulted in this that it **rained not on the earth for three years and six months.** In 1 Kgs. 17, 1, no mention is made of prayer on the part of Elijah, but James does not quote the passage, and Keil's remark is certainly to the point: all the prophets received the power for their work only through faith and prayerful communion with God. — **And he prayed again, and the heaven gave rain, and the earth brought forth her fruit.** Again we find no explicit mention of prayer on the prophet's part in in 1 Kgs. 18, 42-45, but we find the attitude of prayer plainly described, and Keil rightly says that Elijah here continued praying until the promise of rain God had made to him began to be fulfilled. Some find a discrepancy between the three years and six months mentioned here by James, and likewise by the Lord, Luke 4, 25, and 1 Kgs. 18, 1, where "the third year" is mentioned; they conclude that the rain must have come already in the third year. But "the third year" refers not to the period of drought, but to the occurrence last mentioned, Elijah's stay at Zarpat, where he had remained over two years. The O. T. does not state just how long the drought lasted. Jewish tradition without doubt reported the correct length of time of so terrible a visitation, and both Jesus and James corrobate this traditional information as true. There is nothing mystical in the three and a half years, as some have supposed; to think so, simply because other like periods are mentioned in Scripture in prophetical statements, is to follow fanciful analogies. The great fact of Elijah's efficacious prayer is the thing that must impress us and stimulate us to pray with the same assurance of being heard. Like Elijah we must put ourselves in harmony with the words and promises of God and direct our faith wholly according to them, then will every one of our prayers be heard. To turn to desires and wishes of our own, away from the divine promises and directions given to us in our situation and place, is to obtain no answer to prayer and to bring down upon us the divine displeasure instead.

Defection from the truth.

James concludes his entire Epistle by supposing a third case, actual examples of which no doubt were frequent enough: **My brethren, if any among you do err from the truth, and one convert him; let him know, that he which converteth a sinner from the error of his way shall save a soul from death, and shall cover a multitude of sins.** — From the thought of bodily sickness James proceeded to that of sin and a distressed conscience; and from that he naturally goes a step farther to the case of complete defection from the faith, when conscience itself ceases to be troubled and all is still in spiritual death. Here the admonition is altogether to the brethren, not to the fallen man himself. A special appeal lies in the address: **My brethren;** we notice it also in the emphatic way in which James describes the greatness of the deed of converting a sinner. **If any among you do err from the truth** makes the matter personal; such a thing is possible, surrounded as you are with falsehood and deception, weak and unspiritual as many of you are. Let him that thinketh he standeth take heed lest he fall! "The apostle has in mind the sad case of a man who has fallen away from him who is the way, the truth, and the life, who has grown cold in prayer, careless about attending the divine services, who has opened his heart to all kinds of doubts and instead of the Amen of confession has substituted a mere Perhaps, who has not torn out his eye and cut off his foot at once, but succumbed to evil lust, and, after himself falling from the truth, allowed others to persuade him that the truth itself had fallen, or that there never was any truth in the real sense of the word." Koegel. **The truth** is the Word of God, especially the saving Gospel; to **err from the truth** includes a going astray doctrinally as well as morally, either or both are deadly. — **And one convert him,** "turn him" away from the error of his sinful course, back again to the truth, in repentance and faith, shows that it can be done, and implies that we should bend all our efforts toward doing it. To induce us to try, James states a general proposition applicable to all sinners, whether once converted and fallen away again, or never converted before: **let him know** this blessed fact, **that he which converteth a sinner from the error of his way shall save a soul from death.** God alone converts, but he uses you and me as his agents, and in that sense we convert. **A sinner** is entirely general; every "sinner," whose mark is sin, follows **the error of his way,** the deception which makes him think his way is right and good, at least affording him satisfaction, pleasure, happiness. Eve fell into this error, and in its countless forms it has caught thousands and thousands since, and holds them fast with a chain around their very minds and hearts. To **convert** such a sinner is to show him his error, to give him the truth instead, to let that truth enlighten him, destroy the error and thus free the soul. Whoever does this for a poor sinner **shall save a soul from death;** "shall save," viewing the ultimate result, which lies in the future; and "from death," since eternal damnation is the real, complete death, the irrevocable separation of man from the divine fountain of life. If we read αὐτοῦ after ψυχήν, or after θανάτου: "his soul from death," this must mean the soul of him who is converted, not the soul of him who converts another. Hofman tries to uphold the former, but in the face of Scripture teaching generally, and without any real basis in the text itself. The world praises those who save the lives of others, perhaps at risk of their own; these are "heroes," and the state or some one else decks them with costly medals. But infinitely greater is the credit due to him who saves an immortal soul from eternal perdition, and this perhaps with wrestling and prayer, possibly even at great sacrifice and suffering, as in the case of many a missionary. — **And shall cover a multitude of sins,** while added coordinately, really explains how a soul is saved from death; the root of death is sin, and the moment you turn a sinner from the error of his way, you cover up his sins, even if they be a vast multitude. Again this attributes to us what is really God's own work, namely to forgive sins. "Blessed is he whose sin is covered," Ps. 32, 1. "Whither shall we conduct the erring brother, in order that the multitude of sins that he has committed may find pardon and redemption? 'It is finished!' Jesus has the keys of hell and death. Before him the rescued sinner kneels. However great the mass of his sins, here is forgiveness and life, here is redemption from the power of sin, here is sanctification unto blessedness." Koegel.

HOMILETICAL HINTS.

God is hard to find in sorrow, and in joy easy to forget. — Nothing in the world is harder to bear than a long series of beautiful days. Only Christians know that the goodness of God leads them to repentance; only Christians know how to receive with thanksgiving. — The history of our hymns is a living testimony to many a halleluiah amid tears.

Prayer is the accurate barometer of the spiritual life of the individual Christian as well as of the congregation. If not spiritually dead, but a living body, a congregation will again and again appear before its God, in joy and in sorrow, in days of prosperity and in days of adversity, now singing Psalms praising the Lord, now calling upon him for protection in danger and help in distress. Hein.

Here is the place to instruct and warn against the false Romish sacrament, against faith-cures, rejection of medical aid and reliance only on prayer, Christian Science, and the like, showing our people just what to do in case of sickness. We want no faith gone wild, rejecting the dictates of reason, no absence of faith, falling into despair, no superstitious faith, resorting to magic and secret arts; we want the faith that knows how to pray.

It is not necessary, yet often true enough, that pastoral care does not begin until sickness and death enter a family.

Our elders to-day have the duty to visit and comfort the sick. Let us not forget it. Koegel reminds us that we Christians possess both the universal priesthood and the universal duty of teaching and instructing as prophets of God.

Luke was a physician. Jacob sent some balm, a precious salve, to his son Joseph. Isaiah commanded Hezekiah to lay a lump of figs upon his boil. Christ tells us of the good Samaritan who used oil and wine in binding up wounds. Paul urges Timothy to use a little wine for his stomach's sake. The law of Moses commanded him who injured another to pay the physician. — As wrong as it is to despise medicine, so wrong is it to trust medicine alone and neglect, and thus despise, pastoral care and prayer.

No Christian Scientist or faith-healer is able to offer an acceptable prayer to God, because these people deny the divinity of Christ and his mediatorial work by which alone we can hope to come in prayer to God. — According to Christian Science disease is not real, only a delusion of the mind. Their prayers are not intended for God at all, that he remove the sickness, but merely for the patient, that his mind may be freed from the delusion of sickness. Thus prayer is turned into a blasphemous deception.

What is the cause of sickness? The Scriptures answer: Sin. Therefore whenever Christians are sick, that sickness reminds them of their sins, moves them to repentance and to seek forgiveness. For that reason, as James advises, they call the elders.

There is no more terrible disease than a bad conscience, and no more deadly plague than erring from the truth. — The way of error leads to haughty blinding. The picture of God fades from the mind and becomes a mere idea or word. God is something secondary and of no more importance for man. Instead man grows greater and more glorious in his own mind. The less God counts, the less sin means for man. The moral judgment becomes perverted, then this leads to all sorts of sinful deeds. There is but one remedy, namely conversion.

We must die the death of repentance, or we will die the death of judgment. The death of repentance leads to the life that never dies. That which uncovers our sins also covers them again, namely the love of Christ.

True Faith is a living Power Among the Members of a Christian Congregation.

It moves them
    I. *To pray for their sick brethren.*
   II. *To seek their erring brethren.*

C. C. Hein.

Help Each Other!

    I. *In the affliction of sickness.*
   II. *In the affliction of error.*

Riemer.

The Prayer of the Righteous Availeth Much.

    I. *In joy and in sorrow.*
   II. *In sickness and in sin.*
 III. *In time and in eternity.*

Matthes.

The Prayer of Faith.

Used by Christians for each other
    I. *In bodily sickness.*
   II. *In spiritual sickness.*

Langsdorff.

Brethren, let us Bring Back the Erring.

    I. *See their danger.*
   II. *Think of the means for rescue at our command.*
 III. *Remember the reward that awaits us.*

Koegel.

The Mutual Aid in a Christian Congregation.

    I. *In sickness the best help.*
   II. *In distress of conscience the only relief.*
 III. *In defection from the truth the only rescue.*

THE TWENTIETH SUNDAY AFTER TRINITY.

Rom. 14, 1-9.

The value of this text, which treats of *the strong and the weak members in the Christian congregation,* is apparent at a glance. There will always be some of the latter class among us, and both we and they need the apostle's advice in shaping our conduct. This centers around the so-called *adiaphora,* or things indifferent, on which likewise the apostle here expresses himself. The Formula of Concord devotes an entire article to the subject. The text itself may be divided into three sections, the first describing the conduct of the strong and weak members toward each other (1-4), the second the conviction on which this conduct must rest (5-6), the third the principle from which this conviction must grow.

The strong and the weak in their conduct.

Our text has no special connection with what precedes. Paul has laid down the principles of the Christian life and made a number of practical applications suitable to his first readers. He now makes another at some length, the first section of which constitutes our text. **But him that is weak in faith receive ye,** *yet* **not to doubtful disputations. One man hath faith to eat all things: but he that is weak eateth herbs. Let not him that eateth set at nought him that eateth not; and let not him that eateth not judge him that eateth: for God hath received him.** — Just whom Paul meant by one **weak in faith** commentators have had trouble to decide. No errorist can be meant, for then the apostle would not be so lenient; no Judaizing Christian, for the general abstinence from meat and wine does not fit him; and so with

269

others who have been suggested. It is best to take the
apostle's own description as given in this chapter and not
go beyond that. There were a few in the congregation at
Rome who, while they had living trust in Christ as the
Redeemer and believed the doctrines of the Gospel, were
weak in regard to the liberty which this faith grants in regard to the things God has neither commanded nor forbidden; they made it a rule not to eat meat nor to drink wine
at all, using the latter only in the Lord's Supper. Some
of them, and perhaps all of them, also observed days, not
the Jewish Sabbath or other holy days of the Jews, but
days set apart by themselves for religious instead of secular use. The weak Christians in Rome thus differed considerably from a similar class in Corinth who hesitated
only about meat offered to idols and afterwards sold in the
markets, and who were not concerned about wine at all.
Nor were they Judaistic legalists imagining that certain
outward observances were necessary to salvation. We,
therefore, cannot put them into one class with those in our
day who think that all alcoholic beverages are forbidden of
God, and consider it a sin to partake of them; they are
also unlike those who make a legal Sabbath of Sunday and
insist that the Jewish form of the third commandment is
binding upon Christians (compare Augsburg Confession,
66, 61 *etc.*). All these are not merely weak in the faith,
but evident errorists, who must be treated accordingly, and
their demands rejected and refuted by the Word of God.
Sometimes, however, some of their ideas disturb the minds
of our people and cause them to hesitate in using their God-
given liberty; such are "weak in faith," and with them all
others who cling to the crutches of outward observances
and forms and timidly shrink from using the full and
blessed liberty given us by the Word of God. — Paul bids
the Roman Christians to **receive** him that is weak in the
faith, that means in a fraternal, friendly manner, as a true
brother in the faith. It would have been a bad mistake to
cast such out, or to withdraw from them, just because
they considered certain things as necessary to the Christian

life, which God had not commanded, and with timid consciences feared to let them go. Of course, this does not
apply to those who adhere to sinful practices and connections, or to erroneous doctrines, which militate against the
faith and endanger not only their own souls but also those
of others. — *Yet* **not to doubtful disputations** appends a
warning. The word διαλογισμοί is regularly used for the
wrong ideas and thoughts with which one troubles himself, and here refers to the ideas of him who is weak in
faith, the thoughts in which this weakness appears. In
only two of the church fathers is διάκρισις used in the sense
of "doubt;" its regular meaning is "decision" or "judgment." The margin has: *for decisions of doubts*, meaning by "doubts" the peculiar ideas of him that is weak.
Paul does not want the reception of the weak brother to
lead to disputes with him; the strong are not to judge and
condemn his ideas when they get together with him. They
are to let him alone, and gradually his faith, nourished by
the Word, will of itself grow stronger and get rid of weak-
ening notions. The wisdom of this is apparent. To keep
up debate with a weak Christian and to pass harsh judgment on his ideas may upset him entirely, or drive him to
carry his weakness to the point of actual error. Luther
writes: "In the fourteenth chapter he teaches that we
should deal gently with consciences weak in faith and forbear with them, so that we use our Christian freedom not
to the injury, but to the advancement of the weak. Where
this is not done, dissent and a despising of the Gospel follow. It is better to yield a little to the weak, until they
become stronger, than that the doctrine of the Gospel be
entirely suppressed." — Paul now describes the strong and
the weak: **One man hath faith to eat all things;** "knowing that all creatures of God are good, and nothing to be
refused, 1 Tim. 4, 4, he knows that sin or holiness does not
depend on the food that is eaten or is not eaten" (*Luth.
Com.*). *"All things"* here refers to all kinds of food, including wine and meat. This person has the conviction
and confidence, and one well founded on the teaching of

the Gospel that he may eat any kind of food. Winer, 44, 2b. Of course, this does not mean that he thinks himself free to indulge in harmful food, or to excess. — On the other hand **he that is weak eateth herbs,** only herbs, excluding meat and wine. He has certain scruples about the latter, although God has in no way forbidden them. Just what these scruples are we are not told, only we see that they are not of a legalistic kind, and not based on false doctrine. They probably felt that there was a certain danger in the eating of meat and in the drinking of wine, because they saw all about them the excesses to which the heathen carried their gluttony and drunkenness; in order to keep on the safe side and to cultivate proper Christian holiness they therefore avoided meat and wine altogether. — What does Paul advise? **Let not him that eateth** all things, in the full liberty God has given us, **set at nought him that eateth not** some things, here meat and wine. To look down on the weak in this matter, to despise and make mock of them, would be a sad sin against Christian charity. It is the very thing, however, which the strong are liable to do regarding the weak, in almost all cases where weakness of this kind occurs. — On the other hand: **let not him that eateth not judge him that eateth,** censuring, possibly even condemning him, for using his God-given liberty with a free conscience. And this is the very thing he who is narrow in his views of Gospel liberty is liable to do. He must not judge and condemn as sinful what God has left free; that would turn his weakness into dangerous error. Christian love and fellowship, so helpful and beneficial to us all, would be sadly disrupted both by the sin of setting others at nought, and by that of judging others where God has made no law. True unity is furthered by Christian kindness and forbearance. — The warning against unbrotherly judging is made stronger by showing why it is out of place: **for God hath received him** who eateth all things, as a true servant of his. Such judgment then conflicts with God's judgment on the essentials of membership in his church. He who requires more than God requires will have to answer to God himself.

The point is so important that Paul elucidates it more fully: **Who art thou that judgest the servant of another? to his own lord he standeth or falleth. Yea, he shall be made to stand; for the Lord hath power to make him stand.** It is presumptuous for a weak brother to set himself up as if he were the very strongest of all, yea, himself the real master in the house of God. This is Christ, who himself judges every οἰκήτην, *household servant* of his, and needs no man to help him. To be sure, when one servant reminds the other of the Master's commands and requirements as laid down in his Word, this is no presumption, but the very best service we can render each other. It is a different thing entirely when we go beyond the Word and start to judge according to our own foolish ideas. — It is a general rule, a fixed principle, applicable to all lords and servants, that a servant stands or falls to his own lord. No matter what others may say or think, his case is wholly in the hands of his own master. There is no reason why we should drop the idea of judgment in the phrase: "to stand or to fall to his own lord." Some substitute for it the idea of continuing or failing to continue in Christian life and service, to the advantage or the disadvantage of the Lord. But the reason assigned for thus changing the figure, namely that the following sentence fits this thought better, rests on a misconception. **Yea, he shall be made to stand** is emphatic; Christ *will* make him stand. How so? **for the Lord hath power to make him stand,** δυνατεῖ, stronger than δύναται, "can, or is able;" the Lord is mighty and powerful enough to make his servant stand in the judgment. It is objected that Christ's servants "stand" in the judgment not through the power, but through the grace of the Lord — which is true enough when the question of their sins and shortcomings is put forward. But here Paul urges that Christ is mighty and powerful to keep his servants true and faithful in their work during the

18

time of their service, so that they resist every temptation to abuse the liberty he has given them, and thus stand in his judgment, now already, and finally at the last day. Christ does not need the assistance of the weak brethren in getting his servants to stand. In giving all of us the liberty of the Gospel he has shown no weakness that now must be made good by the addition of rules about meat and drink, such as the weak brethren try to follow. Let us hold fast and make proper use of our liberty, using the Lord's might that is in it; it will preserve and keep us in every way, and we may be constantly sure of the Lord's commendation: "Well done, thou good and faithful servant!" It is a mistake to count weakness as strength, and to overlook the true strength which Christ offers us all; and again it is a mistake to reduce all the Lord's servants to the level of the weak, as if their weakness were the true ideal, when the reverse is true, and the weak should all be brought to the higher plane of the Lord's liberty and strength.

The strong and the weak in their conviction.

One man esteemeth one day above another: another esteemeth every day *alike.* **Let each man be fully assured in his own mind. He that regardeth the day, regardeth it unto the Lord: and he that eateth, eateth unto the Lord, for he giveth God thanks; and he that eateth not, unto the Lord he eateth not, and giveth God thanks.** — The chief point which Paul urges in these words is that each man must "be fully assured in his own mind;" he must follow the conviction that he is serving the Lord in the best way possible for him. Zahn thinks that the apostle introduces the question of esteeming days merely by way of illustration, this question with the difference in conduct between different members being well understood by all. But nothing points to such illustrative use, the apostle makes no application from the question regarding days to the one regarding eating. It appears, from the similarity with which Paul states the two cases, that they are simply parallel. There were in Rome weak Christians who esteemed one day above another. Perhaps they were identical with those who abstained from meat and wine. The fact that Paul does not dwell at length upon the question of days is quite generally interpreted as indicating that this question caused less trouble than the other, perhaps none at all. Still the two belong together as involving the very same principle. **One man esteemeth one day above another,** κρίνει, he judges it to be so; when he puts one day beside (παρά) the other, he sees a difference, one seems more sacred to him than another. It is best to refer this distinction of days to the Jewish Sabbath and holidays. What other days would anyone in Rome think of putting above others? The most natural explanation is that there were Jewish Christians in Rome, perhaps some of them from the old mother congregation in Jerusalem, who still clung to the early practice of the apostles in using the Sabbath for worship. They did not insist on any legal observance of the day or try to compel its observance by others, as did a number of Judaistic errorists elsewhere; still they could not separate themselves from their old customs. When the Sabbath came they shut their shops and stores, ceased work, and counted the day holy; likewise the old Jewish festival days. — **Another esteemeth every day** *alike,* judges every day, *i. e.* makes no difference between them. Godet points to the slight irony in this second use of κρίνειν, for when we judge or distinguish every day, we wipe out all difference. The idea is not that all days are secularized, but that all are sanctified and used for the Lord's service. — Again the apostle does not condemn the one action, and uphold the other as according to a divine command. The entire question is one of Christian liberty and must be treated accordingly. The thing to avoid is intolerance in such questions. He who makes no distinction of days is strong in that he makes full use of his liberty; he who hesitates about doing this is weak, in that he is afraid of using so much liberty. Yet it would be wrong for either to condemn the other, seeing that the Lord has not done so in his Word. So Paul advises: **Let each man**

be fully assured in his own mind. That cannot mean: Let each be assured in his own mind that he is right, and the other wrong, and then each honor the conviction of the other as if that too were right. The apostle never puts truth and error on a level, and never urges tolerance between them. The entire question here is not in the field of truth and error, or right and wrong, but in the field of liberty, where God has neither commanded nor forbidden. The apostle's injunction therefore is: Let each be fully convinced that his own course is really best and most profitable for himself. — How this works out he at once shows: **He that regardeth the day, regardeth it unto the Lord,** which, of course, involves the other alternative, not found in the best texts: *and he that regardeth not the day, to the Lord he doth not regard it,* A. V. It really is not a question of days, but one of serving and honoring the Lord in the best way. He who thinks he needs some special day for this, let him be fully certain in his own mind, and then use the day for that purpose; but let him not judge and condemn others. On the other hand, he who rejoices in his freedom and uses every day as a day of worship and service, let him be sure in his own mind, and then employ all his days accordingly; only let him not mock and despise his weaker brethren, who cannot feel right unless they adhere to certain days. As regards days the church soon settled on one certain day for public worship, namely the day of Christ's resurrection and of the pouring out of the Holy Ghost, the first day in the week, the Lord's day. The course of the weaker brethren who clung long to the Sabbath, the seventh day in the week, was abandoned entirely. Truly, and in the fullest exercise of Christian liberty, Sunday was chosen, because good order for public worship and the best interests of the church seemed to require the setting apart of such a day. In the same spirit of liberty we now should use the day, glad that it serves our needs so well and that the vast majority of professing Christians have all united on this day. The legalistic ideas which some still connect with it we must always reject as con-

trary to the whole apostolic doctrine of liberty and prone
to lead to error, if not already the fruit of error. See
Augsburg Confession, Article 28, § 53 *etc.;* also *Eisenach
Gospel Selections,* Seventeenth Sunday after Trinity. —
Paul, however, is concerned chiefly about the question of
meat and wine: **and he that eateth, eateth unto the Lord,
for he giveth God thanks.** Counting all food as good
gifts of God, he eats freely of any kind in the name of the
Lord and for the glory of God, 1 Cor. 10, 31, and shows
this by his returning thanks at table. "For every creature
of God is good, and nothing is to be rejected, if it be received with thanksgiving: for it is sanctified through the
word of God and prayer." 1 Tim. 4, 4-5. — Likewise: **and
he that eateth not,** namely meat and wine, **unto the Lord
he eateth not,** if his motive be right at all, as that of the
Jewish Christians at Rome certainly was, **and giveth God
thanks** for the herbs or vegetables with which he thought
best to content himself. At heart, Paul shows, both are one
in trying to serve the Lord; as. to their being true Christians there is no difference between the weak and the
strong. "The apostle renders no objective decision, because in the matter of a moral adiaphoron the main thing is
our subjective conduct, our personal inner attitude to the
thing. Objectively and in itself the freer attitude is more
correct, although subjectively it may be more false than
the other which feels itself bound; this will be the case
when the latter attitude avoids judging others, while the
former boasts of its freedom. Whether a person feels
himself bound to a certain mode of life in itself indifferent,
or whether he feels himself free, the chief thing in regard
to others is that he avoid judging them or despising them,
and in regard to himself, that for his own person he be
sure in his own mind. For when the weaker Christian with
his wavering conscience allows himself to adopt the freer
mode of life, he will sin, verses 20 and 23; and in the same
way, when the freer Christian is not divinely certain of his
case in the Lord who has made him free, but turns to the
freer mode of life in fleshly desire for liberty from re-

straint and with an injured conscience." Philippi. "Using
and abstaining, acting and refraining from acting are to
the Christian no arbitrary matters, determined by his own
caprice, but are determined by his conviction as to what
the will of the Lord is" (*Luth. Com.*), and, we may add,
in all cases where the Lord has not expressed his will, by
his conviction as to what in his own personal case will best
aid him in serving the Lord.

The strong and the weak in their principle.

What Paul has just said about regarding days and
about eating and not eating rests on a grand Christian
principle, namely on our complete subjective depend-
ence upon the Lord. This, embracing our entire life
and death, naturally includes also our course of conduct
in one or the other individual matter. **For none of us
liveth to himself, and none dieth to himself. For whether
we live, we live unto the Lord; or whether we die, we
die unto the Lord: whether we live therefore, or die,
we are the Lord's. For to this end Christ died, and lived**
again, **that he might be Lord of both the dead and the
living.** — Our life and our death depends objectively upon
the Lord; he controls it with his power and providence.
But this is not the point the apostle urges, for this would
show only that we ought to devote our lives to him, to
whom we thus belong. Paul is urging upon his readers
their subjective, personal purpose as Christians, which is
to live and to die unto the Lord. **For none of us liveth
to himself** means that every Christian, whether weak or
strong as regards matters of Christian liberty, has given up
living according to his own blind notions and foolish desires; and the same way about dying: **and none dieth to
himself,** as far as the character of our death is concerned
each one of us has given up the idea of winding up his life
in the blind and foolish way in which so many others are
content to pass into eternity. — Our purpose and principle
is different altogether: **For whether we live, we live unto
the Lord,** devoting our lives and all our activity to him, in

his service and honor; **or whether we die,** when he sets the time for us, **we die unto the Lord,** willingly following his call, confidently commending our souls to him. So that, summing it all up: **whether we live therefore, or die, we are the Lord's** belonging wholly to him. Bengel: *Eadem ars moriendi, quae vivendi.* With this principle of living and dying unto the Lord, of belonging to him and serving him both in life and in death (note the close connection indicated by τέ . . . τέ), fixed in our hearts once for all, even in things indifferent we will inquire and study how best to use them, or to leave them unused, that the Lord may be honored and his work among men promoted. — From the fixed purpose in the Christian's heart the apostle turns to the great soteriological purpose of God himself, showing that the former is in harmony with the latter. The **for** is explanatory: **For to this end Christ died, and lived** *again,* **that he might be Lord of both the dead and the living.** Christ's death on the cross and his vivification in the resurrection belong together; he did not become Lord of the dead by his death, and Lord of the living by his living again, but by dying and living again he became Lord of both. The coordination of terms here is merely formal; "the dead" are mentioned before "the living" only in order to make the terms parallel. The reading: "Christ both died, and rose, and revived," A. V., and several variants of a similar kind, are efforts to explain the original reading and without good textual authority. The aorist ἔζησεν indicates the first moment when life returned to the dead body of Christ, Christ remaining in that life ever after; the word cannot refer to Christ's earthly life anterior to his sacrificial death, there being no occasion to refer to that especially, moreover the Scriptures generally declare that Christ obtained his lordship by his death and resurrection: Rom. 6, 9-10; 8, 34; Phil. 2, 8 *etc.;* Luke 24, 26; Matth. 28, 18. Luther finely expresses what is meant by Christ's lordship: "that I may be his own, and live under him in his kingdom, and serve him in everlasting righteousness, innocence, and blessedness, even as he is risen from the dead, lives and reigns to all eternity." Even such a change as death does not effect this lordship of Christ over us: he rules alike over all his believers living or dead. This is a difference far greater than that between those who eat and those who refuse to eat, between those who regard all days, and those who regard special days. These differences between the strong and the weak thus sink into insignificance. The one supreme divine purpose is the lordship of Christ over us; with that assured for us all who mean to be Christ's in life and in death, othe things do not matter greatly, only so that they do not mili tate against this. Thus the apostle goes back of the rule o conduct he lays down for the strong and the weak, bac of the personal conviction even which must govern the cor, duct, to the great saving principle and truth that lies at th bottom of it all: Christ, our one Lord, to whom we belon, in faith and who rules over us with his power, mercy, and glory for ever and ever.

HOMILETICAL HINTS.

He who is weak needs a support, a child must learn to walk by the help of others. — It would be foolish for an apprentice to imagine that the master must still use all the helps which he himself requires. It would be equally foolish for a master to expect an apprentice to show all the skill and perfection which he himself attained only after long training. — The skilled sailor knows how to conduct his boat through the threatening wind and waves, avoiding the dangers and keeping to the safe course. It would be foolhardy for a beginner to take the same risks, he would surely perish in the dangers. — Shall we despise a child because it is not a man? a beginner who is timid because he is not a master? Shall we not rather be patient, considerate, helpful, that faith may grow, knowledge increase, and the full freedom of the Christian life develop?

Intolerance is the thing that must not be tolerated. When Peter withdrew himself from the Gentile Christians at Antioch and refused to eat with them, he justly deserved Paul's rebuke. — The worst weakness is that which demands that all others shall be equally weak. And many a one who thinks himself strong has a very weak point in his lack of consideration, of patience, and forbearance for the weak.

"Not that which goeth into the mouth defileth a man; but that which cometh out of the mouth, this defileth a man." Matth. 15, 11. "Unto the pure all things are pure." Tit. 1, 15. "Therefore let no man glory in men. For all things are yours. . . . And ye are Christ's; and Christ is God's." 1 Cor. 3, 21 and 23.

In essential things unity, in doubtful things liberty, in all things charity. Augustine.

All men must die, but Christians are willing to die. They are ready in the Lord's service and for his honor, in faith and in love, to weary this body with labor and to sacrifice it in their calling, to be sick with patience and submission, and to die when the Lord appoints their hour. The sacramental prayer ever rings through their lives: "Lord Jesus, thou hast bought us: to thee will we live, to thee will we die, and thine will we be forever. Amen." Others indeed proclaim as the hight of their wisdom: Whether we live or die we are and will remain the children of blind chance, slaves of a stern fate — nothing more!

One evening Luther and Melanchthon had to cross the swollen river Elbe on their way to Wittenberg in a frail boat. Melanchthon hesitated to go: Do not embark, Martin, the stars are against us! But Martin drew his resisting friend in: We are the Lord's, and therefore we are lords, lords also of the stars!

A king's favorite lay dying. The prince deeply moved stood at his friend's bedside and bade him ask one more signal favor. "Save me from death!" pleaded the dying man. "O how I would like to," he replied, "but that is beyond my power." "Fool that I was," exclaimed the despairing man, "to give the service of my whole life to a weak human creature, and never to think of serving him who alone could help me in death." — To die without Christ is to lose the soul in hell; to live with Christ is to move forward toward heaven already in this life.

Strength and Weakness Among the Members of a Congregation.

I. *In regard to knowledge.*
II. *In regard to faith.*
III. *In regard to brotherly conduct.*

How About Things Which the Lord Has Left Free?

I. *You may use them freely, but only in the Lord's name.*
II. *You must not despise those who do not use them.*
III. *You must not judge those who do use them.*

We are the Lord's.

I. *No one is his own lord.*
II. *No one is the lord of others.*

Latrille.

Our Conduct in Regard to Things Indifferent.

I. *When you think of yourself only, follow Paul's word: "We are the Lord's."*
II. *When you think of your fellow Christians, follow Paul's word: "To his own master he standeth or falleth."*

C. C. Hein.

The Christian's Declaration of Independence, "We are the Lord's."

I. *Free from compulsion for all time.*
II. *Bound to the Lord for all eternity.*

Matthes.

Christian Tolerance.

I. *It has definite bounds.*

a) We dare tolerate no error.
b) We are bound to tolerate all things in themselves neither commanded nor forbidden of God.
c) But things in themselves indifferent cease to be such in fact when they become involved in questions of doctrine and a full confession of the truth. See *Formula of Concord,* Article 10.

II. *It requires a definite conduct.*

a) We must not set others at nought.
b) We must not judge others.
c) We must seek and serve the Lord alone.

THE
TWENTY-FIRST SUNDAY AFTER TRINITY.

Eph. 6, 1-9.

This text on *parents and children, masters and servants in the Christian congregation* is exceedingly timely. Here are lessons which thousands have failed to learn, suffering the most distressing consequences as a result; here are lessons which we in the church cannot learn too well, if we would indeed be true to our profession as followers of Christ. Luther somewhere says that parents cannot merit hell any more quickly or thoroughly than by failing to do their duty by their children. Just what that duty is in its higher reaches the apostle Paul here sets forth, supplementing it with the duty of children, of servants, and of masters. After treating of marriage, the foundation of the Christian home, and of the duty of husbands and wives Paul proceeds with children and parents, and then with servants and masters.

Children and parents.

To the apostle it is a matter of course that the Christian home will also contain children. To some this precious gift is denied without the slightest fault on their part; theirs is considered a somewhat exceptional position, unless they fill the sad gap in their homes by adopting one or more orphan children, which should be urged upon childless Christian couples. The apostle does not reckon here, or in any of his letters where he speaks of parenthood, with the modern crime of abortion which commits murder in order to avoid the burden of child-bearing and child-rearing and destroys the chief purpose of marriage as instituted by God. The way in which the apostle assumes the presence of children in the Christian home may be utilized by the preacher on this text to drive home some of the elementary truths that ought to be impressed upon our hearers in these evil times. — **Children, obey your parents in the Lord: for this is right. Honor thy father and mother (which is the first commandment with promise), that it may be well with thee, and thou mayest live long on the earth.** — The direct address and command: **Children, obey,** takes it for granted that the children in Ephesus will be present in the assembly of the congregation to hear what the apostle writes also to them. As Paul did not forget to say a word to the children in such a grand letter as the one to the Ephesians, let not the preacher forget often to address the children in his Sunday sermon. That they should be present at the regular service is so self-evident, that the pastor who continues to let the children go home after Sunday school will never be able to answer to God for his negligence. — The special duty of children is expressed in the words: **obey your parents in the Lord.** God has arranged the natural relation of parents and children so that the former are superior to the latter, and the latter dependent upon the former; he has put a strong natural love into parental hearts and a mighty desire to care for the children and give them prosperity and happiness. The Gospel does not upset this natural arrangement of God, it sanctifies it: **in the Lord,** that is: in Christ, of whom the apostle has been speaking all along in describing the relation of husband and wife. It is in vain for Meyer to argue that the children thus addressed need not necessarily have been baptized; he is answered by the Lord himself who couples the command to baptize with the one to teach all things that he has commanded, Matth. 28, 19-20. Paul is here attending to the teaching, and we may be sure that the baptism was not neglected. The obedience is to be "in the Lord," rendered as in communion with Christ. This is more than a reference to the will of God as expressed in the law; more than if the apostle had said: God wants you to obey.

It is more also than a reference to the example of Christ (Hamann). The entire obedience of Christian children is to be rendered as a fruit of their blessed relation to Christ. Because they are Christ's own, living under him in his kingdom, with a new spirit in their hearts, they are to obey their parents, with true Christian obedience. — **For this is right,** the apostle adds, touching one of the strong motives of true obedience, which is the desire to please God and do what is acceptable in his sight. The rule of right for all Christians, children as well as grown people, is the will of God. To do what he bids us, to do it "in the Lord," moved by love to him and enabled by his grace, is the Christian's constant desire; and it begins in the early days of childhood. — The apostle therefore quotes the fourth commandment: **Honor thy father and mother,** Ex. 20, 12; Deut. 5, 16. Honor is the form which love assumes when directed to those above us. Mere outward obedience is not enough, it must spring from this true motive of honor in the heart, and that must be planted there by Christ himself. Father and mother are equal in this respect, and Christian ethics rightly includes not only natural parents, but also those who in any way take their place and assume a relation like theirs toward any child. — Here Paul inserts the remark: **which is the first commandment with promise,** then adding also the promise. The use of ἐντολαί in the Gospels for the moral law, the ten Mosaic commandments, and the fact that Paul here writes to children, namely the entire body of children in the congregation at Ephesus, makes it certain that he is here thinking only of the decalogue, not, as some suppose, of all the commandments of God, moral and ceremonial. What concern would Christian children have in any ceremonial regulation intended for the Jewish dispensation? Now the fact is that God attached a promise already to the first commandment, Ex. 20, 6, and there is no other commandment, outside of the fourth, with a promise. To say that Paul's words: "this is the first commandment with promise," means that the commandments which precede it are without such a promise, but that of those which follow one or more also have a promise, is manifestly not correct. The absence of the article with ἐντολή ought to be noted. The true meaning of the apostle is brought out by putting a comma after πρώτη: "which is a first, that is chief, commandment"; then follows the addition: "with a promise that it may be well with thee *etc.*" This is the marginal reading in the Greek text of Westcott and Hort, and is followed quite closely by most commentators. The word πρώτη thus indicates rank instead of number, and the rank is indicated by the added reference to the promise: this commandment is one of the chief ones, in point of promise. It resembles the first in this respect: each heads a table of the law, and each has a promise attached. — The promise is in the form of a purpose clause (ἵνα) showing God's kind intention towards those who render obedience to this commandment: **that it may be well with thee, and thou mayest live long on the earth.** Paul adapts the O. T. promise, as originally made to the Jews, to his Christian readers, omitting the reference to Canaan: "that thy days may be long upon the land which the Lord thy God giveth thee," Ex. 20, 12. Here is an example of how we must distinguish between the substance of the law and its old covenant form. After ἵνα we have here first a subjunctive γένηται and then a future indicative ἔσῃ. Winer thinks the latter is not dependent upon ἵνα, and the R. V. offers the translation *shalt* in the margin, according with this view. Yet the N. T. writers use the future indicative after ἵνα, and there are a number of examples where the indicative follows the subjunctive, when two verbs are employed; Blass seems to be right when he attributes this to the influence of the Hebrew, p. 212. The main part of the promise is **that it may be well with thee,** in the highest sense of the word. This does not exclude bodily and temporal well-being, but it places spiritual well-being above it. It cannot be well with us merely when our fields bear so heavily that we must tear down our barns and build greater, or when we grow wealthy enough to wear

purple and fine linen and fare sumptuously every day. It
is truly well with us when we keep in God's grace and
abide under his blessing. How natural the connection of
Christian obedience of children with such well-being in
after life is we can readily see when we observe that from
such obedience there will grow a faithful Christian life
in general. For Christian parents will ask their children
especially to keep in God's paths, to avoid sin and shame,
and to be true to God's Word. Let children rejoice to
obey all such commands; streams of blessings flow from
them for all their future life. The child who disobeys for-
sakes all these blessings, and his disobedience in general,
and especially in the lines indicated, is bound to produce
the most bitter fruit. See the blasted lives of the young
criminals in our reformatories and prisons, and in other
sad institutions. — This well-being will naturally also include that **thou mayest live long on the earth.** Not that
every obedient child will necessarily live to a good old age;
there are other factors which God's providence takes into
account, making an early death a greater blessing for
some than a late death would be. But the rule as such
holds good: Christian obedience leads to quiet, prosperous, undisturbed lives, away from all those sins which
wreck so many a young career and so often blast it with
the penalty of an untimely death.

The apostle now turns to the parents: **And, ye
fathers, provoke not your children to wrath: but
nurture them in the chastening and admonition of the
Lord.** The father is the head of the family, but all his
work in behalf of the children is seconded by the mother.
So both are meant; but certainly the apostle does not
justify the conduct of those fathers who simply feed and
house their children and leave their training wholly in the
hands of the mothers. The chief sin of children is disobedience; the chief sin of parents, who are set in authority over their children, is harshness; hence the apostle
urges: **provoke not your children to wrath,** and Col. 3,
21: "provoke not your children, that they be not dis-

couraged." Authority is easily abused and then becomes tyranny. The danger with many to-day is that they give up their authority as parents altogether and allow their children unbridled license. Paul here shows how parents are to exercise their authority, so that it will not outrage the feeling of justice in the hearts of the children and produce bitterness and resentment in the form of open or secret wrath against their parents. — They are to **nurture them,** to rear them up with care, **in the chastening and admonition of the Lord.** On παιδεία and νουθεσία as here combined read Trench, *Synonyms* I, 152 *etc.* The heathen Greeks used the former only in the sense of "education;" this the Christian writers deepened to mean much more. "Nurture" in the A. V. is not strong enough, it should rather be "discipline" in the sense of "the laws and ordinances of the Christian household, the transgression of which will induce correction." In Heb. 12, 5 this correction (παιδεία) is meant, especially its painful features; here the word includes the whole system of Christian training. By **admonition** is meant the training by word, "by word of encouragement when no more than this is wanted, but also by the word of remonstrance, of reproof, of blame, where these may be required." The first term deals rather with acts and measures in general, the second with words. Both are necessary and must be combined. While the second is a milder term, Trench reminds us that it stands for no Eli-remonstrance, 1 Sam. 2, 24, for of him it is expressly said: "he restrained them not," οὐκ ἐνουθέτει αὐτούς, 3, 13. As children advance in years the παιδεία will more and more turn to νουθεσία, the earnest words of parents controlling the children completely and directing them in their conduct and course. — The addition **of the Lord,** not: *zum Herrn* (Luther), indicates the character of this discipline and admonition. It makes little difference just how we explain the genitive: the discipline and admonition which belongs to the Lord and which he exercises, or which our relation to the Lord requires; it evidently emphasizes the Christian principles of all child-train-

ing. Christian parents mean to rear their children to be
faithful, noble Christian men and women; this they can
do only when their whole work is governed by Christ and
animated by his Spirit.

Servants and masters.

Paul writes of servants who were δοῦλοι, *bondservants* (margin) or slaves, but at the end of verse
8 he also refers to such as are "free." This makes the
application easier, for to-day Christianity has overthrown the institution of slavery. Still, when so many
servants and laborers to-day complain of "slavery," the
apostle's words addressed to actual slaves have a special
value. There will be less tyranny and slavery in the
household and in the industrial world when the apostolic
admonitions are put into the hearts of men and control
their actions. To do this is part of the great work of
the church. — **Servants, be obedient unto them that
according to the flesh are your masters, with fear and
trembling, in singleness of your heart, as unto Christ;
not in the way of eyeservice, as men-pleasers; but as
servants of Christ, doing the will of God from the heart;
with good will doing service, as unto the Lord, and not
unto men: knowing that whatsoever good thing each
one doeth, the same shall he receive again from the
Lord, whether** *he be* **bond or free.** — The obedience
which Paul enjoins is that which pertains naturally to the
position of a slave in the household, and we may add, to
that of a free servant, whether in the household or otherwise hired for work. There is a Lord and Master to
whom we all belong spiritually, and the apostle refers to
him repeatedly in what follows; so he describes the earthly
masters as **they that according to the flesh are your
masters,** as far as mere outward and bodily relation is
concerned. Here too the Gospel does not overthrow the
order of nature, but aims to purify, ennoble, and sanctify
it. This it does by changing the inward character of obedi-

19

ence on the one hand, and of mastery and control on the other. — The obedience is to be **with fear and trembling,** which does not mean dread of punishment, such as might fill the hearts of godless slaves or servants, but dread of shortcomings in matters of duty and proper service. Note how Paul uses the same phrase in 1 Cor. 2, 3; 2 Cor. 7, 15; Phil. 2, 12. — **In singleness of your heart** adds the idea of full devotion to duty as such, without duplicity or ulterior purpose. — **As unto Christ** might be considered a third coordinate modifier, added to the previous two and rising to the highest level in characterizing the prescribed obedience; but its meaning is such that it may well be taken as modifying both of the preceding phrases. Servants are to be so anxious and devoted in their obedience as if their service pertained entirely to the Lord himself. "If a slave might have doubts what kind of service his earthly master had a right to claim from him, he could have no doubt about what kind of service he owed to Christ." *Luth. Com.* — Paul explains more fully, first negatively, then positively. **Not in the way of eye service, as men-pleasers** describes only too truly the action of many servants and laborers, who care nothing about really doing their duty, but only to pass outward inspection and secure their master's or employer's approval. When they think their laziness or dereliction will not be seen or chided, they idle and loaf, do inferior work, or take other advantage of their superiors. Even their diligence in seeking only human approval has a false motive from the Christian standpoint. — **But as servants of Christ, doing the will of God from the heart** states in a positive way how Christian servants work for their masters. They who try to please only men, make these their highest masters, and what that means they will find out when it comes to the reward. The Christians who are in the position of δοῦλοι to earthly masters are at the same time δοῦλοι Χριστοῦ, servants or slaves of Christ. In all their work his eyes are constantly upon them, so they are always **doing the will of God** in all their service to men **from the**

heart, ἐκ ψυχῆς, *ex animo,* for their Master constantly
looks at the heart. And here is the difference between the
service of mere worldly men and that of true Christians.
The grandest effort to secure the applause of men, even
when highly successful, is as nothing beside some obscure
task rendered "from the heart" to please Christ. — Some
commentators draw "from the heart" to what follows, and
Westcott and Hort so punctuate the Greek; but it is best
to take the phrase as the two English versions have it,
stating emphatically that Christian servants put their heart
into the work and never stoop to sham and deception. What
follows is quite complete without the phrase mentioned:
**with good will doing service, as unto the Lord, and not
unto men merely.** Their good will is toward their earthly
masters and employers; though slaves, and thus forced to
service, Christ, their heavenly Master, sweetens their
labor, so that all moroseness and ill will disappears and
they render their service with kindly feeling. This, because they really do their work **unto the Lord,** and not as
others only **unto men.** Their whole work and effort rests
on a higher plane; even in doing the meanest, humblest
labors they serve Christ, and no man, even though he be
King, can do a higher or grander thing. — What lies behind all these specifications, especially behind this emphasis on the Lord and the service rendered to him, now
comes out in a sort of climax: **knowing that whatsoever
good thing each one doeth, the same shall he receive
again from the Lord, whether** *he be* **bond or free.** The
readings differ more or less; we take that of Westcott and
Hort as the best: εἰδότες ὅτι ἕκαστος, ἐάν τι ποιήσῃ ἀγαθόν,
τοῦτο κτλ., which is followed by both English versions.
Christian servants know what worldly workers either do
not know at all or treat as foolishness, namely that as
there are two kinds of masters, two kinds of service, two
ways of serving, so there are also two kinds of pay, and
that of the Master whom none can deceive is the grandest
and most desirable of all. He pays very exactly: every
good thing that we do, he renders it back to us again.

Good thing here stands in the sense of good and acceptable in his eyes, good as coming from a good heart, stamped with the goodness of love to him. That very thing we shall receive again from the Lord, in the shape of commendation and gracious reward. On the judgment day every man shall "receive the things done in his body," those very things, "according to that he hath done, whether it be good or bad," 2 Cor. 5, 10. This rule is general and applies to **each one,** ἕκαστος, and Paul adds: **whether he be bond,** that is a slave, **or free,** serving of his own volition for pay. The future κομίσεται (the form in later Greek) refers chiefly to the final reward at the end of time, but already in this life faithful servants "carry away" many a reward which is a direct counterpart and reflection of their faithfulness. But where earthly masters are blind, indifferent, openly unjust, or even cruel and tyrannous, no Christian servant shall lose a thing by continuing faithful. In fact, the harder their service is made and the more difficult to render it faithfully, the greater will be the final reward for those who have persevered to the end.

And, ye masters, do the same things unto them, and forebear threatening: knowing that both their Master and yours is in heaven, and there is no respect of persons with him. Instead of sketching out in full detail what the conduct of the masters should be, the apostle sums it up: **do the same things unto them.** Before the forum of God's Word there is no essential difference between masters and servants; God measures both now, as he will measure at the end of the world, with the same rule. Commentators generally refer τὰ αὐτά to μετ' εὐνοίας in verse 7, but it seems best, since neither this nor any other phrase constitutes a grammatical antecedent, to take τὰ αὐτά as a general reference to all the acts which Paul has enjoined upon servants; these all, allowing for the difference in station, must be required of masters likewise: they too should fear and tremble lest they fail of their duty; they too must have singleness of heart in treating their servants as though the Lord's eyes were ever upon their every word and act; they too must show good will for Christ's sake; they too must serve Christ in the way they handle and reward their servants; they too must do the good things they expect the Lord to give them back again. Thus it is plain τὰ αὐτά is the key to the whole servant problem, to the whole labor problem; only it must be applied to the difficulties by both sides, masters as well as servants. — Paul mentions especially the vice to which masters are prone, seeing the power and authority is in their hands: and **forbear,** ἀνιέντες, really: "dismiss," **threatening,** from which cruelty and oppression so generally result. Note the article: "the threatening," so customary with masters. In the world of workers to-day this vice with all its brood of violent acts is found also among those who work for others. The spirit of Christ forbids it altogether. — Just as Paul pointed the servants to Christ, so now he does the masters. Masters though they are, they too have one above them, a divine κύριος, before whom they are in the most lowly position, for he is **in heaven.** Let this keep them humble and free from the arrogance which leads to the abuse of petty power. This exalted Master is absolutely just: **there is no respect of persons with him,** as there is here below with foolish men. When a servant is at fault, he is made to suffer; when a master does the same wicked thing, he is allowed to go unreproved. The unequal justice of human laws which would not take a slave's word, but always took a master's, is abolished in the court above. Masters may well walk in fear and trembling before him who will surely avenge the servants whom they have abused. "Think not, Paul would say, that what is done towards a servant, he will therefore forgive, because done to a servant." Chrysostom. Col. 4, 1. Even a king's purple shall not shield him against the complaint of his lowest menial at that day. When masters and servants together begin to serve Christ, their troubles will cease, their blessings will multiply, their positions will be filled with happiness, their consciences will be easy, their reckoning at the last day will be met with joy.

HOMILETICAL HINTS.

Rump calls it strange that it should be necessary in writing to a Christian congregation to safeguard the rights of parents. What an accusation against our sin-cursed race that the very foundations of human society are thus corroded with sin! For children to love, honor, and obey their parents ought to be as natural as for them to run and play, to eat and sleep, yea, to breathe and exist. — A sad commentary on children's love when it is said that it is easier for one father to keep seven children, than for seven children to keep one father. — The root of the human tree is in the family life; where these roots are not sound, all doctoring and propping of the sapling will avail nothing. — Children reflect to a great extent the real character of their parents.

"God has exalted fatherhood and motherhood above all other relations under his scepter. This appears from the fact that he does not command merely to love the parents, but to honor them." Luther. He also writes: "Whomsoever we honor from the heart we must truly regard as superior. Thus the young must be taught to reverence their parents in God's stead, and to remember that even though they be lowly, poor, frail and peculiar, they are still father and mother, given by God. Their way of living and their failings cannot rob them of their honor. Therefore, we are not to regard the manner of their persons, but God's will that appointed and ordained them to be our parents." Lenker, *Luther's Catechetical Writings*, I, 65-66, Large Catechism. — The Reformer vividly brings out how a little child honoring and obeying its parents according to this commandment will on the judgment day put to nought the proudest monk with all his self-chosen works. The same is true of those who to-day busy themselves with many things and forget the elementary duties of the fourth commandment. — "Will you not obey your father and mother and submit to their training — then obey the hangman; if you will not obey him, obey death, the great slayer, the teacher of wicked children." Page 71.

"What a child owes to its father and mother, the entire household owes them likewise. Therefore, men and maids should not only obey their masters and mistresses, but should honor them as their own parents; they should do all that they know is expected of them, not from compulsion and with reluctance, but with pleasure and delight; and they should do it for the reasons mentioned —

because it is God's commandment, and it is more pleasing to him than all other works." Page 72-73.

"All live as if God gave us children as objects of mirth and pleasure; as if he gave us servants to use, like an ox or the horse, only for work, or as if we were to live with those under us according to our own whims — to ignore them, in unconcern about what they learn and how they live. . . . Let everyone know, then, that on pain of the loss of divine grace his chief duty is to rear his children in the fear and knowledge of God; and, if they are gifted, to let them learn and study, that they may be of service wherever needed." Page 77.

Luther's "Table of Duties" ends with the lines:
"Let each his lesson learn with care,
And all the household well shall fare."

It is a legitimate and necessary inference which connects the school-training of our Christian children with this admonition to parents regardng the rearing of their children in all godliness. No Christian parent can possibly consent, with an easy conscience, to place his children in schools where the Word of God is not taught and the apostle's command regarding children ignored. Teachers perform parental duties in all their work; they are the substitutes of parents. No Christian parent can accept a substitute for his children who is not in a position, and perhaps not even able, to help train up these children in the nurture and admonition of the Lord. Where the home and the school clash or go apart in what pertains to the child's soul, that soul is bound to suffer, and may suffer in the most fearful manner. Too many empty churches, and too many indifferent members in our churches show the sad fruitage of schools without the blessed training power of the Gospel.

"There all will go well in all stations, where the Word of God is followed, with a clean heart and an honest faith. That must be the source and foundation. A servant, when he works and looks no farther and thinks only: My master gives me my wages, for that I serve him, and beyond that I care nothing about him — he has not a clean heart and mind. But if he is godly and a Christian, he has this mind: I will not serve for what my master gives me or does not give me, is godly or wicked, but because the Word of God is here and says to me: Ye servants, be obedient to your masters as to Christ himself. Here it will spring out of the heart of itself, if such a word is grasped and valued, and he will say: Very well, I will serve my master and take my wages; but my highest aim in doing it shall be that thereby I serve my God and the Lord Christ who has commanded me, and because I know it pleases him. There you see a true work from a clean heart." Luther.

"The Christian table of duties knows also a service of masters towards their servants. This service is even more serious and important than the outward service which one may demand according to his contract." Riemer. — "You owe those who work for you not only their yearly wages and daily bread, you owe them besides a piece of nourishment for the inner man and a piece of love for the heart."

The Savior is the forerunner of all who serve and their archservant. He who requires service must place himself in the service of God; who desires honor must honor the souls of his subordinates which belong to the Lord. From what we seek of them let us figure out what we owe them. Matthes.

"Let Each His Lesson Learn with Care, and all the Household well shall Fare."

- I. *The children, that they obey their parents in the Lord.*
- II. *The parents, that they nurture their children in the Lord.*
- III. *The servants, that they render their service as to the Lord.*
- IV. *The masters, that they command as themselves under the Lord.*

Hamann.

What makes a Christian Home?

- I. *Christian parents.*
- II. *Christian children.*
- III. *Christian masters.*
- IV. *Christian servants.*

A Visit of the Apostle Saint Paul in the Homes of our Congregation.

- I. *Must you dread it?*
- II. *Can you welcome it?*

Sanctified Homes.

- I. *Let Christ dwell there.*
- II. *Let his Word rule there.*
- III. *Let his blessing abide there.*

Why do we Establish Church Schools?

- I. *In order to train up Christian children and parents.*
- II. *In order to train up Christian servants and masters.*

The Importance of Training up Children in the Nurture and Admonition of the Lord.

I. *This will bring long life and prosperity to the individual.*
II. *This will make godly and happy homes.*
III. *This will produce gentle masters and faithful servants.*
IV. *This will cure a thousand evils in every department of life.*

THE
TWENTY-SECOND SUNDAY AFTER TRINITY.

Heb. 13, 1-9.

This text shows how the brethren in a Christian congregation ought to stand together in love toward each other and in faithful adherence to the truth of the Gospel. Chief among them are faithful pastors whose work is finished and whose example is to stimulate those who bear them in loving remembrance. Our subject then is: *the brethren in a Christian congregation and their chief duties.*

The duty of love among Christian brethren.

The last chapter of Hebrews contains the holy writer's final admonitions to faithfulness in Christian conduct and adherence to the truth of the apostolic teaching. A comprehensive admonition heads the chapter: **Let love of the brethren continue.** The supposition is that ἡ φιλαδελφία is already present. It cannot be otherwise where true faith joins hearts together; there the spiritual bond of brotherhood exists, and it is bound to manifest itself. That it did manifest itself among the first readers of this Epistle the writer has already noted, for instance in 6, 10; 10, 33. But just as faith may be assailed, waver, and decline, so the love which flows from it may grow cold and inactive. It must be stimulated constantly, so that nothing will check its fullest exercise. It will **continue** or abide when day by day, in the various relations of life we show kindness, sympathy, and help to our brethren, and live together with them in purity and contentment, trusting together in God to whom we all belong. In our times, when many false brotherhoods have been established, claiming to be superior to our brotherhood in Christ, and urging their claims and

298

benefits to the detriment and even disruption of this true brotherhood, it is especially necessary to emphasize the divine character of the bond of brotherly love which unites us as believers in Christ, and to urge all our brethren to continue therein, cutting loose from every antagonistic tie.

Some of the ways in which this "love of the brethren" must show itself are now set forth. **Forget not to show love unto strangers: for thereby some have entertained angels unawares.** One form of the φιλαδελφία is the φιλοξενία, love unto strangers. In those troubled times, when Christians were often persecuted and had to leave their homes and wander among strangers, it was highly necessary that their fellow Christians should assist them in every possible way, especially also by giving them food and lodging, *i. e.* entertaining them temporarily. This was the more necessary since there were no public lodging places or hotels for strangers, and since many of the early believers were poor people. Love to such strangers was one of the finest forms of charity. Now we are not called upon to exercise it so frequently, but let us not "forget" it, when occasion arises. There is frequently room for it now when the work of the church calls many of our brethren together for conventions of one sort or another; while not a charity in the sense of the original admonition, the hospitality shown on such occasions is a true manifestation of brotherly love and a material aid in prosecuting the work of the church. — Abraham, Gen. 18, 3, and Lot, Gen. 19, 2, actually entertained angels unawares. The construction ἔλαθόν τινες ξενίσαντες is a Greek idiom, the main idea being expressed by the participle, the Greek verb only adding the idea of concealment: "unawares." The suggestion is hardly that we now should rejoice to entertain strangers, since we too might have the good fortune of receiving angels into our houses in so doing. The O. T. incidents of this kind are too rare to admit of such a generalization. The idea is rather that as some were unexpectedly blessed in receiving strangers, so now we, when we open our houses to some lowly messenger of God (ἄγγελος is "messenger"), may likewise receive a blessing we are not looking for. God has a wonderful way of repaying generous and whole-heartedness toward those who labor and suffer in his cause. Matth. 10, 41; 25, 38 and 40.

But there are other brethren who endure even more for the Gospel's sake: **Remember them that are in bonds, as bound with them; them that are evil entreated, as being yourselves also in the body.** To remember is not to forget, the writer merely varying the expression. Among the many who suffered bonds in the early church we know one especially, Paul, who lay in prison for years. Here the admonition does not state what action is to follow our remembrance of the captives; there is only an implication: **as bound with them,** sympathy being so strong, the feeling of fellowship so intense, that we feel their bonds as our own, and, since we cannot go and open the doors of their prison, that we cry unto God in their behalf. "The supplication of a righteous man availeth much in its working," James 5, 16. The great trouble is that we do not feel ourselves συνδεδεμένοι with those in bonds for Christ's sake, after the manner of Paul: "Whether one member suffereth, all the members suffer with it," 1 Cor. 12, 26. The hardships, sufferings, labors, and persecutions of others do not concern us as deeply as they should; hence our intercessions are so cold and languid. If already in the ancient synagogue those in bonds were remembered in the service, and public intercession for them was made in the early Christian church, we to-day ought to pray with the fullest sympathy and fervor: "Be thou the protector and defense of thy people in all times of tribulation and danger." — **Them that are evil entreated** broadens this Christian sympathy to include all who join their lot to that of Christ's followers and suffer on that account in one way or another, like Moses for instance, "choosing rather to be evil entreated with the people of God, than to enjoy the pleasures of sin for a season, accounting the reproach of Christ greater riches than the treasures of Egypt," 11, 25-26. — **As being yourselves also in the body** refers to our susceptibility to the same evils and like trials. Besides the inward tie of brotherly fellowship and sympathy there is the outward bond of the same bodily condition. Perhaps we have already felt in our own poor bodies what others now endure, or we may yet come to feel it before we lay aside this earthly house of our tenement. So the holy writer touches both sides in order to awaken and quicken our brotherly sympathy into earnest intercession for others. Rieger points to Joseph as suffering evil treatment in his youth, to Job as suffering ill during middle life, and to Peter as suffering his worst trials in old age (John 21, 18). We all walk in the shadow of the cross, and our hearts ought to go out toward each other.

The next admonition deals with the divinely instituted relation of marriage and shows what brotherly love requires in this respect: *Let* **marriage** *be* **had in honor among all, and** *let* **the bed** *be* **undefiled: for fornicators and adulterers God will judge.** The A. V. follows the old interpretation of this passage, which held that marriage is here defended against a false asceticism and overestimation of virginity, translating by supplying only the copula: "Marriage *is* honorable in all, and the bed undefiled; but whoremongers *etc.*" Delitzsch follows this exegetical tradition, although he admits that the passage is hortatory like the context generally. But this context is so strong, and the γάρ, not δέ (A. V.), in the second sentence so plain in pointing out what abuse is to be guarded against, that we are rather compelled to supply ἔστω: "*Let* marriage *be* had in honor *etc.*" Of course, it does not receive its proper honor when the unmarried state is ranked far above it, as this is done in the Catholic Church to-day; but the degradation of marriage here meant is that which consists in defilement and sexual abuse of one kind or the other. — In the N. T. γάμος usually means "wedding" or nuptials, here its second current Greek meaning is evident: the marital union in general, **marriage.** This is to be τίμιος, precious, valuable, **had in honor,** and that ἐν πᾶσιν, **among all,** whether they are themselves in the married estate or not.   The dignity and honor of marriage rests on its divine institution, on the blessings God connected with it, and on the hedge he has thus drawn about it to shield it from violation.   Instead of "among all" some translate "in all respects," but the masculine is to be preferred to the neuter as being decidedly more definite.   Still Vincent's remark has weight when he points to ἐν πᾶσιν in verse 18, and adds: "There are many points in which marriage is to be honored besides the avoidance of illicit connections." — **And** *let* **the bed** *be* **undefiled** states at once, briefly and pointedly, what above all else the honor due to the married state demands.   A defilement would take place either by adulterous intercourse, or by lascivious sensuality on the part of the married themselves. — The holy writer supports his admonition by pointing to the divine threat: **for fornicators** who in their lust indulge in sexual intercourse outside of proper matrimonial restrictions, **and adulterers,** who defile the marriage bed itself, **God will judge,** though they should be able to hide their filthy sins from the vision of men.   The subject ὁ θεός is placed in the emphatic position at the end: *He* will judge and punish accordingly, whatever society or any foolish human authority may or may not do.   Who will say that this admonition is not necessary to-day among Christian brethren?   The tendency of our times is strongly in favor of laxness, as witness the number of divorces, disrupted and unhappy marriages, the spread of the social evil, its auxiliaries in the dance, the theater, the drinking places, the easy tolerance of many parents, the undue liberty of young people, the immodesty in woman's dress, *etc., etc.*   There is a clear boundary line of tact in treating of these things in the pulpit, which must not be transgressed by him who would warn and admonish most effectively; and there is a false hesitation and reluctance on the other side, which closes the lips of some, and which must be overcome if they are to do their full duty by their hearers.

The sixth commandment is followed by the seventh; avarice and greed are often coupled in the Scriptures with adultery and fornication. The general warning here has a special point: Christians sometimes had their goods confiscated and were thrown into dire poverty; this is why God's provident care is so emphatically put forth. **Be ye free from the love of money; content with such things as ye have: for himself hath said, I will in no wise fail thee, neither will I in any wise forsake thee. So that with good courage we say,**

   The Lord is my helper; I will not fear:
   What shall man do unto me?

Note the force of the abruptness and terseness of ἀφιλάργυρος ὁ τρόπος: "unavaricious your way!" Since τρόπος originally means "turn," the margin offers: "Let *your turn* of mind be *free from the love of money.*" Our way, manner, fashion of life is meant, including both the disposition and the conduct. A man may love money even when he has it not; again, possessing it, he may twine his heart about it, and it may hurt him fearfully, even break his heart to lose it. Our whole manner is to be different. — The next is equally terse and forceful: ἀρκούμενοι τοῖς παροῦσιν: "contented with things at hand." **Such things as ye have,** as happen to be ours at the time, may be poor and small enough, but to be satisfied and content with them will keep out the desire that makes unhappy and separates the heart from God. — Such contentment requires more than mere human considerations are able to furnish, hence the addition: **for himself,** namely God, who as Delitzsch finely says "is absolute and ever present to the consciousness of the believer," **hath said** in his Word, Deut. 31, 6, also 8; 1 Chron. 28, 20, what now follows. He "has said" it, εἴρηκεν, perfect from εἶπεν, and so for all time it stands. **I will in no wise fail thee, neither will I in any wise forsake thee;** ἀνῶ, second aorist subjective from ἀνίημι after the intensified negation οὐ μή, "in no wise;" ἐγκαταλίπω likewise, Blass, 209. In no wise will

God let us go or give us up, nor will he in any wise abandon us. The O. T. passages are in the third person, and commentators are puzzled to find Philo quoting in the first person exactly as in our passage. It need not trouble us that the person is changed, for Moses attributes the promise directly to God himself, and Philo and the writer of Hebrews simply take him at his word. This divine promise is better than the signed promissory notes of any bank, financial institution, or most stable government, for all of these may repudiate their promises, God absolutely cannot and will not. — **So that with good courage,** confidence, boldness, θαρροῦντας, **we say,** trusting fully in the promise God has given us. **The Lord is my helper; I will not fear: what shall man do unto me?** Thus making our own the words of Ps. 118, 6, which was Luther's favorite Psalm, his Confitemini, the exposition of which gave him so much comfort in his Patmos at the Coburg. The deviation from the Septuagint is but slight, chiefly the combining of the last two clauses: "I will not fear what man will do." When here the writer of Hebrews together with his readers says: "With good courage we say," we must recall chapter 10, 34, that they had already endured the spoiling of their goods; so if again they should lose all, or nearly all, they would endure it again with all fearlessness, knowing that the God who kept them before would keep them once more.

The duty of faithful adherence to the apostolic teaching among Christian brethren.

From earthly things we now turn to spiritual; from the exercise of love, purity, and contentment to the exercise of faith and faithful adherence to the truth. They that spoil our goods, certainly harm us greatly, and we may grow anxious about our earthly future; they that attack us with "divers and strange teachings" threaten to do us far greater harm. So we are bidden: **Remember them that had the rule over you, which spake unto you the word of God; and considering the issue**

of their life, imitate their faith. This remembrance is to strengthen and safeguard. Let pastors and other leaders of the church also remember that their example is to exercise an influence long after they are dead, and let this remembrance make them more faithful while they live, and strengthen them to crown their labors with a blessed end. Riggenbach shows that ἡγούμενοι was used of secular officers of the leaders of the priests, of the rulers of the Jewish communities and of local Jewish congregations; in Acts 15, 22 Judas and Silas are so called, and the title came to be employed of those who directed the Christian congregations, whether of local pastors or of the church in a more general way. Compare verses 17 and 24. Whether those are meant here to whom 2, 3 refers, we are unable to say. — The leadership here meant is connected with the office of preaching and teaching the Gospel: **which spake unto you the word of God,** and thus brought you to believe it and to advance and grow in the faith of it. A sacred bond of love and gratitude will ever connect true Christians with such leaders in the church. This underlies the appeal here made: **and considering the issue of their life, imitate their faith.** The persons here meant had already died; the issue of their life had been reached; ἀναστροφή is manner of life, "conversation" (A. V.), they had attained a blessed death in Christ Jesus, some perhaps by martyrdom, but not necessarily all. Just who is meant the original readers, no doubt, knew at once; it is idle for us now to speculate on their identity. Their end is to be considered, that is, observed and contemplated attentively, and that in order that their faith may be imitated by a like faith on the part of the readers. Death especially tests our faith; our best confession is to die joyfully in Christ Jesus. See, for instance, how Luther passed away, making full proof of the blessed faith he had preached and lived, to the comfort and strengthening of all who had tried the same faith and of us who now hold that faith. So should be the death of every Christian pastor and leader in the church. If it

20

be not a death by martyrdom, it may be one connected
with much suffering and pain, which when borne with
fortitude and patience in the abundant strength that Christ
gives will surely be of special value for all who behold it
or hear of it.

Men die, even the greatest in the church, but he
whom they believe in is ever the same: **Jesus Christ
is the same yesterday and to-day,** *yea* **and for ever.** Well,
therefore, may we imitate the faith of faithful confessors
who have gone before. Jesus Christ, the Savior who appeared on earth as the Messiah of God is the same, identical
and unchanged, **yesterday** when they whose death was just
referred to lived and died trusting in him, **to-day** at the
moment when this Epistle was being written and when it
was read by its recipients, and not only for these periods,
yea **and for ever,** *unto the ages* (margin), and to all the
generation of believers yet to come. He is ever the same
in all that renders him the object of our faith and trust:
in his mercy and grace, in his power and majesty, in his
divinity, in his meritorious work, in his ability to keep,
bless, and finally to save us. They who died trusting in him
made no mistake, as eternity will show; nor do we make
a mistake in imitating them. Calvin dates "yesterday" back
to the old covenant, Bengel to the time prior to the incarnation, Kuebel and others to the eternal preexistence of
Christ; but the context, the practical bearing of the statement as it occurs in the context, and the historic name
"Jesus Christ" point to the immediate past, to which the
writer had just referred in speaking of the death of former leaders. On the eternal Sonship of Christ he had
already expressed himself very fully, chapter 1, *etc.* The
apostles may pass away, generation after generation may
follow them, all things may change, waver, fall, Jesus
Christ changes not; as he blessed and saved all those who
went before, so he still blesses and will forever bless us
who now prove true to him and all others after us.

Now follows the admonition which the writer has
had in mind since recalling the departed leaders of the

church, a renewal of what he has previously written
and a final deduction: **Be not carried away by divers
and strange teachings: for it is good that the heart be
stablished by grace; not by meats, wherein they that
occupied themselves were not profited.** — In contrast
with the unchanging Christ stood the **divers and strange
teachings** of those who opposed Christ and in various
ways tried to overthrow the Gospel. Here the whole
mass of teachings is meant which at this time disturbed
the Hebrews. They all meant a return to Judaism, namely
its outward forms and ceremonies, and frequently mixed
with these some of the newer speculations from other
sources. All these teachings were "divers," a great variety,
some laying stress on this, some on that side of Judaism,
mixing in now this, now that form of speculation. And
they were **strange,** foreign to the Gospel of Christ, different from it entirely. So error is numerous and more
various than ever to-day, constantly decking itself in a
new mantle; and still all its forms are foreign and strange
to the Gospel. This ought to be enough for us; the newness, the variety ought to repel and not attract us, also
the strangeness. Alas, some are caught by false teaching
just because of this its character. Be not borne or **carried
away** from the sure foundation and the only source of
salvation, which is Christ, the soul and center of the entire
Gospel. — Instead of hanging loosely to him, so that this
or that wind of false doctrine may blow us away, learn
that **it is good,** in the eyes of God, beautiful, καλόν, to all
who are in harmony with him, **that the heart be stablished by grace,** made firm, and solid by being brought
upon an unmovable base. Grace does this, the grace of
God which operates through the Word. It fills the heart
with knowledge, it makes faith strong and robust, it helps
us realize more and more that Jesus Christ and his Gospel
is the only foundation upon which we can rest secure.
When this condition is ours the winds and waves of false
doctrine may beat about us, they will never carry us away.
Too many are in their faith like loose pebbles or sand by

the sea-shore; we must be like the cliff that is one mass with the great bed-rock underneath. — **Not by meats** is added in order to point out the lines of teaching which threatened the first readers most. Commentators devote much effort to the question, just what βρώματα here signify. We may say in general, the whole ceremonial system of the Jews, especially as they then practiced it, is meant; or, more closely, the Jewish sacrificial feasts and regulations about meats: **wherein they that occupied themselves,** literally: *walked,* **were not profited,** that is benefited and helped. All the zeal which the Jews of that day devoted to these outward practices gave them no true peace of soul, no help for salvation. It is so still with all outward forms of holiness. "The kingdom of God is not meat and drink; but righteousness, and peace, and joy in the Holy Ghost. For he that in these things serveth Christ is acceptable to God and approved of men." Rom. 14, 17-18. To none of these divers and strange doctrines were the departed leaders carried away; they stood firm to the end on Christ the Rock of Ages. The great desire and aim of the holy writer is that all his readers may attain the same final issue of life.

HOMILETICAL HINTS.

"For Christians to stand faithfully by each other, even when that involves loss and mockery, is no less necessary to-day than it was of old. There is many a cause and occasion for Christian love to strengthen the faith of the brethren. Even the humblest of us can aid in this work by holding faithfully to the church, the means of grace, Word and Sacrament. . . . If outward protection and help is not as necessary as it was in the early days of Christianity, inwardly the needs and troubles are so much the greater, and there is much work for Christian love of the brethren, to aid the discouraged and doubting, and to stand by the contending. Let us not expect everything of our pastors. In our times especially the testimony of laymen and the work of love has power to convince. When all cooperate the greatest blessing will result. This will tie us together most firmly and support the weak. To all of us the admonition comes: Let your hearts be stablished in brotherly love!" Riemer.

Marriage is a moral union, not a sensual union. — He who belongs to hell with one member of his body may well see to it that he belong not there entirely. — He who continues in one sin is like a bird with one foot caught in the snare. He may flutter as far as the threads allow him to go, but when the bird-catcher comes along, his neck will quickly be twisted.

Rump castigates the sins of impurity by pointing to young girls but recently confirmed hurrying into marriage to escape greater shame, to the birth of fatherless children, to the indifference of the members of a congregation toward such transgression which is a mighty factor in producing them.

. Let us get rid of the idea that secret sins are sins from which we can escape. A secret judgment follows them like a shadow that cannot be thrown off. It kills happiness, it puts a gnawing worm into the conscience, it blights the body, it fills with fear of the judgment day. Be not deceived, God is not mocked.

The avaricious man overestimates the value of money and underestimates the value of the divine blessing. — It is easy to preach contentment, but it requires no less than complete trust in God to practise it. No Christian is to live thoughtlessly, but to use carefully what God gives him and to save of the abundance of his gifts. To be frugal and saving is a Christian duty. But he who uses it as a mantle for his filthy love of money, abuses the gifts of God in a twofold way, to his miserable idolatry he adds hypocrisy. Many a Christian so-called himself twists the rope by which the devil will hale him to hell, and he uses his precious dollars for the strands. The worst use you can put money to is to make of it a stone to drown your soul as you try to swim to the heavenly shore. Not one so loaded ever reached the other side.

The world is full of divers and strange teachings, and every now and then a brother is carried away by the superior show of wisdom, the attractive novelty, the plausible argument, the supposed progressiveness of such teachings. The old apostolic doctrine, sealed by the blood of many a martyr and the living and dying testimony of God's greatest workers and saints, wears the humble robe of repentance and the white garment of faith in Christ. It tells you nothing but the simple story of Christ, the same yesterday, to-day, and forever. Like moths all these strange doctrines shall have their gaudy wings burned by the flame. Remember the faithfulness of your spiritual fathers and learn to be their equally faithful sons and daughters. — The more God gives the churches faithful leaders, the more will he require of the churches that they follow them to the end.

Be True to the True Church!

I. *The church of the true doctrine.*
II. *The church of the faithful confessors.*

Remember Your Faithful Teachers!

I. *The Word of God which they spake unto you.*
II. *The love and purity of their lives.*
III. *The faith that sealed their death.*

A Firm Heart.

I. *Assailed by many a storm.*
II. *Grounded on Christ and his Word.*
III. *Made strong by God's grace.*

It is a Good Thing That the Heart be Stablished by Grace!

I. *In love to the brethren.*
II. *In the hatred of sin.*
III. *In the faith of the truth.*

It is a Good Thing to be a Member in the True Church.

I. *There God's Word is properly taught and error exposed.*
II. *There clean morals are inculcated and all vice rebuked.*
III. *There loving brethren give us their sympathy and extend their help.*
IV. *There faithful pastors give us their service and leave us their noble example.*

Jesus Christ, the Same Yesterday, To-day, and For Ever.

I. *The basis of our faith.*
II. *The fountain of our love.*
III. *The cleansing power of our lives.*
IV. *The crown of glory in our death.*

THE
TWENTY-THIRD SUNDAY AFTER TRINITY.

---

1 Tim. 4, 4-11.

'This text closes the third subcycle of the after-Trinity series. Here one pastor is writing to another and marking out for him how he must conduct himself in his holy office. The reference to pastors in the previous text took in only those whose labors were already finished, and viewed their character and conduct from the standpoint of the people whom they had served and who still had them in loving remembrance. This text views the pastor from the standpoint of the holy office itself; a master in the work, Paul the apostle, lays down for his assistant, Timothy at Ephesus, what must be required of him in order to be "a good minister of Jesus Christ." Our subject then is: *the pastor in the Christian congregation and his chief duty.*

Himself nourished in the words of faith and good doctrine, he must put the brethren in mind of these things.

Stellhorn has the heading for this chapter: "The pastor must be a leader in doctrine and in conduct." The heart of the chapter comprises our text. Paul begins with a brief description of the devilish character and ungodly contents of the doctrines which are bound to appear soon, some of which had already indicated their approach. Men would forbid to marry and command to abstain from meats, thus bringing forward a false doctrine of sanctification subversive of the entire Christian system of teaching as derived from Christ. Paul holds up the truth of God beside this error and shows Timothy how false it is, and then bids him to go on preaching that truth for the benefit of the

311

brethren committed to his care. **For every creature
of God is good, and nothing is to be rejected, if it be
received with thanksgiving: for it is sanctified through
the word. of God and prayer.** — "For" introduces an
elucidation of what Paul has just written, namely that God
has created meats to be received with thanksgiving by them
that believe and know the truth.   Certainly we may eat
"meats," food of all kinds, which God has created, since
every creature of God is good, παν κτίσμα, every thing
made by him, a word especially applicable to the inanimate
creatures of God. "Good" here means good for its purpose, as God intended it, namely beneficial for man in supporting and making pleasant his earthly life. The "all" is
especially emphasized by the negative clause: **and nothing
is to be rejected,** ἀπόβλητον, thrown away, as morally defiling, so that the mere fact of partaking of it or using it
would be sin and contaminate the soul. To imagine and
teach such a thing is to contradict God himself and his
judgment in creating such things. This applies in our day
to many prohibitionists who condemn all alcoholic beverages as products of the devil and "poisons" which to touch,
taste or handle is sin; they even condemn the use of wine
in the Sacrament, tampering with the Lord's own institution, and disturbing the faith and consciences of the simple. — There is, however, one condition, when we come
to use what is good in itself, that it be good also in our use
of it: **if it be received with thanksgiving,** with a feeling
and expression of gratitude to him who gave it. . Of course,
this will exclude all abuse of God's creatures, for it would
be mockery to misuse his gifts and to add thanksgiving to
such a sin. So also he sins who takes and uses God's gifts,
but does so without thanking him; not that his using them
in itself would be sin, but his wrong manner of using them.
"In itself, to be sure, food and drink, like everything belonging to the domain of nature, and also its use, bears no
religious relation to God, has nothing to do with Christianity
and salvation, lies in the province of the first and not in
that of the second or third article, hence is not 'holy' in a

religious sense. But in the case of a Christian everything
is to be holy, whatever he is and does; in the case of a
child of God everything must be put in relation to God,
benefit also his soul, and serve to honor God." Stellhorn.
Of course, this applies also to "meats," the use of food and
drink. — **For it is sanctified through the word of God
and prayer,** and this is the reason for the "thanksgiving."
"The word of God" here is not some special saying of
God, but the Word as employed in prayer in general, as
when we call upon Jesus to be our guest, or appropriate
directly Ps. 145, 15-16; 106, 1; or the substance of other
passages in prayer. The word will thus be the substance,
and prayer (ἔντευξις, converse, intercourse, petition) the
form in which our grateful acknowledgment is made to
God. This **sanctifies,** makes sacred and holy by bringing
into connection with God, the use of food or any of his
created things. So the eating of a Christian will differ essentially from that of a worldly or ungodly man. "Paul
says of marriage, of meats, and similar things: It is sanctified by the Word of God and prayer, *i. e.* by the Word, by
which consciences become certain that God approves; and
by prayer, *i. e.* by faith which used it with thanksgiving as a
gift of God." *Apology,* 251, 30. Our passage is used also
as a directive in determining how the consecration of the
earthly elements in the Lord's Supper must be performed.
Stellhorn adds that here we have an apostolic injunction
to prayer at table, agreeable to the example of Christ, Matth.
14, 19; 15, 36; Luke 24, 30; something so necessary for
our day, since many eat without "saying grace." "A true
Christian is sanctified to God, stands in God's service with
all that he is and does; he therefore feels that he must sanctify to God all that he does and uses, place it into his service, use it for his honor; and this he does in the case of
food and drink, when he partakes of it with thanksgiving,
with the Word of God and prayer. This proper use necessarily excludes also all other misuse."

Now Paul takes up the duty of Timothy as a Christian pastor, using the doctrine just elucidated as an

illustration of what he must do in his office in general.
**If thou put the brethren in mind of these things, thou
shalt be a good minister of Christ Jesus, nourished in
the words of the faith, and of the good doctrine which
thou hast followed** *until now:* **but refuse profane and
old wives' fables.** The supposition is that Timothy will
indeed put the brethren in mind of these things, in fact, will
continue to do so: ὑποτιθέμενος, the present participle denoting continuance. The verb ὑποτίθημι means literally "to put
under," and thus here "to suggest," to keep putting in mind.
There is a certain gentleness in it, showing how a pastor
keeps on with patient and quiet instruction and admonition,
instilling the truth more and more deeply into the hearts
of his members. — So, Paul says to Timothy, **thou shalt
be a good minister of Christ Jesus,** διάκονος, one who is
active in service for the benefit of another, the stress being
on the service he renders, not as in δοῦλος on his condition
as in servitude. The word is used here in a general way,
not as an official title, although Timothy, and Paul also,
were called ministers of Christ. In doing what the apostle
has just said Timothy will be a **good,** καλός, minister of the
Lord, whose eyes will rest upon him with pleasure and approval, who will accept his work. This must be the aim of
every pastor in all that he does. Our highest title of honor
is not D.D., even if bestowed by the greatest university, nor
any fame or honor that may come from men, but that simple and divine title: διάκονος καλός. — Of course, if Timothy
does what Paul expects of him in laying the things just
mentioned again and again upon his hearers, this will mean
something more, he must then be constantly **nourished in
the words of the faith, and of the good doctrines which
thou hast followed** *until now.* All divine truth hangs
together, and to teach any section of it well one must be
nourished, ἐντρεφόμενος, or (if the middle voice is preferred)
nourish himself constantly, raise up and train up himself.
in the entire system of divine truth. It must be food and
drink, house and home, teacher, master, friend, and lover
to him. Thus every pastor must live in the Word to be a

good pastor; his purpose will be double, to grow in the
truth and grace himself, and to help others grow likewise.
The same thing holds true of every Christian, but of the
latter only in respect of the universal priesthood, outside
of the special pastoral calling. — **The words of the faith**
are those which express and declare the faith, the divine
truth given us to believe. Wohlenberg has: "the words
with which faith has to do, with which it must always be
concerned." Stellhorn: "the words which produce faith,"
which is here less acceptable than the other renderings of
the genitive τῆς πίστεως. — Paul adds a second genitive:
and of the good doctrine which thou hast followed,
namely by giving it constant attention; not: "whereunto
thou hast attained," A. V. Paul here refers to his own
work of instructing and teaching Timothy; for it was from
the apostle that he heard "the words of the good doctrine,"
and followed them carefully by learning and heeding them,
so that now he had developed to good stature in their
knowledge and strength. No greater blessing can come to
pastors than able and faithful teachers; no better work can
they do for themselves than to keep on nourishing themselves in "the words of the good doctrine" those teachers
have given them. A just and severe judgment will meet
those who sat at the feet of such godly teachers, and afterwards cast off their words and followed wisdom of their
own that did not tally with "the words of the faith." —
But refuse profane and old wives' fables, namely the
speculations and fancies to which Paul had already referred in 1, 4, which very likely consisted of all sorts of traditional supplements to the Jewish law, allegorical interpretations, stories of fanciful miracles, and similar Rabbinical fabrications in the line of history or doctrine. These
"myths" are called **profane,** βεβήλους, allowed to be trodden
on, with nothing sacred about them, although they were put
forth as religious and in the interest of religion; and "old-
womanish," γραώδεις, silly, like **old wives'** tattle, that a
sensible man who has serious work to do could not for a
moment listen to. It is evident from this characterization

that the apostle is not describing "the doctrines of devils" in verse 1, nor anything as serious as the Jewish legalism. So he also tells Timothy simply to **refuse** these foolish fables, to request that he be not troubled with them. He is to keep to God's Word only, and to disdain this nonsense which some tried to take seriously; by thus scorning it he is to help crush it the more effectually, for some things become serious only when taken seriously.

Himself exercising unto godliness, he must labor and strive that the brethren do likewise.

It is not enough to teach and remind others, a Christian pastor must do more. One of the old church-fathers has put it in a striking way: He must not only thunder in the pulpit, he must also flash like lightning in his walk and conduct. **And exercise thyself unto godliness: for bodily exercise is profitable for a little; but godliness is profitable for all things, having promise of the life which now is, and of that which is to come.** The apostle does not use the middle voice γυμνάζου, but the active together with the reflexive pronoun, γύμναζε σεαυτόν, most likely because he has in mind some one else who exercises *himself* differently. Whatever others may do, a Christian pastor must **exercise** himself unto godliness, that is discipline himself inwardly in thought and will, and outwardly in all that he allows and denies himself, so that **godliness** may be fostered and strengthened in him, the disposition to respond in all things to the fear and reverence of God. Such exercise will include self-control, self-denial, a constant crucifixion of the flesh, a steady effort to do one's duty, though disagreeable at times. This is not a peculiar exercise for pastors, but one necessary for all Christians alike, first among whom, of course, Christian pastors should stand. — Paul puts this kind of exercise ahead of all other: **for bodily exercise is profitable for a little,** to a small degree, not indeed worthless, yet far below the spiritual exercise just mentioned. It seems too trivial to make "bodily exercise" here mean the physical training in

the palaestra, running, boxing, *etc.*, as practiced by the
Greeks, who delighted in beautiful and strong bodies.
Much less is there a suggestion here that exercise and care
of the body will be of some benefit to Timothy in his work
as a tent-maker (Wohlenberg). It certainly makes a peculiar impression to have Timothy pictured as an athlete,
doing stunts in the arena. Bodily exercise here is what
Luther has well described, when he calls fasting and bodily
preparation a fine outward training. Such forms of asceticism do have a certain value, and Paul made use of
them for himself, 1 Cor. 9, 27. It is never good to give full
rein to our bodily desires and inclinations. Stellhorn is
right, however, when he points out that we are so foolish,
that either we imagine, when we use this sort of training,
we are doing a meritorious thing in the sight of God, or
that we neglect such exercise altogether. — The apostle
would have Timothy attend also to "bodily exercise" and
gain whatever profit might be so derived, but the chief
thing must ever be godliness itself: **but godliness,** which is
fostered and strengthened directly by the spiritual exercise
of Christian virtues, **is profitable for all things,** since there
is never a situation in which it would not be of the greatest
help and benefit to a Christian, to say nothing of a pastor, to
have a highly developed fear and love of God in his heart,
and a readiness in his heart to respond to it at once in his
conduct. — How far "all things" reach is shown by the addition: **having promise of the life which now is, and of
that which is to come.** Since godliness is itself a form of
the spiritual life, the promise which it has can hardly be
"life" itself, *i. e.* true life while on earth and eternal life
hereafter. So we decline to follow those commentators
who press the word "life," and either make the life "which
now is" of the same essence as "that which is to come," in
order to show that this is what is promised to godliness, or
figure out a difference. A promise "of life now" is one
which belongs to the present life; and a promise "of life to
come" is one which belongs to that future life in heaven.
Meyer, B. Weiss, and Vincent have this interpretation,

which is followed also by nearly all who incidentally use
the apostle's statement as a proof passage.   Instead of the
absence of the article before ζωῆς militating against this
view, Meyer rightly says the other view, that the life is the
thing promised, would require the article.   Moreover τὰ
πάντα points to a multipicity of blessings, not to one solitary
grand blessing.   The godly man, who keeps on exercising
unto godliness, has the promise of God's favor and blessings for all the days of his earthly life.   So numerous are
these blessings that Paul does not begin to mention them.
Timothy knows them himself.   On the other hand, they
who think they gain a great deal by now and then, or by
permanently forsaking godliness, shall presently to their
dismay discover that they have lost even the good things
of this life: a good name, a good conscience, *etc.*, and often
the divine curse brings them very low in other ways.   Besides, the godly life has a promise which belongs to the life
to come; the stream of divine blessings does not end at the
grave, it flows on into eternity.   All that is promised to
faith belongs also to godliness, for faith is the heart and
center of it, and without faith godliness is impossible.

**Faithful is the saying, and worthy of all acceptation.
For to this end we labor and strive, because we have our
hope set on the living God, who is the Savior of all men,
specially of them that believe. These things command
and teach.**   The "saying" which the apostle means is
the one just uttered concerning godliness and its great
promise.   Of this, much better than of anything that follows, he can say that it is **faithful,** dependable, because God
always keeps his promises, **and worthy of all acceptation**
by us in shaping our lives accordingly. — Paul, and with
him Timothy, has accepted this precious "saying" as the
guiding principle of his life; their actions prove that they
consider this "saying" just what Paul says it is, "faithful
and worthy of all acceptation:" **For to this end we labor,**
κοπιῶμεν, work hard and tire ourselves, both in our position
as Christian believers and as pastors, **and strive,** ἀγωνιζόμεθα,
or contend, **because we have our hope set on the living**

God, to whom our hearts are devoted in all their godliness, and who as the "living" God can and will fulfil his promise here and hereafter. The reading: "suffer reproach," ὀνειδιζόμεθα (A. V.), instead of "strive," ἀγωνιζόμεθα, as in an athletic game, is less well attested. The perfect ἠλπίκαμεν means that the hope once set on God now rests there; it is permanently placed on him. "To this end" refers back to the promise accorded to godliness; this seems better than to make it refer to the following clause: "to this end that (ὅτι,) we have our hope etc." — The power and ability of God to justify such hope set on him is further indicated by the relative clause: **who is the Savior of all men, especially of them that believe.** His desire and effort is to make all men godly and thus to save them; for this purpose he prepared the whole plan of salvation and had his Son and Spirit carry it into effect. To be sure, many refuse to be led to godliness, preferring the allurements of sin, so God's saving grace is fully realized only in "them that believe." — But all that Paul has urged upon Timothy personally has a wider application; godliness is the business of us all. Therefore: **These things command and teach:** order that the members in your congregation do these things, and instruct them that they may know how and may succeed well. This is the duty of the pastor. He proclaims the divine command, and true believers heed it as such; at the same time, just as Paul here teaches and explains in detail, he must unfold the truth to the minds of his hearers, and they will gladly receive the Word and walk faithfully in the light of it.

HOMILETICAL HINTS.

The relation existing between a Christian congregation and its pastor is one of the most important in the entire life and work of the church. That congregation is blessed indeed which has "a good minister of Jesus Christ," recognizes the fact, and makes the fullest use of his ministration. — A great many foolish, unnecessary, and some wrong things are expectetd of Christian pastors. Just what is their real work? St. Paul here states both sides of it: nourished in the words of faith and good doctrine, they are to teach and remind the brethren; exercising themselves in true godliness, they are to bring others to do the same. These are the essentials about which all else is grouped, and from which all else grows. Whatever lacks proper connection with these fundamental duties is no part of the minister's work, and must not be required of him.

There is but one standard of truth and morality for pastors and for people. We must not imagine that some doctrines are well enough for pastors to believe, but not necessary for their people; or that the pastor ought to live up to certain commandments, which could hardly be required of the people. Or, turning the thing about, no pastor must imagine that he can be freer in his doctrinal views than the simple, honest biblical teaching his people should have; or that, being a pastor, he may allow himself various liberties in conduct which would be out of place for his people. Any double standard is not only dangerous, but contrary to God's own Word, who will deal with all who pervert it. — Still, the pastor, as Paul shows in his letter to Timothy, is to take the lead, to show the way, to lay hand to the work himself first. This is his high and holy office. It is thus that he has a duty which comes to him especially and in a particular way; others share it to a certain degree, like the teachers in the church schools, the members of the church council, but since he alone is pastor, he is the one to lead all the others, and he has a duty which exceeds that of all the rest.

Intellectual appreciation of doctrine is far inferior to spiritual appreciation; and this is what Paul means by being nourished with the words of Scripture. The greatest doctor of divinity has not finished his course of training in the Word. — The old wives' fables that troubled Timothy at Ephesus have disappeared; to-day the empty, chaffy "fables" that even some pastors pay far too much attention to are novels, stories in the popular monthlies and other "light literature." A mind nourished on such wind will not be rich in truth and well-equipped to guide others.

Let no pastor or layman think that "bodily exercise" is good for nothing; it has a benefit, and one that we need and may well secure. Temperance in food and drink, moderation and balance in all legitimate forms of pleasure, a curbing of desires in themselves not wrong, a regular time and form for devotion, certain set duties, and other things of this order, will be beneficial if rightly employed; and the example thus given to others will always be helpful.

There are two views of life which often clash with each other. The one has for its motto: Enjoy thyself! It gives free rein to the desires, many of them quite natural, and some of them unnatural. The other comes with the demand: Deny thyself! It has a severe look to it and tries to make life as hard and dreary as possible. Neither is true nor safe. Religion is often identified with the latter, although the former too is often proclaimed as in harmony with the Gospel. But the Gospel has its own principle which is to enjoy and to deny whatever is pleasing to God. You may freely and cheerfully enjoy all things for which you can thank God; you must unhesitatingly and unflinchingly deny and reject all things for which you cannot thank God. Our part is neither to be conformed to this world, nor to flee from this world, but to be conformed to God, and to flee from what is opposed to God.

Do not think that you can shake godliness out of your sleeve when the hour comes in which you need it greatly; godliness is of gradual growth, and you must cultivate it by constant practice, then when you need some form of it unexpectedly it will be on hand. — Remember, it was easier yesterday to attain it than it is to-day; easier to-day, than it will be to-morrow. — Godliness in youth preserves from many a temptation and protects against many a bitter experience. Godliness in business preserves a clear conscience and gives us prosperity that is untainted. Godliness in pleasure puts a clean cup to the lips and makes us drink no bitter dregs. Godliness in friendship and love gives our lives a true uplift and spares us the miseries of those who let others drag them down. Thus, indeed godliness is profitable for all things.

What Must a Christian Congregation Expect of its Pastor?

I. *That he be nourished with the Word, and nourish his congregation likewise.*
II. *That he practice godliness, and help others to practice it likewise.*

What Must a Good Minister of Christ Jesus Offer to his Congregation?

I. *The Word of truth that has filled his own heart.*
II. *The example of godliness that he has cultivated in his own life.*

A Good Minister of Christ Jesus.

I. *He ministers well with the Word.*
II. *He ministers well with his conduct.*

21

The Meaning of Life in the Light of the Gospel.

I. *A grateful reception of God's good gifts.*

II. *A serious discipline under God's gracious care.*

Adapted from Riemer.

The Profit of True Godliness.

I. *For the body.*

It sanctifies our food; also our appetites and desires, verses 3-6.

II. *For the soul.*

It produces a desire for good spiritual nourishment; also a dislike for what is shallow and useless; verses 6-7a.

III. *For time.*

It makes us ready for tiring labor; also eager for the contest to win the prize; also patient in suffering; verses 7b, 8, 10.

IV. *For eternity.*

It brightens our hope in the living God; also it carries us forward to eternal joy; verses 8 and 10.

Heffter.

How a Pastor and his People are to Work Together.

I. *In the Word of faith and good doctrine.*

II. *In the exercise of godliness and Christian virtue.*

THE
TWENTY-FOURTH SUNDAY AFTER TRINITY.

1 Thess. 5, 14-24.

The last four texts in the after-Trinity cycle deal with the consummation of the Christian life. The burden of the first is that we may be found *without blame at the coming of our Lord Jesus Christ*. This is the only one of the four texts in which the coming of Christ is directly mentioned, and here it is only mentioned and no more; the emphasis is all on us and our life, its various sides, and the form it must have to appear blameless at the last day. And it is noteworthy that in this text, as in the remaining three, the holy writers either use the plural or address an entire congregation as a body. We are to walk hand in hand as our life reaches its consummation, and when it merges into eternity we will stand at last as one great glorious host before the throne of God. — Concerning the church at Thessalonica and the reason why Paul wrote his two letters to this church, see the Fifteenth Sunday after Trinity. Our text constitutes the conclusion of the first letter. The apostle has written of the things which were especially necessary for the Thessalonians, he has explained about those who have fallen asleep, and also about the coming of the day of the Lord, ending now with the exhortation that they build each other up. Just what this building up includes he sketches in detail, all his admonitions and instructions being given with a view to the great day when Christ shall at last return. There are three sets of brief admonitions, closing with a prayer to God.

Let us care for our brethren.

In verse 12 the apostle has addressed the "brethren," the members of the congregation in general, in regard

323

to the elders who had been appointed to labor among them and to guide and admonish them; to this was added the exhortation that they should be at peace among themselves. Now follows a set of admonitions, forming a little circle of its own, in which our entire round of duties toward the brethren is traced out in a masterly way. **And we exhort you, brethren, admonish the disorderly, encourage the fainthearted, support the weak, be longsuffering toward all. See that none render unto any one evil for evil; but alway follow after that which is good, one toward another, and toward all.** — The δέ here merely adds a new line of thought. The apostle and his assistants, Silas and Timothy, who had brought the Thessalonians to faith in Christ, **exhort** them to exercise brotherly love and care for each other. When some failed to heed this gentle exhortation and call to right conduct. Paul used a stronger term, 2 Thess. 3, 12: "we command and exhort." A loving, kind exhortation ought to be all that is necessary among true Christians. — Those among us who in any way fall behind ought to have our first loving care. Paul mentions several classes, first **the disorderly,** τοὺς ἀτάκτους (from ἀ, not, and τάσσειν, to draw up, arrange), those who are out of line, like soldiers who fail to keep their proper places in the ranks. The expression is general, although here the apostle has in mind such as ceased to do their regular work, became busybodies, failed to provide their own bread, and became a burden to the congregation, 2 Thess. 3, 10-12. Disorderly conduct takes on many forms; often it is of a fleshly and worldly character, breaking away from the rules of quiet, steady Christian conduct and causing more or less disturbance and offense. The first thing we are to do with all such is to **admonish** them, to put them in mind of what their conduct really is and of what their calling as Christians requires of them. This ought to suffice to bring them into line again; of course, if it does not, stronger measures, such as discipline, must be used. — Besides the disorderly there are **the fainthearted,** who are easily discouraged in

one way or another. This too is a general class, although
the apostle probably had in mind such as grew discouraged
when death removed some of their friends, 4, 13. The
loss of dear relatives still discourages many. Besides this
the hardships and trials that come upon us and the battles
we are called upon to fight cause many to grow fainthearted. These we are to **encourage,** to console and thus
spur on to do their part. Brotherly sympathy and encouragement, strengthening words are especially necessary
in the case of all who incline to give up. Many a Christian
would not hold out if others did not take him by the hand
and lead him on. — Then there are **the weak,** whose faith
is not robust to stand the knocks it receives in this wicked
world, whose knowledge is too limited and who hold to
wrong and mistaken ideas, whose conscience thus gets into
various difficulties. These we must not despise, but **support,** ἀντέχεσθαι, hold ourselves against them, cling to them,
so that they do not fall and sink down. The devil likes to
destroy the weak, to pull them down and make them his
prey. He knows the weak side of every one of us.
Brotherly love braces up the weak and helps them attain
new strength. The apostle's idea is certainly not that the
weak should continue in their weakness, and that the strong
are to reduce themselves to the same condition. When
weakness becomes chronic and spreads, the enemy will
finally succeed in dragging many completely down. By
brotherly support weakness must be overcome. — Instead
of naming other special classes the apostle now thinks of
faults and shortcomings which may appear anywhere
among Christians, and of ill treatment which may come
to us from such as do not share our faith at all, and he
admonishes: **be longsuffering toward all,** hold back
patiently under provocation and do not blaze up in anger
or passion. Prov. 16, 32; 1 Cor. 13, 4; Eph. 4, 2;
Col. 3, 12. — The inclination of the natural man will
always be to avenge himself; if he cannot do so at once,
he will wait for a later opportunity. But this would be
blameworthy indeed in a Christian: **See that none render**

unto any one evil for evil, see that none of you do this
wicked thing. Of course, the Christian, where he can,
will dissuade his brother from taking vengeance, but, as
Luenemann rightly remarks, there will not be much
opportunity for this; the apostle is thinking of each one
of us and the wrong conduct into which we may fall
when someone greatly injures us. Our natural sense of
justice may prompt us to retaliate, but the spirit of Christ
will move us to overcome evil with good and thus remain blameless in our conduct, Rom. 12, 19-20; 1 Pet.
3, 9; Matth. 5, 44. — Instead of ever taking vengeance:
alway follow after that which is good, τὸ ἀγαθόν, pursue,
strive to attain what in the widest sense is good, beneficial in any way, certainly also in a moral way, **one toward another,** in the circle of the congregation, **and toward all,** no matter who may be involved.   The
Christian's motto must ever be to do only good to others.
It may be a small kindness for which he has opportunity
now, again it may be great help which he is able to render,
as when the Samaritan went to the aid of the man who
had fallen among thieves.   It may be bodily relief which
he is able to extend, but it may also be the freeing of a
soul from the doom of sin, as when the aged John went
out to bring back the youth who had broken away from
his guidance and become the leader of a robber band. —
If we want to be blameless at the coming of our Lord
Jesus Christ, we must constantly watch our conduct toward others, especially toward those who are one with
us in the faith.

Let us accept what God sends.

**Rejoice alway; pray without ceasing; in every thing
give thanks: for this is the will of God in Christ Jesus
to you-ward.** — Here is Paul's philosophy of the Christian
life in a nutshell; it is the highest kind of optimism, resting wholly on the wisdom and love of God. Not only
does it keep the heart truly happy, even amid the most
painful and trying circumstances; it also keeps us from

many of the worst forms of sin, such as presumption, murmuring against God, doubt, secret unbelief, ingratitude, *etc.* **Rejoice alway,** be delighted and pleased at all times! How is that possible, you will say, when so many things happen to us that are bound to distress us? Are we to laugh when one of our relatives dies? Are we to smile and talk pleasantly when some calamity plunges us and many others into the gravest loss and trouble? This is not a rejoicing like that of the world, mere gayety and frivolous pleasure, but a rejoicing "in the Lord," Phil. 4, 4. It is the secret delight, always filling the soul, that God is our Father, Christ our Savior, and that in even the most painful experiences God's grace, love, and kindness is blessing us and leading us upon the paths of righteousness for his name's sake. This joy abides even amidst tears, nor can death blot it out. Whatever God would send the Thessalonians, they should be glad, it would be blessing only. — **Pray without ceasing,** προσεύχεσθε, turn the heart in devotion to God, and this uninterruptedly, incessantly. While Paul indicates no special connection between this and the foregoing admonition, it is quite evident that we can rejoice alway only when we pray alway. Formal, audible prayer cannot be meant, although certain monks tried, on the basis of this passage, to maintain an ἄπαυστος λειτουργία, and a certain sect of Euchites established an *indesinens oratio.* Paul has other admonitions to constant prayer: Eph. 6, 18; Col. 4, 2; Rom. 12, 12. His conception of prayer is deeper than the utterance of set forms of words, in a special attitude, and for some special purpose perhaps; prayer for the apostle is the constant communion of the Christian with God; in a hundred ways, consciously and unconsciously, his heart turns God-ward. His grace and help is the center toward which his soul constantly gravitates. There will, of course, be set times and seasons for special prayer and worship, but these will only be the more marked evidences of a life, the very warp and woof of which is prayer. — **In every thing give thanks,** because every thing that God sends us is for our good, including pain, loss, sorrow, and other crosses. It is evident how constant joy depends on constant thankfulness. If we would have cause not to thank, but to complain, joy would be at an end. The phase ἐν παντί means in every condition and relation of life, in joy and in sorrow. The deeper our gratitude, the higher our joy. — Paul adds: **for this is the will of God in Christ Jesus to you-ward.** Some restrict τοῦτο to the giving of thanks, but there is certainly an inner connection between constant joy, constant prayer, and constant gratitude, hence τοῦτο embraces all three. God's θέλημα, his will or wish, his desire and requirement as directed toward us is what these apostolic admonitions declared. He wants our entire lives to be formed on these lines, then they will please him and escape his censure, in other words be "without blame." **In Christ Jesus** points out the sphere and domain of this will; it is his Gospel-will, good and gracious, giving us in Christ the very thing that enables us to conform to his will.

Let us use the Spirit well.

To pray is to draw from God, and his will in Christ Jesus to us-ward is an extension of his grace and blessing to us. This naturally leads to the following admonitions: **Quench not the Spirit; despise not prophesyings; prove all things; hold fast that which is good; abstain from every form of evil.** — By τὸ πνεῦμα the Holy Spirit is meant as he dwells and operates in the hearts of the members of the church. Various commentators suppose that Paul here has in mind the special charismatic manifestations and operations of the Spirit, such as the speaking with tongues, inspired utterance in the form of prophecy, and the like. But the expression is entirely general: and every motion, prompting, and work of the Holy Spirit in the hearts of his people is meant. The context points rather to the ordinary and regular operations of the Spirit than to extraordinary and exceptional manifestations. All that Paul has written in regard to our conduct toward the brethren, verses 14-15 must be a fruit of the Spirit, likewise joy, prayer, thanksgiving; so also what follows, prophesyings, holding fast what is good and shunning evil. The apostle is addressing all the Christians at Thessalonica, and all of them are to let the Holy Spirit rule and guide them, prompt and move them, quicken and empower them to do what is pleasing in the sight of God. So they must not **quench** the Spirit, extinguish his holy fire in their hearts. This is done when the fervor and ardor he awakens in us is put out altogether or greatly lessened by fleshly, worldly objections. Many a noble, generous, godly impulse thus dies unfruitful of action, or bringing forth only a fraction of the good it might have produced. And this applies not only to the individual and his own circle of motives and impulses, but also to our united efforts. Many a good suggestion, plan, appeal, certainly coming from the Spirit, is quenched altogether or in part by the unspiritual thoughts and objections brought against it by other brethren. There are always some who do not respond aright to the Spirit's promptings, sometimes do not even recognize them. All such are blameworthy. — The highest and most helpful operation of the Spirit is found in prophesyings, hence: **despise not prophesyings,** do not set at nought or mock the utterances of those who tell you the Word of God for your instruction, admonition, warning and spiritual betterment in general. In the early church there was the special gift of prophecy, the Spirit of God working directly and markedly through some believers, even giving them revelations concerning future events, Acts 11, 27, *etc.;* 20, 10; 21, 9. But prophecy consisted more generally in an explanation and application of the revealed will of God to Christian hearers. The apostles were prophets in both senses of the word, their assistants and the elders they ordained in the churches were prophets in the latter sense of the word. See Meusel, *Handlexikon,* the article *Prophetie.* Here **prophesyings** is used in the most general sense, as a product of the Spirit of God, and refers

chiefly to the instruction and admonition by men enlightened and moved by the Spirit in the Thessalonian congregation. Their words might not suit some of the members of the church, and they might be inclined to make
light of them and to offer flippant and unspiritual objections. This is what Paul warns against, and the same
warning is necessary to-day. — Instead of despising the
word spoken for our special benefit, the apostle admonishes us: **prove all things,** examine and test them,
δοκιμάζετε, as metal is assayed and tested; "all things," of
course also prophesyings, but not only these. That
prophesyings were to be tested Paul shows especially in
1 Cor. 14, 29; and some had the gift of the Spirit to
discern the spirits, 1 Cor. 12, 10. Of course, all such
proving, whether of prophetic teaching or of other matters in the congregation, had to be in accord with the
Spirit of God and the truth he had revealed. Prophecy
itself had to be "according to the proportion of faith,"
Rom. 12, 7, had to measure up to the faith as held and
confessed by the true church in accordance with the Word
(*analogia fidei*); so also whatever else was proposed and
done by the members of the church. — In thus proving
all things our aim must be positively to **hold fast that
which is good,** and negatively to **abstain from every form
of evil.** "Good" here is whatever is beautiful and fair
in the eyes of God; that, and that alone, ought to appear
καλόν, or as τὸ καλόν, to us. It alone graces our life, evil
disfigures it, however fair our perverted vision may pronounce it. It alone benefits us, however pleasurable and
profitable evil may seem at the time. To hold fast that
which is good means to approve and choose it, and then
to carry it into effect in spite of any objections that may
be raised against it. There is energy in the word
(κατέχετε), battle if necessary. — On the other hand we
are to abstain from **every form of** evil, ἀπὸ παντὸς εἴδους
πονηροῦ. The margin offers *appearance of evil,* but εἴδος
is never the mere appearance of a thing which may not
accord with its real nature; it is the special **form** which

the thing takes. No matter in what form evil may come
to us, no matter how fair its cloak may be, how seductive
or deceptive, we must hold ourselves away from it, for
after all it is **evil,** πονηρός, evil in an active sense, malig-
nant, working mischief, oppressing and hurting him who
comes in contact with it. Who would want anything to do
with such evil in any form? It blasts, poisons, kills: hold
yourself entirely aloof from it. Spiritual evils are worst,
such as perversions of the truth, which many to-day count
quite harmless, and moral defections, which always react
upon the inner life to its hurt or total destruction. Only
he will be "without blame at the coming of our Lord
Jesus Christ" who follows the Spirit, obeys his Word,
holds to the good, rejects the evil.

Let God sanctify you wholly.

In an entirely natural way Paul, whose heart is full
of prayer, turns his admonition into a fervent petition to
God. He has spoken of the Spirit's activity, and of the
divine help of the Word, so it is easy for him to lay
full stress upon what God must do for us in all our life
if we are to be and remain blameless in his eyes. **And
the God of peace himself sanctify you wholly; and may
your spirit and soul and body be preserved entire, without blame at the coming of our Lord Jesus Christ.
Faithful is he that calleth you, who will also do it.** — The
position of αὐτὸς ὁ θεός is emphatic; all depends on him.
He is called **the God of peace,** as so often in Paul's letters
(Rom. 15, 33; 16, 20; Phil. 4, 9; *etc.*), because of the
heavenly gift of true peace which he offers and bestows
upon us. Wohlenberg thinks this alludes to strife among
the Thessalonians which the apostle wanted to counteract
and overcome, but this idea is both shallow, when we
consider the apostle's prayer in its comprehensiveness, and
far-fetched when we consider the context. Peace is the
inner harmony of our whole life with God, and as the one
who gives us this great gift Paul prays that God would
sanctify the Thessalonians **wholly,** separate and set them

apart for himself completely, so that his sanctifying influence penetrates them through and through. No nook nor corner of your life is to be left to the control and possession of the world and the flesh. The peace of God is to reign undisturbed in every province of our being. Too many are satisfied with a partial Christianity, one side of life with a show of holiness, — and this usually not too strong — and the other still very worldly. All the admonitions of Paul are forever trying to prod into every corner of· our nature, that none may escape purification. And here he prays that his efforts may succeed, that God himself by his Word and Spirit may sanctify us 'wholly. Sanctification here embraces the whole work of the Spirit which follows the enkindling of faith in the heart. The adjective ὁλοτελεῖς belongs to ὑμᾶς, it is quantitative, not qualitative; not "total sanctification" in the sense of the sects who think that Christians can be brought to a state of perfection in which they will sin no more, but a sanctification that extends through every member and faculty of our ·person and every part of our life. This sanctification will not be wrought all in an instant, like the gift of the "second blessing" some dream of, but gradually, like a steady growth and development, 2 Pet. 3, 18; Eph. 4, 15. — Paul explains his meaning more fully by referring to the **spirit, soul**, and **body** of his readers; sanctification is to extend to all three. The effort to establish the doctrine of trichotomy from this passage is in vain; for in substance spirit and soul are identical. Where the two are distinguished, as here, the **spirit** designates the highest, deepest, noblest part of man, that side of his being with which he is able to grasp the incomprehensible, invisible, eternal things of God, the house where faith and the Word of God dwell; while **soul** designates the same spirit as animating the body and working through it, its nature then being to grasp what reason is able to know and comprehend. Luther. See *Eisenach Gospel Selections*, I, 519, *etc.* "Spirit" and "soul" may often be used interchangeably, and "soul" may stand for man's entire being as properly describing a spirit joined to a body. Both soul and spirit designate man's higher nature, each word, when used distinctively, expressing a special relation. The apostle in our text aims to describe all sides of our being (ὑμᾶς ὁλοτελεῖς), hence this enumeration of three. — His desire is that spirit, soul, and body **may be preserved entire, without blame at the coming of our Lord Jesus Christ.** The A. V. incorrectly draws ὁλόκληρον as an attribute to τὸ πνεῦμα: "your whole spirit;" the word is not attributive, but predicative, and though neuter to agree with the first of the three nouns (πνεῦμα), belongs to all three alike. Winer, 59, 5. **Entire** (ὅλος, whole, and κλῆρος, allotment) means complete in all its parts, and is thus synonymous with ὁλοτελής. The Greek παρουσία, or presence, denotes the glorious and visible presence of Christ when he returns to judgment at the last day. To appear "blameless" (A. V.), then, must be the one great aim of Christian life and effort, the one prayer that underlies and overshadows all others. For in that day we shall be judged according to our works, namely according to the true fruit of faith, or its absence, as the case may be. So Paul's wish for our sanctification and preservation is nothing else but the wish that our faith may show its fruits in the fullest development. The two optatives ἁγιάσαι and τηρηθείη are used in the regular way to indicate a practicable wish, one whose fulfilment is hoped and expected. Luenemann says that the spirit will be kept entire, without blame, when the voice of truth constantly dominates it; the soul likewise, when it conquers the allurements of sensuousness; and the body, when it is not abused as an instrument of shame. Each in its totality is thus to be put wholly to God's service and kept there, by the guarding care of God, to the end. — Paul's wish and prayer, and its echo in the hearts of his readers, has the fullest assurance of realization: **Faithful is he that calleth you,** trustworthy, dependable. God is called ὁ καλῶν ὑμᾶς, the present participle being used as a noun, without any reference to time, Winer, 45, 7. His intention in calling us and bringing us into his kingdom shall be fulfilled; his call will not be in vain: **who also will do it,** namely carry into effect what his call implies. How can he abandon us after calling us? How can he begin such a great and blessed work, and then leave it unfinished for lack of effort or care on his part? That is impossible But with such complete assurance for us as regards God, how active, confident, hopeful, and joyful should be our work of using his grace and help and thus attaining the glorious goal he has set for us!

HOMILETICAL HINTS.

When we speak of a blameless life everything depends upon him who is to pass judgment upon us. Many are blameless enough in their own eyes, some nearly blameless in the eyes of their friends; but who is blameless in the eyes of God? — Yet blameless is not exactly the same as sinless. All those whom Christ shall accept at the last day are sinners; but when they came to faith their sins were pardoned and all blame for them disappeared; and then more and more their faith asserted itself in the service of Christ, and the Lord delighted therein. He pardoned their imperfections and shortcomings and he accepted the fruit his own grace had produced in their receptive hearts.

The kingdom of God here on earth is a fellowship of labor. God employs us all, but while he accepts our labor as a service to himself, its fruit and product is to be entirely ours. The more love and labor you put upon others in God's service, the greater will be your own spiritual riches. Yours is to be not only the talent placed into your hands in order to trade for the Master, but yours also all the talents you gain by trading. Only a king of untold wealth is able to treat his servants thus.

There is only one way to overcome evil; you must use good. Some fight fire with fire; but to meet evil with evil only heaps new fuel upon the flames and makes the conflagration greater.

Some think it a sign of superior strength on their part when they look down upon the weak; alas, this is a weakness on their part, perhaps greater than that upon which they look down in their pride. True strength is like a parent stooping down to a child; like a master showing a novice how; like an old experienced guide pointing out the safe steps and the danger places to a new traveler;

like a hero in battle carrying the wounded comrade to a place of safety.

The human heart is like a pendulum swinging between laughter and tears, wreathes of roses and thorny briars, dirges and marriage festivities. How then can it ever rejoice alway? Answer: in the Lord, who puts a blessing into our weeping as well as into our play, into our crosses as well as into our crownings, into our wailing as well as into our songs. — You meet many jolly people in the world, but not so many joyful people. True joy grows only where the blood of Christ has moistened the soil. — Thankfulness is happiness. How much of it is yours? — Daily, hourly, momentarily you enjoy gifts that come from God. To realize it is to thank alway, and thanksgiving is one form of prayer.

Riemer has a paragraph on preaching in his sermon on this text. How many Christians count it a matter of indifference to stay away now and then from the public proclamation of the Word. This is the sin of despising prophesyings, and this quenches one of the brightest flames of the Spirit. — No admonition is more necessary to–day than the one which bids us prove all things. The world is full of dangers, errors in religious things. But many do their proving by using a false test, namely their own blind reason, their woful ignorance, or the opinions of men, especially those that happen to be popular. Use God's Word only as the test-stone, and make yourself a master of that Word, especially of its chief doctrines.

The Blameless Christian Life.

I. *Its outward marks.*
II. *Its inward power.*

Let God Sanctify you Wholly!

I. *By grounding your spirit in truth.*
II. *By filling your soul with love.*
III. *By keeping your body from evil.*

What Influence Must the Lord's Coming Exert Upon our Lives?

I. *It must move us to exercise ourselves in holiness.*
II. *It must impel us to equip ourselves for holiness.*

The Happiest Life in the World.

I. *It sparkles with love.*
II. *It is upborne by prayer and thanksgiving.*
III. *It is crowned with truth.*
IV. *It is joined to God.*

Helps for Holiness.

I. *The brethren.*
II. *The Word.*
III. *God.*

"Prove all Things!"

I. *How? By means of the Word.*
II. *Why? That you may hold fast the good, and abstain from every form of evil.*

THE
TWENTY - FIFTH SUNDAY AFTER TRINITY.

Heb. 10, 32-39.

In this text the writer of Hebrews aims to encourage his readers. He has shown them at length Christ, the true High Priest (7, 1—10, 18), and then, following this elaborate didactic section, he has added first an admonition, verses 19-25 (our text for the First Sunday in Advent), then a strong warning, verses 26-31, and now a hearty word of encouragement, verses 32-39. This ends with a reference to faith, giving the cue for the grand chapter to follow, on faith and its heroes. We may sum up our text in the call: *Cast not your boldness away!* It would stir us all up to go on confidently to the end. There is first a statement in regard to former courage and faithfulness, verses 32-34; then, based on this, the appeal not to shrink back.

Call to remembrance the former days.

The readers of this Epistle were no novices in Christian experience. They had had a strong taste of what it means to follow Christ in a wicked world. But they had been faithful, and here their faithfulness is acknowledged to their great credit and made the basis of an appeal not to shrink back at this late date. **But call to remembrance the former days, in which, after ye were enlightened, ye endured a great conflict of sufferings; partly, being made a gazingstock both by reproaches and afflictions; and partly, becoming partakers with them that were so used. For ye both had compassion on them that were in bonds, and took joyfully the spoiling of your possessions, knowing that ye yourselves have a better possession and an abiding one.** — 'Αναμιμνήσκεσθε, call up to remembrance, separates more widely the past to be recalled from the present, than μιμνήσεσθε would do; the latter is followed by the genitive, while the former has the accusative of the thing remembered. — It is impossible to fix exactly the period meant by **the former days,** nor the occurrences here detailed as having taken place in them. Some commentators make no attempt in this direction, the others offer tentative suggestions.   Two things seem certain, that the persecutions following the martyrdom of Stephen are not meant here, and that the terrible outbreak under Nero in the year 64 is likewise out of the question; the former cannot be meant because the affliction mentioned in our text took place shortly after the conversion of the readers, and they certainly did not belong to those who first formed the congregation at Jerusalem (2, 3) ; and the latter cannot be meant because, aside from other points, this persecution was exceedingly bloody, and our text makes no reference at all to martyrdoms.   So there are left to us only incidental persecutions, not otherwise especially recorded, by which the readers of this Epistle were made to suffer considerably in various ways, but not unto death. — **After ye were enlightened,** φωτισθέντες, refers to enlightenment produced by the Gospel, when it first shed its radiance into the hearts of the Hebrews.   The word is used in the same way in 6, 4; compare also 10, 26.   This, of course, was a memorable time for those people, even apart from the trials it ushered in; for it was then that the darkness of error and delusion fell from their minds, and the grace of God, his glorious plan of salvation, and all the blessings he had in store for them shone in their true splendor before their eyes. — But at once the severest kind of cross was laid upon their young faith; those were the days **in which ye endured a great conflict of sufferings.**   It seems that when these Hebrews forsook the synagogue, their former brethren became enraged and stirred up the authorities against them, so that these young believers had to go through a painful test of their faith.   An ἄθλησις is a **conflict** such as athletes undergo when straining for victory and a prize.   But this was a conflict of **sufferings,** it consisted of them, and it could be won only by "enduring," by holding out in spite of all the hurt that blind hate and fanatical opposition was able to inflict. **Ye endured,** ὑπεμείνατε, means that they did so without growing discouraged, without wavering and giving up. They were victors in the conflict to which their faith was thus called. Let us note that this is no small praise, especially when it is bestowed upon beginners in the faith. To be sure, the first love was still in their hearts, yet while this often burns brightly for a short time, it is apt to give way at last; but with these Hebrews it held out till their enemies grew weary. — The following particulars are added by means of τοῦτο μὲν . . . τοῦτο δέ, found only here in the N. T., but frequently in the classics: **partly, being made a gazingstock both by reproaches and afflictions; and partly, becoming partakers with them that were so used.** Their conflict involved suffering on their own part; through **reproaches,** the accusing, damaging things said against them, and **afflictions,** oppressive acts done to their actual hurt, they had been **made a gazingstock,** θεατριζόμενοι, as if exposed as a spectacle in the theater for all people to stare and wonder at. The hostile attention of everybody had been drawn to them, and all who thus regarded them spoke ill of them and aided in doing them despite. The verb θεατρίζειν occurs only here and in the patristic literature, it matches well the preceding ἄθλησις. In part these Hebrews suffered also indirectly, by **becoming partakers,** through sympathy, and the help and comfort they offered, **with them that were so used,** τῶν οὕτως ἀναστρεφομένων, really: "with them that fared thus," or "that conducted themselves thus," *i. e.* allowed themselves to be made a gazingstock, as just stated. Thus they had displayed both the courage and the self-forgetful love that goes with faith. — **For** adds a few explanatory details, reversing the order, however, in the form of a chiasmus: **Ye both had compassion on them that were in bonds, and took joyfully the spoiling of your possessions.** The A. V. follows the incorrect reading: "on me in my bonds," τοῖς δεσμοῖς μου, instead of τοῖς δεσμίοις. This incorrect reading seems to be due to the supposition that Paul wrote the Epistle, and this while a prisoner in Rome; even so, there is no reason why the writer should bring in himself at this point when his whole argument turns on the heroic bravery of his readers. Some were actual δέσμιοι, prisoners, put in bonds for their faith's sake. This, it seems, was the worst that was done in these persecutions. The others who were not arrested **had compassion on them**, and evidently showed it by word and deed, although they ran the risk of similar treatment. They would not deny their brethren, nor would they forsake them in their hour of need. It was a noble and brave thing to do. 2 Tim. 1, 8 and 16. Moreover, when persecution turned their way, they **took joyfully the spoiling of their possessions,** the confiscation of their goods which the authorities inflicted upon them. Riggenbach points out that this is more likely what τὴν ἁρπαγὴν τῶν ὑπαρχόντων means, since it is mentioned here after imprisonments; not a spoiling by mob-violence. Confiscations in Roman law always accompanied other penalties. This they received or accepted (προσδέχεσθαι) **joyfully**, not as if they had suffered a severe loss, but as a distinction and honor conferred upon them. — **Knowing that ye yourselves have a better possession and an abiding one** explains this joyfulness, which must have greatly puzzled their enemies. Here too the A. V. follows an inferior reading: "knowing in yourselves that ye have in heaven a better and an enduring substance." There is very little authority for ἐν ἑαυτοῖς; not enough for ἐν οὐρανοῖς. As between the accusative ἑαυτούς and the simple dative ἑαυτοῖς, the former has the best attestation. The marginal translation: *that ye have your own selves for a better possession,* while grammatically possible, makes no good sense, and appears like a curiosity. Delitzsch thinks that the reflective pronoun is superfluous and tautological, but he overlooks that it is meant to contrast the readers who were despoiled with their enemies, who despoiled. Whatever they thus lost, they on their part, unlike their despoilers, had **a better possession and an abiding one,**

superior in every way and more excellent, and one that
remained theirs and that no one could deprive them of.
It is not necessary to name this ὕπαρξις, every Christian
knows what it is, "the heavenly inheritance, the world to
come, whose powers are already stirring within us" (Delitzsch); or, naming it more as now we possess and enjoy it, the spiritual riches, forgiveness of sin, sonship
and heirship, and all the peace, comfort, power, and joy
that go with these. All the gold in the world could not
buy release from one sin; and all the glory of the world
could not secure for us one drop of true comfort or one
spark of real joy, or one ounce of true spiritual strength. —
While these Hebrews were not called upon to give the
supreme proof of their loyalty to Christ, we feel that
they would have been ready to give it, if their enemies
had required it. Nor have they been alone in the world;
the history of Christian missions presents many examples
of supreme loyalty on the part of recent converts. All
such belong in the class which the next chapter so grandly
describes, setting the finest examples of true faith and
attachment to the Gospel promises before us. Do we
belong to this class also? But it is one thing to belong
to it for a time, and another to hold out in it to the very
end.

Never cast your boldness away!

On the basis of the description just made the writer
of Hebrews puts forward most effectively the admonition which his readers need just now. It is an en-
couraging, stimulating call to persevere unto the end.
**Cast not away therefore your boldness, which hath
great recompense of reward. For ye have need of
patience, that, having done the will of God, ye may receive the promise.**

For yet a very little while,
He that cometh shall come, and shall not tarry.
But my righteous one shall live by faith:
**And if he shrink back, my soul hath no pleasure in
him.**

But we are not of them that shrink back unto perdition; but of them that have faith unto the saving of the soul. — After having endured so much and proved faithful so far, it would be sad indeed if after all the Hebrews would give up in discouragement. This very thing has happened: Christians have begun exceedingly well, and have ended by weakly surrendering. So the call here is, not to act cowardly and despondent, not to lose the victory when the battle is nearly over, not to throw away the great reward when it is almost due. The verb ἀποβάλλειν may denote involuntary loss, but here it evidently has its original meaning: **Cast not away** your παρρησία, your assurance and confidence as regards Christ, in particular as regards the sure fulfilment of his promise, verse 36. The word denotes the liberty to tell everything, see Heb. 10, 19 in First Sunday in Advent, and is thus properly rendered **boldness;** then also it is naturally modified to denote the confidence and assurance that one must have to speak freely to another, and this is what the word naturally means here. It cannot refer to the confident confession of the Hebrews before their adversaries, since throughout the Epistle it is made to refer to God: 3, 6; 4, 16; 10, 19, and our passage where the same meaning is required by the context. The Hebrews may have grown discouraged, when after their first victory other battles awaited them; the sense of God's grace, the power of his promises may have grown weaker in their hearts as time passed on. But whatever the cause, it would be folly for those who had once risen to full confidence in God and the Gospel, to cast this aside now and thus ultimately miss its reward. — **Which hath great recompense of reward** shows what the Hebrews would lose; with their confidence they would cast away also this μισθαποδοσίαν, the paying over to them of their just reward, which is especially described as "great." Not that our παρρησία is such a meritorious work in God's sight as to deserve payment of reward on his part; it is like faith in general, not a matter of law, work, and legal claim of earnings at

all, but a matter of the Gospel, of the grace and goodness
of God, who gratuitously bestows the greatest blessings
upon those who trust in him to the end. Our best works
could claim but little, but when we come with full, free
confidence in God, he opens up all the fountains of his
love, 1 Cor. 2, 9. This negative call, not to cast away
our boldness, is but the other side of those positive admonitions which run through the entire Epistle, to keep on
in confidence to the end, 3, 6; 4, 14; 6, 18; 10, 23; *etc.* —
The thing that is necessary now that their boldness may
not cease is ὑπομονή, endurance, the brave, manly steadi-
ness which bears whatever may be required in the course
once chosen as right before God. **For ye have need of
patience** (ὑπομονή)**, that, having done the will of God,
ye may receive the promise.** Patience is described by
Delitzsch as "that unshaken, unyielding, patient endurance
under the pressure of trial and persecution, that steadfastness of faith, apprehending present blessings, and of
hope, with heaven-directed eye anticipating the glorious
future, which obtains what it waits for." The word is
placed first for emphasis: "Patience you have need of,"
that is the one thing you must try to secure. The purpose in this is that, **having done the will of God,** namely,
continue in patience, **ye may receive the promise,** ye
may carry away the great and glorious reward God has
promised to all wo endure to the end, which is eternal
blessedness in the heavenly kingdom of Christ. To give
up, to cease your efforts, to let go God's grace is contrary
to his good and gracious will, and therefore must forfeit
all that the promise holds out. There is no reason to
take the aorist participle ποιήσαντες in any but its natural
sense, as action preceding the main verb. — In order to
impress his call to continued confidence and perseverance
the writer makes use of prophetic utterances, which his
readers, well versed in the O. T., will understand without
further explanation. There is no intention to quote exactly, as no formula for introducing a quotation is used.
Moreover, the writer here puts the prophet's words into

the light of the N. T. and thus in using the words explains just how he wants them understood. The point
in the quotation is twofold, namely: that the Messiah will
return soon, so that our endurance will need be but for a
short time, and that only he who holds out shall please the
Lord. **For yet a very little while,** emphasizes the brief-
ness of the time till the Lord's return. We find μικρὸν
ὅσον ὅσον in Is. 26, 20. The words in our text are simply a
verbal appropriation and no more. Their meaning here
comes from the context entirely: "yet a little, how very,
very (little)." It makes little difference whether we read
the case as an accusative of time, or as a nominative with
a copula to be supplied. The two ὅσον ὅσον express the
superlative: "very little." — Now follows an appropriation of Hab. 2, 3 *etc.*: **He that cometh shall come, and
shall not tarry;** so that "a very little while" stands for
the interval between any sufferings and trials of the Christians and the Lord's final coming. Our writer puts in
ὁ before ἐρχόμενος, making it plain whom he means, namely,
the glorious Messiah, Ps. 118, 26: "Blessed is he that
cometh in the name of the Lord." For the time of the old
covenant this coming and "he that cometh" meant the
coming of Christ in general, in grace, as well as in judgment, and the prophets usually viewed both as one grand
vision, without distinguishing in their perspective of the
future the interval between the two parts of this coming,
the incarnation and the judgment at the end of time. Of
course, our writer here applies the prophet's words only
to the latter event, the former already lying in the past.
He shall come is an emphatic declaration, intended to overcome all doubt; he will not deny his own name ὁ ἐρχόμενος,
the Coming One. **And shall not tarry** or delay when the
hour arrives; he shall come promptly and will not cause
us to wait needlessly. This is cheering news for those
who in part have already grown weary under trials while
they waited for the Lord. In the Hebrew the prophet
does not speak of a person, but of a vision which is for an
appointed time and will surely come and not tarry; this

vision refers to the Messiah, so that really it is he whom
the prophet bade the people wait for. The Septuagint already used a personal subject, and the writer to the Hebrews uses the prophet's words still more clearly of the
Messiah. — Instead of using the entire passage from Habakkuk our writer appropriates only what he needs; and
instead of following the order of the sentences in the original or the Septuagint, he uses an order that suits his own
purpose; so that we see, he is bent not ·on adducing a
regular proof passage by way of authoritative quotation,
but merely on appropriating the essential meaning of what
Habakkuk had said, the fact of his having spoken thus being
enough to duly strengthen the present writer's admonition and to impress his readers. — **But my righteous one
shall live by faith,** or, as other authorities read: *the
righteous one,* margin. The original has: "his faith," and
the Septuagint: "faith in me" ($\mu o \upsilon$). It is a textual question whether in our passage we should use the $\mu o \upsilon$ at all,
or where we should read it. The passage is here used because eternal life is made so clearly dependent upon faith,
which is the heart of all true $\pi a \rho \rho \eta \sigma i a$ and $\upsilon \pi o \mu o \nu \eta$. On
the interpretation see Rom. 1, 17, Third Sunday after Epiph-
any. Faith is the source of eternal life ($\epsilon \kappa$ $\pi i \sigma \tau \epsilon \omega s$)
because it is the only means by which we can apprehend
Christ, the Life; nor is any synergistic or Pelagian sense
connected with the word "faith," for God alone works and
maintains faith in us, and we hold it fast solely and
alone by his grace. — But it is possible to have faith and
not to retain it. Faith must meet opposition, must endure one contest after another, must exercise itself in
bearing the cross. He who has faith must therefore use
God's grace diligently in order to keep his faith till the
end. — **And if he shrink back, my soul hath no pleasure
in him** points out the danger and its fearful consequences.
Our author simply attaches this statement to the foregoing
one by means of "and." He makes no effort to go back
to the original words of the prophet: "Behold, his soul,
which is lifted up, is not upright in him," which the Sep-

tuagint failed altogether to translate correctly: "If any one draw back, my soul hath no pleasure in him." The prophet was speaking of the proud, puffed up Chaldean, whose soul was not upright in him, and he is foretelling how God will deal with him. Over against this picture of the Chaldean the prophet placed the picture of the just man, whose faith, firm in trust and reliance on God, shall secure him life. The writer of Hebrews takes the incorrect translation of the Septuagint, which even grammatically has a false sense in that the subject of the sentence, "his soul," instead of referring to the proud Chaldean, refers to him who is spoken of as coming, and he transfers the whole sentence into a new place, and thus gives it a sense which is at least biblically correct. It is very plain, therefore, why the writer of Hebrews does not say: "These are the words of the prophet," or something to that effect. He is putting, not the original meaning indeed, but one at least scripturally correct, into the old, incorrect words of the Septuagint. In general, however, we may add that the idea of not being "upright," of having a soul which lacks true uprightness in the presence of God, is held fast by our writer when he speaks of a man "shrinking back." What made the ancient Chaldean displeasing in God's eyes, certainly will, if it appear in a new form now in the Christian, be no less displeasing to God. **If he**, namely "the righteous one," instead of standing firm by faith in affliction and trial, **shrink back**, ὑποστείληται, draw himself back, in fear, cowardice, weak surrender, from the conflict which all who have faith must endure, **my soul,** that is God, **hath no pleasure in him,** and must turn from him, especially at the last day, when the great reward is to be bestowed upon the faithful and enduring. To shrink back means to cast away the παρρησία, to let go the ὑπομονή, in which true faith always manifests itself. God, who gives to every believer abundant grace to hold out and persevere to the end, is always deeply offended, when we fail to use this grace, but, looking away from it, let the conflict about us cause us to shrink back and give up. On

Hab. 2, 3, *etc.* compare the excellent commentary of Keil; on our passage in the text Riggenbach will be found helpful. — Only to encourage and stimulate his readers did our author point out what God thinks of those who grow cowardly and afraid. Of course, the dread possibility of their sinking down into this class underlies the entire discussion, see 26-31. Of his first readers our author has better hopes: **But we are not of them that shrink back unto perdition.** The more effectively to touch their hearts he uses the emphatic ἡμεῖς, connecting himself with them. But here, as in a flash, he shows what shrinking back implies: he who draws back to save himself from persecutions and trials, does not draw back to safety, but to the very worst possible fate, **unto perdition,** eternal death and damnation in hell. Is. 7, 9. The genitive ὑποστολῆς after οὐκ ἐσμέν expresses quality or character: we are not of this sort. To what can we shrink back, if we draw away from God? what is there left away from him? Certainly no safety, no life, no peace, no joy; nothing but terror, gloom, wretchedness, death, in one word: perdition. And this is not annihilation, as some suppose, contrary to all teaching of Scripture, but an existence away from the one source of life and light; a self-chosen existence, from which there is no escape once death takes us away from the means of grace in this life, Luke 16, 31. — **But** (we are) **of them that have faith unto the saving of the soul,** this is the glorious antithesis to the previous negative statement. Here πίστεως is again used predicatively, Blass 35, 2. **Faith** is now used to bring out fully what was before described by the essential manifestations of faith, such as "boldness" and "patience." The Greek has: *unto the gaining of the soul,* margin; really, so that we gain possession of it and keep it safe. To lose the soul (Luke 9, 25) is to let it fall away from God, into the night of eternal death; hence to gain it is to bring it into permanent connection with God and the blessedness that is ever present with him. Here ψυχή designates the immaterial part of man, but not as contrasted with the body: if the soul is saved, man altogether is saved. But it is the soul that decides his fate; there faith has its seat, and all the spiritual attributes of man, and the body is the instrument and servant of the soul, and shall share its fate ultimately, whatever that may be.

HOMILETICAL HINTS.

Our religion has sometimes been mocked as fit only for women and children. It is fit for them, but this text shows what it would make even of them, strong and courageous heroes, enduring all trials valiantly to the end. And there are thousands of men who have not one tenth of the courage in their hearts which true faith in Christ requires. — How often has not the church been declared dead! Think of the storms she has weathered, the conflicts from which she has emerged, always with her strength unbroken and her prestige greater than before. Her grave-diggers have never quite finished the tomb for her interment, for always before they were done they themselves sank down overcome and began to turn into dust.

Study well the history of those who have suffered for their faith; let it impress you how they endured and held out amid jeers and scoffs, slanders and accusations, blows and fetters, prisons and dungeons, fines and confiscations, and other losses and mistreatments. Then tell yourself that these are the marks of your own religion, and it would not be what it is, if to-day it could not produce a fortitude and heroism like that of by-gone days. Let us get rid of the idea that Christianity is a bunch of roses, a sweet song of love and peace, a balmy zephyr that lulls asleep in gentle ease. It is iron in the blood, it is a shout of battle, it is a storm that rocks us to the bottom of our being. If it is to overcome death and hell and carry you through them to the skies, it must overcome every trial in this life and establish you here on a rock that men may assault, but shall never overthrow. — No power on earth is able to overcome Christian patience. — Many cannot understand that patient suffering is of more value than bustling diligence. But patience is the will of God, and he teaches it to every son of his.

"By grace we have been saved in the beginning of our faith, by grace we are to be saved at its end, from start to finish by faith which alone is able to receive grace, and the reward of which it always is; and this salvation is not of ourselves, it is God's gift alone." Stier.

How does Christ to-day exercise his dominion over the hearts of men? What makes them rise to meet him? His wondrous patience is what attracts our eyes. Alway patient and lowly, howe'er vile scoffers offended! This is what reveals the conquering power of Jesus' passion, what draws even cold hearts into the arms of his love. The more men humbled him, the more we see revealed this patience of his which never for a moment forsook him. When Judas with a kiss betrayed him to his captors, when Rome's soldiers bound him and maltreated their captive with hellish hate, when Caiaphas and Pilate contrary to their own conscience tried to stamp him a blasphemer by means of false witnesses, and a disturber of the people, when Herod mocked him for his pleasure and when Peter in his cowardice denied him, when the fever pains of the burning oriental sun began to scorch his veins as he hung upon the cross, and even then his foes, instead of silently witnessing his death, reviled with their hatred to the last — no matter how terrible his suffering, how desperate his woe, he continued in patience, waiting till the Father would receive his spirit and all his work should be done. Learn beneath the cross the patience that will help you persevere and win the victory in the end. Rump.

He who deserts the colors in time of war is branded as a traitor. — There are too many fair-weather Christians. Like miserable wrecks they are left behind in the march to victory. There is no crown for them on yonder day.

Cast not Your Confidence Away.

I. *Remember the courage of those who have gone before.*
II. *Use diligently the grace that now offers itself to you.*
III. *Look forward to the recompense of reward which the Lord has in store for you.*

The Hearts That Hold Out.

I. *They are full of faith.*
II. *The are full of patience.*
III. *They are full of obedience.*   Pueschmann.

Cast not your Confidence Away!

I. *See what it has brought you in the past.*
II. *See what it shall bring you in the future.*

Adapted from Boy.

Blessed are They That Persevere!

I. *The world knows nothing grander than their confidence and patience.*

II. *Eternity can offer nothing grander than their crown.*

Are you of Them That Draw Back?

Then

I. *Think of their mistake.* They forsake the only sure ground of confidence there is.

II. *Think of their folly.* They prefer temporal ease and profit to eternal glory.

III. *Think of their crime.* They reject Christ and all his grace after having found them.

IV. *Think of their fate.* They have chosen perdition instead of salvation, and they shall have their choice

---

The Damnation of the Backslider.

I. *His broken vows.*

II. *His shattered faith.*

III. *His guilty disobedience.*

IV. *His eternal doom.*

THE
TWENTY - SIXTH SUNDAY AFTER TRINITY.

Rev. 2, 8-11.

The last two texts of our epistle series are from the last book in the Bible. Smyrna, 40 miles from Ephesus, with the Turkish name Ismir, lies on the coast of Ionia, at the head of the gulf into which the Hermus flows. Of the seven cities to which Christ addressed letters in Revelation it is the only one which has retained its importance to the present time. It has some 250,000 inhabitants and an extensive trade. There are now large numbers of Christians at Smyrna, and in this also it exceeds the other cities in a notable way. Ephesus lies altogether in ruins, Sardis and Laodicea likewise. Thyatira, long in ruins, is now a Turkish village with a few Christians among the inhabitants. Pergamus is a small town now, with a small Greek and an equally small Armenian congregation. Philadelphia has but 250 Christians among its 2,000 inhabitants, and has undergone in recent times a terrible massacre of its Christian population. Smyrna alone, "the city of myrrh and martyrs," flourishes, having a number of Christian churches with large membership. The Germans established a school here for girls, with about 200 pupils, the instructors being deaconesses. This was the work of Fliedner in 1853, and was followed in due time by the erection of an orphanage and a hospital. A German evangelical congregation, belonging to the Prussian state church, was also formed; moreover the American Board does missionary work here among the natives and the Jews. — The letter addressed to "the angel of the church in Smyrna" is quite brief, and one of the two in which no fault is found with the church to which it is addressed. Its burden is a call to faithfulness which has found a constant echo in Christian hearts everywhere:

351

"Be thou faithful unto death!" Here we have it in its full
historical setting, which ought to help us to steer clear of
platitudes and generalities in our preaching, and make our
treatment both more concrete and interesting, and thus more
effective.

**And to the angel of the church in Smyrna write:
These things saith the first and the last, which was dead,
and lived** *again.* — The form of the so-called "letters,"
as we see in the one before us, is not epistolary, but rather
like messages sent to each of the churches. There is in
each case, first, a command to write to the angel of the particular church named; secondly, a sublime title of the Lord,
who himself dictates the message; thirdly, a summary characterization of the church addressed, beginning with the
words: "I know," and continuing with an exhortation
either to repentance or to constancy; and fourthly, a promise
to him that overcometh, generally accompanied by an earnest
call to attention: "He that hath an ear *etc.*" — **The angel
of the church** is God's messenger to the church; not, therefore, an actual angelic being, or "a guardian angel" (Weiss),
not the personified spirit of the congregation (Lange, and
others), not the collective presbytery, but the chief minister
or pastor, the individual elder or bishop who presided over
the church. Trench and others of the Anglican Church
insist that ὁ ἄγγελος designates "the bishop" in the
Anglican sense of the word, but this imports a modern conception into the general term, and one foreign to the text
and to the N. T. generally. The glorified Lord himself,
described fully in his majesty, power, and grace, in the first
chapter of Revelation, here addresses the pastor of the
church at Smyrna personally, as the one who is responsible
for the church and for its spiritual condition. An inspection of the seven letters shows that besides this personal
note, there is the idea of representation. The character of
the church as such is embodied in its "angel," and as he is
so is his church. As the shepherd, so the flock. Accordingly, in addressing "the angel" the Lord addresses the
church itself and all its membership. Pastor and people

belong together, and are treated by the Lord himself as practically one. This idea of solidarity between a pastor and his congregation, and of his responsibility for the condition of his congregation cannot be emphasized too much in our time. Our flocks are what we make them and what we allow them to become or be. God will judge every "angel" of the church by his works as these appear in the church itself. — In the case of each of these seven letters we have a clear command from the Lord to the apostle John to **write,** and the very words of the message to be written are dictated to him. Note also 1, 19, where the same command embraces much more. As the prophets of old received their messages from God, and this down to the actual words, so John here is used by the Lord as his *calamus* or pen, as his mouthpiece, as his secretary. Not that the Lord is bound to this one mode of controlling the writers of his Word, he has other modes, but this one is here clearly described to us, and like all the others employed by the Lord, is fitted to convey to us directly and inerrantly his own Word in his own words, as he himself intended them to be our one safe and sure guide for all time. — Instead of beginning at once in the first person, the Lord first dictates a sentence in the third person, in which he seals the message about to be uttered as his very own, imprinting his divine authority upon it: **These things saith the first and the last, which was dead, and lived** *again.* The designation "the first and the last" is used by Isaiah three times for Jehovah, Is. 41, 4; 44, 6; 48, 12; and in Revelation 1, 17, in our text, and in 22, 13 we have it used three times by the glorified Redeemer of himself. It expresses his eternity. There is none before him, there is none after him, for he is the eternal God himself. "First, because all things are from me; last, because all things are to me; from me, the beginning; to me, the end. First, because I am the cause of origin; last, because I am the Judge and the end" (cited by Trench from St. Victor). This title shows what authority supports the message about to be given, what at-

23

tention and obedience it ought to receive. What he who is
the first and the last says is final; and when we give ear to
that and follow it we certainly shall be safe. — The addition: **who was dead, and lived** *again,* brings to mind the
fact that the eternal God himself became our Redeemer
from sin and death. He **was dead,** ἐγένετο νεκρός, aorist,
became dead (margin) ; a definite act in the past is meant,
when the Lord of glory gave his life for us on the bitter
cross. **And lived,** again an aorist, ἔζησεν, a definite past
act, when the dead arose from the tomb and reentered life,
the glorious life he now has and shall have to all eternity.
He it is who says these things to the believers at Smyrna,
whose redemptive love is therefore in all his words, to whom
our hearts are bound by the most blessed ties. Simcox and
others think that the attributes of death and life are here
especially ascribed to Christ, because his message here is a
promise of life to them who die for his sake. He who belongs to Christ who died need fear no death; he who belongs to Christ who lived, can be assured forever of life.

Now follows the body of the message, and first of all
the Lord's own estimate of the church at Smyrna: **I
know thy tribulation, and thy poverty (but thou art
rich), and the blasphemy of them which say they are
Jews, and they are not, but are a synagogue of Satan.**
The A. V. reads: "I know thy works, and tribulation,"*etc.*,
but the best authorities compel us to omit τὰ ἔργα καί. The
θλίψις of the church at Smyrna was the persecution which
pressed hard upon its pastor and the members; it was the
result of Jewish and Gentile hostility. We are unable to
furnish any details, except that the church here must have
suffered like the churches in other localities at this time. —
The special mention of **poverty** naturally leads us to suppose that this was connected with the "tribulation," also a
result of Jewish and heathen hostility. Those who had possessions may have lost them through confiscation by the
authorities; and in general, being hated and reviled by their
fellow citizens, they could not prosper in temporal things.
And being poor they were the more readily despised and

had no means to defend themselves. Such poverty for Christ's sake is one of the afflictions most difficult for some Christians to bear; when they see their property and money disappear, when their livelihood is gone, and there is dearth even of daily bread and the ordinary necessities of life, then their courage is liable to sink, and many are ready to yield. It belongs to the special credit of the Christians at Smyrna that they endured "poverty" without flinching, and the Lord gives them credit for it. — He adds the special comfort: **but thou art rich,** namely spiritually, in the true wealth that abides forever. The church at Smyrna had "the kingdom of God," Matth. 6, 20; was "rich toward God," Luke 12, 21; "as having nothing, and yet possessing all things," 2 Cor. 6, 10; Jam. 2, 5. This is wealth that the world fails altogether to appreciate, and even Christians often undervalue it greatly; and yet all other riches are as nothing against it. — The third affliction which the Lord mentions is **the blasphemy of them which say they are Jews, and they are not, but are a synagogue of Satan.** These, evidently, were actual Jews, not Judaizing Christians, and they vented their hostility in mockery and revilings against the Christ whom these faithful ones believed in. Of course, this was a blasphemy against their precious faith, and was meant to strike them personally in the directest manner. Christ and his believers are not separated in the antagonism of those who hate and oppose him. The ἐκ is stronger than the genitive alone would be; it indicates more strongly the origin of the blasphemy. They, indeed, boasted of being **Jews,** God's chosen people, but their saying so did not make them so, for they were doing the work of Satan himself, and were thus nothing but **a synagogue of Satan,** John 8, 44. In a twofold way we see here how the Lord regards men: outward appearances and claims do not count with him or deceive him for a moment. He knows who are his own, and he marks every evidence of faithfulness on their part. He also knows his enemies, and every wrong they inflict upon believers is recorded against them. What a reckoning that will be when all the things that thus the Lord "knows" are brought forward in the final judgment! Blessed Smyrnæans, in his summary statement of their condition the Lord had no special criticism to add, as in the case of no less than five others of the churches of Asia Minor! What of our congregation to-day? Could the Lord, if he were to address a message to us to-day, stop with words of commendation and praise alone, or would he have to add, as in the case of Ephesus for instance: "But I have this against thee"? or, worse yet, as in the case of Sardis: "I know thy works, that thou hast a name that thou livest, and thou art dead," or of Laodicea: "that thou art neither cold nor hot"? The glory of Smyrna was not a multitude of works in the Lord's service, but what ranks even higher with him, faithfulness under painful persecution, patient endurance for his name's sake.

Now comes the admonition to continue in the blessed course they had chosen: **Fear not the things which thou art about to suffer: behold, the devil is about to cast some of you into prison, that ye may be tried; and ye shall have tribulation ten days.** — Four things deserve notice in these words: the encouragement, not to fear; the announcement of this greater tribulation; the statement of the Lord's purpose in permitting this tribulation; and the comforting assurance that it will not continue long. The injunction: **Fear not,** or, if μηδέν is read instead of μή, "fear nothing," is found about three hundred times in the Scriptures, a testimony that the real purpose of the Bible is to bring us a comfort that shall cast out all fear. — **The things which thou art about to suffer** points to a variety of persecution still greater than the things already past. The use of μέλλειν with the infinitive to express the future is found in the classics and is repeatedly used in the N. T.; here we have it twice in succession. — **Behold** draws special attention to some of the impending persecutions. These are referred back to their real originator **the devil,** who would use men as his tools and agents. The real fight is always between the prince of darkness and the King of light, between principalities, powers, the rulers of the darkness of this world, and spiritual wickedness in high places (Eph. 6, 12) and their great conqueror Jesus Christ. "There is nothing more remarkable in the records which have come down to us of the early persecutions, than the sense which the confessors and martyrs and those who afterwards narrate their sufferings and their triumphs entertain and utter, that these great fights of affliction through which they were called to pass, were the immediate work of the devil." Trench. By ὁ διάβολος, the slanderer, the same being is meant as by Σατᾶν, the adversary, in the previous verse. Those who attempt to deny the personality of the devil can find no possible foundation for their claim in the Scriptures; here the Lord himself, long after his walk on earth, speaks of the devil as his personal foe and the prime author of all the persecutions of believers on earth. — The prince of darkness, using the synagogue of his own servants, the pseudo-Jews, in bringing accusations against the Christians before the Gentile authorities, **is about to cast some of you into prison,** usually the first serious move in pagan persecutions and liable to usher in other measures still more serious. We see that the Lord has such in mind when he urges the church to be faithful "unto death." **Some of you,** ἐξ ὑμῶν, contains a dread uncertainty — who would these brethren be, who would have to endure imprisonment and face possible death? Most likely the more prominent and influential members in the church, the foremost of whom would, of course, be "the angel of the church" himself. — In ἵνα πειρασθῆτε, **that ye may be tried,** proved, tested, as to your faith and its real strength, we see the divine hand behind all the machinations of their enemies. Duesterdieck thinks that this clause states the intention of the devil, and not that of the Lord, a trying unto evil, unto a denial of the faith, and not unto good, unto a brave confession of the faith even in the face of death. The Lutheran Commentary likewise: "Satan seeks their ruin, for he hopes that those cast into prison may fall away." While it is possible to take the words in this sense, we decidedly pre-

fer the reading of Kuebel and others that here the Lord's
intention and purpose in the tribulation of his saints is expressed.   If the devil's were meant there would have to
be a δέ or an ἀλλά, or some other contrasting expression,
indicating what on the other hand the Lord wants of his
people, as for instance: *"But* be thou faithful unto death"
etc.   There is nothing of the kind; all these sentences lie in
one plane: "that ye may be tried — and ye shall have tribulation ten days. — Be thou faithful unto death," there is
no adversative particle anywhere; it is the Lord who here
tells us his own thoughts.   This puts a comfort into the
words: "that ye may be tried;" the Lord's good and gracious intentions shall be carried into effect even through the
malice and hatred of the devil.   Our faith is only tested
and thereby strengthened and purified when the devil is
permitted to bring persecution upon us.   Let us keep the
Lord's intention before us, in order that we may do nothing
to counteract it by any yielding, weakness, or fearfulness
on our part. — **And ye shall have tribulation ten days,**
the Lord adds, specifying the time.   All is under his control, and beyond the bounds he has set even the devil cannot go, as we see so clearly in the case of Job.   Duesterdieck, in order to fortify his interpretation of the previous
clause, prefers the marginal reading, making this sentence
also express the devil's intention: *and may have tribulation
ten days.*   But the "ten days" are fatal to this conception,
for the devil's intention would never be to fix a narrow
limit or any limit at all; he would want to continue the
tribulation until he had brought the last saint to a denial
of his faith.   The Lord fixes the limit, and we must read,
not the subjunctive ἔχητε, but either the future indicative
ἔξετε, **ye shall have,** or the present indicative ἔχετε "ye
have," the former being preferable.   It is the Lord's intention to try his saints, but not beyond their strength, he
shortens the days.   Some are inclined to take the **ten days**
literally, Kuebel adducing the reason that this is not an account of a vision, but a matter of fact message to the people
at Smyrna.   But the analogy of nearly all the other num-

bers in the Apocalypse leads us to prefer the symbolical
sense of the number "ten" in this prophetic announcement.
But among the many who take this sense there is much
diversity as to what the symbolic number is to indicate;
some interpret ten years, some even the ten great persecutions of the entire church, including thus the church of
Smyrna. But these are able to furnish no proof for their
conceptions. The number ten denotes a fixed and limited
period, one pertaining to the local church at Smyrna alone.
Ten is best taken to denote completeness, and is so used in
many places, the ten commandments, the ten virgins *etc.* It
seems entirely proper to take "ten" here in the same way:
"ten days" is the complete period of the coming persecution; the trial of the Smyrnæan church shall be finished in
that period. And "ten" is the smallest number for such
completeness, unlike its multiples which denote greater
multitude or extent; so the coming tribulation, whatever
its actual duration in days or weeks, shall be brief. And
this too furnished a measure of comfort; the Christians at
Smyrna could steel their hearts for the coming severe but
brief trial, knowing that if they held out valiantly their
tribulations would soon be passed.

Forewarned is forearmed. And doubly so when the
negative: "Fear not," is followed by a positive: "Be
faithful," with a glorious promise attached. **Be thou
faithful unto death, and I will give thee the crown of
life. He that hath an ear, let him hear what the Spirit
saith to the churches. He that overcometh shall not
be hurt of the second death.** — The admonition is, of
course, addressed to the entire church, to all its members
collectively. Thus far only "tribulation" and "prison" was
mentioned, now we hear that **death** itself is to be anticipated by some. This is evidently a martyr's death, and the
true and original sense of our passage is not that we keep on
believing until we reach the natural end of life, but that
we keep on believing and confessing in spite of all persecution, even to that which takes our earthly life. When we
use the passage for a general application, beyond the

thought of actual persecution by anti-Christian foes, and beyond the thought of actual martyrdom, we ought still in every case to start from this original sense as the foundation of the sermon. If the believers at Smyrna were to be faithful unto martyrdom, much more should we be found faithful in lesser trials and temptations, with no actual martyrdom threatening us. The imperative γίνου is really: "become," and is more expressive than ἴσθι: "be;" faithfulness is to be constantly achieved, attained, won; there is always an effort, often a battle in it; it is not merely a fixed and established quality that one can rest and quietly continue in. — **Faithful,** πιστός, is here used in its full Christian sense: faithful, reliable in holding fast the Christian faith and confession without wavering or yielding to contrary influences. **Unto death** marks the extreme limit, beyond which no hostile forces can go, and therefore includes all lesser afflictions and sacrifices which adherence to the faith may require of us. What is here urged upon all the saints at Smyrna may well have had special reference to "the angel of the church," the pastor himself. The Apocalypse was written, according to the best evidence, including also all the oldest tradition, at the end of John's life, about 95 or 96 A. D. See the Lutheran Commentary. Introduction, where the question is fully treated. This makes it probable that "the angel of the church in Smyrna," to whom the Lord addressed this message, was Polycarp. the disciple of the apostle John. He was martyred A. D. 168, which was 86 years after his conversion, and he served as the pastor of the church at Smyrna for many years. probably extending back to A. D. 95 and even earlier, although positive evidence is not at hand in regard to the actual length of his ministry. Smyrna had its Olympian games, which always excited the populace and elicited its interest in the highest degree. It was on occasions of this kind when the Christians, holding aloof, appeared highly anti-social and unpatriotic to their heathen fellow citizens. This accounts for the ferocity exhibited against the aged bishop Polycarp. The people clamored that he should be

cast to the lions; the proconsul opposed it, but, impotent
to restrain their fanaticism, let him be tied to the stake.
The Jews with their own hands carried the logs for the
pile which burned him in the great amphitheater. A cir-
cular letter from the church at Smyrna describes his
martyrdom. When urged to recant he said: "Four-score
years and six I have served the Lord, and he never wronged
me; how then can I blaspheme my King and Savior." In
this letter it is further reported that the devil devised many
things against the martyrs, but, thanks to God, did not
prevail against all. This implies that others besides Polycarp were made to suffer, and that some did not hold out
in faithfulness as he did. Of him we are told, that he "by
his patience overcame the unrighteous ruler, and received
the crown of immortality." — This allusion fits our text
admirably: **and I will give thee the crown of life;** also
verse 11: "He that overcometh" *etc.* We need not decide
whether the idea of "the crown" here is derived from the
crowning of the victor in the Olympian games, these games
being viewed with extreme aversion by the Jewish Christians at this time; or whether the image is taken from the
crown-wearing of the leading priest at Smyrna, who was
thus honored at the end of his year of office (Fausset; also
Smith, *Dict. of the Bible*). Vincent remarks that it is
doubtful whether any symbol in the Apocalypse is taken
from heathenism. So, even if inscriptions found at Smyrna
mention persons of both sexes as "crown bearers," **the
crown of life,** that special crown (note the article) con-
sisting of the true and eternal life itself ($\tau\tilde{\eta}s \ \zeta\omega\tilde{\eta}s$) promised
to the faithful, is sufficiently explained as the Christian
symbol and reward of victory in the trials of faith. There
is no reason to think of a royal crown, since the close of
our text mentions overcoming, which refers to battle and
strife. This crown the Lord **will give** as a reward of
grace; we win it, because he who won it for us now makes
us faithful to endure all things for his name's sake, and
then himself lifts us from the conflict to a life of glory and
blessedness; compare Jam. 1, 12; 1 Pet. 5, 4.

Each of the seven letters has the solemn appeal: **He that hath an ear, let him hear what the Spirit saith to the churches,** a repetition of what Christ had said on various occasions when he taught on earth, Matth. 11, 15; 13, 9 and 41; *etc.* Always it is used to impress deeply some great truth upon the hearers. It reaches out to every believer in the church; whoever has faith, the inward ear to receive and appreciate truth, especially also the precious truth of the Lord's promises, is bidden to use his ear now. — **By the Spirit** here is meant the Holy Spirit, who is the Spirit of Christ, Rom. 8, 9. He speaks **to the churches,** to all Christian congregations in general, through the written Word, taking the things of Christ and giving them to us. So in the Apocalypse we have both the word of Christ and of his Spirit. — In each of the seven letters we have a promise beginning with the words: **He that overcometh,** ὁ νικῶν, although in each case the following promise is varied. If we take all these statements together, we have a glorious view of what is promised to those who win the victory of faith. "To overcome," which is the same as to be faithful unto death, is to resist all the forces of evil to the end. In this battle there will be scars, and there may be temporary defeats, but the Lord's help is able to carry us through victoriously to the end. — Here the special promise is that the victor **shall not be hurt of the second death.** Note that the reward is here designated to fit the work done: he who is faithful "unto death" shall not be harmed by "the second death." He may die a temporal death under persecution, but the resurrection shall undo the work of this death by reuniting body and soul. **The second death** is defined by the Apocalypse 20, 14: "And death and hell were cast into the lake of fire. This is the second death;" and again 21, 8: "the lake which burneth with fire and brimstone: which is the second death;" also 20, 6. The negation οὐ μή with the subjunctive is most positive: "he shall *in no way* be hurt" *etc.* Blass 64, 5. Just as the gift of true life is added to us now who already have this earthly and bodily life, so in addition to the bodily death we all die here, the real, eternal death, a separation of body and soul from God forever, is added to all those who fail to overcome, but are themselves overcome by Satan and his temptations. To escape this death is to have the crown of life; and it shall grace the head of every victor.

HOMILETICAL HINTS.

The early days of the Christian church were marked by severe tribulation; so shall the last days be also. The more necessary to remember that through much tribulation must we enter into the kingdom of God.

There are three crowns for the Christian. The first is the crown of grace, of which the Psalmist sings: "Who crowneth thee with loving kindness and tender mercies" (103). The second is the crown of thorns of Christ's sufferings, which the disciple must bear after his Master. The third is the crown of life, which the Lord gives to those who are faithful to him. There are three crowns, and yet in reality only one: Christ himself is our crown. He is our grace with God, our cross before the world, our life in the glory to come. From the crown of grace there grows the crown of thorns, and from the crown of thorns the crown of life. M. Frommel, *Pilger-Postille,* 101.

Koegel asks the question, what the poor man has who belongs to the circle of Christ's followers, and he mentions first of all: the glorious fellowship of the saints, reaching back to the very beginnings of the church, reaching out to the farthest borders of the mission fields, reaching up to the spirits of just men made perfect in heaven. He has his Bible with the golden message of peace in the King's Son who became a Servant and a Savior of all the weary and heavy laden. He has access by prayer to the throneroom of God, which is more than any access to courts and royal palaces. He may call to God: Abba Father! which is more than titles of nobility and coats of arms. As God's child he is God's ward and favorite, and Christ's coheir, and that is more than to possess treasures that thieves steal and that moths and rust corrupt. He has the great apostles John, Paul, Peter, and others to visit him in the Word, and is able to receive their highest messages and God's own promises' from their lips, and he looks forward to the day when the angels of God themselves shall call for him to give him safe-conduct to his eternal home. To be poor with such riches is to exceed all the boasts of earthly aristocracy and wealth. —

To be rich toward God is wondrous wealth; but there is one kind of riches still greater: to make many rich in the same way, 2 Cor. 6, 10.

The synagogues of Satan still persist: all those places of worship which scorn the blood of Christ, which preach the old Jewish doctrine of salvation by works, which use the holy name and Word of God to blind men's eyes and damn their souls. These all do Satan's own work, no matter what fair name they may bear before men.

You cannot be faithful if you fear men. — The Lord mentions the tribulations of the Christians at Smyrna, he even says that these shall be added unto, but he does not utter words of pity and sentimental comfort. He intends that we shall suffer and be tried; for faithfulness grows only in the shadow of the cross.

Compare your lot with that of the faithful ones who have gone before. How little we are beside the glorious sufferers and victors! And yet we often complain as if too much is laid upon us.

Faithfulness for Faithfulness.

I. *Christ's faithfulness toward us.*
II. *Our faithfulness toward him.*   G. Mayer.

"Be Thou Faithful unto Death!"

I. *Around you a hostile world.*
II. *Above you a faithful and mighty Lord.*
III. *Before you a crown of life.*

The Word of Him Who is the First and the Last, who was Dead and is Alive.

I. *I know mine own.*
II. *I try mine own.*
III. *I crown mine own.*   Matthes.

Smyrna: A Word for Those in Tribulation.

I. *The Lord knows your tribulation.*
II. *The Lord controls your tribulation.*
III. *The Lord rewards your tribulation.*

What does Faithfulness unto Death Include?

I. *Faithfulness in life.*
II. *Faithfulness in suffering.*
III. *Faithfulness, if the Lord wills it, unto death.*

"He that hath Ears, Let Him hear What the Spirit Saith Unto the Churches!"

   I.   *Concerning Satan and his work.*
  II.   *Concerning Christ and his church.*
 III.   *Concerning death and the crown of life.*

THE TWENTY-SEVENTH SUNDAY AFTER TRINITY.

Rev. 7, 9-17.

For the last Sunday of the church year we have a vision of *the saints in heaven*. The consummation of the Christian life takes place in the glorious world to come, and to John it was given to behold this world and its blessed inhabitants, in such a way as this is possible for mortal man, and to record what he saw for our comfort and hope. The full reality of the things here described must be held fast, and in connection with this the true character of the saints in glory: "These are they which come out of the great tribulation, and they washed their robes, and made them white in the blood of the Lamb." The sermon on this text will not omit the admonition which naturally flows from this characterization. The text describes the outward appearance of the saints in heaven, verse 9; their heavenly worship, verses 10-12; their character, verse 14; and their blessed and glorious state.

Their heavenly appearance.

After these things I saw, and behold, a great multitude, which no man could number, out of every nation, and of *all* **tribes and peoples and tongues, standing before the throne and before the Lamb, arrayed in white robes, and palms in their hands.** — "After these things" refers to what John describes in the first eight verses of the chapter, the sealing .of the 144,000 "servants of our God" "out of every tribe of the children of Israel." Some commentators are fully convinced that these 144,-000 are converts from Judaism, especially since the different tribes are all mentioned by name, verses 5-8. By

a great multitude in this second vision they understand either the great body of Gentile Christians, or these together with the Jewish Christians as one great unnumbered host. But Philippi and others are right in pointing out that the distinction here is not one between Jewish and Gentile Christians, but one between the church militant and the church triumphant. John sees first the great company of those who shall face tribulation, then the great company of those who have faced it, verse 14: "These are they which came out of the great tribulation." He sees the host of God's "servants" sealed, verse 4, so that by the Spirit's help they shall not fall amid the tribulation, and then he sees the same host safe and secure in the heavenly world, their sealing having indeed answered its purpose, and now all the marks of the great tribulation are removed from them, verses 16-17. The number 144,000 is symbolic, twelve being the number of the tribes of Israel, and twelve the number of the apostles. These are multiplied together, combining the two fountains from which the church has sprung; and this number is multiplied by the cube of ten, that is ten times ten times ten, indicating the fullest completeness. "Israel" here is the spiritual Israel of the Christian church. The mention of the tribes cannot well refer to the historic tribes of the Jewish people, for this distinction of tribes has long been lost altogether; Dan is omitted in the list, Ephraim is replaced by Joseph, and there are other changes, which can scarcely be accounted for satisfactorily, if the literal interpretation is insisted on. But chiefly the fact that 12,000 are mentioned for each tribe enumerated, shows that the historic Jewish tribes cannot be meant, for the number is plainly symbolic, and so then must be the tribal names. That this interpretation is correct we see in chapter 14, 1 and 3, where the number 144,000 is used again of all believers on earth, and here without any mention of Israelitish names. In both cases the same host is meant, once as it enters the great tribulation, then again as it has left this tribulation, "the name of the Father" still shining on their foreheads. — It is

argued that the 144,000 is a fixed and definite number, and
that the clause: **which no man could number,** both exceeds this and forms a contrast to it, so that both could not
designate the same host. But the moment we take 144,000,
as we must, to be symbolic, this conclusion cannot stand.
John did not count the 144,000, he "heard" this number
by revelation, verse 4, and its meaning is completeness for
him and us. God knows his own, and not one of those
whom the Father has given the Son shall be lost. Their
actual number, while definite, we cannot know, that God
alone knows. So also John did not see the 144,000 or tell
us how they looked to him, he only "heard" the symbolic
number. But in his vision of heaven he actually saw, and
this with astonishment (**behold!**), the great multitude
itself, and it was so great that he despaired of any man
numbering it. To say that the 144,000 could be numbered,
and that this heavenly host could not, and that therefore
the two could not refer to the same multitude, is to be
misled by a cheap surface argument, which falls to pieces
the moment we look more closely. God knows the actual
number of his saints on earth as well as in heaven, the
actual number at any actual time, and the complete number for all time, and for eternity. We know neither; we
have only the symbolic 144,000, used in chapter 7 of all the
saints on earth through all the ages of Christendom, and
in chapter 14 of all the saints in heaven at the end of
time; and to John and us this is a host "which no man
could number." Still, considering the church at any one
definite point of time, and in comparison with the children
of the world, it appears as "a little flock." So much the
more, for our courage and joy, we should look through
John's eyes to the end of time: what a multitude stands
there before the throne and the Lamb! On the pleonastic
use of αὐτόν after the relative ὅν see Blass, 50, 4. The greatness of the number of saints in heaven is further brought
out by the addition: **out of every nation, and of** *all* **tribes
and peoples and tongues.** Not only are the many nations
represented, but in these the tribes that may make them

up, as in the Jewish nation, the peoples, as in our American nation, and the tongues or languages, as likewise in our own nation and in others where different· languages are spoken. Here is a glorious vision of the fruits of mission work in all the corners of the earth. — But whatever the diversity of nationality, race, color, language, or anything else, all these in heaven are one: **standing before the throne,** in the face or presence of it (ἐνώπιον), and of him who sits upon the throne: **before the Lamb.** The plural ἑστῶτες refers to the collective ὄχλος, both in the nominative case after the exclamatory ἰδού; a mixed construction results when this is followed by the accusative περιβεβλημένους as the object of εἶδον. These are peculiarities of the Apocalypse, see Winer for an explanation, 59, 11; Blass, 31, 6. The standing before the throne of the Lamb points to the eternal communion of the saints with their glorified Redeemer, who still bears the name **Lamb** because he was once slain for the sins of the world, and our highest joy will ever be to behold him as the personal source and author of our salvation. — **Arrayed in white robes,** like the garment of light of God and of his angels, in its purity and glorious beauty representing the holiness and righteousness of their wearers. The verb περιβάλλειν means to throw around, and fits well with the long and flowing robes which clothe the saints. — **And palms in their hands,** as a sign of joy and victory. Some attach to the palms the idea of a feast of tabernacles, the old Jewish harvest-home festival; but there is nothing in the text to support such imagery, and it is not good to give the imagination too much rein in heavenly things.

Their heavenly worship.

The narrator becomes more vivid in his language; he writes as if he were now beholding the vision anew, using the present tense: **and they cry with a great voice, saying, Salvation unto our God which sitteth on the throne, and unto the Lamb. And all the angels were**

24

standing round about the throne, and *about* **the elders
and the four living creatures; and they fell before the
throne on their faces, and worshipped God saying,
Amen: Blessing, and glory, and wisdom, and thanksgiving, and honor, and power, and might,** *be* **unto our
God for ever and ever. Amen.** — There is no need of
asking why **with a great voice;** when an innumerable
multitude cries aloud, its voice must resound mightily. So
the heavens ring with the praises of the saints as they worship God and the Lamb. — Their song is of **salvation**
(ἡ σωτηρία, note the definite article), deliverance, rescue,
"salvation" in the highest, completest sense of the word,
as even then they possess and enjoy it. Already here the
saints sing of "salvation," but their song is weak, their
voices often faint, the full glory and blessedness of their
salvation they have not yet realized; and the world utters
its discordant note and tries to silence the song of salvation. What a wondrous thing it will be, when all the
thousands of heaven, in one grand harmonious burst of
praise before the very throne of God and in the presence of
his angels, sing out: "Salvation!" — And this they ascribe
wholly **unto our God which sitteth on the throne,** who
in all eternity formed the wonderful counsel of salvation
and carried it into effect in time; **and unto the Lamb,**
who shed his blood in sacrifice and thus brought our
salvation actually to pass. There are no synergists in
heaven. — This song of the saints is answered by the
angels, their worship uniting with that of the heirs of
salvation to whom they ministered while they were still
on earth. **And all the angels,** likewise an innumerable
multitude (5-11), **were standing round about the throne,**
had placed themselves there (ἑστήκεσαν, pluperfect; some
read εἱστήκεισαν) and were thus standing in this position,
like the saints themselves, all centering in God and the
Lamb, the great fountain of their life and joy. — Within
the grand circle thus formed, and nearest to the throne,
were **the elders,** πρεσβύτεροι twenty-four in number, and
according to 4, 4 themselves seated upon thrones. They

are usually taken to represent the one Church of Christ
as at once the church of the old and of the new covenant,
figured by the twelve patriarchs and the twelve apostles.
Dante is quoted by Vincent:

> "Then saw I people, as behind their leaders,
> Coming behind them, garmented in white,
> And such whiteness never was on earth.
>
> *   *   *   *   *   *
>
> Under so fair a heaven as I describe
> The four and twenty elders, two by two,
> Came on incarnate with flower-de-luce.
>
>   *Purgatorio,* 29, 68-84.

— Encircled by the angels and saints were also **the four
living creatures,** ζῶα, unfortunately translated "beasts"
by the A. V. They are described in Rev. 4, 6-8 in symbolic terms, and are taken to be spirit beings of the highest
orders, resembling the cherubim and seraphim; compare
Ezek. 1, 5-10; 10, 5-20; Is. 6, 2-3. Because one is said to
be "like a lion," the second "like a calf," the third with "a
face as of a man," and the fourth "like a flying eagle," some
have taken these ζῶα to be representatives of the whole
animate creation; but this is fanciful, like many other interpretations which have been offered. Let us note that
they worship God unceasingly (4, 8), and that there seems
to be an analogy between them and the twenty-four elders;
as the elders are the chief among the saints, so these "living creatures" are the chief among the angels; and both are
nearest the throne. — Answering to the shout of salvation
by the saints, the angels **fell down before the throne on
their faces,** in the profoundest act of adoration, **and worshipped God** by so doing and by **saying,** first of all: **Amen,**
"verily," thus sealing as true and also making their own
the praise just uttered by the saints. "Amen" is a tran-
scription of *ameen,* the Hebrew adverbial accusative for
"verily," "certainly," used also as an abstract neuter noun
for verity or truthfulness. — Then they add their own
praise in the form of a sevenfold, and thus most sacred,

ascription of excellence: **Blessing, and glory, and wisdom, and thanksgiving, and honor, and power, and might,** *be* **unto our God.** The definite article accompanies each term of praise. The order of these differs from that of 5, 12, the substance is the same. By εὐλογία is meant **the blessing** which the angels and saints utter in praise of God. The δόξα is **the glory** which shines forth from God in his great attributes as manifested to his creatures. The σοφία is **the wisdom** which underlies all the plans of God and shines out in all his works, especially also the works of salvation. The εὐχαριστία is **the thanksgiving** which all the beneficiaries of God owe and express to him. The τιμή is **the honor,** the supreme dignity and worthiness which belongs to God, and which all his worshipers recognize. The δύναμις is **the power** as God possesses it, and the ἰσχύς **the might** as he puts it forth in his works. There seems to be no definite order in the arrangement of the terms. "The *Amen* which the angels utter proclaims the unison of the whole spirit-world with that redemption of which the earth is the scene (Col. 1, 20); and their present understanding of the great fact so long hid from their gaze (Eph. 3, 10; 1 Pet. 1, 12) is expressed in their *doxology.* In accordance with their universal standpoint, they merge the praise of the Lamb in the general praise of God." Lange. — **For ever and ever,** really: "unto the ages of the ages." The whole closes with a second mighty **Amen.**

Their spiritual character.

The vision as described is now interpreted to John as to its chief points. **And one of the elders answered, saying unto me, These which are arrayed in the white robes, who are they, and whence came they? And I say unto him, My lord, thou knowest. And he said to me, These are they which come out of the great tribulation, and they washed their robes, and made them white in the blood of the Lamb. Therefore are they before the throne of God; and they serve him day and night in his temple: and he that sitteth on the throne shall**

spread his tabernacle over them. — It was fitting that **one of the elders** should make this explanation to John; even here, it would seem, the Lord honors the ministry and uses it, instead of angel service. The elder **answered** to John's unspoken question, or to the question intended to be raised by the vision; he formulates this himself, and it refers to two points: **These which are arrayed in white robes** — not the angels, the other beings, the throne, *etc.* — **who are they, and whence came they?** The angels naturally belong in heaven, and to see them there causes no comment; but when men, and men in such numbers are seen there, the beholder may well ask, at least now before the great day of judgment has arrived, who they are and whence they came, to be thus in heaven and blessedness. — John replies: **My lord, thou knowest.** On the perfect tense of εἴρηκα, literally: "I have said," instead of the aorist εἶπον, Blass says, 59, 4, that this is in consequence of the popular intermixture of these tenses, in cases where the reduplication is not clearly marked. John addresses the elder with the reverence his heavenly exaltation and his position among the heavenly beings required. In positively stating that the elder knows, John requests that he be told, and in advance declares that he will consider what is told him as reliable and trustworthy. — So the elder proceeds: **These are they which come out of the great tribulation.** The present participle οἱ ἐρχόμενοι describes the saints as even now coming up out of the tribulation, one band after another, to the throne of God. It is a vivid answer to the second part of the elder's question: "whence came they?" **The great tribulation,** whence all this countless multitude comes, is the tribulation of the last times, which according to the view of the Scriptures extend from the ascension of Christ to the day of his return to judgment. This great tribulation has been intensified at various times, as in the great persecutions of the early church, and will again be intensified when the end is at hand. Acts 14, 22: "Through many tribulations (διὰ πολλῶν θλίψεων) we must enter into the kingdom of God."

The idea that "the great tribulation" means only the final woes preceding Christ's return, and that this innumerable host consists all of martyrs, is on the face of it untenable, for John here beholds all the blessed, and the entire following description pertains to all saints, not merely to some special class. In the great tribulation, whatever share of it each had to bear, the Lord sustained them, and they held out faithfully, so that now they are where no tribulation can ever touch them again. — **And they have washed their robes, and made them white in the blood of the Lamb;** the washing, by removing all stains, makes white. It is all one act, not two as Hengstenberg puts it, the one a washing, the forgiveness of sins, the other a making white, the living a holy life. The robes are mentioned because they make visible to the eye the person of the wearer. We wear our garments in the daily walk and work of life, where in a thousand ways they may become soiled; and so they picture vividly our walk and work in this sinful world, where stain after stain disfigures the soul. The only medium for the removal of the sin and guilt that comes upon us is the blood of Christ, shed for the atonement of our sins. To wash our robes with this blood means to believe in the saving merits of his atonement and thus to appropriate their saving efficacy for ourselves. The aorists ἔπλυναν and ἐλεύκαναν refer to an act which took place while these saints were still on earth, but this act is that comprehensive one, which constantly trusts in Christ's merits and day by day receives abundantly the forgiveness of sins. The whole theology of this elder and of the white-robed saints in heaven differs from that of the modern doctors, who want no mention of blood, of satisfaction and propitiation, of substitution and sacrifice. — **Therefore,** διὰ τοῦτο, for this reason, and not for any worthiness of their own, **they are before the throne of God,** in heaven, in communion with God, in the place God intended man to be from the beginning. So the blood of Christ saves indeed; all God's saints owe their salvation to it alone. — **And they serve him day and night in his temple,** as John has al-

ready seen part of this service. The verb λατρεύειν is used
in the N. T. of that service which it is the duty of all to
render, and it is used of the service we owe to God. It is
that priestly service which all the saints as white robed
priests of God shall render in the sanctuary of the heavenly
temple in the very presence of God. What here below our
worship in earthly sanctuaries pictures imperfectly, there
our heavenly worship shall perform in supreme perfection.
No weakness shall hinder, no fault in us shall mar, no disturbance from without shall interrupt or in any manner
spoil. That worship shall be our highest delight, and all
who there shall be privileged to render it, have begun by
worshipping together with their brethren here below.
Concerning the phrase **day and night** the Venerable Bede
has already said the proper thing: *More nostro loquens
aeternitatem significat.* There is no actual day and night
in heaven, Rev. 22, 5. Here our service is interrupted by
the changes incident to our earthly existence, there no interruption shall interfere. — **And he that sitteth on the
throne,** God himself **shall spread his tabernacle over
them,** σκηνώσει ἐπ' αὐτούς. What the Shekinah above the
mercy-seat in the tabernacle typified, what the pillar of
cloud in the desert journey of the Israelites illustrated, that
shall be fully realized in heaven. Is. 4, 5; Ezek. 37, 27.
Another description is given in Rev. 21, 3. God's presence
shall ever be with his saints, as if he dwelt in one tent with
them, yea, as if he spread his presence like a tent over
them.

Their eternal blessedness.

The previous description has already told of this
blessedness, but now a number of exceedingly comforting
things are especially added: **They shall hunger no
more, neither thirst any more; neither shall the sun
strike upon them, nor any heat: for the Lamb which is
in the midst of the throne shall be their shepherd, and
shall guide them unto fountains of waters of life: and
God shall wipe away every tear from their eyes.** —

These words of the elder will be better understood if we
recall the hardships and sufferings of the Israelites' journey
through the desert.   So all our life is a journey through
the wilderness to the heavenly Canaan.   The reference to
hunger and **thirst,** to the **sun** striking the weary traveler,
and the **heat** of the desert parching his tongue intends to
picture all the hardships, trials, tribulations, pain, weariness, *etc.,* experienced in a faithful Christian life.   All
these shall be forever gone when the saints reach the
Jordan of death and walk dry-shod to the shores of
Canaan, the land where milk and honey flows, the country
of rich pastures and beautiful flowers, full of refresh-
ment and solace — their true home. — A new figure is
added when the elder says that **the Lamb shall be their
shepherd,** which recalls the 23rd Psalm with all its beautiful imagery.   The Lord is our Shepherd now, and he makes
us lie down now in green pasures, and leads us beside the still
waters.   All this refers to the gifts of his grace, as now we
follow him.   But in heaven the Lamb **which is in the midst
of the throne,** with all his heavenly glory, shall be our
Shepherd, ποιμανεῖ, shall cherish and tend us as a shepherd his
flock.   There is a striking combination of terms in making the
Lamb our shepherd; it is made possible by the fact, that
this Lamb is such only because of his sacrifice for us,
the other ideas connected with the figure do not apply to
Christ.   The modification τὸ ἀνὰ μέσον τοῦ θρόνου, toward
the middle or the center of the throne, means that the
Lamb has its position *before* (Am. Com.) the throne,
namely before the center of it.   This expresses Christ's
mediatorial position, and as such a Mediator he shepherds
and leads his flock even in heaven. — The figure is carried
a step farther when the elder adds that the Lamb **shall
guide** the saints **unto fountains of waters of life;** compare Rev. 22, 1-2.   God himself is the author of this life,
and the joy of heaven will be that we can constantly drink
in this life and taste of the sweetness and strength.   But
we must note, that however much we may ourselves have
received of this life and possess as our own, we never

become independent of God, its author. Even in heaven our life will be only in communion with God, in constantly letting the Lamb lead us to the fountains of the waters of life; although there, of course, nothing can possibly interrupt such communion or ever remove us from the flock the heavenly Shepherd leads. Note the emphatic position of ζωῆς (not ζώσας, A. V.). — **And God shall wipe away,** ἐξαλείψει, shall obliterate, wipe out and thus remove, **every tear from their eyes** ("all tears," A. V., is not close enough). Here the reference is to the actual sorrows of the Christian life on earth, which shall cease forever in heaven, God himself making them come to an end. The underlying image is that of a mother wiping the tears of her weeping child and comforting it. Much of the biblical imagery of heaven is negative, because it cannot be put into positive and direct statements in our poor human language. Heaven is in thousands of respects the opposite of earth. Our tears, every single one, shall be obliterated by the joy we shall receive. But Starke adds very fittingly: "He who does not want to weep on earth cannot have part in this joy." And Roos: "A Christian must weep honest tears here, if God is to wipe them off in the world to come." He who prefers to laugh here with the world cannot expect to be among those at last whose faces, tear-stained, shall feel the touch of the gentle heavenly hand that turns their tears to everlasting joy.

HOMILETICAL HINTS.

There are people who do not like to hear death mentioned; they feel hurt when we remind them of their end. Perhaps the tree has already been cut from which the boards for your coffin shall be taken. What folly to go on eternally planning for life, when this very night your soul may be required of you! — But some prepare for death; they make all arrangements concerning their property, and even their funeral. Their will is duly signed and sealed; their likes and dislikes about coffins, graves, and ceremonies for the dead have all been impressed upon their relatives. They feel assured all will be well and properly carried out when their eyes are closed in death. But have they provided the white garment which alone shall admit them to the company of God's saints above? — Dying alone never saved any man; only dying in the faith of Christ the heavenly Lamb saves.

When John sees the innumerable multitude in white glorifying God and the Lamb in heaven, he has not the courage to say who he thinks they are, namely those, concerning whose salvation amid the strife and terrors of the world he has worried so often. Here he views with his own eyes the great justification of God, who knows how to bring home all his own, in spite of all our doubts, anxieties, and perplexing questions, when we see how he leads them here below. Let us learn to trust God and be content; we too shall sing his praise at last.

God's saints will not appear in heaven in the pride of their own valor and heroism, but in the humble garment which grace has thrown around them. The best shroud is the publican's confession: "God be merciful to me, a sinner!" Cleanse your soul in the blood of the Lamb; this will wash out all vanity and self-praise, all impure desire and all bitterness of enmity, all guilt of any kind; it will make your soul white in divine pardon, and will keep it so to all eternity.

Do not imagine that suffering saves. Men are generally inclined to this thought, and often they speak loosely about the sufferer's recompense in heaven. When one dies who has suffered much, they say that he has overcome at last and is now at rest. But alas, too often sickness and death has overcome the sufferer and he has gone down in defeat, and only the poor torn body rests in the grave, while the suffering of the soul is intensified a thousandfold. Even the sufferings of a Christian do not save him: Christ's blood alone does that. Christian suffering is to make us cling more closely to Christ, to realize more fully that he alone can save, to show that indeed we believe and will not let cease our trust in him.

Whence have these come? From an arid desert, where burning thirst and gnawing hunger filled their souls — from the world. It could not quiet their inward longing, it could not satisfy their souls. All its joys and treasures were but for a day, and they craved what would abide to all eternity.

Human language is all too inadequate to describe heaven, yet God condescends to tell us as much as we are able to grasp. Who will picture the glory of the throne, the great center of all the heavenly world, where God himself sits in the midst of all the heavenly beings? Who will tell us of the glory of the Lamb, our

Mediator, as he stands before the throne, himself God from all eternity, and yet man, slain for us on the cross? And the great cherubim, with their countless eyes and inconceivable power of sight, their six wings, and their glory-stations about the throne. And the twenty-four elders, patriarchs and apostles, whose names have shone in Holy Scripture through many an age, themselves on thrones, sharing in the glory of God and the Lamb. Then the angel host, ten thousand times ten thousand, and thousands of thousands, bowing down before God, and worshipping him with praise such as our poor earthly ears have never heard. And for us, even more glorious than this, the saints of God themselves, the 144,000 of symbolic reckoning, the multitude that no man can number, with not one believer, how poor, lowly, and neglected he may have been in this life, forgotten and left out; and all this host singing *salvation* unto God, the one word which sums up what to all eternity must be sweetest and best to every human soul. As we look with glowing hearts through the eyes of St. John, let every heart yearn and pray that by the Lamb's divine help we too shall have our places in that glorious circle, and with our own eyes see, and with our own ears hear, what God in heaven has prepared for those who love him.

The Saints in Heaven.

I. *Who are they?*
II. *Whence came they?*

The Glorified Church.

I. *Its members.*
II. *Its blessed state.*
III. *Its worship.*

What Admonition Comes to us from St. John's Vision of the Blessed?

I. *The admonition to continue in faith, that we too may be saved at last.*
II. *The admonition to continue in love, that we may help save many others.*
III. *The admonition to continue in hope, that we and others may overcome every tribulation and stand in glory before the throne of God to all eternity.*

C. C. Hein.

The Church Triumphant.

   I. *An innumerable multitude.*
  II. *All in robes of white.*
 III. *All proclaiming God's praise.*
 IV. *All conquerors in tribulation.*
  V. *All eternally blessed.*

Will You be There?

   I. *Is your heart washed white in the blood of the Lamb?*
  II. *Is your heart staunch against the tribulations of this life?*
 III. *Is your heart filled with the longing for the blessedness to come?*

Salvation, the Song of the Saints in Heaven.

  I. *They learned it here in faith.*
 II. *They sing it there in glory.*

THE REFORMATION FESTIVAL.

1 Cor. 3, 11-23.

The assumption in the choice of this text for the Reformation festival is that Luther in his great work in the sixteenth century built upon the one foundation laid of God, built upon it gold, silver, and costly stones, not wood, hay, or stubble, that thus he did not destroy, but did truly build the spiritual temple of God, the church, discarding his own wisdom, glorying not in men or anything that is of men, but in God, in and through whom all things were his. The admonition that naturally connects itself with the text and this assumption, is that we to-day should do likewise. Paul has in mind first of all the preachers of the Gospel and their work in its result for themselves; but his vision could not restrict itself to these alone, he sees the effect which the work of the ministry must have upon the church as such, a destructive effect if it be work of the wrong kind. So he urges the Corinthians in general to cast aside all worldly wisdom, to glory in God and not in men, and to remember their riches in Christ and God. The subject of the text is *the building of the temple of God*. Paul shows us first of all the work, verses 11-15; secondly the sacred structure itself, verses 16-17; and finally, the spirit that must animate us all, verses 18-23.

The work.

The apostle has spoken fully of his own work and the way he pursued it, referring at the same time to the work of others who followed him in Corinth, and to God who blessed the labors of them all. He goes on with the warning: "But let each man take heed

how be buildeth" on the true foundation. A great deal
will depend on it, first of all for himself, then also for
the church as such. **For other foundation can no man
lay than that which is laid, which is Jesus Christ. But
if any man buildeth on the foundation gold, silver, costly
stones, wood, hay, stubble; each man's work shall be
made manifest: for the day shall declare it, because it
is revealed in fire; and the fire itself shall prove each
man's work of what sort it is. If any man's work shall
abide which he built thereon, he shall receive a reward.
If any man's work shall be burned, he shall suffer loss:
but he himself shall be saved; yet as through fire. —**
There is no discrepancy whatever between the statement in verse 10: "I laid a foundation," and the one
now made: **Other foundation can no man lay than that
which is laid,** namely by God himself, **which is Jesus
Christ.** Paul laid a foundation in Corinth by his preaching Jesus Christ there and establishing a church; God
laid the foundation for the entire church in sending his
Son as our Redeemer. It is the latter to which Paul
here refers. He is speaking in general now, of all the
work of building done in the Christian church, which,
of course, includes also the work of Corinth. One thing
is certain: "Other foundation can no man lay than that
which is laid." Whether a man go to Corinth or elsewhere, all he can do is to preach Jesus Christ. If he
refuses to do that, if he preaches something else, he is
laying no foundation at all, he is building on the sand
away from the foundation. So when Paul came to
Corinth, he says: "As a wise masterbuilder I laid a
foundation," laid by preaching in Corinth the one foundation laid by God for the church of all time. If any man
now would want to reject Paul's work and start one of
his own on a different basis, his whole proceeding would
be a piece of folly, for there is no other foundation to
lay than the one God has already laid for us and which
we now lay by bringing it like Paul to heathen com-.
munities. By **foundation,** θεμέλιος, is meant that upon

which the Christian church rests, without which it would
fall to pieces and cease to exist. This foundation is
Jesus Christ, in his person, work, and doctrine. The
name must be taken in its fullest soteriological meaning.
In regard to παρὰ τὸν κείμενον see Blass, 43, 4. Compare
also Eph. 2, 20 in the text for Pentecost. Luther laid
this one and only foundation of God anew in the work
of the Reformation, just as Paul laid it in Corinth. And
now no man can come and lay another foundation; if
he rejects the true Savior and doctrine of salvation as
proclaimed to us by Luther, there is no other foundation he can possibly find or bring. All that any of us
now can do is to build upon the one foundation of God
brought to us anew by the great Reformer.

But it is possible to build two kinds of material
. upon the one foundation: **gold, silver, costly stones,** or
wood, hay, stubble. Hofmann thinks that the former
refers to true believers, the latter to hypocrites or sham
Christians; Bengel adds to this idea the notion of true
doctrines on the one hand, and false on the other. Other
commentators speak of the moral fruits, *etc.* The entire
imagery, as the great majority of commentators recognize,
compels us to think of doctrines or teaching alone.
"Gold, silver, costly stones," such as granite and marble,
designate the true doctrines of the Word of God as apprehended and taught by the ministers of the Gospel, and
we may add, also by the confessing church. The image
is that of a fine and costly temple, in the erection of
which only the most precious and enduring materials are
used. "Wood, hay, stubble" are the opposite, all manner
of mere human ideas, speculations, and errors. Some of
these were used already by errorists in apostolic times,
and our day is full of them. But we must hold fast the
apostle's idea that these errorists do not reject or overthrow the foundation itself; they hold fast in one way
or the other to Christ and his atonement, but instead of
abiding by the full truth of the Word, they mix in their
own false wisdom. The apostle's image thus takes in all the

different Christian churches of our day, so many of which cling to error of one sort or another, and it shuts out all who are really non-Christian, who give up faith in the divinity of Christ and his atonement for our sins. Paul paints a strong contrast: here a great temple all of gold, silver, granite, marble, with nothing perishable or inferior in it; and there a mean hut, wood for the doors and posts, hay or dried grass (χόρτος) mixed with mud for the walls, and straw with the ears cut off (καλάμη), stubble, for the roof, all of these very perishable and inflammable. When Paul writes: "If any man buildeth," he includes every Christian preacher and teacher, also himself. In naming two classes of materials he does not mean that each builder will use exclusively either only the one or the other; some may try to combine gold or silver with wood, or costly stones with hay and stubble. "Let each man take heed how he buildeth thereon." The apostle's warning is necessary also for us who have the fine work of Luther to precede us; many bear the Lutheran name, subscribe the Lutheran confessions, boast of their Lutheran heritage, and yet find some of the wood, hay, and stubble of the errorists about us so attractive that they try to embody it in the structure they are called to help erect. — **Each man's work shall be made manifest;** here for a while he may deceive himself and others, but all such deception must end. Wood may be painted to look like gold or silver, but looks do not make it such. **For the day shall declare it,** ἡ ἡμέρα, the day κατ᾽ ἐξοχήν, the last day when Christ shall judge every man's work; compare 4, 5. **Because it is revealed in fire,** ὅτι ἐν πυρὶ ἀποκαλύπτεται, impersonal: in fire revelation is made. Some make τὸ ἔργον the subject, others ἡ ἡμέρα, but neither is good. Paul's meaning is simply this, that every preacher's and teacher's work shall be brought to a supreme test as to its real character and value at the last day, and the revelation shall be by fire, since this forms the true test. "Fire is the constant symbol of trial and judgment. The meaning therefore is, that the day of the Lord will be a day of severe trial. Every work will then be subjected to a test which nothing impure can ' stand." Hodge. "Fire" is, of course, figurative, like the materials, gold, *etc.*, wood, *etc.*, which it shall test. — **And the fire itself shall prove each man's work of what sort it is,** or, as the margin has it, translating still more closely: *and each man's work, of what sort it is, the fire shall prove it,* δοκιμάσει, assay, or test, as is done with metals. The moment this fire touches the gilded or painted wood, the hay and stubble, it shall burst into flame, but the gold, silver, and stone shall stand untouched and unconsumed. The Romanists try to make the verb mean "purge" and use the passage for their doctrine of purgatory; but Bengel rightly says: "This passage does not sustain the fire of purgatory, but entirely extinguishes it; for only at the last day shall the fire try every man's work. The fire of purgatory, therefore, does not precede." "False doctrine," writes Hodge, "can no more stand the test of the day of judgment, than hay or stubble can stand a raging conflagration." This is true also of much of Hodge's own doctrine who is a Calvinist.

The apostle carries the figure a step farther: **If any man's work shall abide which he built thereon, he shall receive a reward,** "according to, but not on account of his labor," Calov. The work that "shall abide" is all preaching and teaching of divine truth; and it abides not because of the learning or skill of the teachers, but because of the quality of truth that is in it. "Heaven and earth shall pass away, but my words shall not pass away," Matth. 24, 35; they are the gold, silver, and costly stones, and blessed is he who teaches these words, and these alone. The **reward,** μισθός, is not salvation, for this even those who built wood, *etc.*, upon the foundation shall receive; salvation is God's gift to every believer. By the reward is meant the especial honor and glory promised to all faithful teachers, Dan. 12, 3; 1 Cor. 15, 41; com-

25

pare also Luke 19, 17, *etc.* — On the other hand: **If any man's work shall be burned** (κατακαήσεται, late form of passive future, instead of καυθήσεται), burned down, **he shall suffer loss,** all his labor shall be in vain, he shall lose the reward which the other receives and which he too might have had if he had built aright. How shall many a proud name be humbled at that day! Great religious leaders with all their following, men with high titles and greatly honored here on earth, shall stand before the judge crushed and broken when they see the fire of his just judgment consume all that they have proudly reared and left behind as monuments to their credit; while many a poor, unknown, untitled pastor, who sought for no honor except to keep true to the Word, and perhaps suffered the sneers of these supposedly greater men, and persecutions for his faithfulness by errorists and worldings, shall receive the highest reward and shine as a star of the first magnitude in the heavens of the blessed. — Still Paul adds: **but he himself shall be saved; yet so as through fire.** "Saved" here has its usual meaning, rescued from damnation and taken to heaven. This is because these teachers still remained on the one foundation Jesus Christ. Robertson thinks they are saved because of their sincerity, and that anyone who is sincere and means well, no matter what he teaches, will be saved. But this is entirely false, although many believe it. It is not anything in us, but it is Christ Jesus who is made for us salvation. Any degree of true faith in him saves. But as some have supplied to them richly the entrance into the eternal kingdom of our Lord and Savior Jesus Christ, 2 Pet. 1, 11, so others enter with difficulty, Jude 23; Zech. 3, 2: "a brand plucked out of the fire." Baldwin: "When one who has taught saving and useful things will rejoice and enjoy his labor, as a useful workman of the church, he who introduced vain and useless things will see that they are of no value, and that they have no use. Hence his teachings will perish, while he himself, not overthrowing

Christ the foundation, will be saved, as though snatched
from threatening flames; inasmuch as he will then discover with what peril to souls he taught those things which
he formerly held in high esteem." Let us note, however,
that false doctrine is often not satisfied to remain on
Christ the foundation; the moment it leads an errorist
or his followers to forsake that, salvation too is lost for
them.

The sacred structure.

The office of the ministry and the entire work of
preaching and teaching in the church bears so grave
a responsibility with it because it is intended to build
up the spiritual temple of God, the church composed
of living stones, immortal souls. The Corinthians deserved to be sharply reminded of this, since they picked
and chose among their preachers according to worldly
considerations, eloquence, appearance, personal likes,
etc. The pupils in the heathen schools of philosophy
might do this, but not true Christian people: **Know ye
not that ye are a temple of God, and** *that* **the Spirit of
God dwelleth in you? If any man destroyeth the
temple of God, him shall God destroy; for the temple
of God is holy, which** *temple* **ye are.** — By *ναός* is meant
the *sanctuary* or dwelling-place of God (see margin), and
Paul himself defines the word as here used: "the Spirit
of God dwelleth in you." Paul's question is one of surprise, implying blame. The Corinthians should have
known what they were, but their actions showed that if
they had any such knowledge at all, it was only intellectual
and not spiritual. The same thing is true of many a congregation today, so often they forget that they are holy,
a sanctuary of the Spirit, and that only the holy Word of
God, and no destructive error, should be allowed in their
midst. The translation "a temple" must not mislead us
to think that Paul had in mind many temples of which the
Corinthians were one. The genitive *θεοῦ* makes *ναός*
definite enough. The entire church is God's temple, and

every Christian congregation, in fact every true believer, as part of the entire church, deserves the same designation. "As in the Jewish temple the Shekinah, or glory of God, was constantly present, and conferred on the building its awe-inspiring power and rendered any profanation of it a direct offense against God; so does the Holy Spirit now dwell in the church, the profanation of which by false doctrine is therefore sacrilege." Hodge. — In the most emphatic way Paul now drives home the warning the Corinthians need: **If any man destroyeth the temple of God, him shall God destroy.** Note the juxtaposition of the two verbs, making the statement the more striking. The verb φθείρω must be translated in the same way in both parts of the sentence, not "defile" in the one case, and "destroy" in the other (A. V.). Hodge takes the verb in a general sense: "If any man injure the temple of God, him will God injure." But this is too mild. The penalty for defiling the temple was death, Lev. 15, 31; Num. 19, 20, because defilement was equal to destruction of the sanctity of the temple; God cannot live in a defiled place. So Paul warns the Corinthians that he who destroys the temple of God shall himself be destroyed in just retribution for his crime. Here the apostle has in mind the worst effects which false doctrine and its preaching and promulgation is liable to produce: it may destroy the temple of God, cause the Spirit of God to leave the hearts of those who accept such teaching, kill saving faith within them. It is only just that they who cause such destruction be themselves destroyed by suffering the just wrath of God and its temporal and eternal penalties. Let us remember the sternness with which Jesus twice cleansed the courts of the temple in Jerusalem, saying that these people had turned God's house of prayer into a den of thieves. Much worse is the error that overthrows faith by filling the heart with self-righteousness, puffing it up with human wisdom, or plunging it again into sinful lusts and worldly vanities. — The reason why God shall destroy the destroyers of his temple is clearly stated:

for the temple of God is holy, which *temple* **ye are.** We are made pure, clean, and holy, a fit place for the indwelling of God, when our sins are washed away by the blood of Christ; ours is thus the holiness that comes by imputation. There is no greater crime than to destroy this holiness in us. This is for all God's people to know, in order that they may guard themselves against every person, every teaching and influence that would rob them of this holiness and the divine blessings that go with it. In our day of indifference to soul-destroying error the earnest warning of the apostle is especially necessary. And this also for us of the Lutheran faith, who are so liable to undervalue the saving influence of the precious truth committed to our care.

The spirit of the workers.

They who have anything to do at all with the work of building the church, both the preachers and the hearers, must be animated by the right spirit if they are to abide in the truth, hold fast the faith, and continue as the temple of God. Paul describes this spirit in the following admonitions: **Let no man deceive himself. If any man thinketh that he is wise among you in this world, let him become a fool, that he may become wise. For the wisdom of this world is foolishness with God. For it is written, He that taketh the wise in their craftiness: and again, The Lord knoweth the reasonings of the wise, that they are vain. Wherefore let no man glory in men. For all things are yours; whether Paul, or Apollos, or Cephas, or the world, or life, or death, or things present, or things to come; all are yours; and ye are Christ's; and Christ is God's.** — A man would indeed deceive himself grievously if he acted contrary to what Paul is now urging upon the Corinthians. Human wisdom has misled many to their eternal destruction, and they who followed them shared their fate. — **If any man thinketh that he is wise among you in this world** (or: *age*), if he have a lot of the knowledge, the learning, the philosophy, *etc.,* that counts among men, and thus thinks himself wise, **let him,** if he wants to become truly wise, **become a fool,** by discarding all such human wisdom in matters of spiritual import, **that he may become wise** in the true sense of the word, by filling his soul with nothing but the divine truth of the Word. Paul is using a paradox: Become a fool in order to become wise! The paradox is easily solved: a fool in the eyes of the world, in order to be wise in the eyes of God. The wisdom that is no wisdom must be cast aside in order that the wisdom, which looks to many like foolishness, but is the only wisdom, may be attained. "We must be empty, in order to be filled. We must renounce our own righteousness, in order to be clothed with the righteousness of Christ. We must renounce our own strength, in order to be made strong. We must renounce our own wisdom, in order to be truly wise. This is the universal law. And it is perfectly reasonable. We are only required to recognize that to be true, which is true. We would not be required to renounce our own righteousness, strength, or wisdom, if they were really what they assume to be. It is simply because they are in fact worthless that we are called upon so to regard them." Hodge. — Paul states this directly: **For the wisdom of this world is foolishness with God.** The wisdom of this world is not the legitimate knowledge which the human mind is able to secure concerning the things of nature, nor the natural knowledge of God which may be derived from a proper contemplation of his works and ways, but the haughty reasoning and speculation of the human mind concerning God and things spiritual apart from and contrary to the Spirit of God and the revelation he has made of himself. All such "wisdom of this world" is "foolishness with God;" it is not only not true, it is false, silly, ridiculous, and therefore dangerous and also wicked. Even true knowledge becomes folly when the perverted mind attempts to use it for ends for which it was never adapted, as when mathematics, metaphysics, philosophy, *etc.* are used to se-

cure holiness or happiness. Thus many things true enough
in themselves are used so as to become false and foolish. —
Paul proves his statement by two Scripture passages. The
first is from Job 5, 13, the only passage from this book
quoted in the N. T.: **He that taketh the wise in their
craftiness,** ἐν τῇ πανουργίᾳ αὐτῶν, in their knavery or villainy.
The apostle here translates the Hebrew himself; the Septuagint, however, is similar: "Who entangleth the wise in
their wisdom." God thus shows what estimate he places
upon the foolish wisdom of men, and the passage thus illustrates Paul's maxim. The statement is from the speech
of Eliphaz, and expresses an important truth. When men
seek to defeat God by their craftiness and cunning, they
are caught in their own net. There are striking examples
of this in the tempting questions propounded by the Jews
on various occasions to Christ. — The second proof is
from Ps. 94, 11: **The Lord knoweth the reasonings of
the wise, that they are vain.** The original, as well as the
Septuagint, has "the reasonings of men" (A. V.:
"thoughts," διαλογισμούς); Paul defines the kind of "men"
he has in mind, when he uses "wise" in place of "men,"
thus making his translation interpretative. "Vain," μάταιος,
is fruitless, bringing no good results. They make a great
effort and pretense, promise much, but are like blossoms
that fail to set fruit. The entire elaboration of the apostle
is a mighty indictment against the introduction of human
speculation and reasoning in theology or Christian teaching in general. It only perverts, injures, and destroys; it
never builds up the church or a single soul in that which
aids unto salvation.

Wherefore, concludes Paul in a further admonition,
let no one glory in men, in them merely as men and in
what they possess as mere men. Even the proudest and
greatest things they have are vain in the sight of God. —
Why are we not to glory in men? **For all things are
yours,** the whole universe with all the good gifts of God
therein, men themselves included in so far as God has
wrought any good in them. Let us remember our true

wealth, which is immense, and we will never become beggars, following some one man because we see something
great in him. — The apostle elucidates: **whether Paul,
or Apollos, or Cephas,** namely as ministers of God (3, 5),
the one planting, the other watering, *etc.* It was a mistake to pit one against the other, to prize the one for
some special gift or ability, and to discard the other. For
all that was good in each of them was a gift of God to
the church. But let us note that all three were true
teachers of the Word, not one an errorist. So it is a mistake to apply this list, as the Lutheran Commentary does,
to Calvin, Wesley, and Pascal, as well as Luther. No errorist
is ours in the sense in which Paul, Apollos, and Peter were
the Corinthians'. At best only what was true and good in
them is ours, and this we must separate with constant
care from their dangerous false teaching and harmful influence. But in the good and true teachers which God
gives us let us be careful to prize not what is merely
human, but what is divinely wrought in them; this is ours,
and as we appropriate it and benefit by it we thank God.
So we prize Luther and Melanchthon and all the faithful
heroes of the Reformation, for what God has given us
through them. Our glorying is not in them as men, but as
ministers of God, as instruments through which he bestowed the riches of his Gospel upon us. — Paul adds a
few other items, such as are very comprehensive: **or the
world, or life, or death, or things present, or things to
come; all are yours.** Not only does the church possess
the ministry, and such great men as Paul, Apollos, and
Peter in the ministry, but it can call the whole **world** its
own, since the whole of it is directed and governed for
the promotion of the great work of the church. Meyer
thinks of the Christians judging the world at last, when
they are made to participate in Christ's royal power; but
this is strange to the context. **Life** and **death** likewise
are dispensed of God with reference to the interests of his
kingdom. And this not merely the life or death of the members of the church, but life and death in the most general

way. So also **things present,** ἐνεστῶτα, things that have
begun, and **things to come,** μέλλοντα, about to begin. All
are ours in the great plan of God which makes all subservient to our highest and best interests as his children.
With such great and vast possessions at our command,
why should we ever reduce ourselves to depend on the
small and weak abilities of any one man? — But the apostle adds: **and ye are Christ's; and Christ is God's,** thus
referring everything to its ultimate source as well as goal.
Christ has redeemed us, his Spirit has reborn us, and so
with all that we are and have we are his. Blessed is this
ownership for us who are thus owned. All things are
indeed given by the Father into Christ's hands, John 13,
3, and are thus his own, but here Paul means that we believers belong to Christ in a special sense, as those bought
by his own blood, Acts 20, 28; we are his in the sense
that he is in us and we in him, John 14, 20. And Christ .
is God's, as the Son of God who is one with the Father.
This includes his human nature, now forever inseparable
from his divine nature. In explaining this possession of
Christ by God all subordination of the Son to the Father
must be carefully excluded. Christ with all his mediatorial work was indeed subject to the Father and carried
out his will; yet he was God himself, and so the will which
he carried out was his own divine will, in all respects
one with that of the Father. When Paul here writes
"God's," he means the Triune God to whom we belong by
faith in Christ Jesus. Schnedermann adds the warning
to all pastors that they must never attach the members
of their congregations merely to their own persons, because of some gifts, excellencies, tendencies, or even faults
which they may have, but only to Christ, to his Word
and church, and thus to God. This applies also to the
great Reformer, whom we honor and revere, but whose
name and person merely in themselves would be nothing to
us; we behold in him the divinely chosen instrument to bring
us the pure and precious Gospel and thus to attach us forever to Christ and to God.

*26

HOMILETICAL HINTS.

When the blows of Luther's hammer sounded upon the doors of the castle-church at Wittenberg, as on the last of October, in 1517 he nailed up his 95 theses against indulgences, the great corner-stone Jesus Christ was laid anew for us all. Then at last the work of clearing away the great mass of Romish rubbish from the old apostolic foundation began in earnest, and the church was built anew upon this its own real foundation which even the gates of hell shall never overthrow.

Rome left the true foundation, when in the place of Christ it elevated its vice-god, the pope. The papacy, the hierarchy, and the priesthood, these are Rome's earthly mediators; Mary and the saints her heavenly mediators. Both usurp the place of Christ; neither can mediate in reality. Luther proclaimed the old apostolic doctrine anew: Christ our Mediator alone! Christ's blood our righteousness — justification by faith; Christ's Word our only rule, norm, and guide — every doctrine for faith and life drawn from this most limpid fountain of Israel alone. Hence we repudiate the pope, the authority of human reason, and all the glory of men and all the glamour of human wisdom.

Behold what the workers of God have built upon the foundation Jesus Christ! They have taken the precious metals and marble of the Word and have reared up sound and glorious confessions, the most precious of which is Luther's Catechism; they have composed sweet and pure Scriptural hymns, full of truth, comfort, joy, and strength to the praise of God; they have established a true Scriptural worship; they have built up a pure body of theology; they have written books upon books which reflect the glory of the Gospel. And more than this: they have embodied Christ and his Word in their lives. Behold the men of faith, true confessors of the Lord and his saving Gospel; the men of love, who served their brethren in the spirit of Christ, some of whom were enabled to lay down their lives in martyrdom for the Master. See thus the gold, the silver, and the costly stones that have been built upon the one foundation, just as St. Paul and his fellow workers built in the very first age of the church. — Others indeed came with wood, hay, stubble, human wisdom and reasoning, false ideas and ideals, and they too wrought them out in their lives. Many of these the judgment of the Lord has already overtaken, the fire of destruction has already begun to consume them. Still men bring on all sorts of similar material, none of which can endure, all of which shall turn to ashes at the last day.

Lutheranism is nothing but biblical Christianity. Therefore the stones at Wittenberg shall continue to cry in the words engraved upon them:

> "God's Word and Luther's doctrine pure
> To all eternity endure."—

What the earth brings forth, wood, hay, stubble, shall perish; what God has created at the beginning, gold, silver, stone, shall endure. — Many a statue of Luther has been erected in his native land and elsewhere, and every one of them places the Bible in the great Reformer's hand. "In all things," he wrote to Pope Leo X., "I gladly yield to every one, but God's Word I will not, and also cannot, forsake and deny. That I should recant my doctrine cannot come to pass." — We have the sword of the Word, but often we fail to wield it. The cobwebs of neglect are often stronger than iron chains in binding the Word. When necessity presses us we often fly to the Word, but hand and heart are without practice and skill, and so many an enemy triumphs at our expense.

With all its extensiveness the Romish church is narrow. Its monks and nuns fly the world, yet the world is ours; its priests dare not marry, yet marriage is ours; its people are forbidden to eat many foods in Lent, and meat on Friday, yet all things are ours, to use as Christ's people and God's children. — All things are ours to sanctify in the service of Christ; only sin is not ours, it is removed by Christ, and things sinful, they are repudiated by all who have the spirit of Christ. — Ours is a free church, but its freedom is wholly of the Gospel.

The Children of the Reformation Must Build the Church of the Reformation.

I. *On Christ the foundation.*
II. *With gold, silver, and costly stones.*
III. *As a holy temple of God.*
IV. *For the glory of God, who has made all things ours.*

The Glory of The Lutheran Church.

I. *Her impregnable foundation.*
II. *Her imperishable structure.*
III. *Her immortal power.*

We are Children of the Reformation.

That means:

I. *We are Lutheran:* Christ alone is the foundation of our salvation.

II. *We are evangelical:* The Gospel is the sole rule of our faith and life.

III. *We are Protestant:* We protest and contend against every doctrine or practice that dims the glory of Christ and militates against his Word.

Langsdorff.

Luther's Doctrine is Fireproof.

I. *Now, when human wisdom tests it.*

II. *At that day, when Christ himself shall test it.*

THANKSGIVING, OR HARVEST HOME FESTIVAL.

2 Cor. 9, 6-11.

The imagery in this text fits perfectly the idea of the festival for which the text is chosen. It speaks of sowing and reaping, of God supplying seed for the sower and bread for food, enriching us to all liberality in thanksgiving to God. The subject of the text is *Christian giving*, and there are two parts: how we should give, verses 6-7; and how God gives to us and enables us to give, verses 8-11.

How Christians should give.

Our text is from the section of Second Corinthians (chapters 8-9) which deals with the collection the apostle Paul was gathering for the relief of the famine-stricken Christians in Palestine. It is well to observe how much space the apostle allots to this subject, and also how deep down into Christian faith and love he reaches when he bids the Corinthians to do their part. There is an utter absence of any schemes on the apostle's part for raising a goodly sum of money in Corinth or in any of the other congregations; he countenances no worldly form of giving, he depends wholly on Christian love and willingness. This appeal animates also the passage which constitutes our festival text. Paul is sending special messengers to the Corinthians to make up beforehand their aforepromised bounty, that their offering might be ready when now the apostle himself comes to receive it and carry it to the sufferers in Palestine. He is anxious for two things, which he urges in our text, first that the offering may be abundant, and not niggardly, and secondly that it may

397

come from truly willing and ready hearts and thus prove a blessing to the givers themselves. **But this I say,** **He that soweth sparingly shall reap also sparingly; and he that soweth bountifully shall reap also bountifully.** *Let* **each man** *do* **according as he hath purposed in his heart; not grudgingly, or of necessity: for God loveth a cheerful giver.** — It seems simplest and best to supply with τοῦτο δέ either λέγω or φημί, as in our translation, instead of reading it as an accusative absolute: "but as to this." Paul is drawing special attention not to what he has just said in verse 5, but what he is about to say in verse 6. — He uses the thought of Prov. 11, 24: "There is that scattereth and yet increaseth; and there is that withholdeth more than is meet, but it tendeth to poverty." **He that soweth sparingly** has the same figure of scattering seed in order that a harvest may result. The sentence is entirely general, stating a universal truth or experience. Here the special reference is to the act of giving, to a work of charity. It is in itself a fine interpretation of such acts to do them as a sowing. A sower always expects a return, a multiplication of the seed he puts into the soil. So all our good works are a sowing, also our acts of Christian giving; they shall bring in a harvest. Not, however, as the Romanists pervert our passage, as a reward ´of merit on our part. No sower earns his harvest; that harvest is God's unmerited and most wonderful gift to the sower. It is conditioned indeed, the soil must be plowed and the seed planted, but that condition when we meet it is no work of merit on our part and by no means justifies a demand or claim on our part that God now owes us the harvest. We merely obey God's order, and his great goodness showers an unmerited blessing upon us. But how foolish to sow φειδομένως, **sparingly,** holding back the seed and saving it as much as possible, thinking that it is a loss to put the seed into the ground. This is exactly what many foolish Christians do; not indeed when they sow grain, there they are wiser, but when they sow deeds of charity, offerings for the poor and needy and for the cause of Christ. The more seed they hold back, the richer they think they will be, while the very reverse is true. — Such a sower **shall reap also sparingly.** Note the striking way in which Paul combines the two φειδομένως: "He that soweth *sparingly, sparingly* also shall he reap." God, as it were, has placed the matter into the sower's own hands; he in a great measure controls the harvest himself. If the seed looks so precious to him that he cannot part with it, so much the less seed shall he have at last. He who begrudges charity and offerings and holds back selfishly from giving, so much less shall he have in the end. — **And he that soweth bountifully,** or rather: *with blessings,* both in spirit and in quantity differently from the other, **shall also reap bountifully.** Here again the emphatic phrases are put side by side in the Greek. The force of ἐπί with the dative is like the phrases in Rom. 4, 18; 1 Cor. 9, 10, expressing the condition under which a thing is done. To sow "with blessings" (note the plural) is to sow so that many blessings accompany and proceed from the act. Of course, that will be a generous scattering of seed. The result will be a reaping likewise "with blessings," a harvest full of blessings for the reaper. Already in this life we come to do considerable reaping. The generous giver receives many a fine blessing from the bounty of God. Only the grain is often transmuted: we sow one kind of blessing to others, and we receive another kind in return. But the final reaping will take place in heaven, where the glory of those who sowed sparingly will be far less than the glory of those who sowed bountifully. Our lives are like cups which God stands ready to fill in his grace. He who gives himself and his goods sparingly to God comes with a small cup, perhaps only as large as a thimble — he shall have it filled, but think how little he thus receives. He who gives himself and his bountifully, comes with a large cup — and he shall have it filled, and the greater the cup the more pleasure to God to fill it.

Yet the apostle does not want to be misunderstood.

The doing of good works, the giving of alms is not a mere mechanical exchange, so much of gifts, so much of returns. *Let* **each man** *do* **according as he hath purposed in his heart.** The whole matter is one of the heart, and therefore every giver should do just what his heart purposes (προαιρέομαι, to choose for oneself, to prefer). — The apostle explains: **not grudgingly,** as when one is pressed to give more than he really wants to give and is sorry to see so much go; ἐκ λύπης is: *of sorrow,* grieving to give up so much. God always looks at the heart in every gift, and the harvest of our gifts is measured according to the way our hearts give. — **Or of necessity** adds the other manner of giving which Paul wants to avoid, compulsion, or undue outward pressure, when one gives, while really he would rather not give, or gives more than he really would like to give. Both kinds of giving are displeasing to God, and though great sums may thus be offered, little or no blessing can follow in return. — **For God loveth a cheerful giver,** one who carefully considers what he is doing, acts intelligently in the light of God's Word, and then gladly, joyfully brings his gift. Without quoting, Paul appropriates the thought and almost the very words of the Septuagint in Prov. 22, 9. The Hebrew reads: "He that hath a bountiful eye shall be blessed," which the Septuagint renders: "God blesseth a man who is cheerful and a giver." Of course, this is Christian cheerfulness, not the jollity of buyers at bazaars, fairs, raffles, lotteries, and the like, which is worldly in spirit and in form. The cheerful giver whom God loves is one who delights to give for God's sake, in the service of others because he can thus carry out the will of God and please him. This is spiritual giving, a sweet odor in the nostrils of God. It is found only where the heart is filled with the love of God. To have God love us is the highest kind of reward, for in his love grow all the fairest flowers of blessings for this life and for that to come.

How God gives and enables us to give.

And God is able to make all grace abound unto you; that ye, having always all sufficiency in everything, may abound unto every good work: as it is written,

> **He hath scattered abroad, he hath given to the poor;**
> **His righteousness abideth for ever.**

And he that supplieth seed to the sower and bread for food, shall supply and multiply your seed for sowing, and increase the fruits of your righteousness: ye being enriched in everything unto all liberality, which worketh through us thanksgiving to God. — All that is good in us, also any Christian giving we may be able to perform, is something that God graciously works in us, a gift of his to us as it were. The verb δυναται is emphatically put forward; and God's ability is emphasized in the sense that what he is abundantly able to do he also most certainly will do. **To make all grace abound unto you** certainly cannot be restricted merely to the grace of earthly possessions, God furnishing us sufficient so that we can give abundantly to others. **All grace,** and the verb **abound,** (περισσευειν, to exceed, to be more than enough), are altogether too inclusive for that. So also the purpose clause: that ye may abound **unto every good work,** not merely to the one good work of cheerful giving. By "all grace" or favor of God is meant the entire sum of his good gifts to us, both the spiritual and the bodily. He is both able and willing to give us all that may be required in order that we may abound in good works; the only trouble is that we so often are not ready for such an inflow of his grace, we are not enamored enough of good works. — **Having always all sufficiency in everything** likewise reaches out in every direction of the Christian life. Note the repetitions of the word "all" in various forms in the whole sentence. The Stoics used αὐτάρκεια of the feeling of contentment, which is satisfied with what it has as suf-

ficient. Various commentators think that Paul here uses
the word in the same sense; but Bachmann is right when
he points to the modifiers here added: "all sufficiency in
all things," and this "always," which evidently means that
God will supply us with all that we may need inwardly,
in our hearts, and outwardly, in our circumstances, to do
good works, among them also the work of Christian giving. Such works require abundant spiritual grace, such
as proper enlightenment, a strong measure of faith, fervent love, tenderness, pity, and the like. "All sufficiency"
includes these. Then also, whatever the work may require outwardly: if it be giving, that we have something
to give and a worthy object of our gifts; if it be help,
that we have the strength and some weak brother to help;
and so with other good works. — God's abounding grace
is to be matched by our abounding unto every good work.
His gift is always first, and ours is to follow. Both are
to be like an overflowing stream. Too many of us hold
back and act as if we were afraid we might do too much
good. What blindness, when the full store of God's grace
is open for us, always providing all sufficiency in everything for us, so that all we need do is to take of this abundance and dispense it!

The apostle here introduces an effective quotation
from Ps. 112, 9: **as it is written, He hath scattered
abroad,** as one that sows grain with a lavish hand, **he
hath given to the poor,** showing what kind of scattering
or sowing the apostle has especially in mind. The Psalm
describes in detail the blessedness of the man that feareth
the Lord, that delighteth greatly in his commandments;
and one notable item in this blessedness is his great generosity to the poor and needy. The result of this spirit and
work of charity is: **his righteousness abideth for ever,**
i. e. his acquired righteousness, the quality of righteousness in his life which makes him acceptable to God. It
is the righteousness of good works, the proper fruit of
living faith, which Christ shall commend and reward with
his heavenly grace at the last day: "Verily, I say unto you,

inasmuch as ye have done it unto one of the least of these my brethren, ye have done it unto me," Matth. 25, 40. This righteousness shall endure or abide for ever, because its possessor shall enter heaven with it. The quotation is finely chosen and directly to the point; it follows the Septuagint almost exactly, and this renders the Hebrew with great closeness. — The thought of righteousness leads the apostle to say that this especially in all its beautiful fruits is the aim and desire of God. He has said what God *can* do, implying his willingness; now he says directly what God *will* do. Without quoting, he makes use of the thought and imagery of Is. 55, 10: **And he that supplieth seed to the sower and bread for food** in the domain of our earthy life, he will do no less in the spiritual domain: he **shall supply and multiply your seed for sowing** in all manner of good works. "Seed" is the same as "grace" and "sufficiency" above, not merely earthly goods, as Meyer for instance makes it. The A. V. makes this sentence a wish, following a text which has the optatives instead of the future indicatives; the best texts have the latter, making the sentence declarative. The A. V. also connects "and bread for food" ($\beta\rho\tilde{\omega}\sigma\iota\varsigma$, eating) with the verb following: "shall both minister bread for food, and multiply;" but this is unnatural, the obvious construction being that of the R. V. There is little difference between $\dot{\epsilon}\pi\iota\chi o\rho\eta\gamma\dot{\epsilon}\omega$ and $\chi o\rho\eta\gamma\dot{\epsilon}\omega$; the verb here has the derived meaning "supply," as when one stands the cost. And God will do this in the amplest way, he will even "multiply" or increase this blessed seed. — A simple **and** carries the thought farther, showing really what God's object is in offering this seed; it is to **increase the fruits of your righteousness.** The seed of his grace growing in our hearts will naturally bring forth all manner of good works. God's grace makes us righteous, that is eager, willing, and able to do his will, all that is right and good in his sight, harmonizing with his rule or law of right; and every righteous and good work we do is a fruit of this quality of righteousness in us. Now God desires a great abun-

dance of such fruit, John 15, 8; hence his supply of the
necessary seed or grace. Thus Paul has swung around
completely the figure he started with: first we are sowers
who ought to sow bountifully in order to get a good harvest; now God is the sower, who indeed does sow bountifully, and is anxious to get a good harvest, only we who
are the soil are often so barren that his efforts are in
vain.

Paul adds a participial clause to specialize his general
statement and to emphasize the work of giving, which
now is the fruit of righteousness God desires of the
Corinthians. There is no need whatever to make verses
9-10 parenthetical, in order to line up the participle
πλουτιζόμενοι with the subject of the final clause in verse
8; the construction is anacoluthic, ὑμεῖς, the logical subject, being in the writer's mind: **ye being enriched in
everything unto all liberality, which worketh through
us thanksgiving to God.** Hodge makes the enrichment
consist of worldly goods, just as he does with "grace" and
"sufficiency" above, making the apostle's meaning shallow
and poor. To be enriched in everything includes first of
all the spiritual enrichment necessary for good works, then
also temporal blessings and the call and occasion to use
them in God's service. **Unto all liberality** expresses the
special fruit which the apostle desires now of the Corinthians, yet the word "all" includes any other similar fruit
as subsequent opportunity for it may arise. The word
translated 'literally," ἁπλότης, really means "singleness."
so also the adjective and other forms; it is derived from
the verb which means to spread out so that there is no
fold in the cloth. Here, however, it is evident what singleness of heart is meant, namely that which looks only to
the will of God in ministering to the poor. "Liberality"
thus constitutes an interpretative translation, making the
apostle's meaning entirely plain. The εἰς shows what is
God's purpose and aim in enriching the Corinthians with
his grace and gifts. He has sowed the good seed of his
blessings upon them, and desires to reap the harvest of

liberality from them. — This, Paul adds, **worketh through us,** the apostle himself and his assistants whom he is sending in advance to Corinth, **thanksgiving to God.** Getting the Corinthians to contribute of their gifts cheerfully and liberally, and transmitting these gifts to the sufferers in Palestine, Paul and his helpers will be the agents who cause the beneficiaries of the Corinthians' liberality to utter fervent **thanksgiving to God.** This thanksgiving is another fruit of God's sowing. It, too, will be to the credit of the Corinthians, for it will be wrought by their liberality. Yet Paul is happy and proud to have a hand in producing this fruit, by receiving and transmitting the Corinthian offering. In this he may serve as an example for all pastors and collectors now, whose work is often quite arduous, but who have all reason to rejoice in being able to perform it.

HOMILETICAL HINTS.

"Almsgiving impoverisheth not." — "For our God will not have it said of him, that we give more to him than he to us." Luther. — Just as a hundred grains grow from one, so God's blessings reward our gifts of love.

"He that showeth mercy, (let him do it) with cheerfulness," Rom. 12, 8; where instead of cheerfulness there is "grudging" (1 Pet. 4, 9) on account of the compulsion put upon us by our Christian name and calling, our alms have lost their sweet savor. "For the term 'of necessity' is used for that to which any one is forced against his will or otherwise, so that he acts externally for appearance, but nevertheless without and against his will. For such hypocritical works God will not have, but wishes the people of the N. T. to be a 'willing people,' Ps. 110, 3, and 'sacrifice freely,' Ps. 54, 7. 'not grudgingly or of necessity, but to be obedient from the heart,' 2 Cor. 9, 7; Rom. 6, 17. 'For God loveth a cheerful giver,' 2 Cor. 9, 7. In this understanding, and in such sense it is correctly said and thought that truly good works should be done freely or from a voluntary spirit by those whom the Son of God has liberated; as the disputation concerning the voluntariness of good works has been introduced especially with this intention." *Formula of Concord,* 585, 17-18.

Laurentius was a deacon in Rome during the persecution of Christians under the Emperor Valerian. The imperial captain had heard of the ecclesiastical treasures of the Christians, and Laurentius received orders to produce them. The young hero of ministering love came, followed by the poor and wretched, the lame and crippled, and bringing these to the captain he said: "These are our treasures!" On a red-hot iron stool he was slowly roasted to death, and died with the exclamation: "Lord, enter not into judgment with thy servant, for in thy sight no man living shall be justified." The church, however, honors in him a successor to St. Stephen, and applies to him the word of the prophet and of the apostle: "His righteousness endureth forever; his horn shall be exalted with honor," Ps. 112, 9. "As little as Rome can remain hid," says Augustine, "so little can the crown of Laurentius remain hid." Besser.

Rump writes in his sermon, that when he sees the stately houses of the members of his congregation, their verdant fields and fruitful gardens, he is moved to exclaim: What riches, and what blessings! and he thanks God in behalf of his members. So also when he sees them gathered at church, and beholds the signs of their prosperity in clothing and hats and in many adornments, he is moved to exclaim: What wealth, what blessings of God! and again he thanks God in their behalf. But when he counts the gifts they bring as offerings to God and measures the gratitude of his members as indicated by these gifts, he is amazed and grieved, and led to exclaim: What wretched poverty! What has become of all my wealthy members? Hear it, all ye that should hear: "He that soweth sparingly shall reap also sparingly; and he that soweth bountifully shall reap also bountifully."

What if God were to take us at our word when we say that we cannot give, and give so little and so grudgingly? What if he would measure the blessings he bestows upon us with the same measure with which we measure our offerings to him?

God expects more from a child than from some strange beggar who takes his gift and goes. — There are tremendous quantities of money in the world. But think how fearfully much is withheld from God and devoted to the world and the flesh! England spends for intoxicants in two and a half days as much as it spends in a whole year for the cause of missions.

How did Paul induce the Corinthians to give? Not by sharp words of blame and stinging rebukes, but by stimulating their love and by pointing them to the grace of God and its rich gifts. God's giving must precede ours, but his chief gifts to us are a new heart, love, gratitude, trust, cheerfulness, and joy. He who is poor in these may be a millionaire, he will not be a true Christian giver.

Christian Thanksgiving.

I. *Grows from the gifts of God's grace,*
II. *And expresses itself in cheerful giving unto God.*

"He that soweth Bountifully shall reap also Bountifully."

I. *What does such sowing include?*
II. *How does such reaping take place?*

Roemheld.

A Cheerful Harvest Home.

I. *Fields rich in earthly fruits.*
II. *Hearts rich in the fruits of righteousness.*

"God Loveth a Cheerful Giver."

I. *Because God has been able to give him so much.*
II. *Because God is able to give him still more.*

Soli Deo Gloria!

CPSIA information can be obtained
at www.ICGtesting.com
Printed in the USA
BVHW031119180819
555871BV00004BA/111/P

9 781167 316326